Edexcel GCSE (9–1)
Geography B

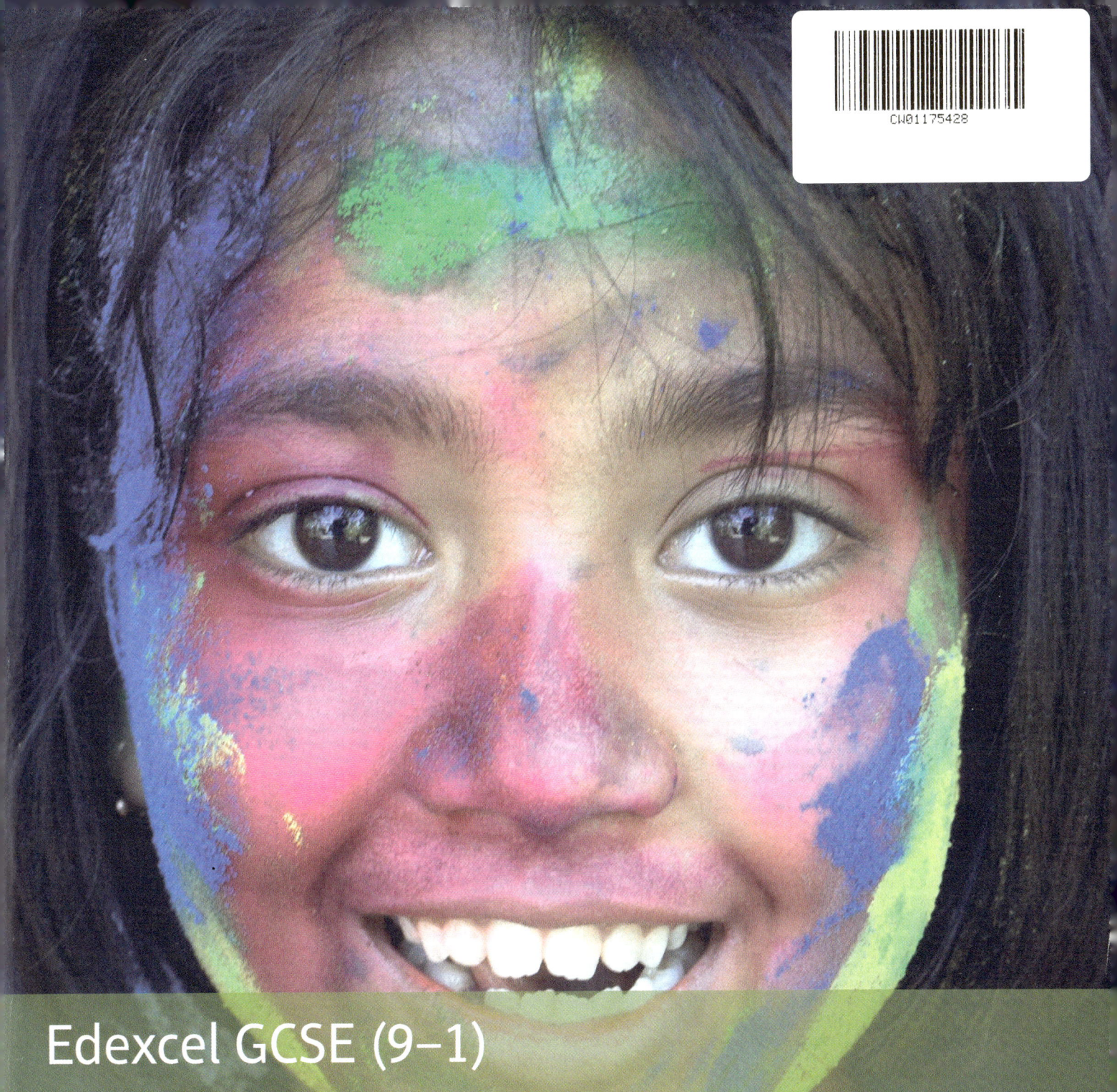

Investigating Geographical Issues

Series Editor: John Hopkin
Authors: Rob Bircher   Michael Chiles   Rob Clemens   Kevin Cooper   Phillip Crossley   David Flint   Paul Guinness

ALWAYS LEARNING

PEARSON

Published by Pearson Education Limited, 80 Strand, London, WC2R 0RL.

www.pearsonschoolsandfecolleges.co.uk

Copies of official specifications for all Edexcel qualifications may be found on the website: www.edexcel.com

Text © Pearson Education Limited 2016
Designed by Colin Tilley Loughrey for Pearson
Typeset, illustrated and produced by Phoenix Photosetting, Chatham, Kent
Original illustrations © Pearson Education Limited 2016
Cover design by Malena Wilson-Max for Pearson
Picture research by Jane Smith
Cover photo/illustration by Corbis: Partha Pal/ 2/ Ocean

The rights of Rob Bircher, Michael Chiles, Rob Clemens, Kevin Cooper, Phillip Crossley, David Flint and Paul Guinness to be identified as authors of this work have been asserted by them in accordance with the Copyright, Designs and Patents Act 1988.

Additional material provided by Lindsay Frost, David Grant, Stephen Schwab and Susan Schwab.

First published 2016

19 18 17 16
10 9 8 7 6 5 4 3

British Library Cataloguing in Publication Data
A catalogue record for this book is available from the British Library

ISBN 978 1 446 92776 2

Copyright notice
All rights reserved. No part of this publication may be reproduced in any form or by any means (including photocopying or storing it in any medium by electronic means and whether or not transiently or incidentally to some other use of this publication) without the written permission of the copyright owner, except in accordance with the provisions of the Copyright, Designs and Patents Act 1988 or under the terms of a licence issued by the Copyright Licensing Agency, Barnards Inn, 86 Fetter Lane, London EC4A 1EN (www.cla.co.uk). Applications for the copyright owner's written permission should be addressed to the publisher.

Printed in Italy by Lego S.p.A.

Websites
Pearson Education Limited is not responsible for the content of any external internet sites. It is essential for tutors to preview each website before using it in class so as to ensure that the URL is still accurate, relevant and appropriate. We suggest that tutors bookmark useful websites and consider enabling students to access them through the school/college intranet.

A note from the publisher

In order to ensure that this resource offers high-quality support for the associated Pearson qualification, it has been through a review process by the awarding body. This process confirms that this resource fully covers the teaching and learning content of the specification or part of a specification at which it is aimed. It also confirms that it demonstrates an appropriate balance between the development of subject skills, knowledge and understanding, in addition to preparation for assessment.

Endorsement does not cover any guidance on assessment activities or processes (e.g. practice questions or advice on how to answer assessment questions) included in the resource, nor does it prescribe any particular approach to the teaching or delivery of a related course.

While the publishers have made every attempt to ensure that advice on the qualification and its assessment is accurate, the official specification and associated assessment guidance materials are the only authoritative source of information and should always be referred to for definitive guidance.

Pearson examiners have not contributed to any sections in this resource relevant to examination papers for which they have responsibility.

Examiners will not use endorsed resources as a source of material for any assessment set by Pearson.

Endorsement of a resource does not mean that the resource is required to achieve this Pearson qualification, nor does it mean that it is the only suitable material available to support the qualification, and any resource lists produced by the awarding body shall include this and other appropriate resources.

Contents

About this book	4
How to use this book	5
Thinking Geographically	6
Where in the world will Edexcel Geography take you?	8

Component 1 Global Geographical Issues — 10

Topic 1 Hazardous Earth	11
1A Climate	12
1B Tectonics	38
Writing Geographically	56
Thinking Geographically	58
Topic 2 Development Dynamics	61
Thinking Geographically	92
Topic 3 Challenges of an Urbanising World	95
Writing Geographically	124

Year 9

Component 2 UK Geographical Issues — 126

Topic 4 The UK's Evolving Physical Landscape	127
Overview	128
4A Coastal Change and Conflict	134
Fieldwork: Investigating Coastal Landscapes	150
4B River Processes and Pressures	158
Fieldwork: Investigating River Processes and Pressures	176
Thinking Geographically	184
Topic 5 The UK's Evolving Human Landscape	187
Fieldwork: Investigating Dynamic Urban Areas	214
Fieldwork: Investigating Changing Rural Areas	226
Writing Geographically	234
Thinking Geographically	236
Topic 6 Geographical Investigations – Fieldwork	239

Year 10

Component 3 People and Environment Issues – Making Geographical Decisions — 242

Topic 7 People and the Biosphere	245
Topic 8 Forests under Threat	263
Topic 9 Consuming Energy Resources	281
Writing Geographically	300

Glossary	302
Index	312
Acknowledgements	318

About this book

Welcome to the Edexcel GCSE Geography Specification B course. This book has been written specially to help you learn about the world you live in. By the end of the course you will know far more about our fascinating and dynamic planet Earth and how it works, as well as developing the understanding and skills that will help you think like a geographer, now and in future.

What will I learn?

There are three parts to your course, called components, each with its own exam paper.

Component 1 Global Geographical Issues

Have you ever wondered:

- How does the world's climate system work, and why is climate change becoming such a hazard?
- What causes extreme weather events and tectonic hazards?
- Why is the world unequal, how can inequality be reduced, and how are some countries managing to develop rapidly?
- Where the world's fastest growing cities are, and how they can be made better places to live?

In this component you will learn about some of the key geographical issues in today's world, and the interaction of the physical and human processes which cause them.

Component 2 UK Geographical Issues

Have you ever wondered:

- Why landscapes in some parts of the UK are different from others?
- What causes coasts and river landscapes to change, and how people can manage them to reduce conflicts?
- How and why cities in the UK are changing, and how they are linked with the countryside?

In this component you will investigate key geographical issues in the UK today. You will also investigate two physical and human environments through fieldwork.

Component 3 People and Environment Issues – Making Geographical Decisions

Have you ever wondered:

- Why natural resources like food, energy and water are under pressure, and how we can manage this demand without damaging the environment?
- Why rainforests and coniferous forests are so different, and how we can manage the world's forests sustainably for the future?

In this component you will use your knowledge, understanding and skills to interpret geographical sources and make a geographical decision.

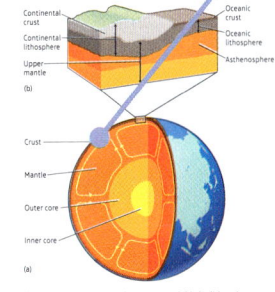

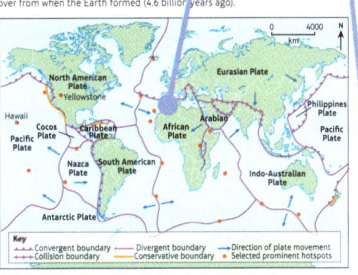

How to use this book

This book is practical and easy to use. The diagram below shows how some of the book's features support your learning.

Learning objectives provide a clear overview of what you will learn in each section. The objectives increase in difficulty.

Clear **diagrams** help you understand key ideas and develop your skills.

Maps at different scales help you locate geographical examples and case studies.

Checkpoints help you review your learning, with activities to strengthen and challenge your knowledge and understanding.

Did you know? features provide interesting facts about the topic, helping you extend your knowledge.

Key terms highlighted in the text help you to develop your geographical language.

Activities help you develop understanding and stretch your knowledge and skills.

Engaging **photos** bring geography to life.

Exam-style questions, tips and **command words** help you practise for your exams. You can get more exam advice at the end of each topic, where there is a checklist, plus sample answers and a commentary.

5

Thinking Geographically

You have already done quite a lot of geographical thinking in Key Stage 3. Through your Edexcel GCSE Geography course you will think more widely and more deeply about the world. Thinking geographically is about asking geographical questions, learning about places, patterns and processes, using geographical language and working with data.

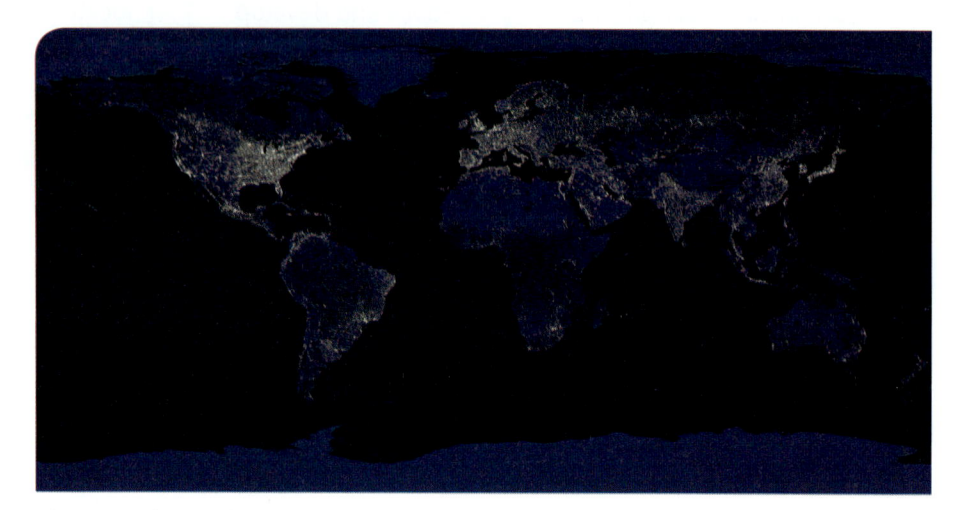

Figure 1 The Earth at night

Activity

1. Think geographically about the satellite image in Figure 1: write out the six W questions, aiming to think of at least one question for each 'W'.
2. Use an atlas to help you try to find answers to some of your questions.

Exam tip

In the exam, including real examples and places in your answers helps show you really know the subject.

Enquiry

Geographers constantly ask questions: good questions help us think geographically about the world. Some useful ones are:

The six W questions: What, Who, When, and especially Where, HoW and Why.

For deeper thinking, try adding 'might', 'could' or 'ought': for example, 'Where might …'.

- **In this book** you will find plenty of these questions in the activities and you will also use them to help structure your fieldwork investigations.

Places

Geographers need to build up good knowledge and understanding of places so they can think geographically – from the corner of a street to whole cities, regions, countries, continents and oceans. We are interested in where places are, what they are like, why they are different and changing, and how they are connected. Investigating places helps build our understanding of the world and develops important skills, including using maps, atlases, photographs and satellite images.

- **In this book** you will study three in-depth case studies of places, as well as located examples from different countries 🌍. Both these are highlighted by green vertical bands alongside the text. You can see where to find these on pages 8–9.
- You will also find mini-case studies throughout the book, showing geography in action in real places.

Patterns and processes

Geographers investigate how and why our world changes – we call these processes. Processes create patterns in the landscape, for example the shape of a river valley or desert, how land is used in a city, where richer and poorer parts of a country are.

- **In this book,** you will learn about the physical and human processes which cause change at the global scale in Topics 1–3.
- Topics 4–6 focus on physical and human processes at the UK scale.
- Throughout the book you will learn about how people and environments interact to change places, especially in Topics 7–9. That will help you understand geographical connections and make geographical decisions.

Finding out about processes, patterns and connections helps you understand the world – and think like a geographer.

Exam tip

In the exam, including diagrams or sketch maps can really help you show your understanding of patterns and processes. In any of the three papers you may be asked about how people and the environment affect each other.

Language and literacy

Geographers use language to think geographically. We use many key geographical words like 'biome', 'urban–rural fringe' and 'globalisation' to help us describe the world and understand how it works.

- **In this book** the key words you will need to learn are highlighted in the text and defined in the Glossary at the end of the book.

When, as geographers, you talk or write geographically, using well-structured sentences and texts helps show your understanding clearly and precisely.

- **In this book** there are extra pages with support for using language and activities to help you improve your writing and grammar. They will help you to write good answers, especially longer written answers which really test your thinking.

Exam tip

In the exam, using geographical language helps show that you really understand the subject. There are four extra marks on each paper for good use of language.

Numeracy and statistics

Geographers use numbers to think geographically. Data helps us to find out more about the world, and to show accurately what we have discovered from different types of maps, graphs and images. We also collect, present and analyse our own data from fieldwork investigations.

- **In this book** each topic includes data presented in different forms, with activities to help you learn the skills you will need.
- There are also extra pages with support and activities to help you improve your understanding of using maths and statistics. These will help where you need to work with data.

Exam tip

In the exam you will be asked to use your number skills in all three papers – you can use a calculator.

Progression

On the 'Preparing for your exams' pages, alongside the sample answers is a symbol containing a number. This symbol indicates that the sample answer has been graded with a numbered step on the Pearson Progression Scale. Our Geography progression scale and map can help teachers and students to assess progress, and can be downloaded free from the Pearson website.

Where in the world will Edexcel Geography take you?

In this book you will use these case studies and located examples, both labelled like this 🌍, to help you get a **big picture of geography**.

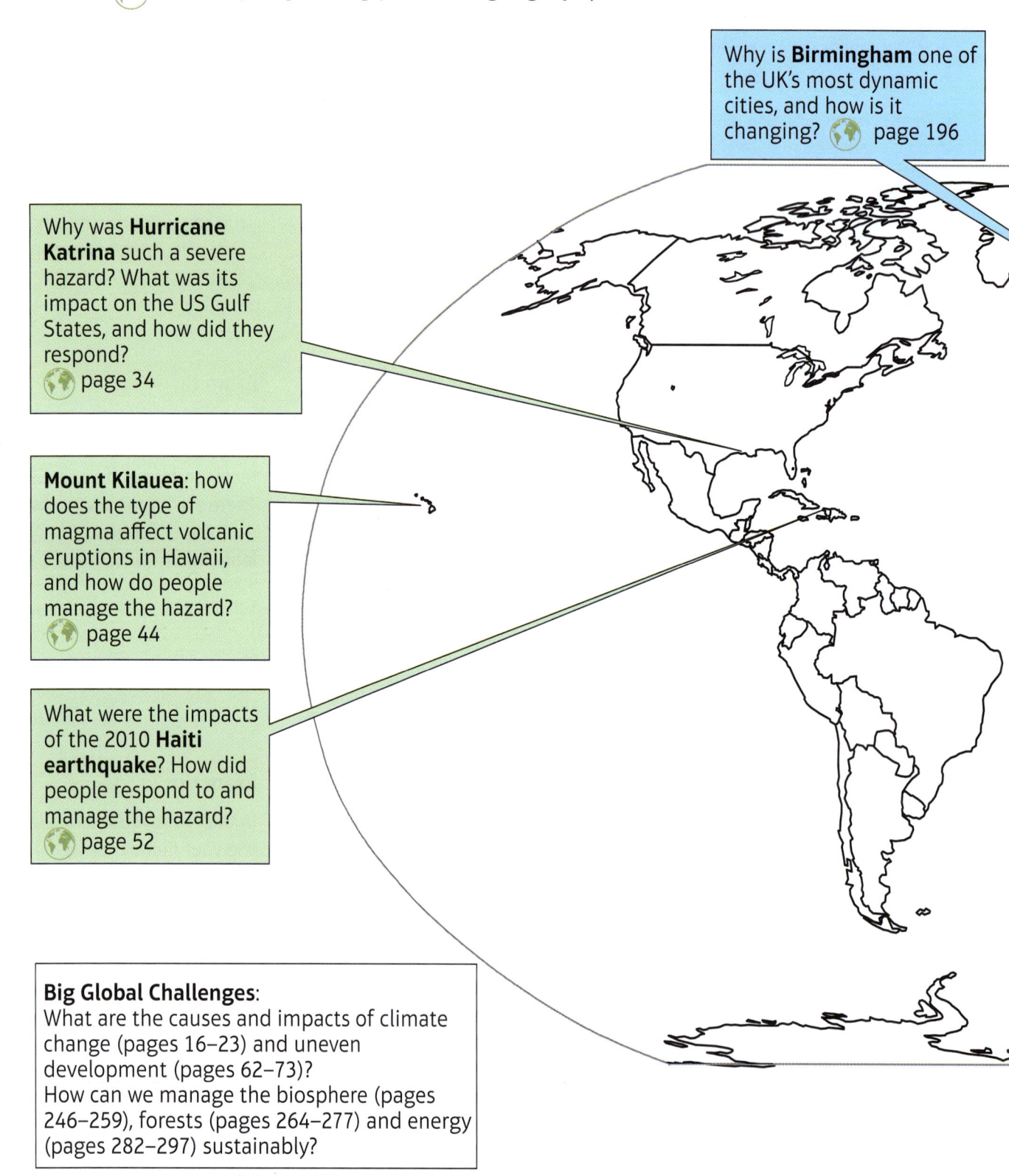

Why is **Birmingham** one of the UK's most dynamic cities, and how is it changing? 🌍 page 196

Why was **Hurricane Katrina** such a severe hazard? What was its impact on the US Gulf States, and how did they respond?
🌍 page 34

Mount Kilauea: how does the type of magma affect volcanic eruptions in Hawaii, and how do people manage the hazard?
🌍 page 44

What were the impacts of the 2010 **Haiti earthquake**? How did people respond to and manage the hazard?
🌍 page 52

Big Global Challenges:
What are the causes and impacts of climate change (pages 16–23) and uneven development (pages 62–73)?
How can we manage the biosphere (pages 246–259), forests (pages 264–277) and energy (pages 282–297) sustainably?

Where in the world will Edexcel Geography take you?

How is the coast of **South Devon** and **Dorset** changing? 🌍 page 145
How is the **River Severn** valley changing? 🌍 page 162
What are the challenges of managing these UK landscapes?

What was the impact of the massive 2011 **Japan earthquake** and tsunami? How did people respond to and manage the hazard? 🌍 page 50

Typhoon Haiyan was one of the strongest ever: how did people in the Philippines respond? 🌍 page 35

Mount Pinatubo, 1991: how did the type of magma here affect this eruption, and how did people in the Philippines manage the hazard? 🌍 page 46

Why is **Mumbai** growing so rapidly? What challenges does this bring? 🌍 page 105

India: How is this dynamic emerging country changing? 🌍 page 74

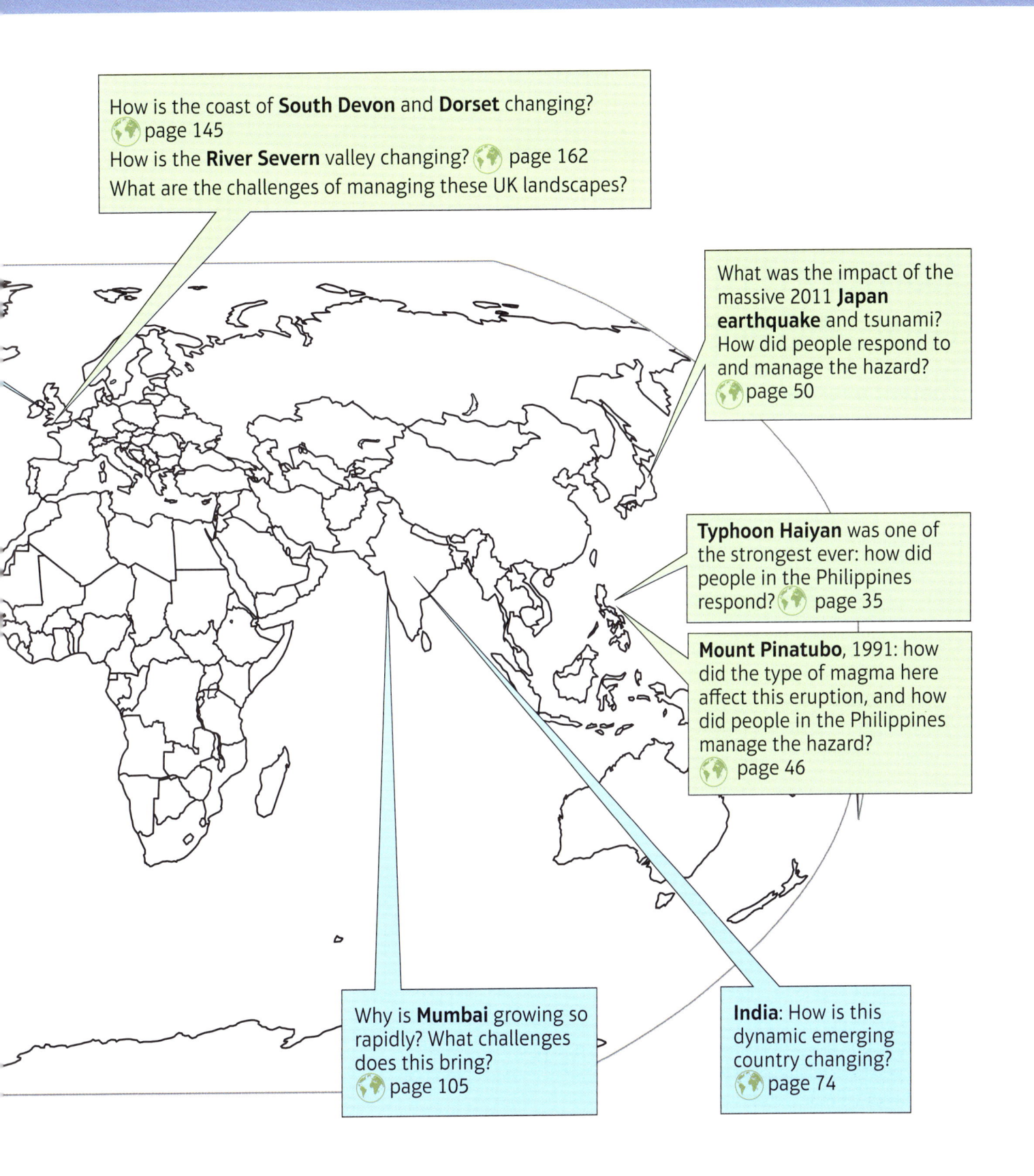

Component 1
Global Geographical Issues

Content overview

In this component you will learn about some of the key geographical issues in today's world, and the interaction of the physical and human processes that cause them.

- Topic 1 Hazardous Earth starts by investigating the world's climate system and climate change. You will then investigate the hazards caused by tropical cyclones and earthquakes or volcanoes in contrasting places.
- Topic 2 Development Dynamics investigates global inequality and development, before focusing on a case study of an emerging country. Here you will investigate development in India and its impact on people and environment and the country's international links.
- Topic 3 Challenges of an Urbanising World investigates the causes and challenges of rapid urban change, before you focus on a case study of the quality of life in a growing megacity, Mumbai.

Your assessment

You will sit a 1 hour and 30 minute exam, with three sections; you must answer **all** the questions in each section.

- **Section A** has questions about Hazardous Earth.
- **Section B** has questions about Development Dynamics.
- **Section C** has questions about Challenges of an Urbanising World.
- You may be assessed on geographical skills in any section, and can use a calculator.
- Each section is worth 30 marks; in addition, up to four marks will be awarded for spelling, punctuation, grammar and use of geographical language (SPAG).
- There will be a variety of different question types, including multiple-choice, calculations and open questions.
- Open questions require you to write a longer answer, from a few sentences to extended writing worth up to eight marks. Eight-mark questions are where you get marks for SPAG.

1 | Hazardous Earth

Our planet is our source of food, water, shelter and protection from the harsh radiation of the Sun. However, it can be a very dangerous place as well. The Earth has many natural hazards that affect the lives of people on different parts of the planet. Investigating natural processes, such as the climate system and tectonics, helps us to understand how they function and how we can prepare for them and deal with their effects. But not all the Earth's hazards are entirely natural. Humans have an increasing impact on shaping the Earth and its climate, making it an increasingly hazardous place to live.

Your learning

In this section you will investigate key learning points about the world's climate and tectonic hazards:

- How does the world's climate system function?
- What are the natural causes of climate change?
- How are human activities causing climate change?
- What are the possible consequences of climate change?
- How are extreme weather events increasingly hazardous for people?
- What impacts do tropical cyclones have on people and environments?
- Why are some countries vulnerable to tropical cyclones?
- How do countries prepare for and respond to tropical cyclones?
- How does the Earth's structure influence plate tectonics?
- What happens when tectonic plates move?
- What are the different types of volcanoes?
- What are the impacts of and responses to volcanic hazards?
- What are the impacts of and responses to earthquakes?

1A | Hazardous Earth: Climate

How does the world's climate system function?

> **Learning objectives**
> - To understand how circulation cells in the atmosphere and currents in the ocean transfer heat from hot areas of the Earth to cooler areas
> - To explore the role of the Coriolis effect and jet streams in explaining atmospheric circulation patterns
> - To explain how the global atmospheric circulation influences the location of arid areas and areas of very high rainfall

Atmospheric circulation

The Earth's atmosphere is constantly moving – over time these wind movements form a clear global circulation pattern. Figure 1 shows the three types of circulation cells that make up this global circulation pattern.

The movement of air within the cells is controlled by heating and cooling. The Earth receives all of its heat from radiation from the Sun. This solar radiation passes through the atmosphere and heats the ground directly. As the ground heats up, it warms the air above it, so warm air rises and transfers heat to the atmosphere. Later this air cools, becomes denser and sinks towards Earth.

The Earth is roughly spherical, so more solar radiation is received at the Equator, the hottest part of the Earth's surface, than at the poles where it is coldest (Figure 2). The Sun's rays hit the Earth's surface at different angles. The Equator receives the most concentrated radiation because the Sun's rays hit the surface almost at a right angle. Near the poles, they reach the surface at a lower angle so the same amount of radiation heats a much larger surface area. Also, near the poles the angle of the Sun's rays means they pass through a thicker atmosphere, which absorbs more energy than near the Equator.

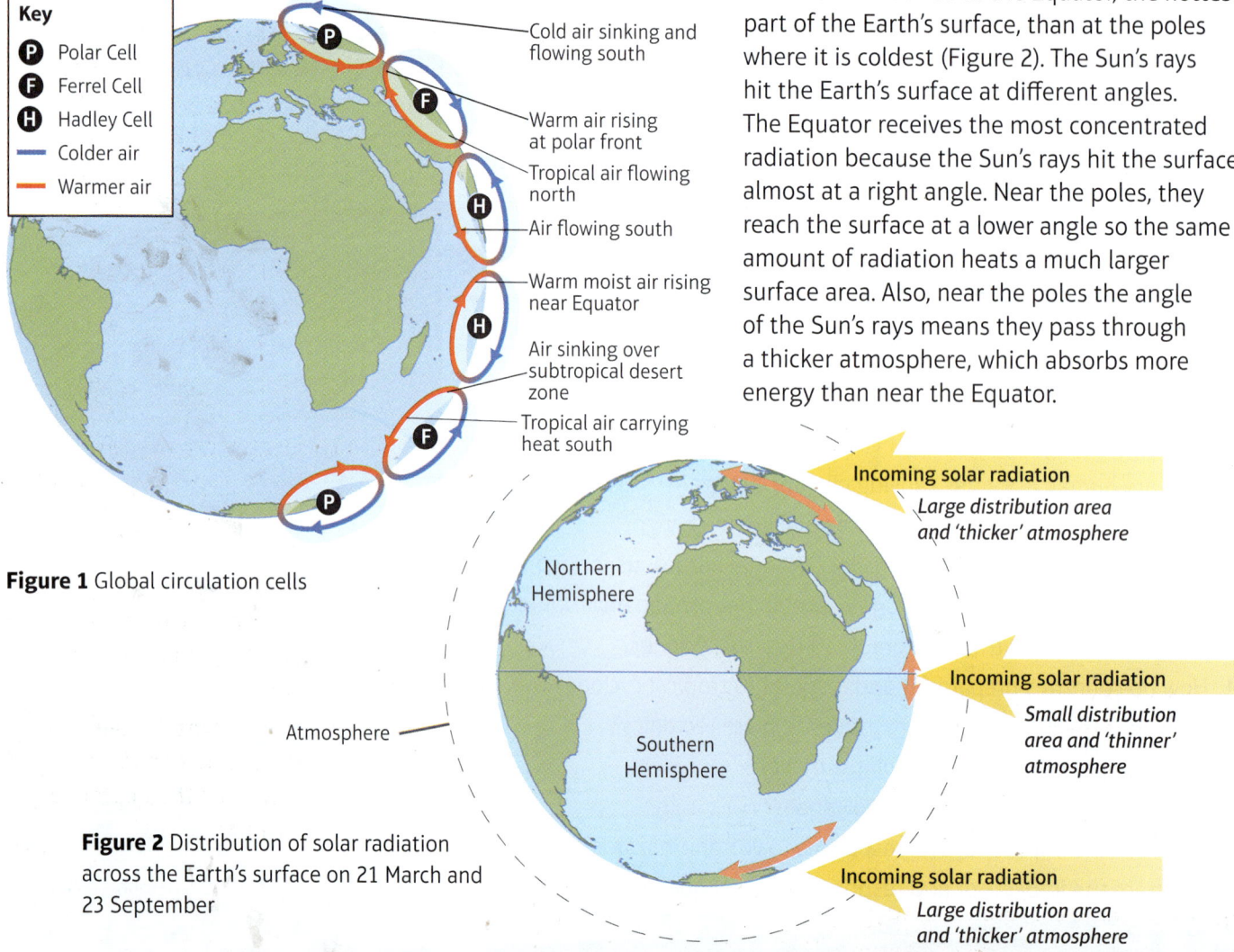

Figure 1 Global circulation cells

Figure 2 Distribution of solar radiation across the Earth's surface on 21 March and 23 September

12

1A Hazardous Earth: Climate

Winds are caused when air moves from high to low pressure. However, because the Earth rotates, the air does not flow in a straight line. As the air moves above the surface of the Earth, underneath it the planet continues to rotate, so winds actually follow a curved path. This is called the **Coriolis effect**. In the Northern Hemisphere the winds are deflected to the right and in the Southern Hemisphere they are deflected to the left. Figure 3 shows the resulting pattern of global winds, blowing from high pressure belts to low pressure belts.

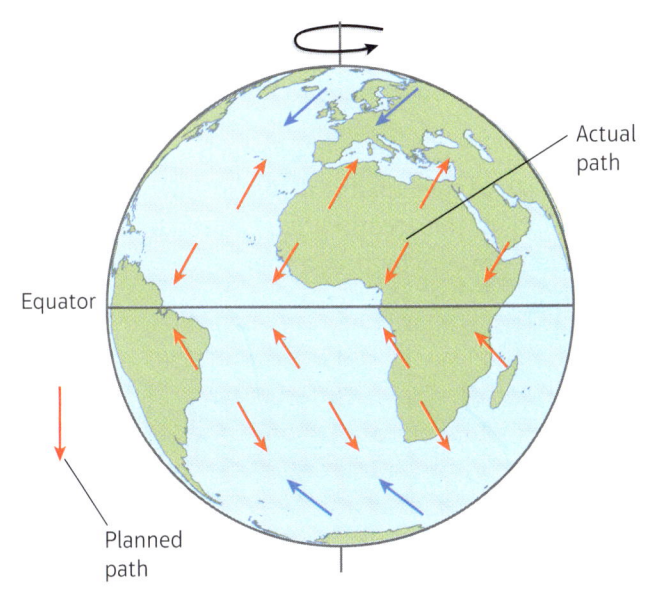

Figure 3 The Coriolis effect

Jet streams can also have an impact on air movement. Jet streams form mostly at the boundaries of the main circulation cells (e.g. at the boundary of a **Polar Cell** and a **Ferrel Cell**) where there is a significant temperature difference (Figure 4). These streams can affect the movement of other weather systems and can therefore change the **weather** for different areas.

Oceanic circulation

The oceans are just as effective at redistributing heat around the Earth as the air is. Also, a location's proximity to the oceans can have a large impact on its **climate** because water can hold heat for a long time.

Surface ocean currents are driven by the movement of wind across the top of the water, whereas deep ocean currents are driven by water sinking and rising because of temperature changes.

Did you know?

Cold, dry air from the northern Polar Cell meets warm, moist air from the Ferrel Cell near the UK's latitude.

Where they meet, rising air causes low pressure and unsettled weather. Surface currents move warm water from the tropics north and south towards the poles. These currents transfer heat away from the tropics. As the water reaches the poles, it cools significantly and sinks towards the depths of the ocean. These deep ocean currents eventually return to the surface and flow back towards the tropics and the cycle starts over again.

Activity

1. Identify two ways in which heat at the Equator can be re-distributed around the world.
2. Use a diagram to explain how ocean currents can affect the climate of an area.
3. How can the Coriolis effect and jet stream impact on the weather of an area?

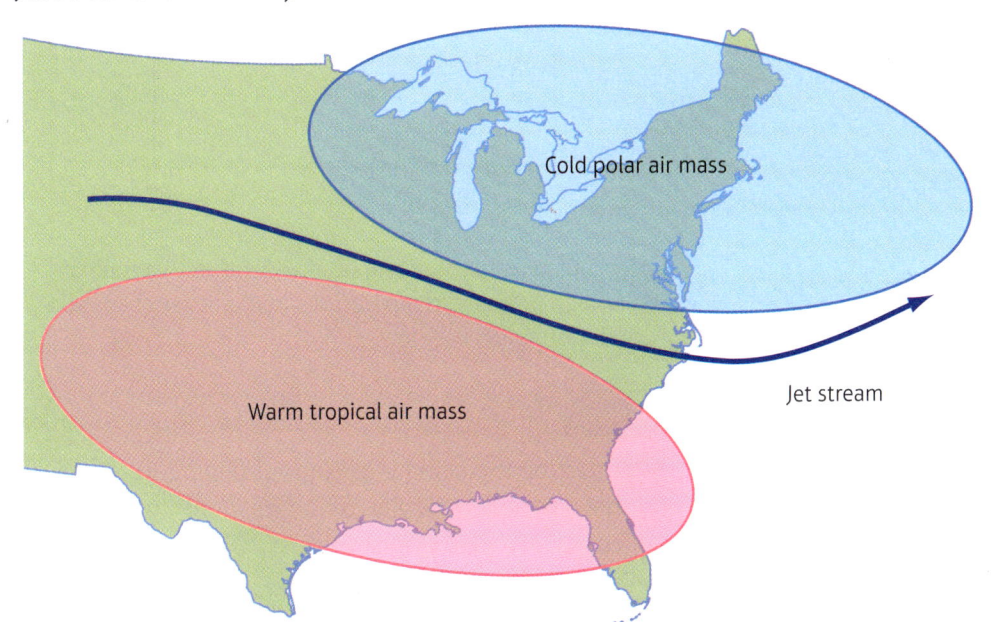

Figure 4 The northern Polar jet stream

13

1A Hazardous Earth: Climate

Atmospheric pressure

Atmospheric pressure is the 'weight' of the air and the force this exerts on the ground. Pressure has a big impact on the climatic features of an area.

As the air continues to rise away from the Earth's surface, the heating effect from the warm ground is reduced and the air begins to cool. Cooler air has less energy and so it begins to sink back towards the Earth.

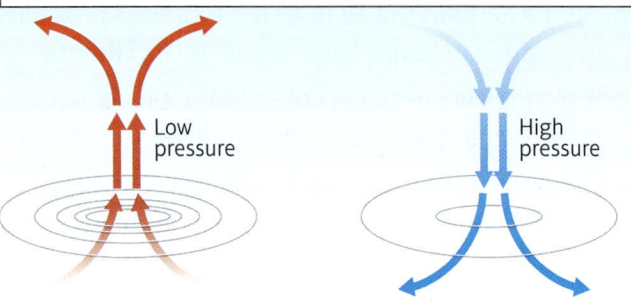

Low pressure | High pressure

The warmth of the Earth's surface heats the air above it, increasing the amount of energy in the air. This causes the air to rise. Rising air exerts less pressure on the ground and so an area of low pressure is formed below it.

The 'weight' of the sinking air exerts more pressure on the ground and an area of high pressure is formed.

Figure 5 Low atmospheric pressure and high atmospheric pressure

Did you know?

Average air pressure is approximately 1000 **millibars**. Below this is low pressure, and above it is high pressure. Pressure is represented on weather maps by **isobars** (lines that show areas of equal pressure).

High pressure usually brings settled weather and low pressure brings unsettled weather. The UK experiences both high and low pressure weather systems as they move from one area to another.

High atmospheric pressure and arid areas

Regular high pressure causes areas to become **arid**, meaning that the area receives low average rainfall – less than 250 mm in a year.

The **Hadley Cells** and the Ferrel Cells meet around 30° north and south of the Equator. Here both cells are returning air back towards the surface of the Earth so there is a zone of high pressure (Figure 1 on page 12). As this air sinks it becomes denser and its pressure increases, causing it to warm up and dry out. The increasing pressure stops any remaining moisture in the air from condensing, so no clouds form. Dry air and no clouds mean no rain.

Regular high pressure causes these mid-latitude areas to become **arid**, meaning that they receive low average rainfall – less than 250 mm in a year. There are two reasons for this.

- The Sun's radiation is intense here and the clear skies mean that daytime temperatures are very high.
- When sinking dry air reaches the surface it blows outwards. Over land this can block moist winds from blowing inland from the sea to bring rain.

Tindouf, in Algeria, is located in one such high pressure area, 27° north of the Equator. Figure 6 shows the climate graph for this location. You can see that average temperatures are very high, and there is very little precipitation.

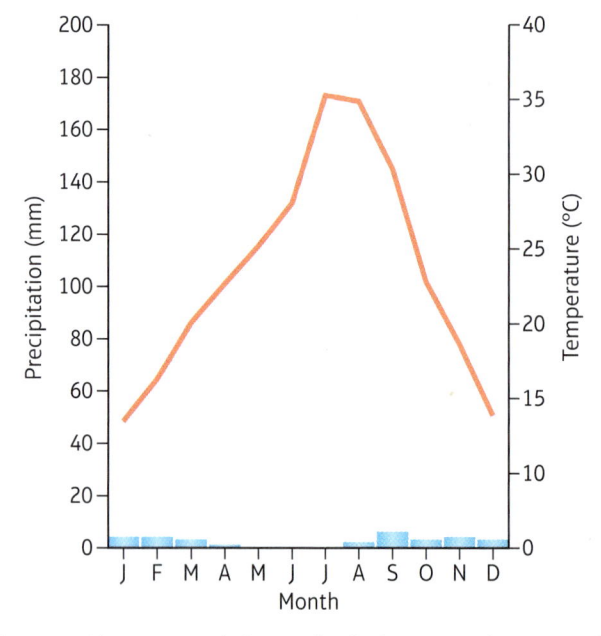

Figure 6 Climate graph for Tindouf, Algeria. In this zone of regular high pressure, temperatures (red) are very high and precipitation (blue) very low

Activity

1. Describe the climate of Tindouf (Figure 6). You will have to look carefully to find its monthly rainfall totals. In a year it receives just 30 mm of rain.
2. Explain how the global atmospheric circulation gives Tindouf its arid climate.

1A Hazardous Earth: Climate

Low atmospheric pressure and high rainfall areas
Areas with regular low pressure experience high rainfall totals. The highest rainfalls are associated with a permanent zone of low pressure called the **Inter-tropical Convergence Zone**, ITCZ for short.

The ITCZ occurs near the Equator between two Hadley Cells, where warm tropical air flows towards the Equator from north and south. Here the Sun's radiation is most intense and high temperatures cause the tropical air to rise rapidly. As this air rises it expands and becomes less dense, causing low pressure. Rising moisture-heavy air causes thunderclouds (**cumulonimbus** clouds) to form, so rainfall in this zone is heavy and regular, especially over land. In these latitudes there are often rainforest ecosystems because the daily heavy rainfall and warm temperatures are perfect for plant growth (see Topic 8). The ITCZ is strongest over the oceans, where it is associated with **source areas** for tropical cyclones (page 25).

Because the Earth is tilted, in June the Sun is directly overhead at 23½° north (the Tropic of Cancer) and in December at 23½° south (the Tropic of Capricorn). The ITCZ also moves through the year, roughly between the tropics, taking heavy rainfall with it.

Figure 7 shows the climate graph for Singapore, which is located 1.3° north of the Equator in a zone of permanently low pressure.

Activity

1. Describe the climate of Singapore (Figure 7). Note how little the temperature changes through the year because of its location near to the Equator. Note how much rain it gets and how rainfall never falls below 150 mm.
2. Explain how the global atmospheric circulation gives Singapore its wet, tropical climate.

Did you know?

Some tropical areas of the world have a wet season and a dry season. This is related to the movement of the ITCZ. The areas are dry when the ITCZ moves away from them, because then they have high pressure. When the ITCZ tracks over them, it brings low pressure and very high precipitation.

Checkpoint

Now it is time to review your understanding of global atmospheric and ocean circulation and how it determines where the areas of regular high pressure and regular low pressure are located.

Strengthen

S1 Explain how low atmospheric pressure and high atmospheric pressure occur.
S2 What is the difference between an isobar and a millibar? (Use the glossary to help you.)
S3 Draw a diagram to explain why the Sun's solar radiation is most intense at the Equator and least intense at the poles.

Challenge

C1 Write a guide for Key Stage 3 students on how to read a climate graph.
C2 What is the term used to describe the effect of the Earth's rotation on winds, making them curve north and south above and below the Equator?
C3 Explain how ocean currents transfer heat energy around the Earth.

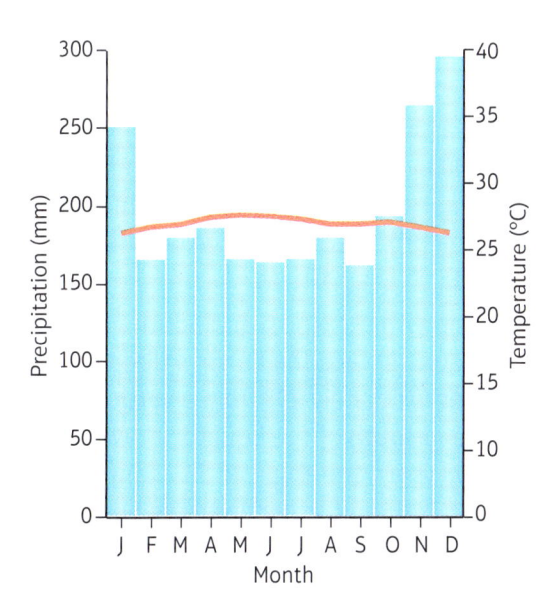

Figure 7 Climate graph for Singapore. In this zone of regular low pressure, temperatures (red) and precipitation (blue) are consistently high

1A Hazardous Earth: Climate

What are the natural causes of global climate change?

Learning objectives
- To know how the Earth's climate has changed over time
- To understand the causes of natural climate change at different times and their impact on the Earth
- To understand how we can use natural evidence of climate change

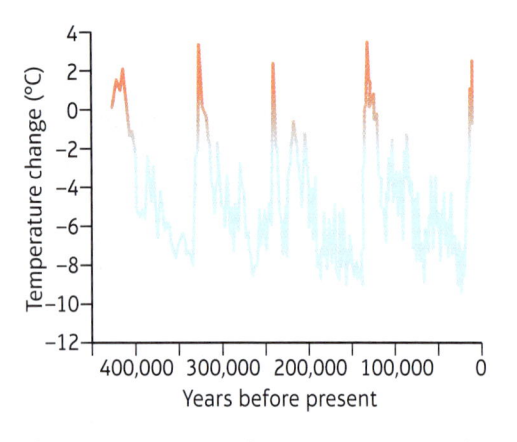

Figure 8 Average surface temperatures over the last 450,000 years

Climate change refers to how the average climatic conditions of the planet vary over time. At some points in our planet's history the Earth has been comparatively warm and during other periods it has been significantly colder (Figure 8). The planet's history is divided into **periods** and the climate during the **Quaternary period** (the last 2.6 million years) has changed many times.

Climate change can occur through both natural and human causes. Natural causes have been responsible for most climate change during the majority of the Earth's history. Human causes have had a greater impact over the last 250 years compared with natural causes, particularly since the Industrial Revolution.

Did you know?
Between about 1550 and 1850 the UK experienced a 'Little Ice Age'. Temperatures were sometimes low enough that the River Thames froze. The ice was thick enough for people to walk across the frozen river.

Natural causes of climate change

Several natural processes can lead to climate change. One such process is **Milankovitch cycles**. These are natural changes to the Earth's orbit and position that affect how much radiation we receive from the Sun. Sometimes these result in the Earth receiving less radiation than normal, leading to cooler periods. At other times in these cycles the Earth receives more radiation than normal, leading to warmer periods or global warming. There are three types of cycle.

- **Eccentricity** – the orbit of the Earth changes shape over long periods of time, approximately every 100,000 years. This means that sometimes the Earth's orbit around the Sun is more circular, making us slightly warmer (**interglacial**), and sometimes the orbit becomes more elliptical, making the Earth slightly cooler (**glacial**).

- **Axial tilt** – the Earth does not sit with the North and South Poles exactly at the top and bottom of the planet. In fact, the Earth is tilted so that the poles are actually rotated approximately 23° from a vertical position. This creates our seasons north and south of the Equator. However, over a period of approximately 40,000 years, the angle of tilt changes. This means that sometimes the Earth is tilted further away the Sun, which makes the difference in the seasons more pronounced (summers are warmer and winters are colder). When it is tilted closer to the Sun, the difference in the seasons is less.

- **Precession** – as the Earth rotates on its axis (which is, of course, what gives us day and night), it does not do so perfectly. In fact, the Earth 'wobbles' on its axis, in a similar way to a spinning top as it slows down.

1A Hazardous Earth: Climate

As this happens, the direction the axis is facing changes. This affects our seasons and creates either greater or smaller differences between summer and winter. This occurs over a period of approximately 24,000 years.

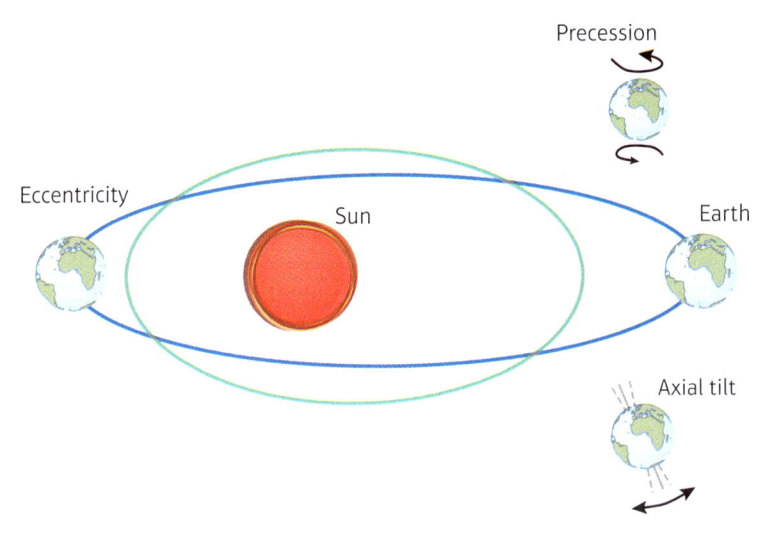

Figure 9 Milankovitch cycles

The other main natural causes of climate change are shown in Table 1.

Table 1 Other natural causes of global climate change

Cause	Description
Solar variation	The amount of radiation the Sun produces varies over time. Periods of lower solar activity are likely to lead to glacial periods and those with higher activity to lead to interglacial periods.
Volcanism	Large-scale volcanic eruptions can eject huge volumes of ash and dust into the atmosphere. Some eruptions produce so much that the volcanic material partially blocks out solar radiation, reducing global temperatures and causing cooler periods.
Surface impact	Large cosmic material, such as asteroids and comets, can impact the Earth's surface. This can eject large volumes of dust into the atmosphere, partially blocking solar radiation and leading to glacial periods. Climate change that is caused by surface impact can have dramatic effects on life. One such impact approximately 65 million years ago is considered to be responsible for the extinction of the dinosaurs. It is not the force of the impact that is thought to have wiped them out however, but rather the massive climate change that was created by the impact.

Activity

1 Describe three natural processes that can cause a cooling of global temperatures.

2 Study Figure 8. Would you agree or disagree that the Earth appears to have regular cycles of warmer surface temperatures and cooler surface temperatures? Provide some evidence (figures) from the graph to back up your answer.

3 Explain how eccentricity, axial tilt and precession might help explain the patterns of changing global surface temperatures that you identified in Figure 8.

Exam-style question

Explain **one** way the climate of the Earth can change because of natural causes. **(3 marks)**

Exam tip

Read the question carefully. The question asks about natural causes, therefore it is only information about these that will earn marks. Don't go off topic.

Command word

Remember to check the command word in the question. **Explain** means that you have to give reasons for your answers, not just identify the correct points.

1A Hazardous Earth: Climate

Evidence for natural climate change

Figure 10 shows how surface temperatures in the UK have changed over the last 1000 years – and Figure 8 on page 16 shows average global surface temperatures over the last 450,000 years. But recording temperatures using thermometers has only been done for a few hundred years (since 1659 to be exact), and really reliable weather and temperature records have only been kept for about 100 years (since 1914). So how can we know what the temperatures were in the UK 1000 years ago, or what global temperatures were 450,000 years ago? Where does evidence for past climate change come from?

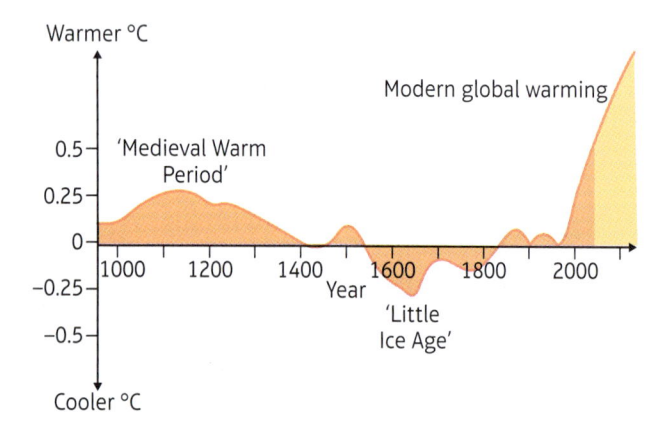

Figure 10 UK climate change over the last 1000 years

This evidence comes from three main sources: **ice cores**, **tree rings** and historical sources.

Figure 11 A researcher with an ice core at an Antarctic research station

Ice cores

In polar regions, such as Greenland or Antarctica, ice has built up over hundreds of thousands of years (800,000 years in the case of Antarctica). In some places the ice is 3000 metres deep. Ice is formed in layers – one every year, like the rings in a tree – so it is possible to work out how many years from the present day the layers represent.

As ice forms, it traps tiny bubbles of air frozen into the ice. These air bubbles contain a sample of the atmosphere from the time that they were frozen. Although humans have only been measuring carbon dioxide in the atmosphere since the 1950s, the ice sheets of Antarctica and Greenland have stored records of carbon dioxide levels in the atmosphere for thousands of years.

Also, water has different isotopes (atoms with different numbers of neutrons) depending on temperature, and these different isotope levels are frozen into the ice. When scientists analyse the isotopes of an ice core they can tell what the temperature was when that ice was formed.

Ice cores are made by drilling down into the ice sheet and collecting a long, thin cylinder of ice. These cores can be as long as the ice is deep – up to 3 km. Climate scientists can then identify which layer in the ice core relates to which year. They can then reconstruct the temperature for that year from the isotope levels and the level of atmospheric gases, such as carbon dioxide or methane, in the bubbles of trapped air in the ice core.

Tree rings

As trees grow they produce growth rings that can be seen in a cross section of a trunk (see Figure 12). Growth rings tend to be wider in warmer, wetter climates and narrower in colder, drier climates. Analysing the rings can tell us what the climate was like throughout a tree's history. Some trees live for hundreds or even thousands of years, but we can also reconstruct past climates from timber used in old buildings – from trees cut down centuries ago – and even from fossilised trees.

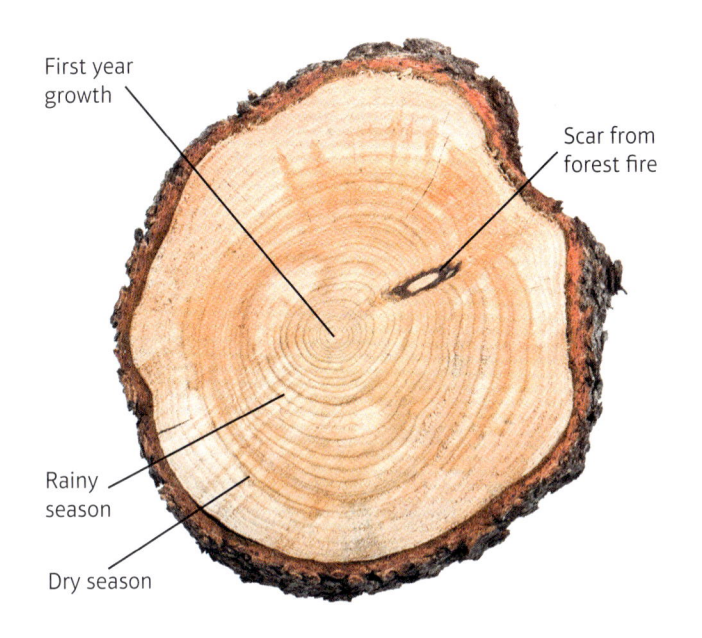

1A Hazardous Earth: Climate

Figure 12 Variations in tree rings, representing different climatic conditions

Labels: First year growth; Scar from forest fire; Rainy season; Dry season

Historical sources

We can also use historical documents, such as personal diaries, paintings and religious records, to examine more recent historical climates. These documents include descriptions of what the climate was like during the past. For example, the Anglo-Saxon Chronicles were recorded by English monks from around 890 to the middle of the 1100s. The Chronicles often record years of drought or heavy rain. We can use these records to cross-check evidence from other sources about climate change.

Exam-style question

Identify **two** sources used as evidence of climate change 1000 to 500 years ago.
- A Tree ring measurements
- B Line graphs
- C Satellite imagery
- D Temperature records
- E Historical sources

(2 marks)

Activity

1. Explain how a tree growth ring would show evidence of higher than normal rainfall.
2. Study Figure 10. Explain how evidence from ice cores, tree rings and historical sources would have been used to generate the temperature data for this graph.
3. Scientists can identify when major volcanic eruptions occurred hundreds of thousands of years ago. Which type of evidence described on these pages would record volcanic eruptions, and how?

Checkpoint

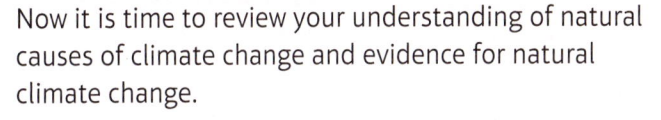

Now it is time to review your understanding of natural causes of climate change and evidence for natural climate change.

Strengthen

S1 What are the three types of orbital change (Milankovitch cycles)?

S2 How do we know that natural climate change has happened?

Challenge

C1 Which of the four main causes of natural climate change do you think would cause the biggest change? Justify your answer.

C2 Why do you think scientists are sure that the 'Medieval Warm Period' and the 'Little Ice Age' (see Figure 10) were caused by natural climate variations, rather than human causes?

1A Hazardous Earth: Climate

How are human activities causing climate change?

> **Learning objectives**
> - To understand how human activity can lead to an enhanced greenhouse effect
> - To interpret the evidence for human activity causing climate change
> - To consider the possible consequences of climate change on people

The greenhouse effect is a natural process which keeps the Earth warm. Greenhouse gases in the atmosphere, such as carbon dioxide and methane, trap some of the heat that is radiated from the surface which would otherwise have been lost into space. Without this effect, the average temperature of the Earth would be significantly cooler (Figure 13).

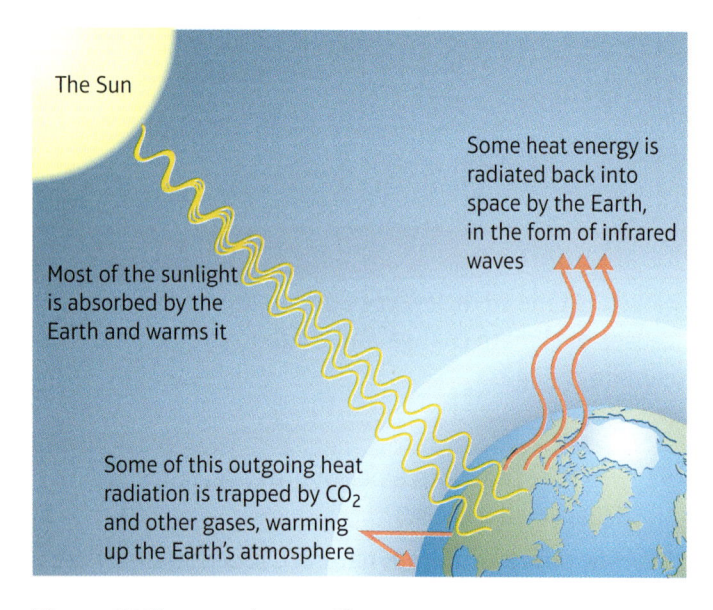

Figure 13 The greenhouse effect

The enhanced greenhouse effect

Human activity has resulted in a large increase in the production of greenhouse gases, leading to the **enhanced greenhouse effect** and global warming. The main human activities that have caused the enhanced greenhouse effect are shown in Table 2.

Evidence for human activity causing climate change

There are three main sources of evidence for the enhanced greenhouse effect – global temperature rise, sea level rise and warming oceans, and declining Arctic ice.

Table 2 Human activities that produce greenhouse gases

Cause	Description
Energy	The demand for electricity is growing because of increasing population and new technologies. Most of our energy is produced through burning fossil fuels (coal, oil, natural gas), which produce greenhouse gases.
Industry	As levels of disposable income rise, increased demand for the production of consumer goods leads to industrial growth and the need for more energy, resulting in more fossil fuels being burnt.
Transport	With cars becoming more affordable and more people taking flights over long distances, huge quantities of fuel are used. Almost all transport relies on burning fossil fuels in some way, again increasing the amount of greenhouse gases released.
Farming	Population growth has led to a higher demand for food production. Mechanisation means more fuel is burnt, and intensive farming of cattle and rice results in increased production of methane, which is a greenhouse gas.

- Measurements of average global atmospheric temperatures show a steep rise from around the 1950s to the present. Although global temperatures have risen before, it is unusual for the increase to be so rapid.
- The rise in global temperatures is closely associated with the rise in carbon dioxide. As you can see from Table 3, the increase in atmospheric carbon dioxide since 1950 has been much higher and much more

1A Hazardous Earth: Climate

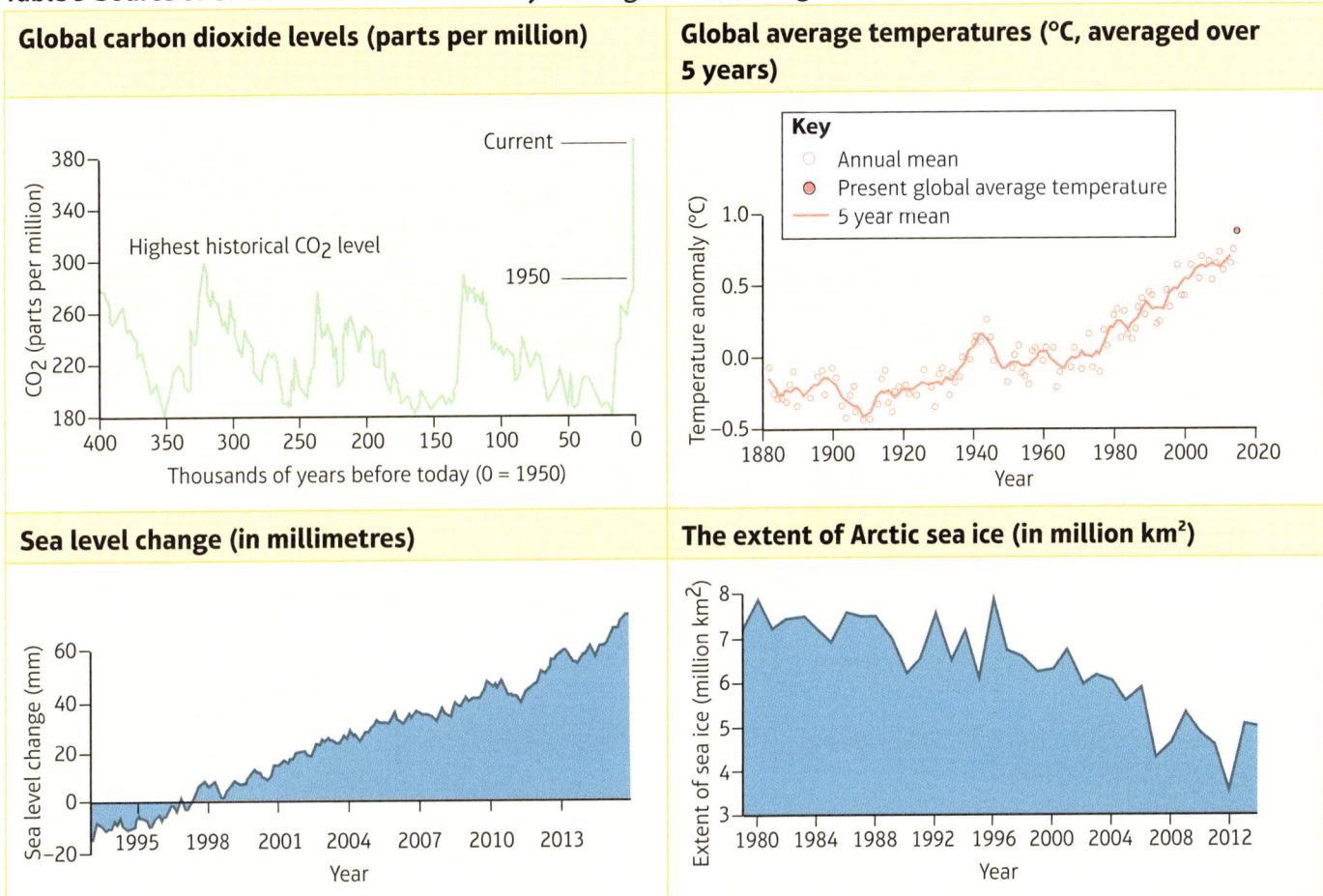

Table 3 Source of evidence for human activity causing climate change

Global carbon dioxide levels (parts per million)	Global average temperatures (°C, averaged over 5 years)
Sea level change (in millimetres)	The extent of Arctic sea ice (in million km²)

rapid than anything recorded for the last 400,000 years. Human activity has produced this increase, especially the burning of fossil fuels to produce energy.

- Long-term measurement of sea levels shows that globally they have risen by about 20 cm since 1900. Rises have increased recently to 3.2 mm a year and are higher in some areas than others. Sea level rise is caused by melting glaciers and ice caps, and significantly by **thermal expansion** – as water gets warmer, it expands. This means that global sea temperatures have been increasing too – the global average increase is around 0.1°C.
- The extent of Arctic sea ice has decreased. Every year sea ice melts in spring and reaches its lowest extent in September. Warmer global temperatures have meant more ice has melted. The sharp decline in the extent of the sea ice cannot be explained by natural cycles in the Arctic.

The evidence shows that global temperatures are increasing, and that the change is too rapid to be explained by natural causes. The rapid increase in atmospheric carbon dioxide is due to human activity, and scientists are certain that more carbon dioxide in the atmosphere will lead to an enhanced greenhouse effect.

Activity

1 Study Table 3. Explain why the increase in global carbon dioxide levels can be used to explain the changes seen in the other three graphs.

2 In Table 3, the four graphs do not show changes over the same time period. Explain how using different time periods can make the rate of change shown by line graphs seem more or less dramatic.

3 Extreme weather events are becoming more common around the world – extreme temperatures are five times more common now than they were 100 years ago, for example. How could more frequent and more extreme weather events be used as evidence of the enhanced greenhouse effect?

1A Hazardous Earth: Climate

What are the possible consequences of climate change?

Climate change is likely to have a range of negative impacts on people. How severe these impacts are will depend on how much global temperatures increase and on where people are in the world, as some places will be impacted more severely than others.

> **Did you know?**
> Climate change could have positive consequences for some people as well as negative ones. For example, large numbers of elderly people around the world suffer ill health because of cold temperatures. If winters become warmer, their health may improve. However, negative impacts are likely to outweigh positive ones. For example, older people also suffer poor health in very hot summers, which are likely to become more frequent as a result of climate change.

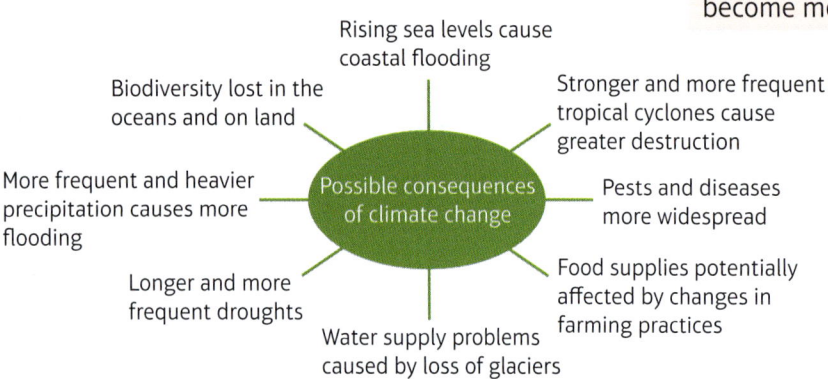

Possible consequences of climate change:
- Rising sea levels cause coastal flooding
- Stronger and more frequent tropical cyclones cause greater destruction
- Pests and diseases more widespread
- Food supplies potentially affected by changes in farming practices
- Water supply problems caused by loss of glaciers
- Longer and more frequent droughts
- More frequent and heavier precipitation causes more flooding
- Biodiversity lost in the oceans and on land

Figure 14 Possible consequences of climate change

Sea level rises

It has been estimated that 23% of the world's population lives within 100 km distance of the coast (2003). Most of these people live in small coastal settlements, however the majority of the big cities in the world are also located on or near the coast. Some of the world's most heavily populated areas are on the fertile deltas of major rivers – where the river meets the sea.

A rise in sea level of 1 metre would have devastating consequences for coastal areas.

- Some low-lying island nations would be submerged – the Maldives, for example.
- Land would have to be abandoned as it flooded – for example, Bangladesh could lose 17% of its land area and 50% of its best farm land. Tens of millions of its people would need new homes and new farms to work.
- New sea defences would need to be constructed. In urban areas this would cost huge sums – US$200 billion for the USA, for example.
- Salt water from the sea would contaminate farmland and groundwater supplies.

Projections for sea level rises

It is difficult to know exactly how much sea levels could rise by, because there are many variables.

- Will greenhouse gas emissions continue to rise (which would increase the rate of warming) or will countries be able to find ways to reduce the level of greenhouse gas emissions? Climate change organisations have modelled four scenarios: (1) emissions peak by 2020 and then decline, (2) emissions peak around 2040 and then decline, (3) emissions peak around 2080 and then decline and (4) emissions continue to rise throughout the 21st century. Figure 15 shows what this might mean for global mean sea level rises.
- Will the ice sheets covering Greenland and Antarctica melt? The loss of Greenland's ice sheet would raise sea levels by 7 metres; the Antarctic ice sheets would add 13 metres. It would take many centuries for all this ice to melt, however.
- Sea level rises will be higher in some places than others because of **prevailing winds** and currents, and where the land is also sinking. These areas are at particular risk if they are also densely populated, like the USA's Gulf Coast.

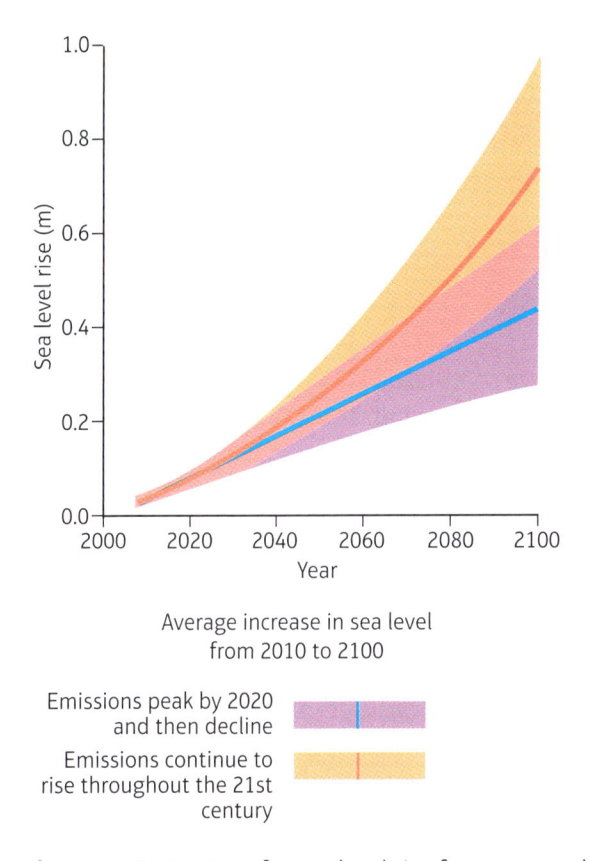

Figure 15 Projections for sea level rise for two greenhouse gas emission scenarios

Activity

Study Figure 15. Explain why climate scientists need to use different scenarios to make projections about the possible consequences of climate change.

Increased temperatures

As well as causing sea level rise through thermal expansion and possible ice-sheet melt, warmer temperatures may also have an impact on food production (changing where different crops can be grown), on the spread of pests and diseases (cold winters currently limit some pests and diseases from spreading), on water supply (if glaciers disappear then many important rivers will be dry during parts of the year) and on people's health. With increasing global temperatures, habitats will change, causing a reduction in biodiversity as animals and plants struggle to adapt to rapidly changing conditions.

Extreme weather events

Because climate is the weather of an area over a long time period, changing climates mean changes to weather also. Experts have already recorded a rise in extreme weather events, such as tropical cyclones; long droughts; flooding from intense, prolonged rainfall; and heavy snowfalls. Extreme weather events kill people and cause very high levels of destruction to property and people's possessions. An increase in extreme weather events is probably most people's experience of climate change so far, although not all extreme weather events are entirely the result of climate change.

Exam-style question

'It is not possible to make accurate predictions about the possible consequences of climate change.' Assess this statement. **(8 marks + 4 SPAG)**

Exam tip

To assess something you must consider the different factors involved and use evidence to decide which you think is the most important.

Checkpoint

Now it is time to review your understanding of the human activities that lead to climate change; the evidence for this; and the possible consequences of climate change on people.

Strengthen

S1 What human activities can cause global climate change?

S2 Study Figure 14. Pick three of the possible consequences shown and explain how they can be the result of climate change

Challenge

C1 How do we know that human activity is leading to global temperature rises?

C2 Why is it difficult for climate scientists to give precise predictions for the possible consequences of climate change?

1A Hazardous Earth: Climate

How are extreme weather events increasingly hazardous for people?

Learning objectives
- To know the key characteristics of tropical cyclones and factors that affect where and when tropical cyclones occur
- To understand how the way tropical cyclones are formed relates to the global circulation of the atmosphere
- To be able to explain the reasons why some tropical cyclones get stronger and why they eventually decline

What are tropical cyclones?
Tropical cyclones are large-scale, rotating storms that form over the oceans in tropical areas. Depending on where in the world they form, they are known as hurricanes, cyclones or typhoons. They can be devastating if they move over land.

Tropical cyclone structure
Figure 16 shows a cross section of a tropical cyclone.

- Above the tropical cyclone is a dense canopy or covering of **cirrus** cloud, caused by the massive uplift of warm, moist air into the atmosphere. When a tropical cyclone is forming, this dense canopy can make the tropical cyclone difficult to spot.
- Swirling round the centre of the tropical cyclone are rain bands – high banks of cloud that can stretch out 1000 km from the cyclone centre and which produce heavy rain and strong winds.
- At the centre of the tropical cyclone is the **eye**, and around it is the **eye wall**. This thick bank of cloud rises 15 km into the atmosphere. The eyewall has the heaviest rain and strongest winds.
- The eye often has no wind and clear skies. It is where air is falling back down to the Earth's surface – a zone of high pressure. It is often the first sign on satellite images that a tropical cyclone has formed.

Formation of tropical cyclones
As suggested by the name, tropical cyclones form in tropical areas. High temperatures cause air to rise away from the ocean surface. The rising air causes thunderstorms. Sometimes these storms group together, creating a strong flow of warm, rapidly rising air, which in turn produces an area of extreme low pressure at the centre of these converging storms.

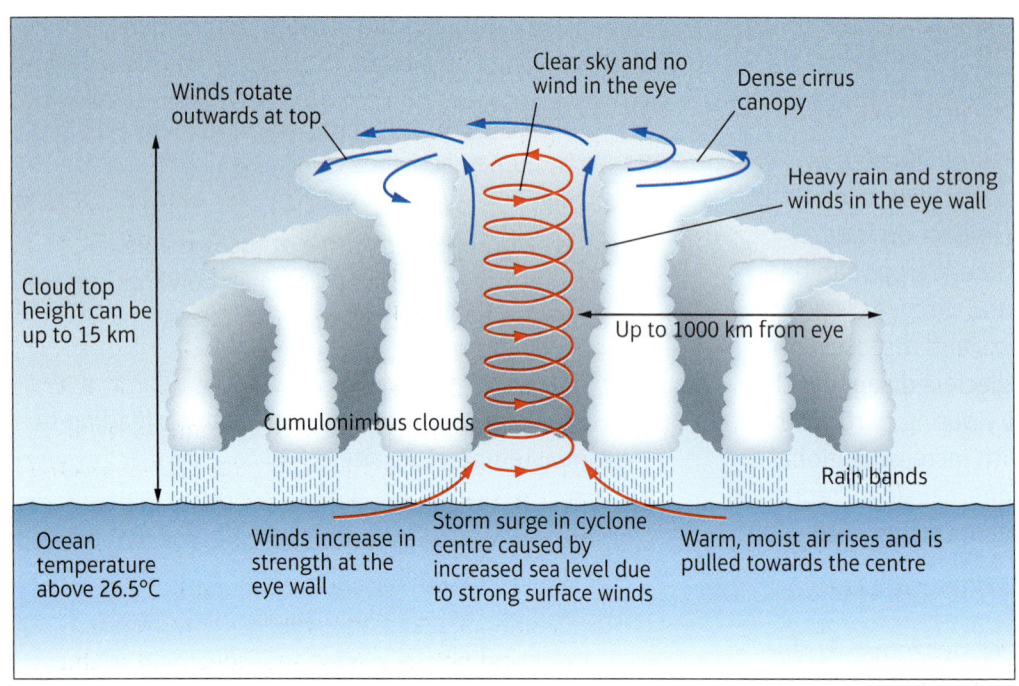

Figure 16 The structure of a tropical cyclone

However, in order for these storms to converge fully into a tropical cyclone, several trigger conditions must be present. These include:

- a source of moist, warm air, normally warmer than 26.5°C (which is why they form in the tropics)
- the time of year (season) when ocean water is at its warmest
- winds converging at the ocean surface, causing the air to rise
- formation away from the Equator so the Coriolis effect (page 13) will cause the storm to rotate.

As the storm rotates, the winds accelerate inwards and upwards, making the depression stronger and forming a tropical cyclone. The eye of a cyclone is dry and calm, because it is the only place for kilometres around where the air is sinking.

Why do tropical cyclones spin?

The rotation of tropical cyclones is a key characteristic and gives them their spiral appearance. Like all winds, the strong winds of tropical cyclones are caused by air rushing from an area of high pressure to an area of low pressure. In a tropical cyclone this process is affected by the Coriolis effect. The rushing winds are deflected into a spin by the rotation of the Earth, which makes all Northern Hemisphere tropical cyclones spin counter-clockwise and all Southern Hemisphere tropical cyclones to spin clockwise.

Tropical cyclones source areas and tracks

The area where a tropical cyclone is formed is called its source area. Source areas have the trigger conditions needed for tropical cyclone formation – particularly sea water temperature of 26.5°C or more. These temperatures are only usually reached between June and November in the northern tropics and between April and November in the southern tropics. Tropical cyclones have **seasonal distribution**.

Tropical cyclones move away from their source area following the direction of the prevailing winds and ocean currents – west for Northern Hemisphere tropical cyclones. Where a tropical cyclone travels is called its **track**.

Figure 17 shows that tropical cyclones in the North Atlantic start by tracking west with the prevailing winds,

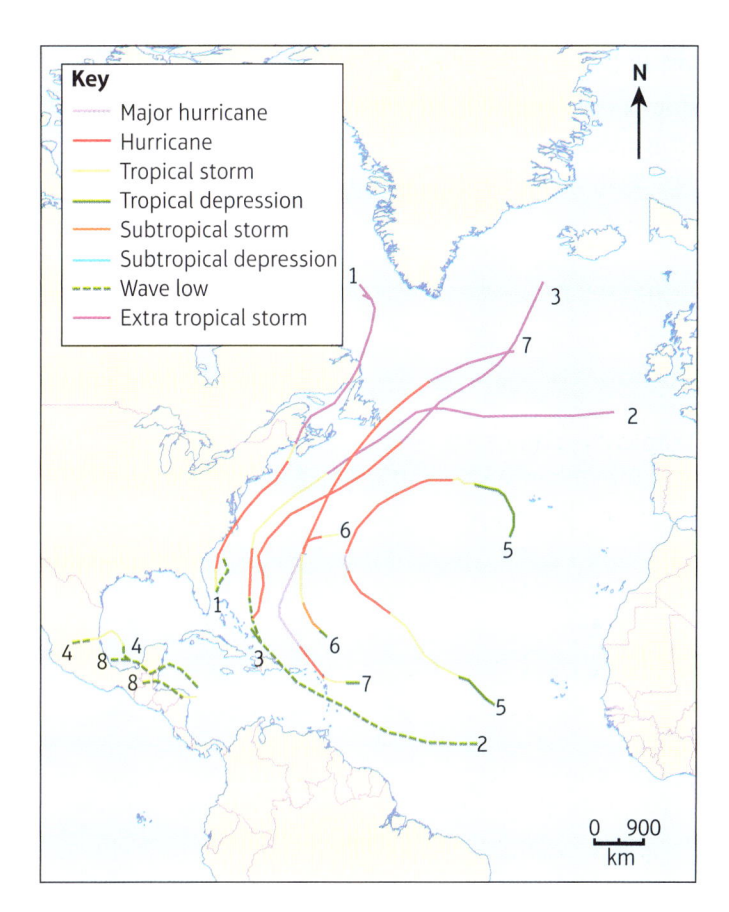

Figure 17 Tracks of eight tropical cyclones in the North Atlantic in the 2014 hurricane season mapped by NOAA

but then curve northwards. This happens when winds in the middle and upper atmosphere change direction and move the tropical cyclone towards the north. If the tropical cyclone reaches as far as 30°N, prevailing winds at that latitude may start to push it north-east, giving the track a hook effect.

Activity

1. Wind speeds in very strong tropical cyclones can exceed 250 km per hour. In which part of a tropical cyclone are winds generally strongest – the eye, the eye wall, the rain bands or the cirrus canopy?

2. Study Figure 17. Use an atlas to identify which countries were affected by tropical cyclones in the North Atlantic hurricane season, 2014.

3. Explain why tropical cyclones have a seasonal distribution and a geographical distribution – between June and November in the northern tropics and between April and November in the southern tropics.

1A Hazardous Earth: Climate

Understanding tropical cyclone intensity
Tropical cyclones and the global circulation of the atmosphere

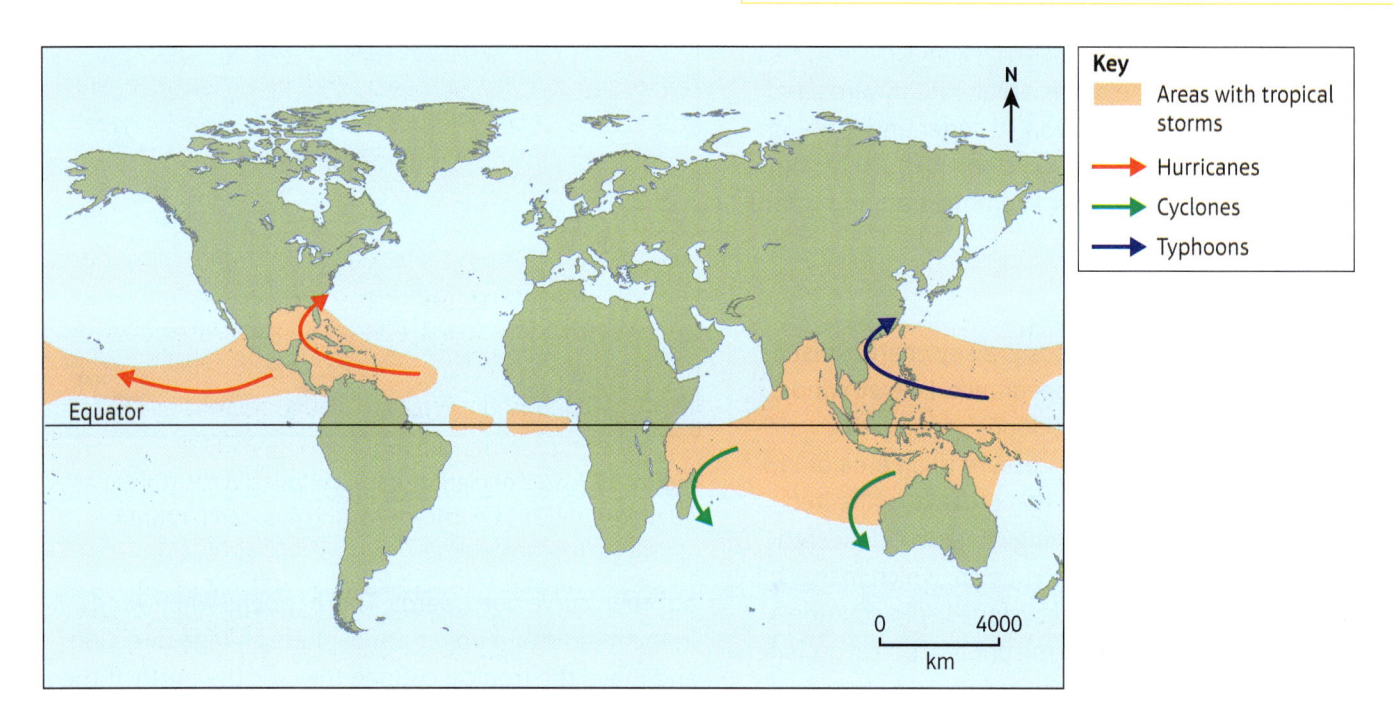

Figure 18 shows the global distribution of tropical cyclones (and the different names they have in different parts of the world). Tropical cyclone source areas are in the tropics, a few degrees north and south of the Equator.

> **Exam-style question**
> Study Figure 18, which shows the global distribution of tropical cyclones. Suggest **two** reasons for the distribution of tropical cyclones shown in Figure 18.
> **(4 marks)**

> **Exam tip**
> As well as identifying each reason you also need to say why it would affect the distribution.

Figure 18 The global distribution of tropical cyclones

As you know, tropical cyclones need warm water to form, which explains their distribution in the tropics. They need the Coriolis effect to give them rotation, which explains why they are not found along the Equator itself – the Coriolis effect begins at around 5° of latitude north and south of the Equator. There are also additional factors required for tropical cyclones to form:

- high humidity – there must be a lot of moisture in the atmosphere
- rapid cooling – rising air must condense quickly to generate the huge amounts of energy to power a tropical cyclone
- low wind shear – if winds are blowing in different directions up through the atmosphere, the cyclone cannot form

- pre-existing low-pressure disturbances – tropical cyclones usually form when smaller storms come together.

The influence of the ITCZ
These additional trigger factors are most likely to occur together in the ITCZ – the Inter-tropical Convergence Zone (see page 15). This is an area of permanently low pressure generated by global circulation of the atmosphere. Its band of thunderstorms extends around the Equator. It forms as part of the atmospheric circulation cell at the Equator (Hadley Cell), where warm, moist air is pushed up by the intense solar radiation. The constant thunderstorms, prevailing strong winds blowing to the west and warm, moist air make this zone the main source area for tropical cyclones.

1A Hazardous Earth: Climate

Factors affecting tropical cyclone intensity

Tropical cyclones are powered by the heat energy that is released when warm moist air condenses. This process generates truly enormous amounts of energy – 600 trillion watts. The majority of this energy is used to push air up to the upper atmosphere, with only a small amount (3%) involved in creating the tropical cyclone's strong winds or forward movement. The physics of this process (the latent heat of condensation) mean that the warmer the water that fuels the tropical cyclone, the more intense (powerful) the tropical cyclone will be.

Figure 19 Satellite photograph of a tropical cyclone in the Gulf of Mexico. You can see the eye in the centre

Dissipation of tropical cyclones

Dissipation is the term used to describe a tropical cyclone that is losing energy and decreasing in intensity. This can happen for three main reasons:

1. when it reaches land it loses energy because it has lost its fuel source – the warm water
2. when it moves into areas of colder water (below 26.5°C)
3. when it runs into other weather systems where winds are blowing in different directions.

Tropical cyclones can only form if the winds throughout the atmosphere's layers are blowing in the same general direction. If winds start to blow in different directions at different levels of the atmosphere, the tropical cyclone may begin to be pulled apart.

If a tropical cyclone makes landfall on an island, it will begin to dissipate, but as the track takes it back over water again, the tropical cyclone can re-intensify as it regains its fuel source.

It usually takes a couple of days for a tropical cyclone to dissipate into a normal low pressure weather system. However, if the tropical cyclone passes over mountainous areas, it will weaken much more quickly. This will result in the release of huge quantities of rainfall that can lead to floods and landslides.

Did you know?

There is a direct relationship between the warmth of the oceans and the intensity of tropical cyclones. So climate scientists predict that one consequence of increasing global temperatures is likely to be more frequent and more intense tropical cyclones. There is some recent evidence that this may already be happening – but so far scientists are uncertain.

Checkpoint

Now it is time to review your understanding of tropical cyclone characteristics and distribution; their link to the global circulation of the atmosphere; reasons why some tropical cyclones intensify; and how tropical cyclones dissipate (lose energy).

Strengthen

S1 Name three of the conditions that must be present before a tropical cyclone can form.

S2 Describe what would happen if a tropical cyclone moved into an area of colder sea water.

Challenge

C1 Study Figure 19, which shows a satellite image of a large tropical cyclone. How many of the following can you identify – eye, eye wall, rain bands, cirrus canopy.

C2 Study Figure 17, on page 25. Why do you think some of the hurricanes intensified more than others in the same season? Why did some track further distances than others before dissipating? Suggest one or more reasons for each of these two questions.

1A Hazardous Earth: Climate

What impacts do tropical cyclones have on people and environments?

Learning objectives
- To know what physical hazards are caused by tropical cyclones
- To understand the impact tropical cyclones can have on people and environments
- To explain why some countries are more vulnerable to the impacts of tropical cyclones than others

Tropical cyclones are severe weather hazards that can bring loss of life and damage on a massive scale. While a tropical cyclone itself can be classed as a hazard, the storm also produces specific physical hazards.

- **High winds** – Tropical cyclones produce winds of over 119 up to 250 km per hour or more. Trees can be uprooted by the force of the wind and infrastructure like power cables damaged. The strongest winds can severely damage or destroy buildings, especially if they are poorly built. Wind-blown debris can impact on people and buildings, causing damage, injury and loss of life.
- **Intense rainfall** – As tropical cyclones move over the ocean they take up a large amount of water, this results in a large release of rain. Weather forecasters can estimate how much rain may fall based on how fast the storm has been travelling over the water. The intense rain created by the tropical cyclone can lead to flooding, damage to property and injury, as fast-flowing water can knock people over, even if it is not particularly deep.
- **Storm surges** – A tropical cyclone creates a large area of low pressure, which allows the level of the sea to rise. When this is combined with the high winds produced by the storm, a large mass of water can be forced towards land by the strength of the wind. When the surge hits land, it does so with severe force. Storm surges can erode beaches and coastal habitats, damage coastal defences and flow inland, contaminating farmland and freshwater areas such as lakes.
- **Coastal flooding** – The combination of intense rain and storm surges puts coastal areas at severe risk of flooding. Not only does this put people and property at risk, but it can also affect the farming and tourism industries. The environmental impact of flooding by salt water will also be very damaging.
- **Landslides** – Intense rainfall affects areas of high **relief** as well as coastal lowlands. High levels of rain can **saturate** the soil very quickly. This makes the soil very heavy and, in areas with steep slopes, can mean that the soil will no longer be able to hold its position and will start to slide down the slope. The **geology** of an area is very significant. For example, where the underlying rock is impermeable, the wet soil and rock above can easily slide over it and downhill. This can cause massive devastation to any settlements at the base of the slope, and will cause river flooding if the landslide blocks river channels.

All of these hazards pose a severe risk to people, property and the local environment. However, it is wind speed that is the most reliable indicator of the damage a tropical cyclone will cause.

Activity

Create a table like the one shown here. Use the text on this page to create a description of each physical hazard and then to identify an impact this hazard could have on people and an impact this hazard could have on the environment. The first one is completed for you.

Name of hazard	Description of hazard	Impact on people	Impact on environment
High winds	Tropical cyclones can produce winds of over 250 km per hour	People can be killed by flying debris	Trees can be uprooted and blown over
Intense rainfall			
Storm surges			
Coastal flooding			
Landslides			

1A Hazardous Earth: Climate

Assessing the impact of tropical cyclones

The Saffir–Simpson Hurricane Wind Scale is the most common scale used to classify tropical cyclones. It is based on the wind speed generated by the tropical cyclone and estimates the likely damage to property and the environment. Tropical cyclones over Category 3 have the potential to cause major loss of life and very significant amounts of damage.

Activity

Study the two photos in Figure 20. Using the Saffir–Simpson scale, estimate the category of tropical cyclone that caused the damage shown in each photo.

Exam-style question

The Saffir–Simpson scale is used to categorise tropical cyclones. Identify which of the following is the most important measurement when deciding the category of a cyclone?

- ☐ A The length of time that the cyclone lasts
- ☐ B The wind speed in the cyclone
- ☐ C The size of the cyclone
- ☐ D The height of the storm clouds   **(1 mark)**

Exam tip

Don't rush questions that carry only one mark. It is easy to make a silly mistake that will cost you the mark. Take a minute to check each option until you are sure of your choice.

Table 4 The Saffir–Simpson scale

Category	Sustained winds (km/h)	Damage	Storm surge (metres)
1	119–153	Minimal: Unanchored mobile homes, vegetation, signs.	1.2–1.7
2	154–177	Moderate: All mobile homes, roofs, small crafts, flooding.	1.8–2.6
3	178–208	Extensive: Small buildings, low-lying roads cut off.	2.7–3.8
4	209–249	Extreme: Roofs destroyed, trees down, roads cut off, mobile homes destroyed, beach homes flooded.	3.9–5.4
5	More than 250	Catastrophic: Many buildings destroyed, vegetation destroyed, major roads cut off, homes flooded.	Greater than 5.4

Figure 20 Damage associated with tropical cyclones

1A Hazardous Earth: Climate

> **Did you know?**
>
> Geographic Information Systems (GIS) data is a good way to track tropical cyclones in space and time. You can use the American NOAA website to track hurricanes in the Atlantic and Eastern Pacific Oceans using GIS, as well as satellite imagery. Australia, India, Hong Kong and Japan have similar websites.

> **Did you know?**
>
> The cast and crew of the original *Jurassic Park* film had to be evacuated from their location set in Hawaii because of the effects of Hurricane Iniki.

Why are some countries vulnerable to tropical cyclones?

Some countries are more vulnerable to the impacts of tropical cyclones than others. There are three main types of vulnerability to tropical cyclones:

1. physical vulnerability
2. social vulnerability
3. economic vulnerability.

Physical vulnerability

As tropical cyclones form over water, coastal areas are at significantly more risk of being affected by tropical cyclones than inland areas. This does not mean that inland areas cannot suffer from the effects of these storms, but the risk is much less. Island nations, such as the Philippines and the Maldives, have most of their settlements in low-lying coastal regions, which makes them much more vulnerable to the impacts of the storms.

The relief of an area also affects how vulnerable it will be to the effects of a tropical cyclone. Areas of low relief will be at risk not only from high winds and rain, but also from the storm surges created by the tropical cyclones, making flooding more likely than it would be in areas of high relief. However, areas of high relief are more at risk from the heavy rain than the storm surge, as this can cause landslides, particularly in the steepest areas.

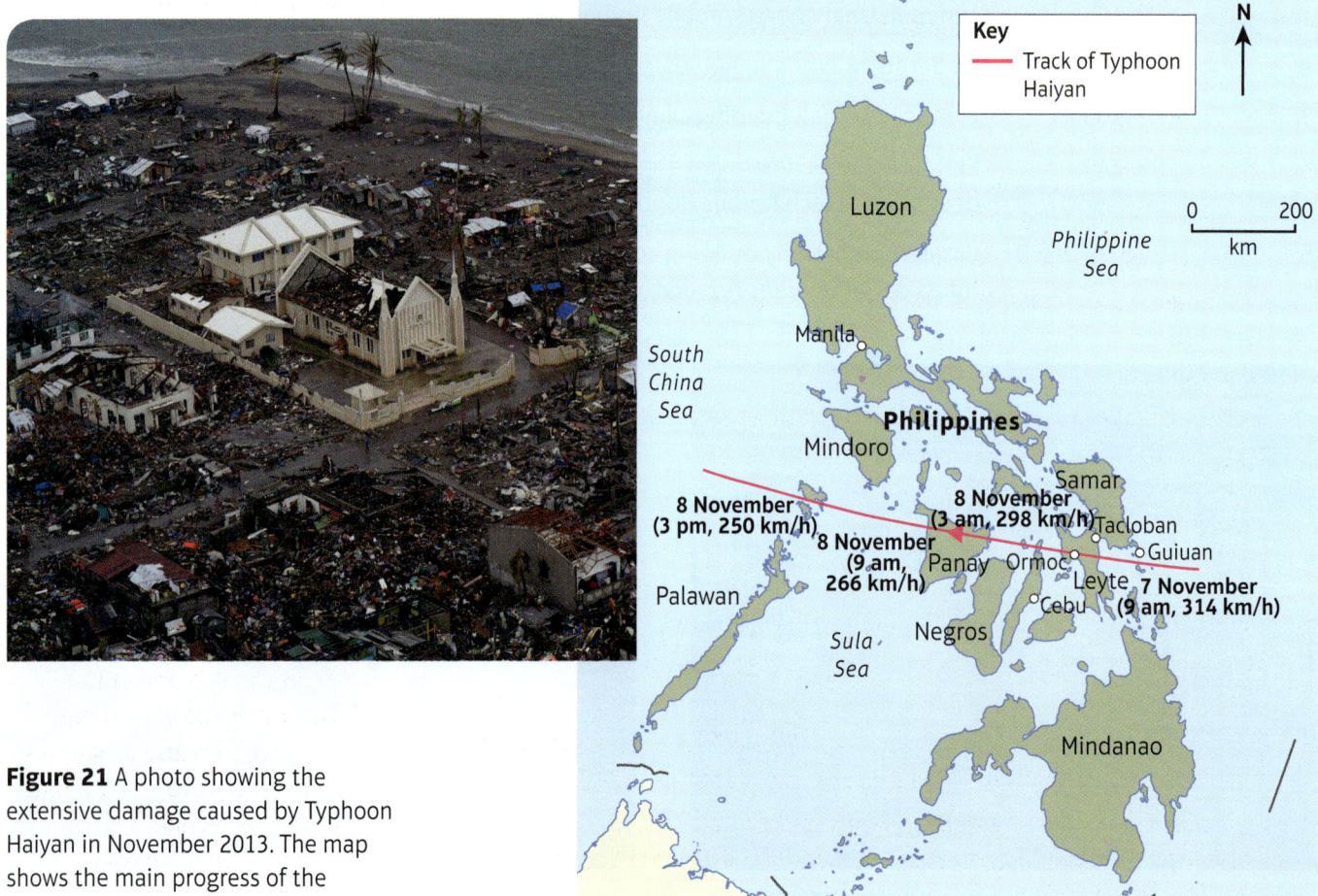

Figure 21 A photo showing the extensive damage caused by Typhoon Haiyan in November 2013. The map shows the main progress of the typhoon through the country

1A Hazardous Earth: Climate

Social vulnerability

Social inequalities can make some areas more vulnerable to the impacts of tropical cyclones. Areas of poverty are more likely to be vulnerable, as housing and other construction may not be of a high standard and is therefore more easily damaged or destroyed. The after-effects of a tropical cyclone are also felt more in poorer areas as people may not have access to shelter, food, clean water supplies and medical care after the event. This means that more people are likely to suffer and possibly die in these areas than in areas that are more affluent and better able to prepare.

Age is another social inequality. Areas with a population of higher or lower average age are more vulnerable to tropical cyclones because older people and young children are more likely to suffer injury during disasters and have more difficulty evacuating the affected area. They are also more at risk from disease in the aftermath of a tropical cyclone, especially if there is a limited supply of clean water.

Social inequalities can be important in developed countries as well as developing and emerging countries. Hurricane Katrina (August 2005) caused 1836 deaths in New Orleans and other parts of the USA's south coast. Many of those deaths were in socially disadvantaged regions of the city. People died in the poorer parts of the city because many did not have access to their own cars in order to evacuate, and because people did not want to leave their homes because of worries about looting.

Economic vulnerability

Countries with high levels of development are more likely to have:

- access to the most accurate weather prediction and modelling data. Being able to predict the tropical cyclone's **landfall** and prepare for it will significantly reduce the impact of the storm
- coastal defences, meaning that their coastal areas will be less affected by storm surges and the damage caused by the tropical cyclone will be greatly reduced
- well-established evacuation procedures and disaster response teams. Poorer countries often have to wait for international aid agencies to help them rescue tropical cyclone survivors. Supplies of food, clean water and medicine are also more likely to be available.

Activity

1. What sort of physical vulnerabilities would increase the risk of damage from (a) storm surges and (b) landslides caused by heavy tropical cyclone rainfall?
2. Explain why a coastal region of the USA should be less vulnerable to the impact of a tropical cyclone than a coastal region of the Philippines.
3. Typhoon Haiyan was a category 5 tropical cyclone. What wind speed, damage and storm-surge size are predicted by the Saffir–Simpson scale for category 5?

Exam-style question

Explain why some areas are more vulnerable to the impacts of tropical cyclones than others.
(4 marks)

Exam tip

Focus on explaining two aspects of vulnerability, including why they affect some areas more than others.

Checkpoint

Now it is time to review your understanding of the hazards created by tropical cyclones; their impact on people and the environment; and why some countries are more vulnerable to tropical cyclones than others.

Strengthen

S1 Identify three physical hazards that can be caused by tropical cyclones.

S2 Explain how a tropical cyclone can cause a storm surge. Figure 16 can help with this.

S3 Name one environmental impact that can result from each of the following physical hazards – high winds, landslides, storm surge.

Challenge

C1 If you were responsible for making a developing country less vulnerable to tropical cyclones, which one of the following would you spend your money on and why – sea wall defences, tropical cyclone monitoring technology, evacuation training for coastal areas?

1A Hazardous Earth: Climate

How do countries prepare for and respond to tropical cyclones?

> **Learning objectives**
> - To know how countries can prepare for tropical cyclones
> - To understand how countries respond to tropical cyclone hazards
> - To investigate how effective methods of preparation and response have been in two located examples: one in a developed country and one in a developing or emerging country

Preparing for tropical cyclones

Preparing for a tropical cyclone depends on accurate forecasting and then effective communication to people who might be at risk.

Atmospheric pressure

Measuring atmospheric pressure is the most common forecasting method, and the one that gives the earliest information on a potential tropical cyclone hazard. Areas of very low pressure are likely source areas for tropical cyclone formation. The problem is that oceans cover very big areas and atmospheric pressure readings need to be made locally. To do this, buoys have been anchored in tropical ocean areas which send in atmospheric pressure readings (they also measure wind speeds). Ships also record pressure and other weather data and send these readings to shore.

When a tropical cyclone gets closer to land, atmospheric readings enable forecasts to be made about possible storm surges. Some countries fly special planes through the upper layers of the tropical cyclone to take very accurate pressure readings to help make these crucial forecasts.

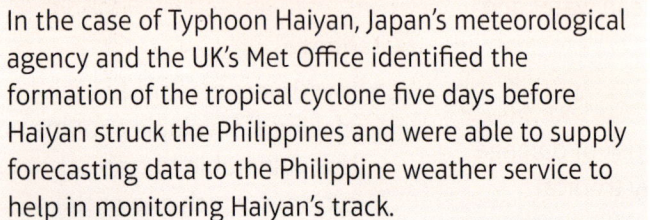

> **Did you know?**
>
> In the case of Typhoon Haiyan, Japan's meteorological agency and the UK's Met Office identified the formation of the tropical cyclone five days before Haiyan struck the Philippines and were able to supply forecasting data to the Philippine weather service to help in monitoring Haiyan's track.

Satellite tracking and radar

Satellite technology allows huge areas of ocean to be monitored for the formation of distinctive tropical storm cloud formations. The progress of the tropical cyclone can then be tracked in real time as it moves over the ocean towards a possible landfall. Once a tropical cyclone has developed an eye, it is easy to spot on satellite images, but in their early stages it is sometimes difficult to distinguish them from other weather systems because of their cirrus cloud canopy. Like satellite images, radar can also provide information from a distance away from the tropical cyclone. Radar registers large banks of precipitation, so it can provide information on rainfall levels. However, radar installations are expensive

Modelling

Atmospheric pressure data, seawater temperature data and information on wind speeds and wind directions are input into sophisticated modelling programs, which generate estimates of likely tracks for the tropical cyclone, likely points of landfall and likely patterns of intensification and dissipation.

> **Did you know?**
>
> In the case of Hurricane Katrina, the USA's National Hurricane Center was able to predict that Katrina would make landfall near New Orleans 56 hours before the hurricane hit the city. It gave specialist advice to local government services while TV and radio broadcasts kept residents informed about the forecast and what they should do to stay safe.

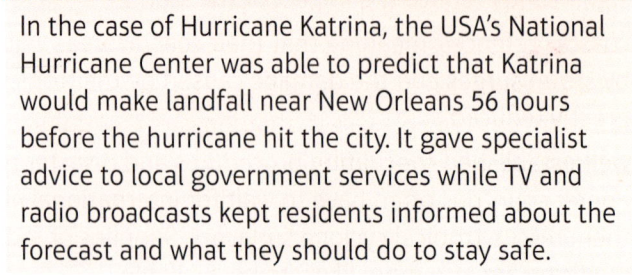

Communicating information

When a tropical cyclone is forecast to make landfall in a country, the government will activate any defences it has in the area (for example, flood barriers or storm surge barriers), order evacuations of people in areas that are at risk and prepare emergency services. Where tropical cyclones are common, governments will usually have constructed emergency shelters and evacuation points on higher ground, away from storm surges and coastal flooding.

1A Hazardous Earth: Climate

In areas that are vulnerable to tropical cyclones, people are regularly given information on and training about being prepared for a tropical cyclone. This includes information on:

- how to secure your house and property from damage and what to do about pets
- preparing an emergency pack of drinking water, battery-powered lights, etc.
- what route to take in an evacuation and what to take with you (e.g. warm clothing and bedding).

Information about the tropical cyclone and what action is needed is broadcast constantly on TV, radio, the internet and social media, or through loudspeaker announcements and posters in areas where media coverage is not fully developed.

Responding to tropical cyclones

Responding to a tropical cyclone refers to how people deal with the effects of the storm after it has occurred.

- Teams of rescue workers search for people trapped in the rubble of collapsed buildings. The speed with which these teams reach an affected area will have a direct impact on how effective the teams will be.
- Providing food, clean water, medical care where necessary and shelter for the victims of the tropical cyclone will mean that people are safe and fewer people will die of injuries, malnutrition or disease.
- Repair and reconstruction of the affected area will have a major impact on the area's recovery. The restoration of power and drinking water, and clearing roads to allow people to get about in cars and public transport is a major priority.

Table 5 Information from the USA's Federal Emergency Management Agency (FEMA) for young people on what to put into an emergency kit

Here are some items you and your family will need:

- Non-perishable food (such as dried fruit or peanut butter)
- First aid kit
- Extra batteries
- Matches in a waterproof container
- Toothbrush, toothpaste, soap
- Paper plates, plastic cups and utensils, paper towels
- Water – at least a gallon (4.5 litres) per person, per day
- Battery-powered or hand-cranked radio
- Sleeping bag or warm blanket for each person
- Flashlights
- Whistle to signal for help
- Can opener (manual)
- Local maps
- Pet supplies
- Baby supplies (formula, diapers [nappies])

Activity

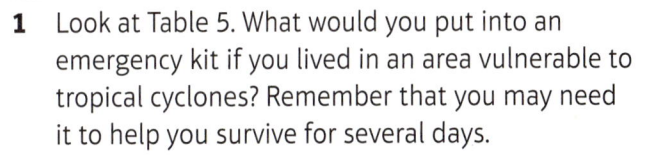

1. Look at Table 5. What would you put into an emergency kit if you lived in an area vulnerable to tropical cyclones? Remember that you may need it to help you survive for several days.
2. Identify **one** advantage and **one** disadvantage for each of the main methods of forecasting tropical cyclones.
3. How would social vulnerability and economic vulnerability affect levels of preparation for a tropical cyclone and the effectiveness of responses to a tropical cyclone?

1A Hazardous Earth: Climate

Tropical cyclone preparation and responses: Katrina and Haiyan

Hurricane Katrina and Typhoon Haiyan are two useful examples to know about when discussing preparations for and responses to tropical cyclones.

Table 6 Typhoon Haiyan and Hurricane Katrina: key facts

Tropical cyclone name and date	Location	Category	Height of storm surge (metres)	Number of deaths	Economic cost (US dollars)
Katrina (2005)	USA (developed)	Category 3	6	1800	100 billion
Haiyan (2013)	Philippines (emerging)	Category 5	5	7000	3 billion

Case Study – Hurricane Katrina, USA, 2005

On the 29 August 2005, Hurricane Katrina, a category 3 hurricane on the Saffir–Simpson Scale, made landfall on the south coast of the USA, having travelled across the Gulf of Mexico.

Preparation
As a developed country, the USA has very good forecasting and tracking services and monitored Hurricane Katrina from its formation as a tropical depression on 23 August. Forecasters were able to predict where the hurricane would most likely make landfall.

In preparation, the Mayor of New Orleans ordered the evacuation of the city. However, many people were unable to leave as they did not have access to a car. The local American Football stadium, the Superdome, was designated as a shelter for people who could not leave as it was on relatively high ground and could hold thousands of people. Approximately 80% of the city's population were evacuated before the hurricane reached the city. Most of those remaining headed to the Superdome: however, some chose to stay at home.

When the storm surge created by the hurricane hit the city, levees and barriers were overwhelmed. Many had not been properly maintained or upgraded. Some areas of the city, such as the Ninth Ward, were under such deep water that people who had remained in their homes had to escape to their roofs to avoid the water: 80% of the city was flooded.

Figure 22 The view of flooded New Orleans from an army rescue helicopter, August 2005

Response
The response of the local and national governments has been criticised for not being fast enough or effective enough.

The people who had been evacuated to the Superdome were trapped there with very limited supplies of food and water; more people arrived after the hurricane hit as there was nowhere else for them to go. The Federal Emergency Management Agency (FEMA) were unprepared for the scale of destruction and there were many more people needing help than FEMA could cope with. Those worst affected were in the poorest regions of the city. These were the people without cars, which made it harder for them to evacuate. Survivors from these areas felt betrayed by their government.

1A Hazardous Earth: Climate

Case Study – Typhoon Haiyan, Philippines, 2013

Typhoon Haiyan was one of the strongest tropical cyclones on record and was the equivalent of a category 5 on the Saffir–Simpson scale. Typhoon Haiyan formed on 2 November 2013 in the Western Pacific Ocean.

Preparation
The Philippines, an emerging country, was assisted in tracking the typhoon with data from Japan. The government used the Public Storm Warning Signal (PSWS) system to warn people across the country of the risk they faced. Originally, only a level 1 warning (the lowest of four levels) was given for some eastern areas. As the typhoon moved closer to the islands, the level of warning was increased and more areas were given warnings. By the time the tropical cyclone made landfall on 7 November, most of the eastern islands were under a level 4 warning. Figure 21 on page 30 shows the track of Typhoon Haiyan across the Philippines.

Those people in areas at risk of flood and landslide (e.g. Samar and Leyte) were evacuated to safer areas. The military were ordered to send planes and helicopters to the regions that were most at risk to be ready to help with the aid effort. In other areas, government emergency shelters were not on ground high enough to escape the massive 5 metre storm surge.

Response
Seven provinces in the Philippines were placed under a 'state of national calamity'. The relief effort was slowed by blocked roads and major damage to local airports. Some areas remained isolated for days. With no sources of clean water available because of burst pipes and contamination from sea water, many people were without safe water for a long time. People needed to be evacuated from badly hit areas, such as Tacloban city, but because there was no electricity for lights, the evacuations could only happen during daylight hours. These delays caused panic and people had to be held back from rushing the evacuation planes when they landed by police and military personnel. The focus of relief efforts in Tacloban meant that people in other devastated areas felt abandoned, as aid was reaching them even more slowly.

Checkpoint

Now it is time to review your understanding of the preparations and responses to tropical cyclones, including the two located examples of Hurricane Katrina and Typhoon Haiyan.

Strengthen

S1 Explain the difference between preparing for a tropical cyclone and responding to one.

S2 Give one example of how preparations for Hurricane Katrina failed in New Orleans.

S3 Give one example of problems for responses to Typhoon Haiyan in the Philippines.

Challenge

C1 Explain why developed countries such as the USA can better prepare for and respond to tropical cyclones than emerging countries such as the Philippines. Use the term 'vulnerability' in your answer.

C2 90% of Tacloban was flattened by Typhoon Haiyan's 230 km per hour winds and the 5 metre storm surge in this area. What preparations should the Philippine government make to help protect more people against this level of destruction in the future?

Exam-style question

'Effective preparation is the best way to reduce deaths from tropical cyclones.' Assess this statement. **(8 marks + 4 SPAG)**

Exam tip

Remember that in an 'assess' question you need to give clear and detailed examples to reinforce and back up your assessment. Using data from case studies will really help you here.

Preparing for your exams

Hazardous Earth: Climate

The Earth's atmosphere is a global system that transfers heat and energy. This system causes great differences in climate, and influences the weather in places such as the UK. The global climate has changed in the past and is continuing to change today as a result of human activity. Changes in atmospheric circulation patterns sometimes cause extreme weather events, including tropical cyclones and droughts. Some places are more vulnerable to these hazards than others, and the way people respond can be different in developed, emerging and developing countries.

Checklist

You should know:

- [ ] how heat is redistributed by the atmosphere and oceans
- [ ] why some areas of the Earth receive more heat than others
- [ ] the impact of the Coriolis effect and the jet stream on atmospheric circulation
- [ ] how the world's climate has changed over time
- [ ] how climate change can occur naturally
- [ ] how we can prove historic climate change
- [ ] how human activity can cause climate change
- [ ] the negative impacts of global climate change
- [ ] the formation and hazards of tropical cyclones
- [ ] how different countries can be affected by tropical cyclones
- [ ] how countries can prepare for the impact of tropical cyclones
- [ ] why some areas are more vulnerable to tropical cyclones than others
- [ ] how countries can respond differently to the effects of a tropical cyclone.

Which key terms match the following definitions?

a   A weather system that forms over the ocean in tropical areas and can produce high winds and heavy rain.

b   Circulation cell near the Equator responsible for storms at the Equator and desert belts north and south of the Equator.

c   The deflection of air movement by the Earth's rotation.

d   A period of time with lower average temperatures causing widespread glaciation.

e   A section of ice drilled from a glacier showing the layers of ice created over time.

f   The increase in volume created when a fluid (e.g. seawater) is heated and expands.

g   The centre of a tropical cyclone; an area of clear conditions created by air converging at the centre of the storm and then sinking.

h   The path followed by a tropical cyclone.

i   A region with little or no regular precipitation.

j   The day-to-day conditions of the atmosphere, e.g. temperature, precipitation, cloud cover, etc.

k   Lines on a weather map that indicate areas of equal atmospheric pressure.

l   The trapping of heat radiation around the Earth by excess greenhouse gases produced through human activity.

To check your answers, look at the Glossary on pages 302–311.

Preparing for your exams

Hazardous Earth: Climate

Question 1 Explain *two* negative impacts of global climate change. (4 marks)

Student answer

A possible negative impact is sea level rise. With ice at the poles, particularly around the South Pole, melting due to higher temperatures, more water will enter the oceans and this will cause sea levels to rise. Another possible impact is the drop in food production that will occur.

Verdict

Part one is accurate and clear. There is correct identification of a possible impact and a clear and accurate explanation. This shows a good level of understanding. Part two does not provide a complete answer. A different possible impact of global climate change is identified but no further detail is provided.

Exam tip

Always check the number of marks available for each question. This question is worth four marks and asks for two impacts. This means that two marks are available for each impact discussed. You will not achieve two marks for only identifying a feature or impact.

Question 2 'Developed countries are able to respond to tropical cyclones more effectively than emerging or developing countries.' Assess this statement. (8 marks + 4 SPAG)

Student answer

Hurricane Sandy hit New York in mainland USA in October 2012. Over 150 people were killed. Typhoon Haiyan was responsible for over 6000 deaths in the Philippines.

The response to these disasters was quite different. Aid was able to reach the areas affected by Sandy much faster. Also, the efforts in the USA were distributed over the whole affected area. With Haiyan, efforts were focused on one city. This meant that other people felt abandoned and some rioting occurred in various areas. Also, the USA did not need to rely on foreign aid agencies to provide support and so was able to act without having to wait for aid to arrive.

Verdict

The first paragraph briefly mentions the impacts of tropical cyclones, but not the responses to it and so does not answer the question set. Paragraph two does discuss responses and so would receive credit. This paragraph compares the responses between two different tropical cyclones in a developed country and an emerging country. However, no assessment is then provided about what factors make responses effective and whether these factors are something developed countries can control better than developing or emerging countries.

Exam tip

You do not have to agree with the statement used in an 'Assess' question. Instead you need to show that you can use evidence to consider and weigh up the different factors that are relevant to the question and decide which you think are most important.

Pearson Education Ltd accepts no responsibility whatsoever for the accuracy or method of working in the answers given.

1B | Hazardous Earth: Tectonics

How does the Earth's structure influence plate tectonics?

Learning objectives

- To know the structure of the Earth and what causes tectonic plates to move
- To know the distribution and characteristics of plate boundaries and hotspots
- To understand the causes of tectonic hazards and why they vary at different plate boundaries

The Earth is made up of several layers – the inner and outer **core**, the **mantle** and the **crust** (Figure 1). They each have different compositions and unique physical properties.

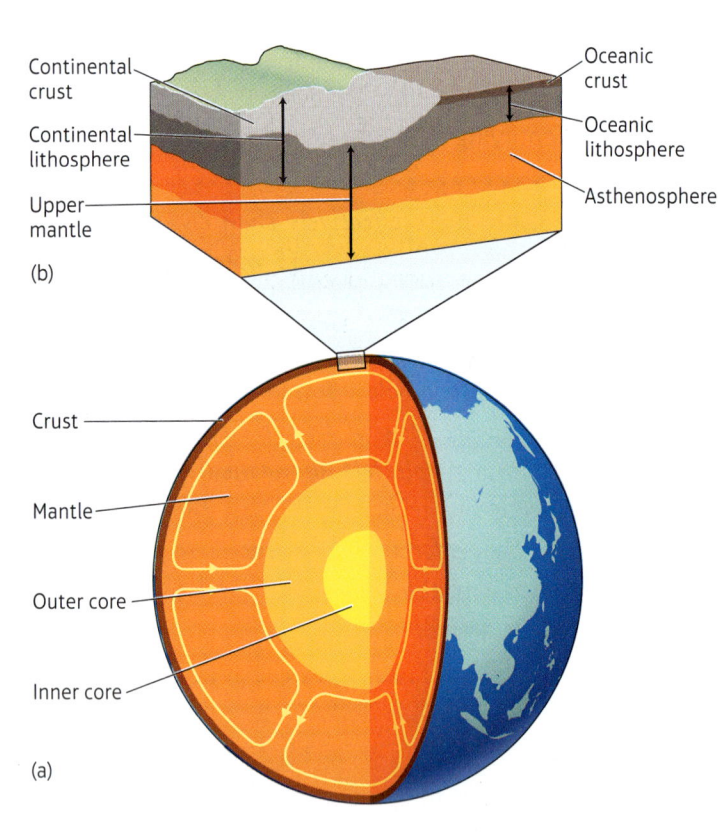

Figure 1 (a) Earth's layered structure and (b) the lithosphere and asthenosphere

- **The crust** – this is the thinnest layer and the one we live on. There are two main types of crust – **oceanic crust** under the sea and **continental crust** under the land. Oceanic crust is relatively thin (5–8 km). As it is made of **basaltic** rock, it is slightly denser than continental crust, at almost 3.0 g/cm³. Continental crust is thick (on average, 30–40 km), but its thickness varies and can reach 70 km under some mountain belts such as the Himalayas. It is lighter than oceanic crust because it is made of mostly **granitic** rock, which is less dense at about 2.7 g/cm³.

- **The mantle** – this is the thickest layer of the Earth at nearly 2900 km. Its temperature ranges from about 1000°C near the crust to about 3700°C near the core. It is divided into two layers – the upper mantle and the lower mantle. The upper mantle is mostly solid, but some melting occurs at **plate boundaries** and **hotspots**. At these locations, the mantle flows very slowly, like warm toffee. The mantle becomes hotter and denser with depth. The pressure also increases, so the lower mantle is solid despite the higher temperatures.

- **The core** – this is at the centre of the Earth and is very hot and very dense. It is made up of two parts – the outer core and the inner core. The outer core is made of liquid iron and nickel and the temperature is between 4500 and 5500°C. The inner core reaches temperatures of up to 6000°C (as hot as the surface of the Sun). It is a dense, solid ball of iron and nickel which, because it is under enormous pressure, cannot melt.

The upper mantle is further divided into two layers: the **lithosphere** and the **asthenosphere** (Figure 1). They are both involved in tectonic activity.

1. **The lithosphere** – this includes both the crust and the top layer of the upper mantle, which is made of **peridotite**. The lithosphere is about 80–100 km thick, although it is thinner under the oceans and in volcanically active continental areas. It is broken up into **tectonic plates** (lithospheric plates) of varying size (Figure 2), which move or 'float' on the asthenosphere below.

2 **The asthenosphere** – this is a denser, mobile layer in the upper part of the mantle, about 100–300 km deep. The temperature in the asthenosphere is high (above 1300°C) and the pressure, while still high, is low enough so that the rocks can flow very slowly.

Convection currents

The tectonic plates are continually moving on the asthenosphere because of rising hot currents called **convection currents** within the mantle. These currents are circular in motion. Rock heated in the lower mantle by the core rises very slowly towards the crust. As it rises, it begins to cool. When it reaches the asthenosphere it is forced sideways because it is blocked by the solid lithosphere above. It continues to cool and, as it cools, it begins to sink slowly towards the core. When it reaches the outer core, it is again forced sideways because of the dense iron/nickel layer, and is heated by the core until it rises again.

Convection currents need a source of heat before they can form. Much of the Earth's heat is generated in the core and comes from two main sources – **radioactive decay** and **residual heat**. The radioactive decay of naturally occurring chemical elements such as uranium releases energy in the form of heat, which then slowly rises to the Earth's surface. Residual heat is heat left over from when the Earth formed (4.6 billion years ago).

Convection currents exert a weak 'pull' on the plate above. They cause tectonic plates to move apart or closer together, or to slide past each other (Figure 2). This movement has greatest impact at the plate boundaries, and can lead to **earthquakes** and the formation of **volcanoes**. Away from the boundaries, towards the centres of the plates, little if any major tectonic activity occurs.

Activity

1 Using Figure 1 for reference, draw a cross section through the Earth.
   a Label the layers of the Earth.
   b Add a brief description of each layer you have labelled.
2 Create a table to compare the characteristics of continental and oceanic crust. Include their location, thickness, what they are made of and their density.
3 Explain in your own words how convection currents cause plate movement.

Tip Processes can often be explained with the help of a simple, labelled diagram.

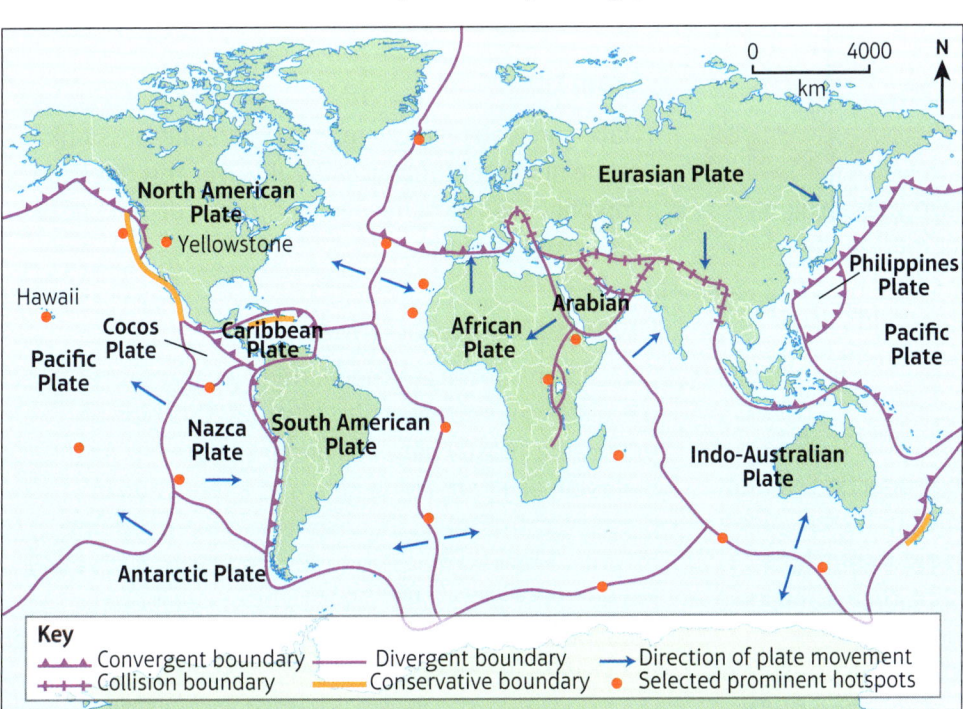

Figure 2 Global distribution of tectonic plates, boundaries and hotspots

1B Hazardous Earth: Tectonics

What happens when tectonic plates move?

Figure 2 on page 39 shows the distribution of the Earth's tectonic plates, the different types of plate boundary and the direction in which the plates move. Most – though not all – volcanoes and earthquakes occur in long, narrow belts along these plate boundaries (also called plate margins).

Convergent plate boundaries

Convection currents in the mantle cause the plates to move towards each other (to converge). Where an oceanic plate meets a continental plate, the denser oceanic plate sinks under the less dense continental plate into the asthenosphere (Figure 3a). This process is called **subduction**, and leads to the formation of a deep **trench** where the two plates meet. As the oceanic plate subducts, the huge increase in temperature and pressure force it to release water and other impurities into the asthenosphere, which begins to melt (like adding salt to ice). This molten rock, called **magma**, rises and may eventually break through the surface of the Earth as a **composite volcano**.

Subduction is not a smooth process. As the oceanic plate subducts, friction causes the plate to 'stick' and pressure builds up in the **subduction zone**. At some point, the plate may suddenly slip and the pressure may be released as an earthquake.

Did you know?

A string of volcanoes and earthquake sites lie along the convergent plate boundaries bordering the edges of the North Pacific Ocean. This so-called Ring of Fire is dotted with about 75% of the world's active volcanoes, 90% of all earthquakes and some of the deepest **ocean trenches**.

Where two continental plates meet, subduction cannot occur. Instead, the plates collide, causing the rock along the boundaries to crumple to form **fold mountains** (Figure 3(b)). As there is no subduction, there is no volcanic activity along these collision boundaries. However, major earthquakes do occur as the pressure of the colliding plates causes rocks to 'snap' along **faults**, such as in Pakistan/Kashmir in 2005 and Nepal in 2015.

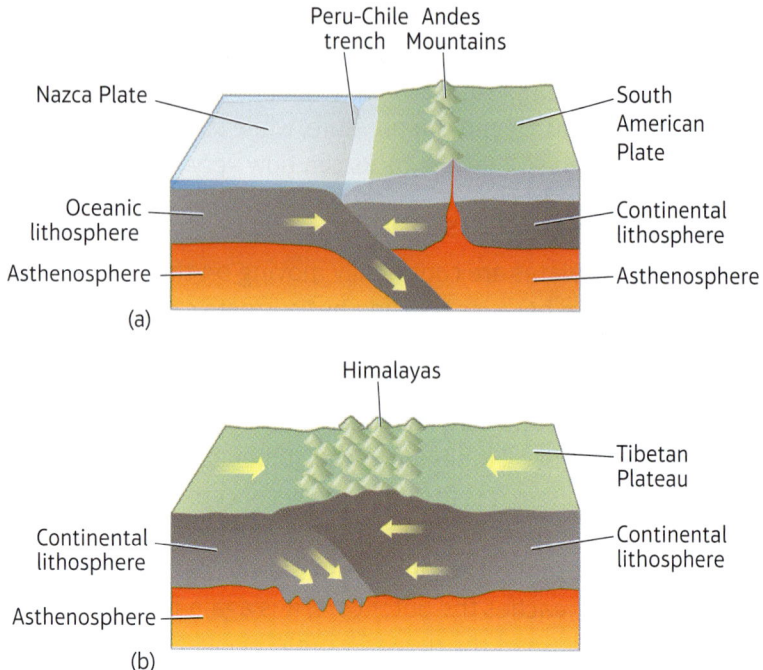

Figure 3 Convergent plate boundaries: (a) continent–ocean convergent plate boundary and (b) continent–continent collision plate boundary

Exam-style question

Name **one** landform often found on convergent plate boundaries. **(1 mark)**

Exam tip

Make sure you read the question carefully and look at the number of marks as a guide. For this question, you only need to name *one* landform – do not waste time naming more.

Divergent plate boundaries

Convection currents in the mantle can also cause the plates to move apart (to diverge). This type of movement mostly happens under the oceans. As the plates break apart, rising heat and a reduction in pressure cause the asthenosphere to melt, forming magma. This magma rises to fill the gap, or **rift valley**, between the plates and cools to form new oceanic lithosphere (Figure 4). Where the magma breaks through the surface of the Earth, it forms a **shield volcano**. As the process continues, chains of volcanoes build up to form a **mid-ocean ridge**. Earthquakes can also occur at divergent plate boundaries as the plates do not always move apart smoothly. However, the earthquakes tend not to be large.

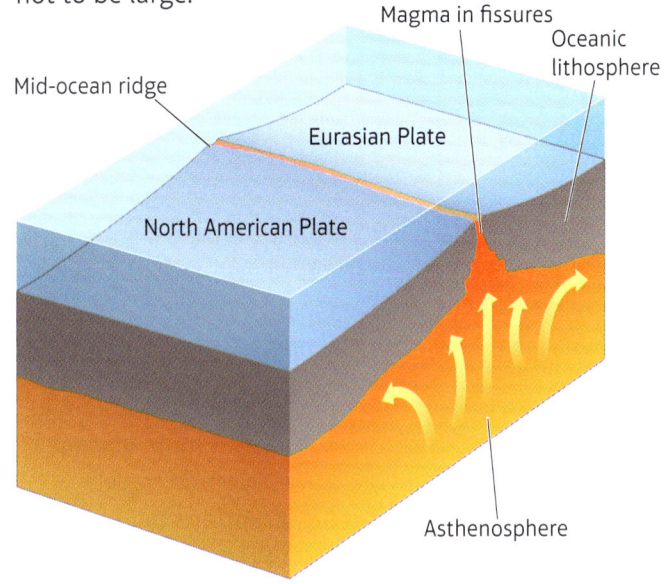

Figure 4 Divergent plate boundary

Conservative plate boundaries

At **conservative plate boundaries**, convection currents cause the plates to slide past each other. In Haiti, for example, the North American Plate and the Caribbean Plate are moving in opposite directions (Figure 5). At the San Andreas fault in California, however, the North American Plate and the Pacific Plate are moving in a similar direction, at slightly different angles and speeds. In both examples, the plates tend to get stuck at some point. Pressure builds along the boundary until one plate jerks past the other, causing an earthquake.

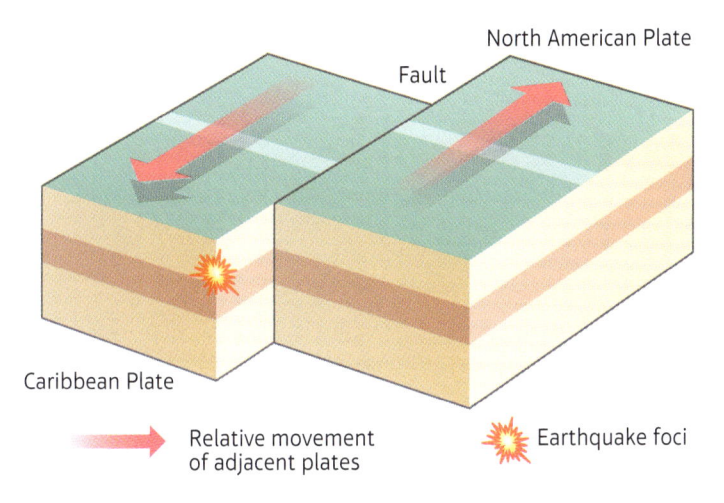

Figure 5 Conservative plate boundary

Did you know?
We know about the composition and physical properties of the crust from drilling into the Earth.

Activity
1. Copy and complete the table below for the three types of plate boundaries

Type of plate boundary	Examples of plates	Features produced	Examples country/area

2. Draw a sketch of Figure 3(a) and annotate it to:
   a. describe the characteristics of the boundary
   b. explain the processes that are taking place.
3. What are the differences between convergent and divergent plate boundaries?

Checkpoint
It is now time to review your understanding of the Earth's structure and tectonic plate boundaries.

Strengthen
S1 Name the layers of the Earth from the centre to the surface.

S2 Explain why drilling deep below the crust would be tricky for scientists.

S3 Study Figure 2 on page 39. Explain why more tectonic hazards occur around the Pacific Ocean than in Europe.

Challenge
C1 Explain the role of the lithosphere and asthenosphere in plate tectonics.

C2 Describe the global distribution of tectonic boundaries shown in Figure 2 on page 39. Remember to describe the general pattern, any exceptions and give examples.

C3 Explain why earthquakes occur along conservative plate boundaries but there is no volcanic activity.

1B Hazardous Earth: Tectonics

What are the different types of volcanoes?

Learning objectives

- To know the different types of volcanoes, and how they are formed
- To know the impacts of and responses to different types of volcanic activity
- To understand how these impacts and responses vary with location

Volcanoes vary in shape and size but are most often cone-shaped hills or mountains. They are formed when molten rock from a **magma chamber** inside the Earth erupts onto the surface through a **vent** in the lithosphere. Molten rock is called magma when it is below the surface and **lava** when it erupts. As well as lava, volcanoes also throw out ash, cinders, pumice, dust, gases and steam from the **crater** when they erupt. These are hazardous, and in extreme situations can kill people.

Volcanoes are divided into two main types depending on whether they are formed along convergent or divergent plate boundaries.

Composite volcanoes

Composite volcanoes are formed along convergent plate boundaries. They are tall, steep-sided cones rising up to several thousand metres from a narrow base (Figure 7(a)). They are made of alternate layers of lava and ash. Two well-known examples include Mount St Helens in the USA and Mount Pinatubo in the Philippines.

Andesitic lava is erupted from composite volcanoes. It has a high silica content, which makes it more **viscous** (thick and sticky) so that it flows slowly and travels shorter distances before cooling. Eruptions tend to be infrequent, but when they do occur they are violent. After an eruption, the vent becomes blocked with solidified lava, causing pressure to build up until there is another eruption. During explosive eruptions the lava shatters into pieces, producing **lava bombs** and very hot flows of gas and ash (**pyroclastic flows**). These are **primary hazards** and can kill people when a volcano erupts suddenly. Further deaths may be caused by **secondary hazards**, such as mudflows (**lahars**).

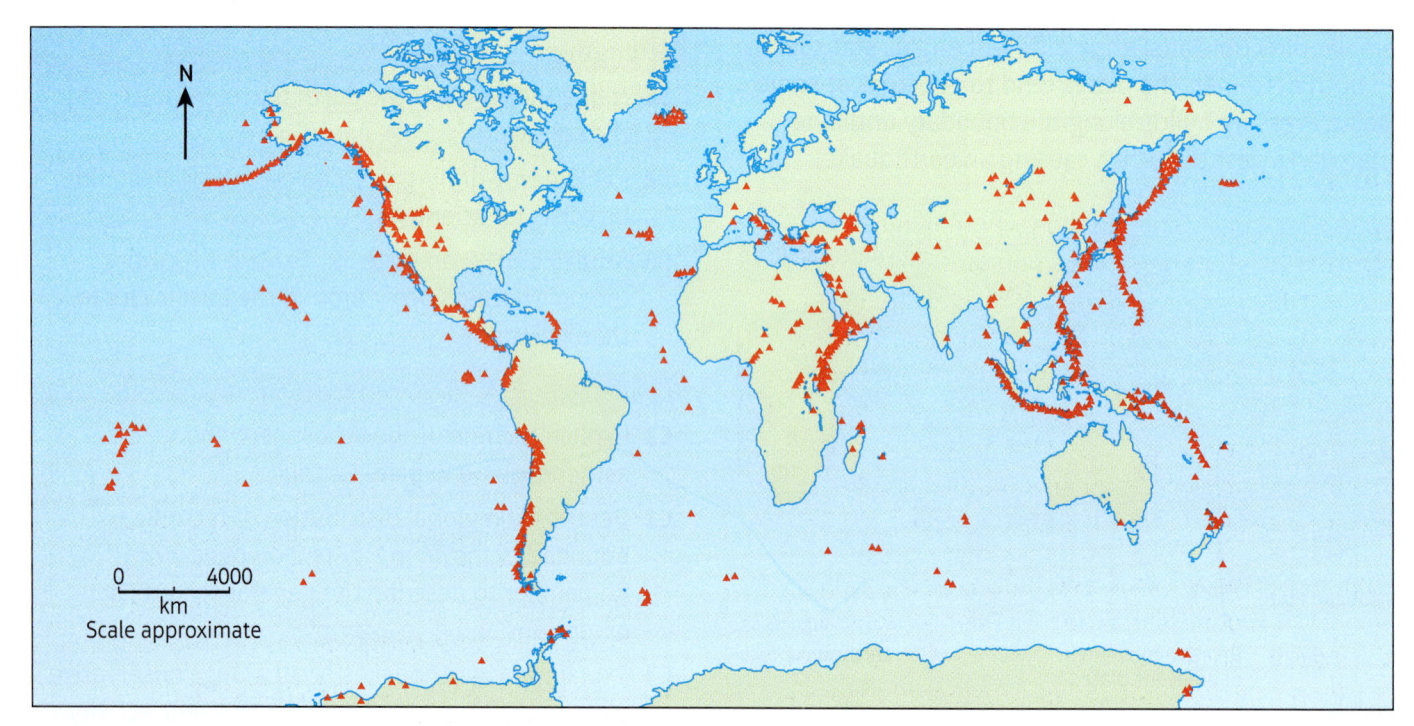

Figure 6 Global distribution of active volcanoes

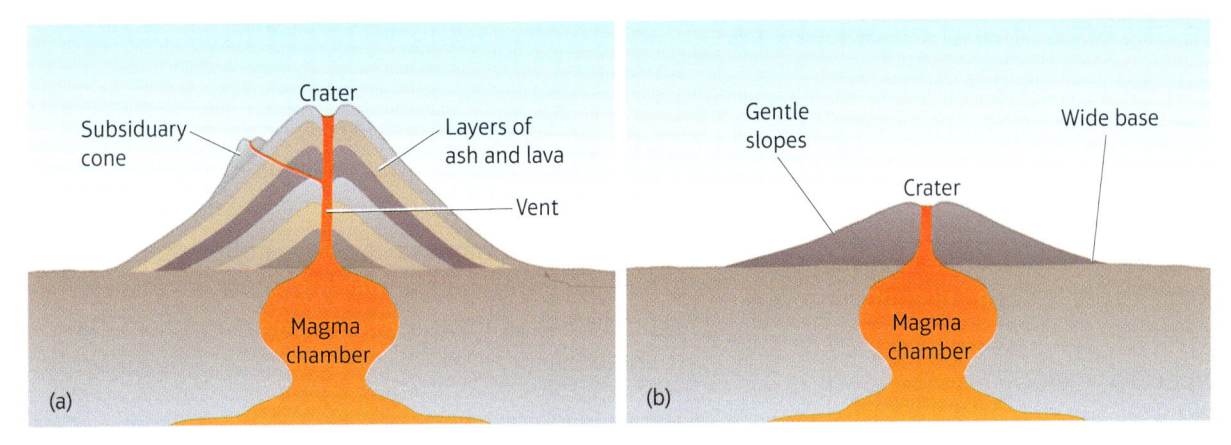

Figure 7 (a) Composite volcano and (b) Shield volcano

Shield volcanoes

Shield volcanoes are formed along divergent plate boundaries and over hotspots. They are low, gently sloping domes with a very wide base – their profile resembles a warrior's shield (Figure 7(b)). They are built from lava only, which in many shield volcanoes, erupts from **fissures** as well as the crater.

Basaltic lava is erupted from shield volcanoes. It has a low silica content, which makes it less viscous so that it pours out of the crater easily, is runny and flows long distances before cooling. Eruptions tend to be more frequent and gentle. While basaltic lava flows destroy property and crops, lives are rarely lost. The Laki fissure eruption in Iceland in 1783–84 was an exception. It threw out a poisonous cloud of volcanic gases, which killed millions of Europeans.

Hotspots

Volcanoes can also be formed away from plate boundaries – these are called hotspots. The Hawaiian hotspot, for example, is in the middle of the Pacific Plate. They are formed by a 'plume' of superheated rock (not magma) rising very slowly through the mantle. Once it reaches the upper mantle, it causes the asthenosphere and the base of the lithosphere to melt. The magma produced then rises through weaknesses in the crust and erupts at the Earth's surface.

Oceanic hotspots erupt basaltic lava, creating huge shield volcanoes. Mauna Loa in Hawaii, for example, is 4168 metres above sea level (8500 metres above the seafloor) and, along with Kilauea, extends for nearly 200 km. Continental hotspots erupt viscous, granitic lava. They have the potential to erupt explosively, throwing out a massive volume of material – at least 1000 km^3. Yellowstone **supervolcano** in the North American Plate is an example of a continental hotspot.

Geologists think that mantle plumes are fixed in place. As the plates move over the hotspots, the volcanoes above get progressively older as they move away from the hotspot location (Figure 8).

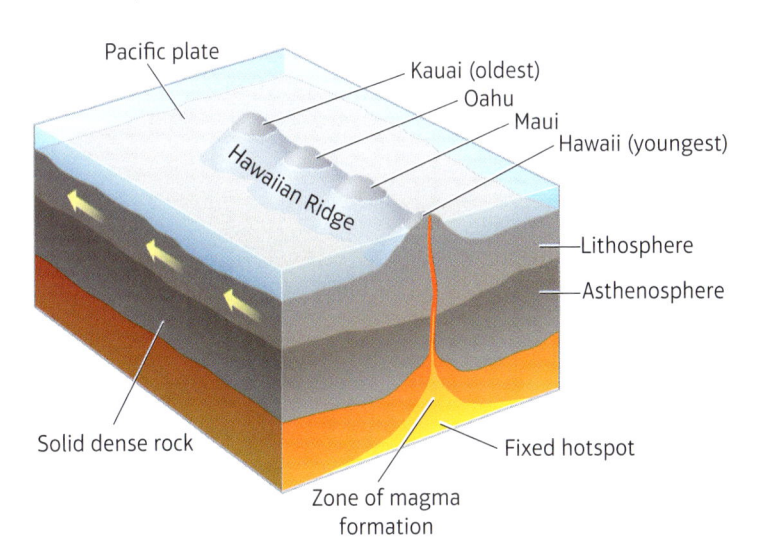

Figure 8 Hawaiian hotspot volcanoes

Activity

1. Create a table to compare composite and shield volcanoes. State where they are formed, describe their formation and list their characteristics. Include diagrams and examples.
2. State **two** differences between oceanic and continental hotspots.

1B Hazardous Earth: Tectonics

What are the impacts of and responses to volcanic hazards?

Volcanoes and earthquakes have both primary and secondary impacts.

- **Primary impacts** are the immediate damage caused by the volcano or earthquake, such as injury or loss of life, destruction of property and disruption to communications.
- **Secondary impacts** are 'knock-on effects' such as shortages of drinking water and food, the spread of disease and longer-term economic and social problems.

The response to a tectonic hazard also works on two timescales.

- **Emergency responses** take place immediately and include rescuing people, providing medical aid, food and water, and restoring water and electricity.
- **Long-term responses** involve restoring the area back to normal and 'managing' future hazards by predicting, protecting and preparing for them (the **three Ps**).

The ability to respond to a tectonic hazard varies – wealthy countries can afford to reduce the impact and respond more effectively through the three Ps.

Case Study – Developed country: The Kilauea eruptions, Hawaii, USA

Kilauea is one of five shield volcanoes on the island of Hawaii (Figure 9). It is one of the most active volcanoes in the world and has been erupting almost continuously since 1983 ('Kilauea' means 'spewing' in Hawaiian). As it is more or less directly over an oceanic hotspot and mantle plume, its eruptions are **effusive** basaltic lava flows.

Figure 9 Location of Kilauea, Hawaii

Primary impacts

Since 1983, lava from Kilauea has covered over 100 km² of land, destroyed more than 200 homes and community buildings, and has damaged utilities and blocked roads. In 1990, Kalapana village was buried beneath 15 to 24 metres of lava. In 2014, residents of Pahoa village were **evacuated** when high lava fountains erupted from a new vent, sending a lava flow towards the sea (Figure 10). When hot lava comes into contact with seawater, steam and lava can explode into the air, endangering lives.

Figure 10 Lava fountain erupting from Kilauea

1B Hazardous Earth: Tectonics

Did you know?
As Truman Taylor photographed Kilauea erupting in 1924, a volcanic bomb exploded out of the crater and landed on him, pinning his leg to the ground. He was rescued, but later died in hospital. Rather gruesomely, on returning to the site the next day, his rescuer discovered Truman's shoe… with his severed foot still in it.

Secondary impacts
In 1986, Kilauea began steadily releasing up to 2000 tonnes a day of sulphur dioxide gas into the atmosphere. This is potentially lethal within 1 km of the volcano, and has led to persistent air pollution (volcanic smog or '**vog**') and acid rain. These damage crops, vehicles and buildings, and can contaminate water supplies.

One positive impact is that around 2.6 million tourists visit the Hawaii Volcanoes National Park each year, generating income for local businesses. The lava also weathers to produce very fertile soil, making Hawaii a good place to grow commercial food crops, such as sugarcane and pineapples, worth US$30 million per year to the local economy.

Responding to and managing Kilauea
Although Kilauea is not generally a threat to human life, the dangers still need careful management. The Hawaiian Volcano Observatory is located close to the crater and **volcanologists** there monitor the volcano (Figure 11) and issue warnings about possible eruptions and evacuations.

- 17 webcams and satellite data are used to monitor activity.
- Gas emissions are monitored; warnings are issued about air pollution levels.
- Seismometers detect minor earthquakes caused by magma movement underground.

Figure 11 Volcanologist collecting samples from Kilauea lava flow

However, weak planning laws and a growing population have resulted in building in areas at risk from the volcano. There is lots of evidence that Kilauea was more explosive in the past. An explosive eruption today could be devastating, as there are thousands of visitors on Kilauea each day.

Exam-style question
Describe **one** way in which people can predict volcanic eruptions. **(2 marks)**

Exam tip
The question asks you to describe *one* way – do not waste time writing about more than one.

Activity
1. Make lists of the primary and secondary impacts of Kilauea, then colour-code them into positive and negative impacts.
2. Why do you think recent deaths from Kilauea's eruptions are few?

1B Hazardous Earth: Tectonics

Case Study – Emerging country: The Pinatubo eruption, Philippines, 1991

Mount Pinatubo is one of many composite volcanoes on the island of Luzon in the Philippines. Here, the Eurasian Plate is subducting below the Philippine Plate (Figure 12). After more than 600 years of inactivity, Pinatubo erupted again on 12 June 1991. Its andesitic lava is relatively thick and full of gas, causing explosive eruptions. A cloud of steam and ash was sent 30 km up into the atmosphere, and pyroclastic flows (burning gases) descended from the crater at speeds of more than 200 km per hour.

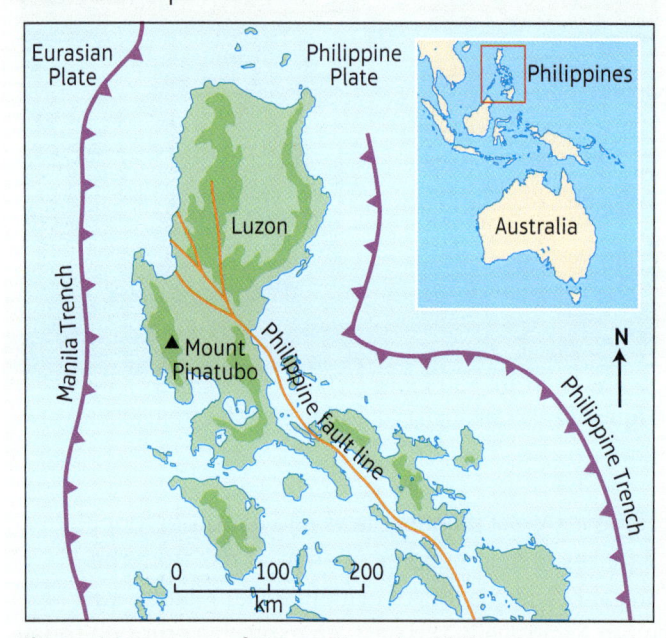

Figure 12 Location of Mount Pinatubo, Philippines

Primary impacts
Volcanologists predicted the eruption and advance warnings allowed thousands of people to evacuate the area. However, the eruption caused serious damage.

- 847 people were killed in the main eruption, many by pyroclastic flows and ash falls.
- The ash cloud caused the region to become cold and dark, hampering rescue operations.
- 5000 homes were destroyed and a further 70,000 damaged. Typhoon Yunya struck at the same time as the eruption. Torrential rain caused much of the ash to be washed back to Earth as mud, causing buildings to collapse under the weight.
- Many people were displaced to shanty towns on the edge of Manila, the capital city, or to evacuation camps (Figure 13).
- Power supplies were cut, and roads and bridges were left unusable; the water supply quickly became contaminated.

Figure 13 Evacuation camp near Pinatubo, Luzon

Secondary impacts
The secondary impacts were arguably more devastating and were felt long after the 1991 eruption.

- As winds dispersed the gas cloud (10 million tonnes of sulphur dioxide), global temperatures dropped temporarily (1991–93) by 0.5°C.
- Hundreds of people died from disease (mainly measles, pneumonia and diarrhoea) in the evacuation camps.
- Crops were destroyed as ash covered 800 km² of rice fields, and around 800,000 farm animals were killed, with the cost to farmers estimated at 1.5 billion pesos (about £20 million).
- Heavy rain mixed with the ash on the ground, causing devastating lahars up to 3 metres high.
- After wet ash destroyed many of its buildings, the US Air Force base at Pinatubo closed and relocated to Singapore. Many Filipinos lost their jobs and local trade suffered great losses.

The response to and management of Pinatubo
Several techniques were used to predict the Pinatubo eruption:

- PHIVOLCS (Philippine Institute of Volcanology and Seismology) seismologists detected swarms

of earthquakes beneath Pinatubo in March 1991, indicating that magma was on the move
- **tiltmeters** were installed to monitor the deformation of the surface as the magma rose (Figure 14)
- helicopters with gas-monitoring equipment flew over the crater daily
- geologists mapped the distribution of lahar deposits from previous eruptions in order to better decide which areas should be evacuated.

Once the threat of an eruption was confirmed, warnings were issued and local people evacuated to camps set up in advance. Vaccinations were given to try to combat the threat of measles and flu. International emergency aid was provided after both the eruption and the lahars.

With the help of international development aid, the Luzon authorities have established some long-term initiatives to better protect the people and their properties, including:

- building dykes and dams to protect against lahars and flash floods
- establishing new farms and employment away from the danger area, including converting the abandoned US air base into Clark International Airport, where tax-free trading attracts businesses which now employ over 47,000 people
- creating new towns and villages outside the area of risk.

Figure 14 A tiltmeter being installed at Pinatubo, Luzon, in 1991

Activity

1. Explain why the impacts of the Pinatubo eruption in 1991 were so much greater than those of Kilauea volcano, which has been erupting since 1983.
2. Describe one similarity and one difference between the management of the Kilauea and Pinatubo eruptions.

Checkpoint

It is now time to review your understanding of the causes and impacts of volcanic eruptions and their management in different locations.

Strengthen

S1 What type of volcano forms above an oceanic hotspot?

S2 What is the difference between a primary impact and a secondary impact of a tectonic hazard?

S3 How are volcanologists able to predict volcanic eruptions?

Challenge

C1 Why are volcanic eruptions more explosive at convergent plate boundaries?

C2 Explain why the impacts of a volcanic eruption are usually more severe in an emerging/developing country than in a developed country.

C3 Describe how the three Ps are used to manage the impact of volcanic eruptions.

1B Hazardous Earth: Tectonics

Why do most earthquakes occur at convergent plate boundaries?

Learning objectives

- To know why earthquakes occur at convergent plate boundaries
- To know the impacts of and responses to earthquakes
- To understand how these impacts and responses vary with location

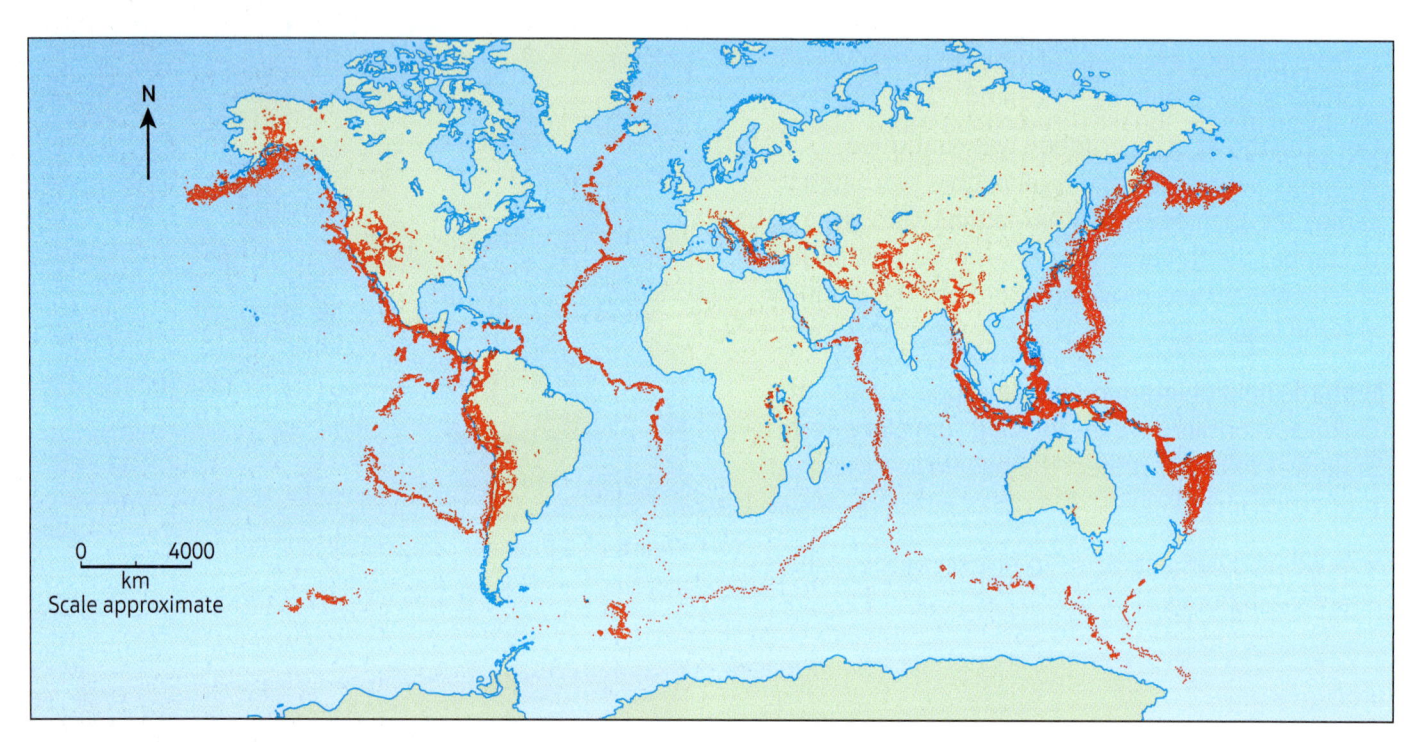

Figure 15 Global distribution of earthquake zones

Earthquakes are intense vibrations within the Earth's crust that make the ground shake. They are sudden and often lethal. Figure 15 shows the location of areas prone to earthquakes. Compare these areas to the tectonic plate boundaries (see Figure 2 on page 39).

Over 90% of earthquakes occur where plates are colliding at convergent plate boundaries. Great stresses build up in the subduction zone as the edge of one plate sinks below the other. Energy builds up until the rock fractures along a fault, and the energy is released in an earthquake. The point of rupture – where the earthquake happens underground – is called the **focus**. **Shock waves** radiate out from this point. The **epicentre** is the point on the ground surface directly above the focus, where the greatest force of the earthquake is felt.

Earthquakes also occur along conservative plate boundaries (see Figure 5 on page 41), and smaller ones occur at divergent plate boundaries, but these can still result in high death tolls and devastation. The amount of damage and destruction caused by a tectonic hazard depends on several factors.

- The scale of the event in terms of its energy, the area affected and how long it lasts. If the focus of an earthquake is shallow (a few kilometres deep) little energy is lost before the shock waves reach the surface.
- The density of human settlement in the area – densely populated cities such as Tokyo can potentially suffer greater damage.
- The time of day/week – there are more casualties if people are inside (offices, factories, homes) than if they are outside.
- The degree to which people are prepared – how far in advance is the warning? Have people been educated

1B Hazardous Earth: Tectonics

in what to do in an emergency? Are there emergency shelters set up? Are homes, offices and factories built in areas of low risk? Are they constructed in a way to withstand a tectonic event?

- The ability of a country to prepare for and cope with a hazard. This depends on the level of development of a country – wealthier countries are better able to afford to reduce the impact through prediction, protection and preparation.

Measuring earthquakes

The size of an earthquake is recorded using a **seismometer**. The **magnitude** (size) is then given according to the **Richter scale**, which gives a value between 1 and 10. The scale is logarithmic, meaning an earthquake measured at 7 is ten times more powerful than one measured at 6, and 100 times more powerful than one measured at 5. Another scale, the **moment magnitude scale (Mw)**, is frequently used today. It is similar to the Richter scale but it works over a wider range of earthquake sizes and is more accurate for larger earthquakes.

Table 1 The deadliest earthquakes since 2006

Earthquake	Magnitude (Mw)	Death toll
Nepal (2015)	7.8	8617
Wenping, China (2014)	6.2	729
Awaran, Pakistan (2013)	7.7	825
Negros, Philippines (2012)	6.7	113
Tōhoku, Japan (2011)	9.0	20,896
Haiti (2010)	7.0	316,000
Sumatra, Indonesia (2009)	7.5	1117
Sichuan, China (2008)	7.9	87,587
Central Peru (2007)	8.0	514
Java, Indonesia (2006)	6.3	5749

Did you know?

Just before a tsunami breaks, seawater retreats from the coastline, exposing the seafloor. This is an important warning sign and gives people the chance to reach higher ground.

Exam-style question

Identify which of the following is the correct equipment to use to measure the magnitude of an earthquake?

- [ ] A Tiltmeter
- [ ] B Seismometer
- [ ] C Satellite image
- [ ] D Webcam (1 mark)

Exam tip

If you know the techniques used to monitor tectonic hazards, this type of question is usually straightforward, but watch out for choices which are nearly correct, but not quite right.

Tsunamis

Tsunamis are usually triggered by earthquakes and, as such, are a secondary hazard. A tsunami is a series of giant ocean waves that send surges of water, sometimes over 30 metres high, onto land.

When a powerful undersea earthquake occurs at a plate boundary, the seafloor at the boundary either rises or falls suddenly, displacing the water above it and setting off rolling waves that build to tsunamis. Tsunamis move across the oceans at speeds of about 800 km per hour. As they approach land, they begin to slow down, grow in height and gain energy. When they crash onto the shore, they cause widespread destruction.

Activity

On a world map, plot the locations of the earthquakes listed in Table 1.

a Explain how the position of the earthquakes compares to the plate boundaries shown in Figure 2 on page 39.

b How many times more powerful was the earthquake in Japan (2011) than the one in Haiti (2010)?

c Explain why many powerful earthquakes occur along convergent plate boundaries.

1B Hazardous Earth: Tectonics

What are the impacts of and responses to earthquakes?

> **Case Study – Developed country: The Tōhoku earthquake, Japan, 2011**

At 2.47 p.m. on 11 March 2011, an earthquake of magnitude 9.0 Mw shook north-east Japan and triggered a tsunami that had a devastating impact in the Pacific region. What caused the earthquake?

- The Pacific Plate, moving at a speed of 83 mm a year, thrust under the Eurasian Plate at the Japan Trench.
- Faulting occurred along 300 km of the Japan Trench, causing the fault to thrust upwards by 10 metres and sideways by 50 metres.
- The earthquake was relatively shallow, with the focus around 30 km below the seabed. The epicentre was about 130 km east of Sendai, on the coast (Figure 16).

This was the strongest earthquake ever recorded in Japan. Hundreds of aftershocks, many between 6.0 and 7.0 magnitude, followed. More fatally, the earthquake triggered a tsunami that raced outwards from the epicentre at speeds of 800 km per hour. Waves up to 10 metres high hit the east coast of Japan and travelled as far as 10 km inland. Waves 3.5 metres high hit the coast of Hawaii and, several hours later, 2.7 metre high waves struck the coast of California.

Primary impacts
Between 667 and 1479 deaths occurred as a direct result of the earthquake, caused mostly by collapsing buildings. Many buildings were severely damaged. Roads and railways were damaged. Electric power, water and sewerage systems were disrupted. Reclaimed land in Tokyo (400 km from the epicentre) suffered from **liquefaction** (the ground turned to liquid), and more than 1000 buildings were damaged.

Secondary impacts
The vast majority of deaths (over 17,000) were due to people drowning in the tsunami; more than half of the victims were aged 65 years or older. A further 5000 or more people were injured or reported missing. Over 127,000 buildings collapsed, and around 1.2 million buildings were severely damaged (Figure 17). More than 2000 roads, 56 bridges and 26 railway lines along the entire east coast of Honshu were destroyed or damaged. The Fukushima dam burst, and the earthquake cut the main power to several nuclear power stations, including to the Fukushima Daiichi plant. Tsunami waves then damaged the back-up generator, causing a nuclear meltdown because the cooling systems failed. The World Bank estimates the damage was in excess of US$300 billion – US$235 billion in Japan alone.

The immediate and long-term response
Advanced warnings of the earthquake and tsunami gave people time to get outside or reach higher ground. The Pacific Tsunami Warning Center warned coastal communities in Japan and other countries round the Pacific. Rescue workers and Japanese soldiers were mobilised to deal with the crisis. The government requested international aid and

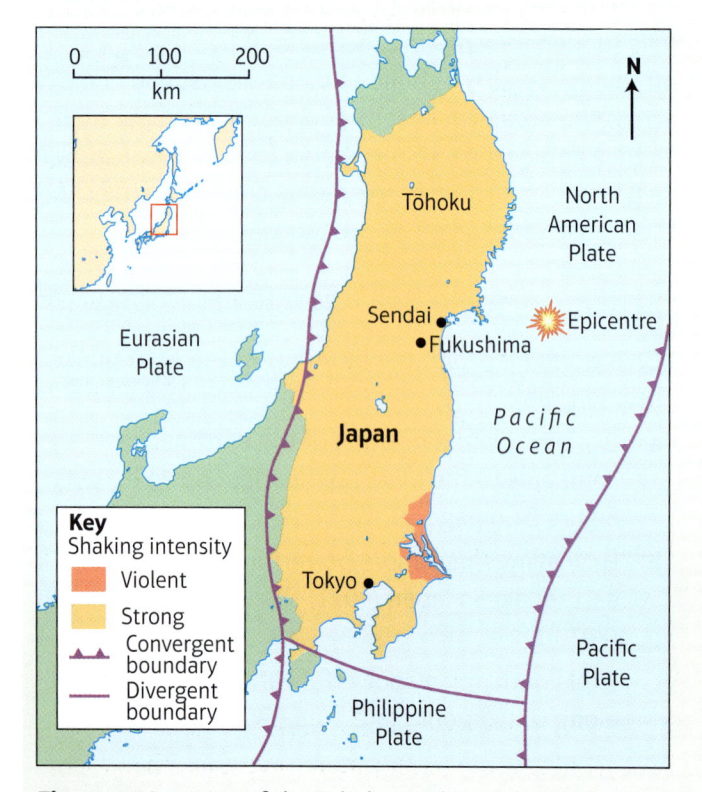

Figure 16 Location of the Tōhoku earthquake, Japan

Australia, China, India, New Zealand, South Korea and the USA sent search-and-rescue teams. Other countries and the Red Cross and Red Crescent provided support, as did private companies and non-government organisations (NGOs) in Japan and around the world. Rescue efforts were hampered by the disruption to roads and communications, and bad weather. More than 130,000 people were displaced, with many in shelters where food and supplies were severely limited. A further 140,000 people were evacuated from a 20 km radius around the Fukushima power plant.

Figure 17 Damage caused by the 2011 tsunami in Japan

Reducing the impact of earthquakes

As yet, earthquakes cannot be predicted. Until they can be, the only effective long-term response is to be prepared. The emergency services need to be trained and ready to respond, and people need to practise both protection and response operations. In Japan, school students and workers take part in the annual National Disaster Prevention Day on 1 September, during which they are drilled in what to do in the event of an earthquake or tsunami.

New buildings are also built according to strict building codes, which ensure that the designs allow buildings to 'move with the quake' (Figure 18). Older buildings are **retrofitted** with some of these design features, too.

Did you know?

Since 2007, all Japanese-manufactured smartphones have been fitted with the Earthquake Early Warning System app.

In the weeks following the disaster, tens of thousands of prefabricated temporary houses were set up in Sendai. Honshu's transportation and communication services were partially restored. The power supply took longer to bring online, reducing the region's manufacturing and business output even further. By late summer, however, the economy was growing again. In February 2012, the government set up an agency to coordinate the rebuilding efforts in the Tōhoku area. The restoration of the region was expected to take 10 years. In early 2015, the agency reported that nearly all the disaster debris had been removed and work had started on a seawall to protect the low coastal zone.

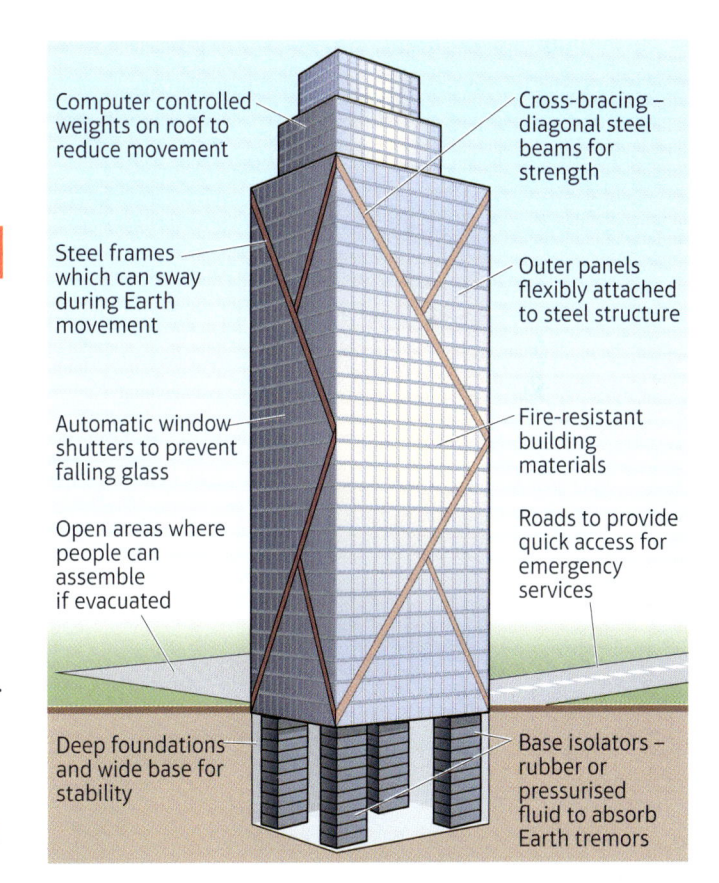

Figure 18 Earthquake-resistant building design

Labels: Computer controlled weights on roof to reduce movement; Cross-bracing – diagonal steel beams for strength; Steel frames which can sway during Earth movement; Outer panels flexibly attached to steel structure; Automatic window shutters to prevent falling glass; Fire-resistant building materials; Open areas where people can assemble if evacuated; Roads to provide quick access for emergency services; Deep foundations and wide base for stability; Base isolators – rubber or pressurised fluid to absorb Earth tremors

Activity

1. Explain how tsunamis are formed and why they can have such devastating impacts, as in the case of Japan.

2. Examine why the primary impacts of an earthquake are usually more severe in urban than rural areas.

1B Hazardous Earth: Tectonics

Case Study – Developing country: The Haiti earthquake, 2010

At 4.53 p.m. on 12 January 2010, an earthquake of magnitude 7.0 struck the Caribbean island of Haiti. It was caused by contraction and deformation along a fault near the conservative plate boundary between the North American Plate and the Caribbean Plate. The epicentre was 25 km south-west of the capital, Port-au-Prince (Figure 19), and the focus was very shallow (13 km below the surface). Aftershocks of magnitudes between 5.5 and 6.0 occurred in the days following the earthquake.

Primary impacts

This was one of the most destructive earthquakes ever.

- The number of deaths was estimated at 316,000 by the Haitian government, and 300,000 injured.
- Around 3 million people were affected by the earthquake. Some 1.5 million were made homeless when more than 180,000 homes were destroyed. They were forced into squalid camps with limited water and sanitation.
- All eight hospitals collapsed or were badly damaged.
- Around 5000 schools were damaged or destroyed and all three universities collapsed – fortunately the time of day meant that most classrooms were empty.
- In total, about 19 million cubic metres of rubble and debris were created.
- One prison collapsed: 4000 inmates escaped.
- The port at Port-au-Prince was severely damaged and the airport control tower collapsed. This hindered emergency efforts and the supply of aid.
- Electricity, water, sanitation and communications were badly disrupted or destroyed.

Secondary impacts

- Cholera spread through the squatter camps, which also provided little protection during the hurricane season.
- With factories closed and tourism stopped, economic losses increased.
- Looting and crime increased as the government and the police force collapsed.

Response to and management of the Haiti earthquake

Haiti is one of the poorest countries in the Caribbean. It was unprepared for such an event and could not respond adequately to the disaster. In the first few days, aid workers reported that no one seemed to be in charge. International aid in the form of search-and-rescue teams were flown into the country to help rescue those trapped by the collapsed buildings. Food, water, medical supplies and temporary shelters were brought into the country from the USA and neighbouring Dominican Republic. American engineers and divers cleared the port so that waiting ships could unload aid. UN (United Nations) and US troops provided security to maintain law and order and to help with distributing aid. The UK's Disasters Emergency Committee (DEC) raised more than £100 million, which was used to provide emergency

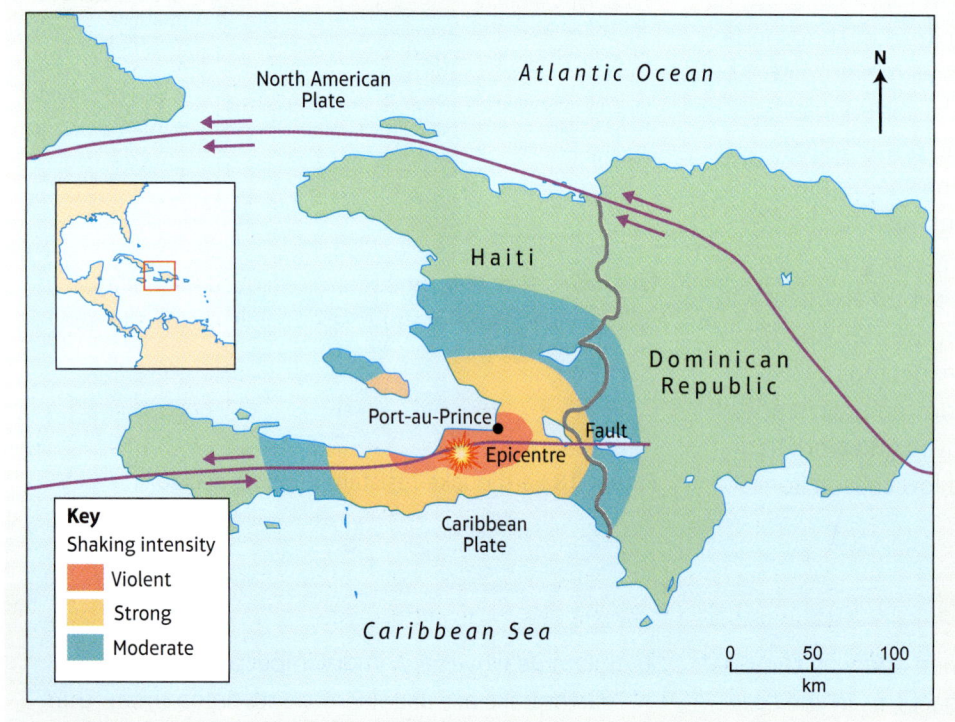

Figure 19 Location of the Haiti earthquake

shelters, medication, bottled water and purification tablets, and sanitation.

Did you know?

The 2010 Haiti earthquake was one of the first where social media and GIS played a significant role in identifying damage and organising relief and recovery.

In the weeks and months that followed, there were several longer-term responses.

- The government moved 235,000 people from Port-au-Prince to less damaged cities. Many subsequently chose to stay away, some even emigrated.
- Three-quarters of the damaged buildings were inspected and repaired. Earthquake-resistant techniques were used in some cases, such as building with old tyres, straw bales or bamboo, with lighter roofs made from large leaves or tarpaulin.
- Some 200,000 people were paid or received food for public work, such as clearing away the tonnes of rubble (Figure 20).
- Money was pledged by individuals and governments around the world, including 300 million euros from the EU, $100 million from the USA and £20 million from the UK. The World Bank cancelled Haiti's debt repayments for five years. However, by 2013, less than half of the US$4.5 billion pledged had reached Haiti. Oxfam estimated that by 2015 there were still 500,000 homeless people without water, sewage systems or electricity.
- A cholera epidemic began 10 months after the earthquake, killing over 8000 people and infecting 6% of all Haitians by 2013.

Figure 20 Clearing rubble after the 2010 earthquake, Port-au-Prince, Haiti

Activity

1. State one physical and one human reason why loss of life was lower in the Tōhoku (Japan) earthquake than in the Haiti earthquake.
2. Compare the Tōhoku (Japan) and Haiti earthquakes. To what extent was each country able to predict, protect and prepare for the event?
3. Look back at your learning in this topic. Examine why tectonic hazards occur, give examples of their impacts and how they can be managed.

Checkpoint

It is now time to review your understanding of the causes and impacts of earthquakes and their management in different locations.

Strengthen

S1 Explain how an earthquake can be measured and what the measurement tells us about it.

S2 Draw a spider diagram to show the impacts of earthquake hazards. Include examples. Use two colours to highlight the primary and secondary impacts.

S3 Design your own earthquake-resistant building. Decide if it is to be built in a developed or emerging/developing country, and annotate it to show its key design features.

Challenge

C1 Describe how and explain why the impacts of an earthquake differ in countries at different levels of development.

C2 Draw a spider diagram to show how earthquake hazards can be managed. Include examples. Use two colours to highlight short-term and long-term management techniques.

Preparing for your exams

Hazardous Earth: Tectonics

The causes and impacts of tectonic activity and the management of tectonic hazards vary with location. There are different processes, and therefore different types of hazards, at convergent, divergent and conservative plate boundaries. The level of development, how 'expected' the tectonic event was and the particular hazards encountered (for example, volcanoes, earthquakes, lahars, pyroclastic flows, fires or tsunamis) are some of the factors that influence the impacts of and the responses to these events.

Checklist

You should know:

- [ ] the composition and physical properties of the different layers within the Earth (crust, lithosphere, asthenosphere, mantle, outer core and inner core)
- [ ] how convection currents occur and how they are thought to drive plate tectonics
- [ ] the distribution of the three plate boundary types (convergent, divergent and conservative)
- [ ] the processes, features and hazards that tend to occur at the different plate boundaries
- [ ] the processes, features and distribution of hotspots
- [ ] how volcano type (shield/composite), magma type/lava flows and explosivity are related
- [ ] how earthquakes and tsunamis are caused
- [ ] that the Richter scale for earthquake magnitude is logarithmic, and what this means
- [ ] the primary and secondary impacts of earthquakes and volcanoes on people and property in a developed and emerging or developing country, and why these can differ
- [ ] how countries respond to and 'manage' or learn to live with volcanic or earthquake hazards in a developed and emerging or developing country (including immediate relief and long-term planning, preparation and prediction), and why these can differ.

Which key terms match the following definitions?

a   The dense, mostly solid layer of the Earth between the outer core and the crust.

b   A plate boundary where two plates are moving apart.

c   The process of one plate sinking beneath another.

d   The fluidity of a lava (or other substance) – how 'sticky' it is.

e   The knock-on, or indirect, effects of a volcanic eruption or earthquake that take place on a longer timescale.

f   A thick and sticky lava erupted from composite volcanoes.

g   A section of the Earth's crust where plumes of magma rise, weakening the crust; these are usually away from plate boundaries.

h   Mudflows resulting from ash mixing with melting ice or water – a secondary hazard of a volcano.

i   The upper layer of the Earth's mantle, below the lithosphere, in which convection currents cause tectonic plate movement.

j   The immediate effects of a natural hazard, caused directly by it.

k   Organising activities and drills so that people know what to do if an earthquake happens.

To check your answers, look at the Glossary on pages 302–311.

Preparing for your exams

Hazardous Earth: Tectonics

Question 1   Describe **one** tectonic hazard that tends to occur at a convergent plate boundary.   *(2 marks)*

Student answer

Tsunamis can occur at convergent plate boundaries when the over-riding plate, having got 'stuck' over hundreds of years due to friction with the subducting plate, suddenly 'flips up', causing an earthquake, making the seafloor rise suddenly, and so causing the whole ocean to rise, setting off a wave. This powerful wave gets higher when it reaches shallow water, and can flood many miles inland.

Verdict

The answer identified a correct hazard (tsunami) that occurs at a convergent plate boundary, and described the tsunami as a powerful wave which gets higher as it approaches the shore, flooding inland. However, most of the answer, about friction and subduction, is not relevant to the question, because it is explaining rather than describing a tsunami. In a real exam, this would be wasting valuable time.

Exam tip

One of the most common errors students make is to confuse 'describe' (say *what* it is like) and 'explain' (say *why* it is like that). Whenever you see one of these two command words, double check that you are writing about the right thing. Never just write all you know about a topic – keep your answer focused on the precise question being asked.

Question 2   Assess the effectiveness of the management of one tectonic hazard event. *(8 marks + 4 SPAG)*

Student answer

Mount Pinatubo in the Philippines erupted in 1991, causing the deaths of 847 people from primary impacts such as pyroclastic flows and ash deposits causing the collapse of roofs – plus hundreds more later on from secondary impacts such as disease. It also severely damaged the farming economy of the area. Almost 1 million farm animals were killed, and rice fields were destroyed.

The management of Pinatubo's eruption has been seen as an overall success. Filipino and American volcanologists predicted the eruption and evacuated around 60,000 people, saving thousands of lives. There is not a lot the government or volcanologists could have done to stop the ash and pyroclastic flows destroying the farms, so this cannot be seen as a criticism of the management.

The main criticism of the management was that many of the local people died from diseases such as measles and diarrhoea in the evacuation camps. As they had mostly been isolated from others, their immunity had not built up. A more effective vaccination programme, especially among the children, could have prevented many more deaths.

Verdict

This student precisely answers the question, by suggesting good and bad things about the management, and giving an overall assessment ('has been seen as an overall success'). There are plenty of place-specific details (data on deaths, number of evacuees) to support the assessment, and geographical terms are used well throughout. Notice that the answer is split into three paragraphs (details of the eruption, successes of the management and then criticisms of the management). You do not need a really long answer to do well.

Pearson Education Ltd accepts no responsibility whatsoever for the accuracy or method of working in the answers given.

WRITING GEOGRAPHICALLY

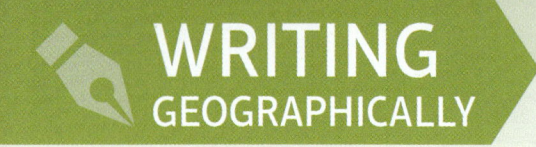

Writing geographically: a clear, well-structured answer

Every response you write needs to be clearly written and clearly structured. To achieve this, you need to **clearly signal that your answer is relevant** and **signal the sequence and structure of your ideas**.

Learning objectives

- To understand how to use key noun phrases, verbs and adjectives from the question to make sure you answer it
- To be able to write a clear opening sentence beginning with a subject-verb construction
- To understand how to use adverbials to link your ideas and signal the sequence and structure of your ideas

Definitions

Noun phrase: a phrase including a noun (an object, idea, person, place, etc., e.g. *wind*) and any words which modify its meaning, e.g. *south-westerly, prevailing wind*.

Verb: words which describe actions ('Chemicals *poured* into the river'), incidents ('Something *happened*'), and situations ('The rock *is* sedimentary').

Adverbial: a word or phrase that can modify a verb, adjective or another adverb; often used to link ideas in a text, e.g. *suddenly, all of a sudden, therefore, firstly*.

How can I make sure I am answering the question?

Look at this exam-style question in which **key noun phrases**, **verbs** and **adjectives** are highlighted:

> 'The causes of past climate change and current global warming are different'. Assess this statement.
> **(8 marks)**

Now look at the first sentences of two different responses to this question.

Student A

> Past climate change and current global warming are the result of both natural events and human activity.

Student B

> A lot of the time people blame global warming caused by natural events on human activity so that's why it's difficult to identify the different causes of climate change.

1. Which student signals most clearly that their response is going to answer the question?
2. Write a sentence or two explaining your choice.

How can I signal the structure and sequence of my answer?

When assessing, explaining, describing or analysing a concept, you can use adverbials to link your ideas. For example:

> Similarly... for example... However... On the other hand... Therefore... Consequently... In conclusion...

WRITING GEOGRAPHICALLY

3. Now look at Student A's response to the exam-style question on page 56. How many adverbials have they used to link their ideas? Make a note of them all.

Past climate change and current global warming are the result of both natural events and human activity. For example, one of the natural causes of climate change is orbital geometry, where every 100,000 years the Earth's orbit changes, affecting the amount of sunlight received. Elliptical orbits lead to warmer periods and circular orbits cause cooler periods. This cannot be managed by humans. However greenhouse gases from human activity can be managed. In the last 200 years, economic development, increasing population and burning fossil fuels has led to the enhanced greenhouse effect and global warming.

On the other hand it could be argued that past and current causes have some similarities. For example, large volcanic eruptions can lead to a period of global cooling, as ash and dust particles are ejected high into the atmosphere, blanketing the earth. In 1883 the Krakatoa eruption is believed to have caused a 1.20 degrees C reduction in global temperature. Similarly, more recently, the eruption of Mount Pinatubo in 1991 caused global temperatures the following year to drop by half a degree Celsius.

In conclusion, whether the causes of climate change are past or current, it is evident that in the past the causes of climate change were mainly natural, whereas today most climate change is caused by humans and could be reduced through more sustainable management.

Did you notice?
Adverbials can be positioned at a number of different points in a sentence.

4. At which point in Student A's sentences are most of the adverbials positioned?

5. Choose one sentence from Student A's answer in which she uses an adverbial. Experiment with repositioning the adverbial at different points in the sentence. What impact does it have on the clarity of the sentence?

Improving an answer
Look at an extract from Student B's response to the exam-style question on page 56.

A lot of the time people blame global warming caused by natural events on human activity so that's why it's difficult to identify the different causes of climate change. One natural event which contributes to climate change is that, every 100,000 years, the Earth's orbit changes from circular when the Earth experiences cooler periods to elliptical which causes warmer periods as the earth gets different amounts of sunlight. Today climate change is mainly caused by human activity. The rise in greenhouse gases in the last two hundred years has been caused by burning fossil fuels as the population increases. There are some causes of climate change which have happened in the past and which we cannot manage. There are other more recent changes in human activity which make a significant contribution to climate change.

6. Rewrite Student B's response aiming to:
   - use a subject-verb start and key words in the first sentence to clearly signal that the answer is relevant to the question
   - use adverbials to link your ideas.

THINKING GEOGRAPHICALLY

Proportion, ratio and percentage

What you need to know

In geography we use proportion, ratio and percentage to break down data sets to describe and understand them better, and to compare them to other data sets.

- **Proportion** expresses one part as a fraction of the whole. For example, the proportion of all tropical storms in a year (80) that develop into hurricanes (30)

  $= 30 \div 80 = \frac{3}{8}$.

- **Ratio** states how many parts make up a whole. Map scales are often shown as ratios. For example, a scale of 1:200 means that the distance shown on the map is $\frac{1}{200}$th the distance in real life.

  5 cm on the map

  $= 5 \times 200$ cm in real life

  $= 1000$ cm

  $= 10$ metres.

  You can use a ratio to describe how two or more quantities make up the whole, e.g. A village population made up of a ratio of 3:4 males to females means there are 3 males for every 4 females in the village.

- **Percentage** is the proportion or ratio expressed as a fraction of 100, e.g. the percentage of days with air frost (40) in a year (365 days)

  $= \frac{40}{365}$

  $= \frac{40}{365} \times 100\%$

  $= 10.96\%$ (to 2 decimal places).

Example

Students were investigating the UK's climate, looking at the amount of sunshine in summer compared with winter where they lived. They measured the hours of sunshine over a year (Table 1).

Table 1 Hours of sunshine over one year

Season	Winter			Spring			Summer			Autumn		
Month	D	J	F	M	A	M	J	J	A	S	O	N
Hours of sunshine	35	70	85	140	222	188	228	202	170	170	94	36

Calculate the annual total hours of sunshine (S_a).

$S_a = (35 + 70 + 85 + 140 + 222 + 188 + 228 + 202 + 170 + 170 + 94 + 36)$

$= 1640$ hours.

THINKING GEOGRAPHICALLY

Calculate the totals for the summer (S_s) and winter (S_w) subsets.

S_s = 228 + 202 + 170   and S_w = 35 + 70 + 85

= 600 hours   = 190 hours.

The decimal proportion of the annual sunshine in summer $S_s \div S_a$

= 600 ÷ 1640

= 0.37 (to 2 decimal places).

As a percentage this is:

0.37 × 100

= 37%.

In winter the proportion would be $S_w \div S_a$

= 190 ÷ 1640

= 0.12

As a percentage this is 12% (to 2 significant figures).

Therefore 37% of the annual sunshine occurs in the summer compared with just 12% in the winter.

An alternative way to present this is using a ratio.

The ratio of summer to winter sunshine, = $S_s : S_w$

= 600:190.

= 60:19.

So, for every 60 hours of sunshine in summer there are only 19 hours in winter.

Apply your knowledge

Students investigating the seasonal distribution of rain falling in parts of the UK were testing the statement that 'Most rain in Wales falls during the winter season'. They had a set of average rainfall data for Valley in Anglesey from the Meteorological Office, from Climate data for 1981–2010 (Table 2).

Table 2 Average rainfall data for Valley in Anglesey

Month	D	J	F	M	A	M	J	J	A	S	O	N	Annual
Rainfall (mm)	91	76	55	63	55	48	54	54	70	72	101	104	843

1. Calculate the proportion of annual rain falling in each season by adding together the averages for each season and dividing by the total annual rain.

2. Express the proportion of rain in each season as a percentage by multiplying by 100.

3. Express your answer as a four-part ratio – winter rain:spring rain:summer rain:autumn rain.

4. Which season was wettest? Does this data support the statement the students were testing or not?

THINKING GEOGRAPHICALLY

Magnitude and frequency

What you need to know

In geography we use magnitude and frequency to help us find out how often or how meaningful an event or its effect is or how geographical conditions differ.

- **Frequency** is the number of times a data value occurs: how often it happens, e.g. the number of storms in a year.
- **Magnitude** is the quantifiable size of an event or piece of data: how large it is, e.g. the force of a wind. It can be numerical or ranked.
- Both can be measured and recorded using a variety of scales, e.g. arithmetic scales to plot frequency of monthly temperature and rainfall; ranked order of magnitude scales such as the Richter Scale for earthquakes and storm surges.
- Ranked scales do not always use equally spaced increases of obvious data values. The Saffir–Simpson Hurricane Scale describes the observed damage (rank 2 is roughly 4 times as damaging as rank 1) but does not imply equal increments of wind speed.

Apply your knowledge

1. Some students were studying whether the frequency and magnitude of hurricane winds and their effect have changed during the last 50 years. Using GSI to access the National Oceanic and Atmospheric Administration (NOAA) database they collected data for hurricane strength on landfall at New Orleans.

    (a) Complete the frequency for 2000–2009 in Table 3 by converting the following wind speeds to their equivalents on the Saffir–Simpson Scale: CINDY (2005) 121 km/h, KATRINA (2005) 236 km/h, GUSTAV (2008) 158 km/h.

    Table 3 Hurricane wind speed magnitude (Saffir–Simpson Scale)

Decade	1	2	3	4	5
1960–1969	1	1	0	2	1
1970–1979	1	0	0	0	0
1980–1989	1	1	1	0	0
1990–1999	1	0	0	0	0
2000–2009					
2010–	1	0	0	0	0

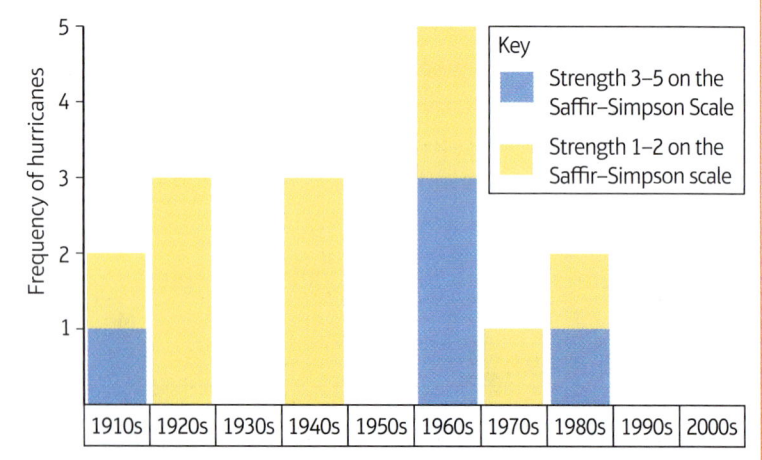

    Figure 1 Frequency of hurricanes from 1 to 5 on the Saffir–Simpson Scale making landfall at New Orleans from 1910 to 2009

    (b) Copy and complete the graph in Figure 1.

    (c) What is the frequency of hurricanes making landfall in New Orleans from 1960 to 2009?

    (d) What is the frequency of hurricanes of magnitude 3 and above from 1960 to 2009?

    (e) Describe how the frequency and magnitude of hurricane storms appears to have changed during the last 50 years.

2 | Development Dynamics

There are different economic, social and political measures that can be used to assess how developed a country is. What are the relative merits of different measures of development? Countries at different levels of development show distinct differences in their demographic data. Over time, a range of factors has resulted in wide global inequality, and there are different theories to explain its causes and how it can be reduced. These include modernisation theory and dependency theory. A number of strategies have been used to try to improve development, including international aid and inter-governmental agreements to set sustainable development goals. Development strategies are often classed as either top-down or bottom-up – what are their advantages and disadvantages?

This section particularly focuses on India's development. You will investigate how India has advanced in recent decades to become an 'emerging country', and whether that progress has been equally shared.

Your learning

In this section you will investigate the following key questions:

- How do we define and measure development?
- How do demographic data vary at different levels of development?
- What are the causes and consequences of global inequalities?
- How do development theories explain development?
- Are top-down or bottom-up approaches to development more successful?
- How has India's development been influenced by its location and global links?
- How are globalisation and other changes in the economy linked to India's development?
- What impacts has rapid economic change in India had on its people and environment?

2 Development Dynamics

How do we define and measure development?

Learning objectives
- To know different ways of defining and measuring development
- To know that demographic data are different for countries at different levels of development
- To understand population pyramids and know how to interpret them

Development is a broad idea linked to improving people's quality of life. One aspect involves money and wealth, which is an **economic development** measure. Other aspects consider **social development** factors such as good health care, or **political development** factors such as freedom of speech. Many people consider good health to be more important than wealth, and people in countries that are not democracies may envy those who live in democratic countries. The sustainability of the natural environment is also an important aspect for long-term development.

Development occurs when there are improvements to individual factors making up the quality of life. For example, development occurs in a **developing country** when local food supply increases because of investment in farm machinery.

Measuring development

Gross Domestic Product (GDP) per capita (per person) is one way of measuring economic development. This is the total value of goods and services produced within a country in a year (GDP) divided by the number of people in the country. Per capita figures allow more valid comparisons to be made between countries with big differences in population size. Figure 1 shows how GDP per capita varies around the world. The **development gap** between the world's wealthiest and poorest countries is huge. For example, in 2014, GDP per capita in the USA was US$54,370; in Malawi it was only US$344.

Today, **Gross National Income (GNI) per capita** is more frequently used as a measure of national wealth. GNI is similar to GDP, but it includes wealth created outside

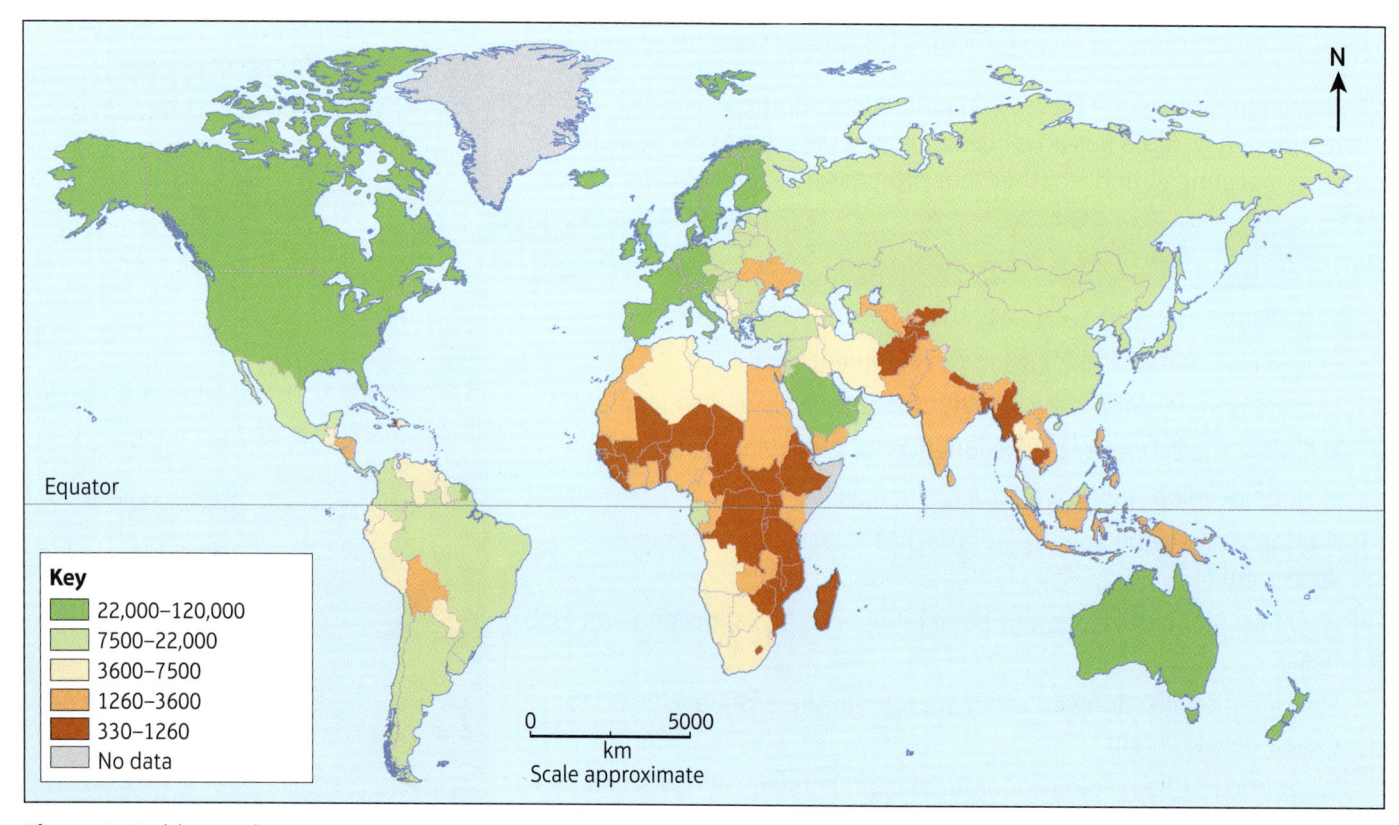

Figure 1 World map showing GDP per capita in US$, 2014

the country by its companies and corporations, and such things as **debt**. However, 'raw' GNI data does not take into account the way in which the cost of living varies between countries. For example, one dollar buys more in India than it does in the USA. To account for this, the GNI at **purchasing power parity (PPP)** is calculated.

No single measure can provide a complete picture of the differences in development between countries. In 1990, the United Nations introduced the **Human Development Index (HDI)**, which considers aspects of both social and economic development, but not environmental considerations. It gives each country a score based on the average **life expectancy**, education and income of the people of that country.

The HDI groups countries of the world into four levels of human development and uses a fixed range of values for each. Table 1 shows how the levels relate to the terms '**developed country**', '**emerging country**' and 'developing country', and the total number of countries in each group in 2014.

Table 1 Levels of human development, 2014

Level of human development	HDI value	Status of country	Number of countries
Very high	0.800 and above	Developed	49
High	0.700–0.799	Emerging	56
Medium	0.550–0.699	Emerging	38
Low	below 0.550	Developing	45

The relative rank position of countries can vary when using a **composite index** such as the HDI compared with a single indicator of development such as GDP or life expectancy.

The scale of inequality *within* countries is often as much an issue as the inequality *between* countries.

The **Gini coefficient** measures the extent to which the distribution of income is unequal within a country and how this changes over time, and allows comparisons to be made between countries. It is defined as a ratio, with values between 0 and 1. A Gini coefficient of 0 would mean that everyone in a country has exactly the same income. A coefficient of 1 would mean that one person had all the income in a country. A low value indicates a more equal income distribution, as in most European countries. A high value shows more unequal income distribution, such as in southern Africa. Richer countries often have a lower income gap, but this is not always the case. As China has developed, it has become more unequal.

The quality of government has a large influence on development. It can affect the lives of ordinary people in many ways. Countries where the quality of government is poor often have a high level of corruption. The **Corruption Perceptions Index** grades countries from 'highly corrupt' (0) to 'very clean' (100). In 2014:

- the five least corrupt countries were Denmark (92), New Zealand (91), Finland (89), Sweden (87) and Norway (86); the UK was ranked 14th (78)
- the five most corrupt countries were Somalia (8), North Korea (8), Sudan (11), Afghanistan (12) and South Sudan (15); India was ranked 85th (38).

Although inequality can be measured in different ways, it is generally thought to be increasing. Many people are concerned about this situation because they see it as unfair and a possible cause of political instability, leading to anti-government protests for example.

Activity

1 Define 'Gross Domestic Product (GDP)' and explain why GDP is often called an economic measure of development.

2 Define 'Human Development Index (HDI)' and explain why HDI is often called a social measure of development.

2 Development Dynamics

How do demographic data vary at different levels of development?

Social measures of development are used to assess how well a country is developing in relation to population, health and education. They are often linked. For example, lack of clean water and medical care cause illness; as a result, people die younger (life expectancy). Young children (infant mortality) and older people are most vulnerable and so the **death rate** is higher.

Table 2 shows some social measures of development in relation to population – these are also known as **demographic indicators**.

As countries develop, the **birth rate** and **total fertility rate** decline for a number of reasons. Education, especially female literacy, is the key to lower fertility rates. With female education comes more knowledge of birth control, greater social awareness and more opportunity for employment. All these factors improve the status of women in societies. In addition, government-directed birth-control programmes have helped to lower fertility rates in many countries. For example, in China the birth rate declined from 43.8 per 1000 people in 1950 to 12 per 1000 in 2014.

Where the **infant mortality rate** is high, many children die before reaching adult life. Parents in these countries often have many children to compensate for the expected deaths, as children are needed to help with the family's work and to provide for parents after their retirement. When countries develop their health care system, infant mortality rates fall, as do **maternal mortality rates**. As more children survive their childhood, people generally decide to have fewer children. In developing countries, children are often seen as an economic asset. This changes as countries develop, when the cost of bringing up children becomes a more important factor in deciding to start or extend a family. As a result, average family size falls.

With progress in development the death rate falls at first, but then increases (Table 2). This is because the death rate is heavily influenced by the age structure of a population.

> **Exam-style question**
>
> Explain **one** factor that causes the fertility rate to vary so much around the world. **(2 marks)**

Population structure

Population pyramids show the structure of a country's population in terms of age and gender (Figure 2). As countries develop, the shape of their population pyramid changes. For example, Japan's population pyramid will have looked like that of Niger in the past. The shape conveys information about the population of a country.

- **Niger** – the wide base reflects a very high fertility rate. The marked decrease in width of each successive bar indicates high infant and child mortality rates. Death rate is high in all age groups so life expectancy is low.

Table 2 Demographic data for selected developed, emerging and developing countries, 2014

Country	Birth rate per 1000	Fertility rate (no. of children)	Death rate per 1000	Infant mortality per 1000 births	Maternal mortality per 100,000 births
Developed countries					
UK	12	1.9	9	3.9	8
Japan	8	1.4	10	2.1	6
Emerging countries					
Brazil	15	1.8	6	19	69
India	21	2.3	7	42	190
Developing countries					
Papua New Guinea	33	4.3	10	47	220
Niger	50	7.6	11	60	630

2 Development Dynamics

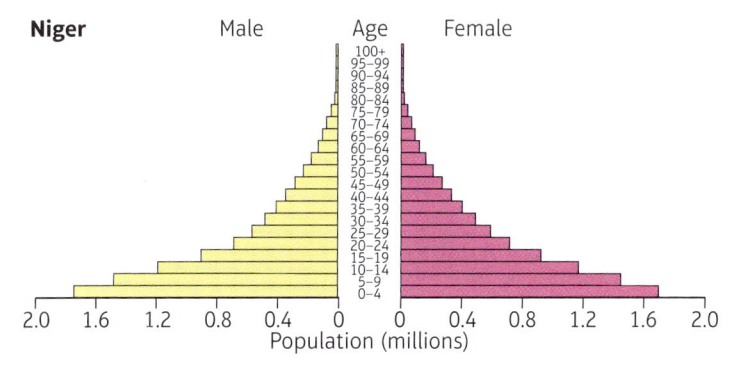

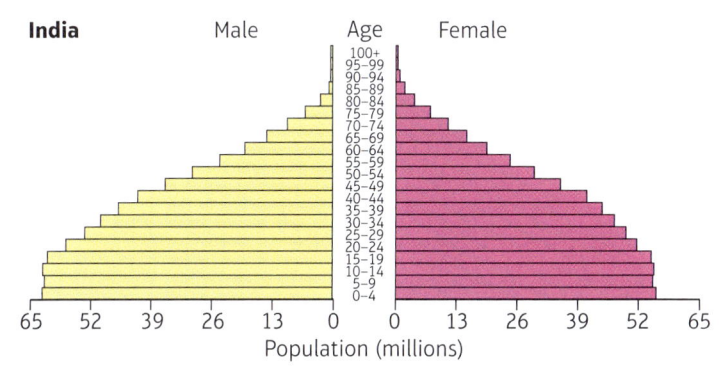

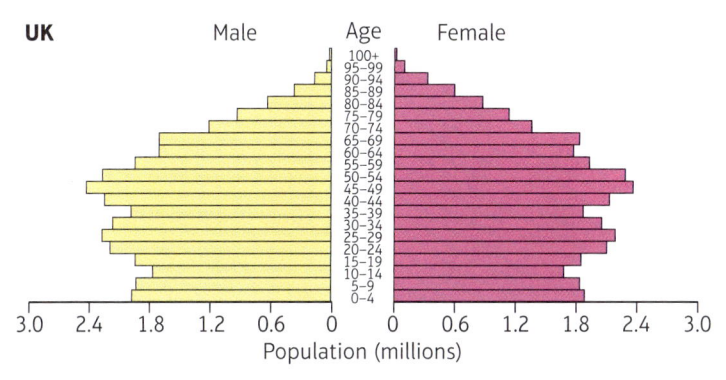

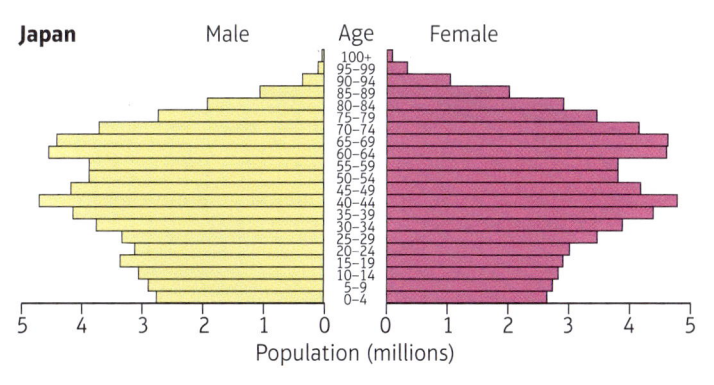

Figure 2 Population pyramids for Niger, India, the UK and Japan, 2014

- **India** – the straight-sided base reflects a decline in fertility rate but also shows that there are many young adults in their child-bearing years.
- **UK** – the narrow base reflects a steady low fertility rate. The fairly uniform width of the bars for the working-age population indicates a longer life expectancy than Niger or India.
- **Japan** – the narrow base indicates the lowest fertility rate of the four countries. The pyramid's broad top shows Japan has the highest population aged 65 and over in the world, 26%. With a higher death rate than birth rate, Japan is beginning to experience **natural population decrease**.

Progress through **demographic transition** is a significant factor in development, with the highest rates of growth experienced by those nations where the birth rate has fallen the most.

Activity

1. Define 'infant mortality rate' and explain why infant mortality generally declines as a country develops.
2. Draw a scattergraph (see page 93) to see if there is a relationship between Infant Mortality and Birth Rate (Table 2). Describe and explain any **correlation** between the data.
3. Sketch the population pyramids for Niger and Japan (Figure 2) and annotate them to:
   a. describe the shape of each graph, making the differences between them clear
   b. explain why the graphs are different.

Checkpoint

Now it is time to review your understanding of the different ways of defining and measuring development.

Strengthen

S1 Describe two ways of defining development.

S2 Describe the global variation in GDP per capita as shown in Figure 1. Refer to all six classes in the key.

S3 State three differences between the **population structure** of the UK and that of India (Figure 2).

Challenge

C1 Explain why the HDI is a better measure of development than GDP per capita.

C2 With reference to examples, explain how the birth rate and the infant mortality rate vary between developing, emerging and developed countries.

C3 Explain how the population pyramids in Figure 2 can be used to describe different levels of development.

2 Development Dynamics

What are the causes and consequences of global inequalities?

Learning objectives
- To know the causes and consequences of global inequalities
- To recognise the role of migration in global inequality
- To understand how different theories can be used to explain how and why countries develop over time

Causes of global inequalities

Studies have shown that a variety of factors have led to inequality in the world.

The physical environment – access to the sea is an important influence. For example, many landlocked and mountainous countries have developed more slowly than coastal nations because trade is more difficult for them. Climate is also influential. Tropical countries have grown more slowly than those in temperate latitudes because they experience a higher incidence of climate-related diseases, which are often carried in the water. Natural hazards, such as earthquakes, hurricanes, floods and drought, can also slow or reverse development in some countries.

History – **colonialism** occurred mainly in the 18th and 19th centuries as European powers, such as the UK, France and Spain, expanded their territories around the world. They exploited their colonies for economic gain, and unequal trading relationships distorted local economies, which meant that many colonies received little benefit. In the modern world, the term '**neo-colonialism**' is used to describe how rich countries can still dominate poorer countries. This now happens in an economic and political sense.

Political and economic policies – **open economies**, such as the UK, encourage foreign investment and have developed faster than **closed economies**, such as North Korea, where imports and exports are not allowed. Investment creates jobs and helps to fund infrastructure. Political mismanagement and corruption can slow or reverse development. Zimbabwe, once one of the most developed African countries, has suffered severe setbacks in welfare and human rights because of poor government and the impact of HIV/Aids.

Social investment – countries that have prioritised investment in education and health care have generally developed at a faster rate than nations that have invested less in these sectors. When Sierra Leone gained independence in 1963, it stopped investing in its health system. Since then, the country's economy has rapidly declined. A healthy and well-educated population attracts investors and therefore encourages development.

Figure 3 shows the percentage share of income in four countries for each fifth or **quintile** of their population. It gives us a good idea of inequality there by comparing the share of income for the poorest fifth and the richest fifth, as well as the shares for the middle earners.

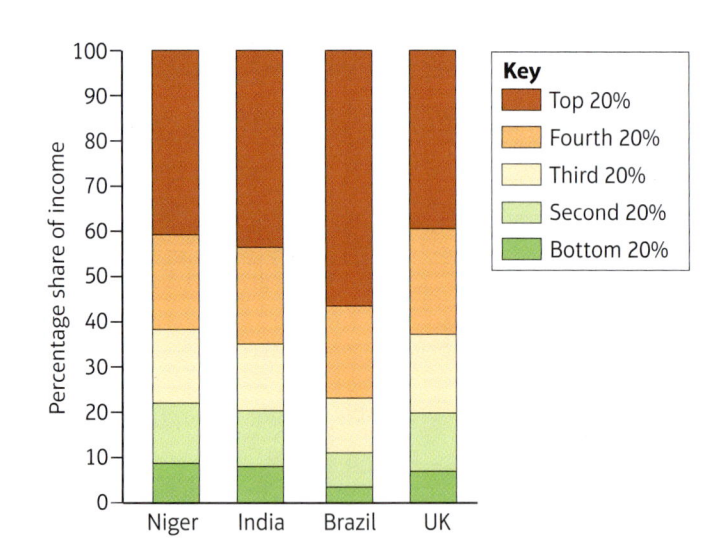

Figure 3 Percentage share of income in four countries, in quintiles, 2009–2013

The consequences of inequality

Inequalities have significant consequences for people, particularly in the least developed countries. The consequences of poverty can be economic, social, environmental and political (Table 3). Development may not bring improvement in all four areas at first, but all four categories should show improvement over time if there is balanced development.

Table 3 Consequences of poverty

Economic	About one in five of the world's population live on less than US$1 a day, almost half on less than US$2 a day. Developing countries frequently lack the ability to pay for food, agricultural innovation and investment in rural development.
Social	More than 775 million people in developing countries cannot read or write. Nearly a billion people do not have access to clean water and 2.4 billion to basic sanitation. Many developing countries do not have the ability to combat the effects of HIV/AIDS.
Environmental	Developing countries have increased vulnerability to natural disasters. They lack the capacity to adapt to climate-change-induced droughts. Poor farming practices lead to environmental **degradation**. Raw materials are exploited with limited economic benefit to developing countries and little concern for the environment.
Political	Some developing countries have non-democratic governments or they are democracies that function poorly. This can worsen the plight of minority groups.

Migration

International **migration** can be a major consequence of inequality between countries. **Globalisation** has led to an increased awareness of opportunities in developed countries. With advances in transportation and a reduction in the relative cost, the potential mobility of the world's population has never been higher.

Did you know?

Currently, about 3% of the world's population live outside the country of their birth. This amounts to about 213 million people, higher than ever before.

One of the largest workforce migrations in the world has been from Mexico to the USA (Figure 4), creating the largest immigrant community in the world. This migration has been the result of:

- much higher average wages and lower unemployment rates in the USA
- the rapid growth in the size of the workforce in Mexico
- the much higher quality of life in the USA.

While migration from Mexico to the USA has brought benefits to both countries (for example, income sent back to families and reduced unemployment pressure in Mexico, and an increased supply of labour in the USA), it is a controversial issue because of its scale. The USA has done more to stop illegal immigration in recent years, including building a high fence along the border.

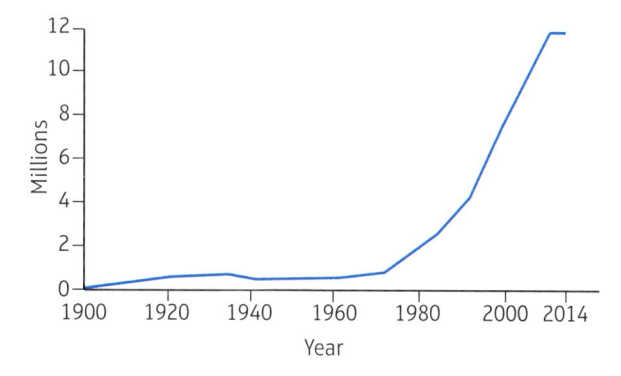

Figure 4 The increase in the Mexican-born population in the USA, 1900–2014

Activity

1. State two physical and two human causes of global inequalities.
2. Nearly 10% of the world population still do not have access to safe water. Is this a cause or a consequence of inequality? Explain your answer.
3. Study Figure 3.
    a. Identify the most unequal country, and state the income share of its bottom and top quintiles.
    b. Identify the two most equal countries, and state the income shares of their bottom and top quintiles.
    c. Write a short summary of the pattern of inequality shown in Figure 3. Explain what a quintile is, and describe the pattern, details and examples. Is it possible to say that one type of country is more equal than others?

2 Development Dynamics

How do development theories explain development?

There are a number of theories to explain how and why countries develop over time. Two contrasting explanations are **modernisation theory** (a capitalist view) and **dependency theory** (a socialist view). The objective of producing theories is to explore and improve our understanding of situations. If we have better understanding, we should make better decisions about how to reduce inequality.

Rostow's modernisation theory

In the 1960s, the American economist W.W. Rostow recognised five stages of economic development (Figure 5).

Rostow based his model on what happened in many European countries. These countries have now reached the final stage, but there may yet be another stage.

High mass consumption: The economic system is almost self-sustaining because people buy products and services, which keeps businesses going. Welfare systems are fully developed, trade expands, e.g. the UK by 1940.

Drive to maturity: Economic growth extends to all parts of the economy. New industries develop to replace old, outdated ones, e.g. the UK in the 1850s.

Take-off: Rapid growth of manufacturing industries and better infrastructure. Steady growth in the economy. Administrative systems (banking and trading networks) develop to support further growth, e.g. the height of the industrial revolution in the UK (1820s).

Pre-conditions for take-off: A few low technology and labour-intensive manufacturing industries begin to develop. Development of infrastructure such as canals and railways, e.g. the UK in the very early years of the industrial revolution (1750s).

Traditional society: Technology is very limited. Most people work on the land and live in rural areas, e.g. the UK in the Middle Ages.

Figure 5 The Rostow model

He suggested that countries further behind on the development path would move through the stages more quickly than those countries before them. For example, the USA reached the final three stages in 1860, 1910 and the early 1920s, respectively. Rostow concluded that the development gap was explained by the fact that countries were at different stages of the model. He argued that **capitalism** was fundamental to economic development.

Modernisation theory has been criticised for its lack of detailed explanation about the progress of development from one stage to another. It also assumes that all countries start with the same resources and other geographical factors, such as population and climate. Many countries have found it more difficult to 'take-off' than Rostow seemed to suggest.

Exam-style question

Identify **two** statements that describe Rostow's modernisation theory of development.

- [ ] A It is based on four main stages of economic development.
- [ ] B The UK was at stage two in the 1940s.
- [ ] C It shows how a country's economy changes over time.
- [ ] D It includes a detailed explanation of how development happens.
- [ ] E The theory was based on European capitalist countries.

(2 marks)

Frank's dependency theory

In the late 1960s, the economist A.G. Frank produced a theory that was critical of capitalism. He argued that:

- colonialism was a major cause of poverty in developing countries. Developed countries had become rich at the expense of developing countries, by exploiting natural resources such as oil, metallic minerals, timber, tea and coffee. In the modern world, neo-colonialism may be having a similar impact
- the capitalist system of world trade has benefited the rich developed countries far more than the poorer developing countries. Rich countries sell their manufactured goods and services at high prices to developing countries. In turn, they buy raw materials from developing countries at much lower prices.

Frank used a simple model (Figure 6) to explain how the '**economic core**' (the developed world) exploited the '**economic periphery**' (the developing world). The model is based on a chain of exploitation. It begins with small towns in the periphery developing at the expense of surrounding rural areas. The core (or metropolis) then develops at the expense of small towns. Frank referred to the economic history of South America to support his arguments. Frank saw **socialism** as providing a fairer society than capitalism.

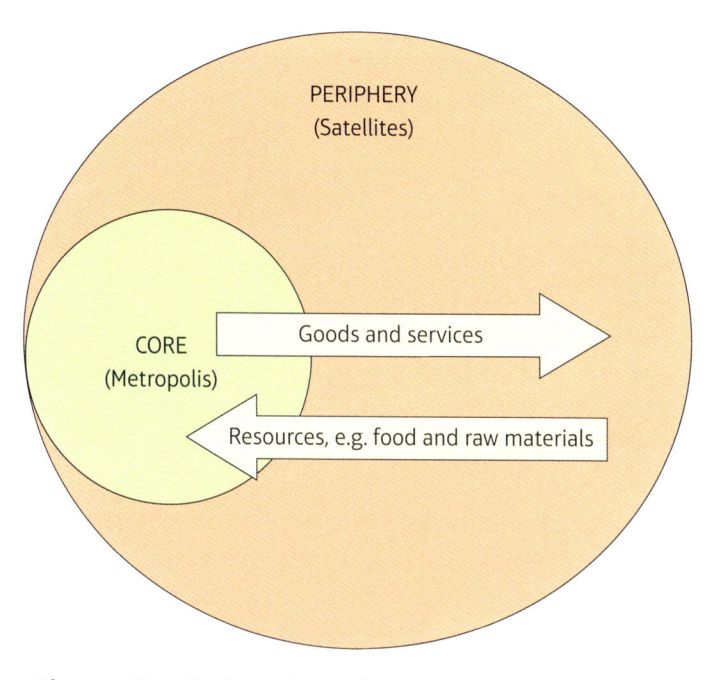

Figure 6 Frank's dependency theory

Criticisms of dependency theory include:

- many countries in the developing world that were never colonised (for example, Ethiopia) remain poor, whereas some former colonies such as Singapore are now developed
- countries that followed the socialist model have mostly remained poor, for example Tanzania
- some poor countries have successfully developed (for example, South Korea)

- rich-country influences today (neo-colonial) may be positive, for example **aid** without ties.

Although neither theory is perfect, they have both provided useful ideas from which to understand the process of development, which is never easy.

Activity

1. Based on your learning so far and Figure 5:
   a. In which Rostow stage would you place Japan? Give one piece of evidence for your choice.
   b. In which Rostow stage would you place India? Give one piece of evidence for your choice.
2. How does dependency theory explain why the world is divided into developed, emerging and developing countries?

Checkpoint

Now it is time to review your understanding of the causes and consequences of global inequality, and the different theories to explain how and why countries develop over time.

Strengthen

S1 Describe two causes of global inequality.

S2 Give examples of the economic and social consequences of global inequality.

S3 Explain why dependency theory is critical of capitalism.

Challenge

C1 Discuss the ways in which differences in the physical environment can help explain the causes of global inequalities.

C2 Explain why international migration may be a major consequence of inequality.

C3 Which theory do you think is most relevant in the 21st century: modernisation theory or dependency theory?

2 Development Dynamics

What are the different approaches to development?

Learning objectives
- To know the characteristics of top-down and bottom-up approaches to development
- To know the role of transnational corporations, governments and international organisations in globalisation
- To understand that other factors such as trade, investment, aid, remittances and debt relief are important in development

A country can try different ways to prompt development. Some use large-scale technology that is often expensive, while others use **intermediate technology** that is more appropriate and beneficial to the peripheral areas of the country. Globalisation is important to any approach to development and describes the increasing global links – economic, social and political – that have occurred over the last 60 years.

Top-down development

Top-down development occurs through the actions of governments and **transnational corporations (TNCs)**. The traditional 'top-down' approach is when experts from developed countries, and the governments of developing countries, plan large-scale projects (requiring technology) with limited involvement of the people who will be directly affected (Figure 7). The motives of government are often broad and not well targeted towards the local people most in need. Sometimes the poorest people are disadvantaged in the process through 'unintended consequences'. For example, for the Three Gorges Dam on the Yangtze River in China, vast areas of land were flooded and the people who lived there were displaced.

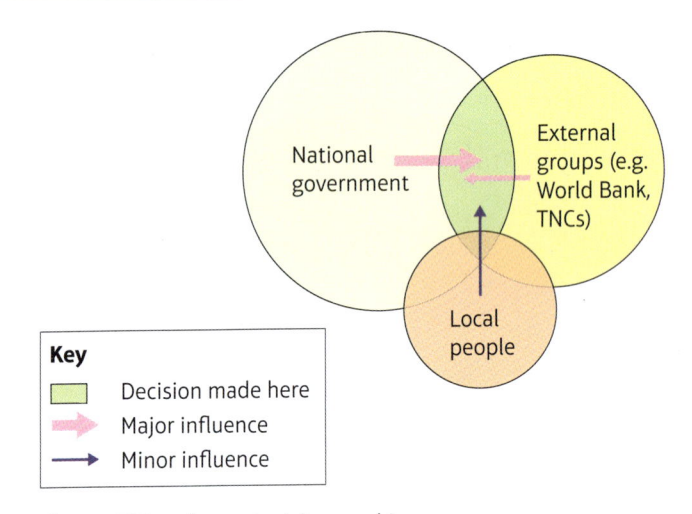

Figure 7 Top-down decision-making

In the past, countries wishing to develop often borrowed money from the World Bank or the International Monetary Fund (IMF). Nowadays, the bulk of investment is through TNCs. A TNC is a firm that owns or controls production in more than one country through **foreign direct investment (FDI)**. TNCs can exploit raw materials, produce goods such as cars and oil, and provide services such as banking. The 100 largest TNCs represent a significant proportion of total global production. Table 4 shows data for the world's ten largest TNCs.

Table 4 The world's ten largest TNCs in 2015

Rank	Company	Revenue (US$ billion)	Industry	HQ country
1	Walmart	485.7	Retail	USA
2	Sinopec	446.8	Petroleum	China
3	Royal Dutch Shell	431.3	Petroleum	Netherlands/UK
4	China National Petroleum	428.6	Petroleum	China
5	BP	358.7	Petroleum	UK
6	ExxonMobil	382.6	Petroleum	USA
7	State Grid	339.4	Power	China
8	Volkswagen	268.6	Automobiles	Germany
9	Toyota	247.7	Automobiles	Japan
10	Glencore	221.0	Commodities	Switzerland/UK

Most TNCs set up operations in rich and poor countries alike, wherever there is an opportunity to make a profit. They take advantage of the fact that overall business operating costs are much lower in some countries than in others. The internet has been essential to the process and speed of globalisation, and has allowed TNCs to manage complex operations all over the world. Some developing and emerging countries, such as India, have been quicker than others to grasp the importance of new technology in economic and social development.

Advantages and disadvantages of TNCs

Countries that are not attractive for TNCs, mainly in Africa and Asia, are among the world's poorest countries. Factors such as landlocked location, political instability, government corruption and wars deter TNCs. Countries where TNCs first set up manufacturing industries followed by tertiary industries, as in Mexico, Brazil and South East Asia, have profited most. Here, TNCs create jobs and bring capital, modern technology and skills into the country. The country's infrastructure (transport and energy supplies) is improved as better access and communications are needed. The initial investment and jobs have a knock-on effect, creating more jobs and providing money to generate services. This is known as a **multiplier effect**.

Concerns have, however, been raised about the power of large TNCs, particularly those operating in developing countries. Such concerns include the exploitation of cheap labour and the presence of poor working conditions, tax avoidance (TNCs may pay few or no taxes in the countries they operate in), their potential political influence and the knowledge that investment in one country could be transferred quickly to a lower-cost location. They cream off large profits to send back to the developed countries, and their industries cause air and water pollution because local pollution controls are either weak or ignored.

Bottom-up development

Non-governmental organisations (NGOs) have often been much better than government agencies at directing aid towards **sustainable development**. The selective nature of such aid has targeted the poorest communities using appropriate technology and involving local people in decision-making (Figure 8). Such an approach is known as **bottom-up development**.

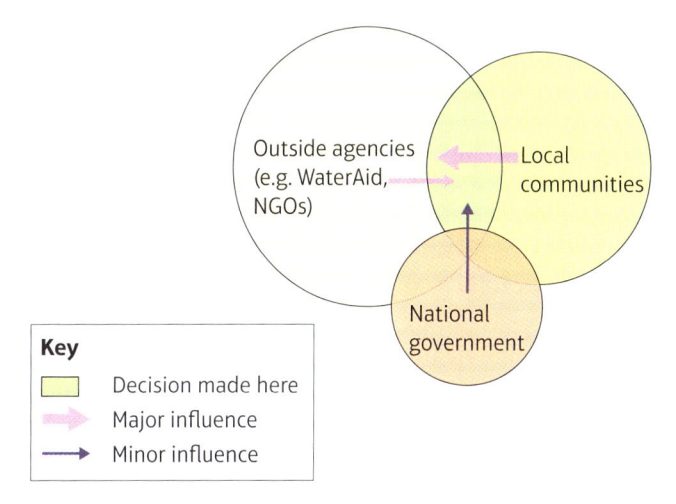

Figure 8 Bottom-up decision-making

The development of the Grameen Bank in Bangladesh is an example of bottom-up development. It shows the power of **microcredit** in the battle against poverty. This is the granting of small, long-term loans (about US$100) on easy terms to poor people. Over 95% of loans have gone to women or groups of women. Experience has shown that this approach ensures the best security for the bank and provides the greatest benefit for the borrowers' families.

Activity

1. Study Figures 7 and 8. Compare the roles of different groups of people in the top-down and bottom-up decision-making processes.
2. Create a table to summarise the economic, social and environmental advantages and disadvantages of TNCs.

2 Development Dynamics

What factors contribute to development?

There has been much debate about the importance of the factors that contribute to development. These include trade, investment, aid, **remittances** and debt relief, as well as good governance and advantages of climate and natural resources (see pages 66–67).

The roles of trade and investment in development

Trade and investment play a key role in economic development. Investment in a country can be the key to it increasing its trade. Some countries, such as China, India, Brazil and Mexico, have increased their trade substantially in recent decades with the help of FDI. It is one factor which has helped these emerging countries to develop strongly in the 21st century and is one of the big successes of globalisation. These countries are sometimes called newly industrialised countries.

However, about two billion people live in countries where trade has fallen in relation to national income. This has resulted in diminishing links to global systems. For example, Africa's share of world trade has fallen in recent decades, and is currently around 2%. NGOs such as Oxfam and CAFOD argue strongly that trade is the key to real development, being worth many times more than aid.

Figure 9 Fair trade banana farmer, Dominican Republic

Fair trade

Poor countries argue that the way world trade operates is unfair. One answer to this is **fair trade**. Many supermarkets in developed countries stock some fair trade products, such as bananas, coffee and tea (Figure 9). Under the fair trade system, small-scale producers group together to form a cooperative. These cooperatives deal directly with companies (cutting out 'middlemen') in developed countries. Companies such as Tesco and Sainsbury pay more than the world market price for the products traded. This gives farmers in developing countries a better standard of living and some money to reinvest in their farms.

Advocates of the fair trade system say that it is a model of how world trade can and should be organised to tackle global poverty. However, fair trade currently accounts for less than 1% of world trade.

Aid

Aid is assistance in the form of grants or loans at below market rates. Aid may provide a vital part of the income of many poor countries. Most developing countries have been keen to accept foreign aid for several reasons:

- **the foreign exchange gap** – countries lack the money to pay for imports such as machinery and oil which they may need for development
- **the savings gap** – population pressures and other factors prevent the accumulation of enough financial capital to invest in industry and infrastructure
- **the technical gap** – caused by a shortage of skills needed for development.

There are two types of **international aid** – official government aid, such as DFID (Department for International Development) and voluntary aid, run by NGOs and charities such as WaterAid and Oxfam.

2 Development Dynamics

Did you know?
Global fair trade sales reached £4.4 billion in 2013. The UK continued as the largest international market for fair trade products at a value of £1.8 billion.

WaterAid has adopted a bottom-up strategy (see page 71), stressing the local and small-scale and putting particular emphasis on sustainability (Figure 10).

At the United Nations in 1970, the developed countries promised to spend 0.7% of GNP on international aid. Almost all donor countries have failed to reach this target. International aid is more of a priority in some countries than others. However, it is not just the total amount of aid that is important, but also the way in which the money is spent. Critics of foreign aid say that it can be wasteful and can create a culture of dependency.

The importance of remittances
Many international migrants send money back to their families in their country of origin. These remittances are a very important source of income. In 2014, remittances to developing countries totalled over US$436 billion, considerably exceeding the amount of official aid received by these countries. They can be very important in the fight to combat poverty and helping economic development.

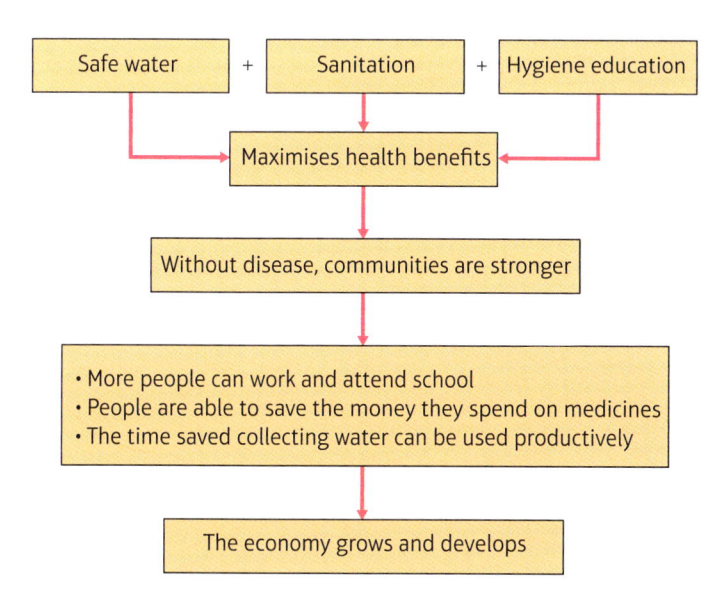

Figure 10 WaterAid's approach to development

Debt relief
Debt is a major problem for the world's poorer nations. In the 1980s and 1990s, many developing countries built up big debts through trade deficits and loans for big development projects. Annual debt repayments can amount to a considerable part of a country's income. There have been a number of initiatives to reduce or cancel the debts of the poorest countries. One solution has been to swap a country's debt for investment in the environment. In 2007, for example, Costa Rica's debt to the USA was US$90 million. Costa Rica has agreed to spend US$26 million to increase its area of protected forest, support local communities and encourage ecotourism. In return, the US government and conservation groups will cut Costa Rica's debts by the same amount.

Another important solution has been the Heavily Indebted Poor Countries (HIPC) Initiative, established in 1996 by the IMF and the World Bank. By 2015, debt reduction under the HIPC Initiative has been approved for 36 countries, 30 of them in Africa, providing US$76 billion in debt-service relief over time.

Activity
1. Explain the role of aid and debt relief in development.
2. Research the benefits of joining a fair trade scheme if you are a banana farmer in a developing country.

Checkpoint
Now it is time to review your understanding of how approaches to development vary in type and success.

Strengthen
S1 Give two advantages and two disadvantages of TNCs located in developing countries.
S2 What are the differences between top-down and bottom-up approaches to development?
S3 Suggest why remittances can be important to low-income countries.

Challenge
C1 Explain the role of technological advance in the process of globalisation.
C2 Why is trade generally viewed to be more important than aid in the development process?
C3 To what extent has globalisation helped development?

2 Development Dynamics

Case Study – How has India developed in recent decades to advance from a 'developing country' to an 'emerging country'?

Learning objectives

- To know India's strategic location in Asia and the world
- To know the range of environments within India
- To understand India's broad political, social and cultural context

Where is India?

India is part of continental Asia. Much of India forms a peninsula which narrows to the south and which divides the Indian Ocean into the Bay of Bengal and the Arabian Sea (Figure 11). There are two major island groups – the Andaman and Nicobar Islands to the south-east, and the Lakshadweep Islands to the south-west.

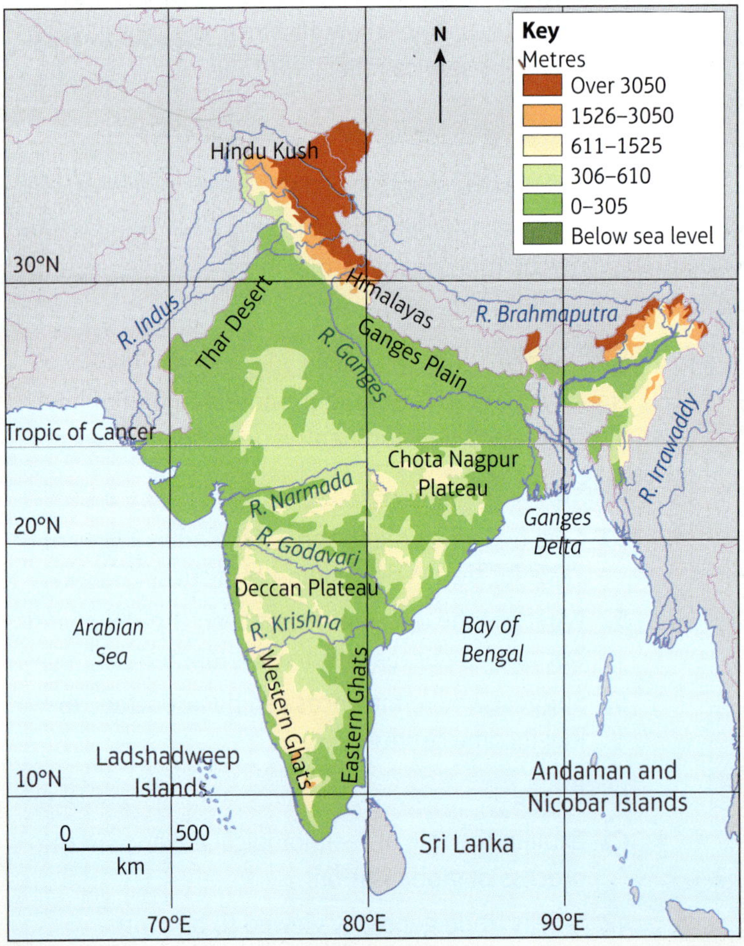

India shares international borders, totalling 15,200 km in length, with six countries – Pakistan, Nepal, China, Bhutan, Bangladesh and Myanmar (Burma). To the south-southeast, a short distance across the Palk Strait, is Sri Lanka. In total, India's coastline is over 7500 km long.

India is by far the largest country in the Indian subcontinent. The subcontinent has an area of 4.4 million km², which is about the size of Europe. Definitions of the composition of the subcontinent vary. It is generally taken to include India, Pakistan, Bangladesh, Nepal, Bhutan, Sri Lanka and the Maldives. This region is increasingly referred to as South Asia.

Exam-style question

Describe the geographical location of an emerging country you have studied.

(3 marks)

Exam tip

A detailed answer should refer to the continent in which the country is located, latitude and longitude, the countries it borders and adjacent oceans and seas.

India has the seventh largest land area in the world, with almost 3.3 million km² (Table 5). An important aspect of India's place in the world is the country's huge population, estimated to be 1.31 billion in 2015. This is not far behind China's 1.37 billion. In less than ten years' time, India will have overtaken China as the most populous country in the world. India's annual population growth accounts for about

Figure 11 India's physical environments

19 million of the 89 million annual increase in global population. This is more than any other country.

Table 5 Largest countries in the world by land area and their populations, 2015

Country	Land area (millions km²)	Population (millions)
Russia	17.1	144
Canada	10.0	36
USA	9.8	321
China	9.6	1372
Brazil	8.5	205
Australia	7.7	24
India	3.3	1314

India is a former British **colony**. It gained independence in 1947 with the partition of British India into India and Pakistan. The former was to be primarily a Hindu state and the latter a Muslim state. In the largest mass migration in history, Hindus fled Pakistan for India and Muslims fled India for Pakistan. These people were fearful of what might happen if they stayed as minority populations. The eastern part of the original Pakistan became the independent nation of Bangladesh in 1971.

Since partition, India and Pakistan have fought four wars (one undeclared) over the 'Kashmir issue'. Despite the region's majority Muslim population, India controls the southern part of Kashmir and Pakistan the northern part. Both countries are nuclear powers, which is perhaps the main reason why other countries are so concerned about the relationship between the two nations. Neighbouring China is also a nuclear power and relationships with India have been difficult at times. The two countries fought a brief war in 1962 (the Sino-Indian War). Current issues of concern between the two countries include potential water resource conflicts in the Himalayan region and increasing Chinese influence in the Indian Ocean.

Did you know?
India is a member of the global 'space club'. India's first satellite was launched in 1975. In 2014, it successfully put a satellite – Mangalayaan (Hindi for Mars vehicle) – in orbit around Mars.

India is a member of the United Nations, the World Trade Organization, the Indian Ocean Rim Association, the Non-Aligned Movement, the South Asian Association for Regional Cooperation, and is a leading and influential member of the Commonwealth of Nations (the Commonwealth). This is an inter-governmental organisation of 53 nations, most of which were former members of the British Empire. The Commonwealth seeks to promote democracy, rule of law, human rights, good governance, and social and economic development.

A major factor in India's strategic position is the country's central location in the Indian Ocean. India is eager to strengthen its global image and sees the Indian Ocean region as essential to achieving its national interests. For example, the east–west shipping routes through which much oil from the Middle East is transported to East Asia are not far to the south of India. India aims to become a **hub** of transport, communication and trade within its wider region.

India's location in Asia has undoubtedly been a factor in its economic development. India has been motivated by the more rapid development of other emerging nations in the region such as Malaysia, Indonesia and China. They provide an example of how India itself could become more globalised.

Activity

1. Study Table 5.
   a. Calculate the population densities of the countries listed.
   b. How does India compare in size and population with the three superpowers: USA, Russia and China?
2. What advantages are there of India's long coastline and central location in the Indian Ocean?

2 Development Dynamics

What is India's environmental, political, social and cultural context?

Environmental contrasts

Mainland India extends from Kashmir in the north (about 37°N) to Nagercoil in the south (about 8°N), and from Gujarat in the west (about 68°E) to Arunachal Pradesh in the east (about 97°E). The **Tropic of Cancer** divides the country almost in two (see Figure 12). India is ahead of Greenwich Mean Time (GMT) by 5 hours and 30 minutes.

In view of the large size of the country and the great difference in latitude, it is not surprising that India has a variety of contrasting physical environments (Figure 11). India has a great range of different landscapes, from the Himalaya mountains in the north, the Thar or Great Indian Desert in the west, the jungles of the north-east, the fertile Ganges plain covering much of northern India, and the Deccan – the high wooded plateau that dominates the southern peninsula of India. India's major rivers are the Ganges, Brahmaputra and Godavari. Rivers have been central to the development of settlement in India from the earliest of times. Some, such as the Ganges, are regarded as sacred in Indian culture.

India's climate varies from tropical in the south to temperate and alpine in the north. The Indian **monsoon** is the Earth's most powerful weather system, blowing from the north-east during the cooler months. Its direction is reversed during the warmer months when it blows from the south-west. The rain brought by the monsoon is vital for water supply and farming, but can also bring costs such as flooding.

Social and religious composition

India is a land of great cultural diversity, as evidenced by the many different languages spoken throughout the country. Although Hindi (spoken in the north) and English (the language of politics and commerce) are used officially, more than 1500 languages and dialects are spoken.

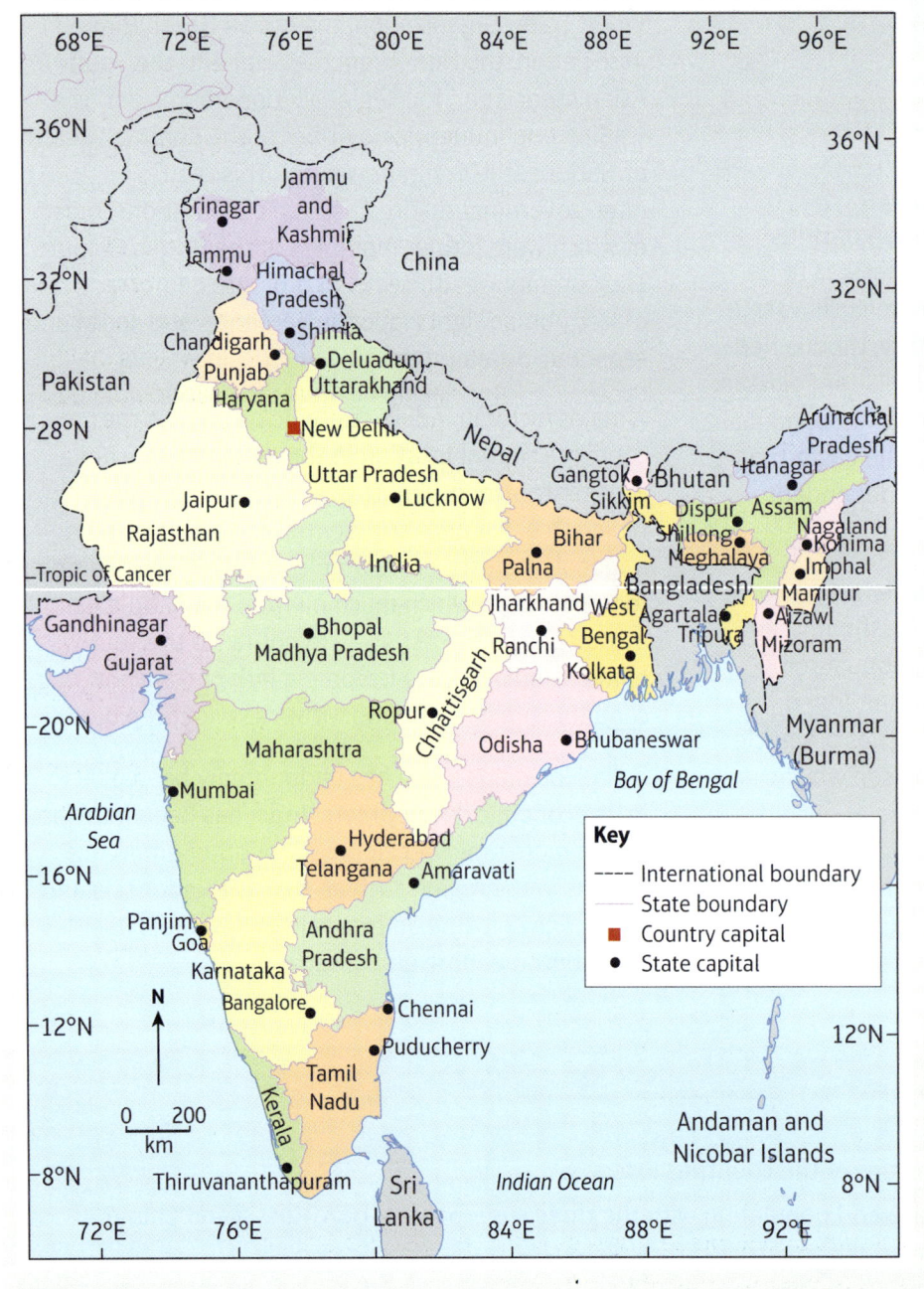

Figure 12 Map of India showing states, state capitals and boundaries with neighbouring countries

Indian society is divided into social ranks known as '**castes**'. A person's caste is determined at birth by their parents' status. At the bottom of these social groupings are the so-called 'untouchables'. These people have no caste and do the most menial jobs. The caste system is understandably controversial and an increasing number of Indians would like it to disappear. This was certainly the view of Mahatma Gandhi, who is regarded as the 'father of the nation'. Gandhi was the leader of the Independence Movement in British-ruled India.

Although India has no official religion, over 80% of the population are Hindu. Of the remainder, 13% are Muslim. Other religions include Buddhism, Sikhism and Jainism which all have their origins in India. Interestingly, India has the third largest Muslim population in the world (10.9% of the total), after Indonesia (12.7%) and Pakistan (11.0%).

Government and states

India is a parliamentary democracy. Its Constitution guarantees the basic rights of citizens and prohibits discrimination on the basis of religion, caste, sex or place of birth. Administratively, India is divided into 29 states and seven union territories. State governors are appointed by the president of India, who is head of state. The largest state is Rajasthan; the smallest is Goa (see Figure 12 on page 76). The country's population is heavily concentrated in the broad fertile northern plains. More than 50% of India's population live in the six states of Uttar Pradesh, Maharashtra, Bihar, West Bengal, Andhra Pradesh and Madhya Pradesh.

There are huge variations in socio-economic development within India. In general, the most advanced states and territories are in the north-west (Chandigarh, Delhi, Haryana and the Punjab) and a line of states in the west and south (Gujarat, Maharashtra, Goa, Kerala and Tamil Nadu). There are lower levels of development in the northern and eastern states.

The colonial legacy

Since Independence in 1947, India's relations with the UK have gone through different phases but have generally warmed in recent years. Opinions vary as to the impact of colonialism on the subcontinent. One legacy is that most of India's population speaks English. This has been an important factor in India's integration into the global economy. In fact more people speak English in India than in the UK!

Economically, India is split between village India, supported by traditional agriculture, and urban India, one of the most heavily industrialised areas in the world, with a fast-growing economy as well as much poverty. The increasing economic power of India has not gone unnoticed in the UK. The latter is anxious to export more goods and services to India, and encourage more Indian investment in the UK.

The Indian diaspora

Another interesting aspect of globalisation is the spread of the Indian population abroad. The 20 million people who make up the Indian **diaspora** are scattered over more than 100 countries. In 2014, they sent US$71 billion in remittances back to India – a source of foreign exchange that exceeds revenues generated by India's software industry.

Checkpoint

Now it is time to review how the development of India is influenced by its location and context in the world.

Strengthen

- **S1** Name the countries that form the Indian subcontinent. What is this region called?
- **S2** Which is the odd one out: USA, China, Russia, India? Why?
- **S3** What is the monsoon and why is it so important to India?

Challenge

- **C1** Why are other world countries concerned about India's disputes with Pakistan and China?
- **C2** Why is the Indian diaspora important to the economy of India?
- **C3** Give examples of the diversity of India's population. Do you think this helps or hinders its development?

2 Development Dynamics

What are India's key economic trends?

Learning objectives

- To know India's key economic trends since 1990
- To appreciate that government policy is a major influence on development
- To understand the role of globalisation in India's economic advance

India has undergone rapid economic advancement in recent decades. All measures of development have shown considerable improvement. Such significant change has meant that India is now considered to be an emerging country rather than a developing country.

GDP and GNI per capita

India's GDP began to steadily grow from 1950. In the 1990s, the rate of growth increased and then increased again in the present century. India's economy has grown by an average of 7% for the last two decades. It became the world's fastest growing major economy from the end of 2014 and is now the world's 7th largest economy by nominal GDP (not adjusted for inflation). When measured using PPP, however, India's economy is the third largest in the world.

As GDP has risen at a faster rate than population growth, GDP per capita has increased, as have other similar measures such as GNI per capita (Table 6). The data show that GNI per capita almost doubled between 2006 and 2014.

Table 6 India – GNI per capita and HDI

Year	GNI per capita PPP (US$)	HDI
2000	2522	0.496
2005	3239	0.539
2010	4499	0.586
2014	5497	0.609

Change in India's economy

As a country develops, the structure of its economy changes. So does the proportion of people working in the three main economic sectors. This happens as people move from less productive to more productive employment which pays higher wages, so each sector's contribution to the country's GDP also changes. Figure 13 shows India's distribution of GDP for four different years, from 1980–1981 to 2010–2011, in the three main sectors. The main trends are:

- a large reduction in the contribution of agriculture to total GDP – from 37.2% to 14.5%
- a small change in the contribution of manufacturing industry – from 16.9% to 18.4%.
- a rapid increase in the contribution of services – from 45.8% to 67.1%

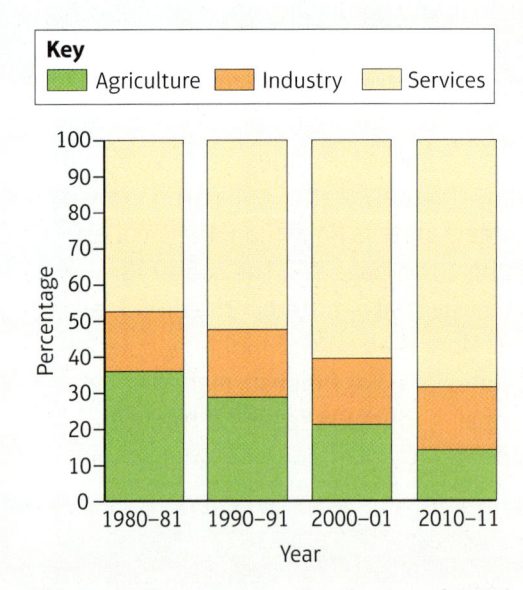

Figure 13 The changing distribution of GDP by economic sector in India, 1980–2011

Trade

As India has become more integrated into the global economy, the volumes of both its exports and imports have increased (Figure 14). Total merchandise trade increased more than threefold from US$252 billion in 2006 to US$794 in 2012. The composition of India's trade has also changed, with higher value goods becoming more prominent in both directions of trade.

- Key exports are petroleum products, gems and jewellery, pharmaceutical products and transport equipment.
- Oil is India's biggest import, followed by gold and silver, and electronic goods.

Asia is the main destination for India's exports, up from 40.2% of the total in 2001–2002 to 51.6% in 2011–2012. India's largest import source is China.

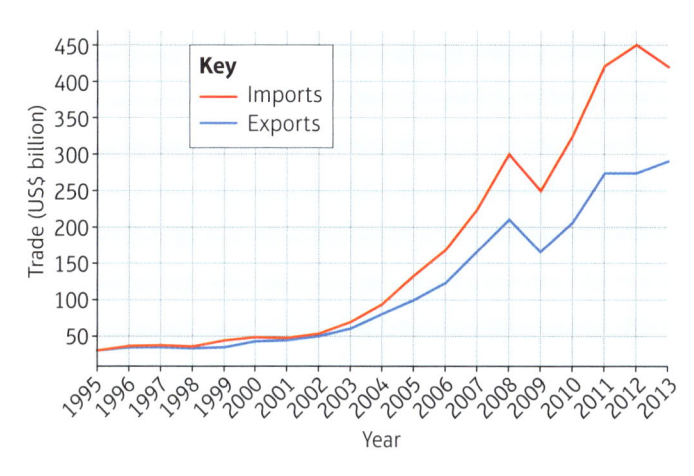

Figure 14 India's trade balance, 1995–2013

Foreign direct investment (FDI)

India's economic development has recently been boosted by a spectacular increase in foreign direct investment, especially since 2000. Table 7 shows inward FDI stocks, or the cumulative level of investment in India for each year. There has been inward investment in all three economic sectors. The Indian government has been particularly keen to encourage FDI in the development of the country's infrastructure. For example, some of the country's largest railway projects will be funded by FDI investment. In 2014–2015, the top two sources of FDI into India were Mauritius and Singapore.

Table 7 India – FDI stocks (US$ billion)

	1995	2000	2014
Inward	5.6	16.3	252.3
Outward	0.5	1.7	129.6

A key indicator of India's economic development is that Indian companies are investing an increasing amount of money abroad. India's outward FDI is much lower than its inward FDI (Table 7), but the gap is steadily narrowing.

Activity

1 Study Table 6.
   a Draw a multiple-line graph to show the change in GNI per capita and HDI between 2000 and 2014.
   b Describe what your graph shows about India's economic and social development.

   Tip With a multiple-line graph you need to mark years on the x-axis and have two y-axes: one for GNI values and one for HDI values.

2 Using GDP data, write a short paragraph to describe how the structure of India's economy is changing.

3 On an outline map of India:
   a draw proportional flow lines to show the difference between India's inward and outward FDI in 2014 (use a scale of 10 mm per US$100 billion)
   b add flow lines to show the value of exports (US$329.6 billion) and imports (US$472.8 billion) in 2014, annotating the most important goods.

2 Development Dynamics

How does government and globalisation influence economic change in India?

Government policy

India emerged as a newly industrialised country in the 1990s when important economic reforms began to open up the country to foreign investment and make it easier for Indian companies to forge international links (see foreign direct investment on page 79). In recent years, the government has stressed the importance of innovation and the country's science budget has increased considerably.

Education is a high priority for the Indian government. It is free and compulsory for all children between the ages of 6 and 14. India has more than 1.4 million schools and 36,000 higher education facilities. Apart from state schools and colleges, there is a strong private sector under state regulation. Improvements in education (Table 8) have been regarded as an important contributor to economic and social development in India. The education sector has attracted a considerable amount of FDI (US$964 million between 2000 and 2014).

Table 8 Improvements in literacy in India

Indicator	2001	2011
Literacy rate (%)	64.8	74.0
Male literacy rate (%)	75.3	82.1
Female literacy rate (%)	53.7	65.5

Aid

India has been the biggest recipient of international aid in history because of the scale of its development challenges. In recent years, however, aid has declined rapidly as the country has developed. For example, the UK planned to end aid to India in 2015 although some 'technical assistance' would continue. India now sends aid to other countries such as Bhutan, Nepal, the Maldives, Sri Lanka and Afghanistan. In 2014–2015, it was anticipated that Indian foreign aid expenditure at US$1.3 billion would be more than double its foreign aid receipts. India is one of a few emerging countries to change from being an aid recipient to a donor. Advocates of international aid say this shows how successful aid can be.

The role of globalisation

As India has improved its connectivity with the rest of the world, its rate of economic growth has increased. India attracts FDI from TNCs for several reasons, including:

- an increasingly skilled labour force along with low labour costs
- rapid growth of India's economy based on a large population and rising incomes
- the increasing competitiveness of Indian enterprises
- a large and well-educated English-speaking workforce
- international developments in trade, transport and communications
- government incentives such as tax exemptions.

TNCs in India have also steadily moved up the 'value chain' by producing more sophisticated and higher value products, such as computer software and hardware. They combine low-cost production with high-level technology from Western countries and then export these products back to Western markets.

The importance of the service sector

The software and ICT services sector in India has been at the forefront of the country's economic growth. The exports from this sector alone were worth about US$100 billion in 2014–2015.

Outsourcing has been a major global strategy by Indian companies. India's low-cost labour has been used to provide ICT and other services to companies in developed countries. For example, many British and American companies have **call centres** in Bangalore and other Indian cities. Medical transcription and expert knowledge services are other examples of the back-office functions that India supplies to large companies elsewhere in the world.

The tourism sector (Figure 15) is growing rapidly. In 2014, it accounted for 6.8% of India's GDP, with over 22 million tourist arrivals. More than 39 million people are employed in tourism.

2 Development Dynamics

Figure 15 Taj Mahal, Agra, Uttar Pradesh

Transport and communications technology

India's road system more than doubled in length, from about 3 million km in 1990 to over 6 million km by 2012. There has also been significant investment in railways, seaports and airports.

- India's rail network is more than 63,000 km long.
- India has 12 major and 185 minor seaports; about 95% of India's foreign trade by volume and 70% by value is carried by ship.
- India has 11 international and 86 domestic airports.

Did you know?

Over 35.1 million passengers pass through Delhi International Airport each year. This is more than the total population of Australia.

However, while India's transport networks are much more developed than they were 20 years ago, more investment is needed to sustain future growth.

India has not only benefited from increasing global connectivity, but has developed its own communications technology (ICT) industry to a high level. It now has the second largest wireless network in the world after China.

Did you know?

India receives and increasingly gives three types of aid.

- Voluntary aid, from NGOs – some based in India.
- Bilateral aid, from one country's government to another. India does not accept tied aid, where the money has to be spent in the country that gives it.
- Multilateral aid, from international agencies like the UN and World Bank.

Activity

1. List some examples of how the government is supporting India's development process.
2. Study Table 8.
    a. Describe the improvement in literacy in India.
    b. Explain, with examples, why education is so important for development. What challenges do the figures show?

Checkpoint

Now it is time to review your understanding of how globalisation has caused rapid economic change in India.

Strengthen

S1 What is the difference between inward and outward foreign direct investment?

S2 Read again about globalisation on page 80. Draft a definition of globalisation, then check your draft against the glossary. Skim through pages 79–81 to add examples of globalisation.

Challenge

C1 Explain why India has changed from being a net recipient of foreign aid to being an aid donor.

C2 Explain why India attracts foreign direct investment from transnational corporations, and how this helps economic development.

2 Development Dynamics

What impact has economic growth had on Indian people?

Learning objectives

- To know that economic development has contributed to demographic change, urbanisation and regional contrasts in India
- To know the impacts of economic change on different age and gender groups in India
- To understand that economic growth impacts people and the environment in terms of air, water and land pollution

Demographic change

India's demographic characteristics have changed at the same time as its economy. Fertility rates have declined rapidly. India's total fertility rate, which was 5.2 in 1971, is now down to 2.3 (Figure 16). This is not far above **replacement level fertility** which is 2.1. There is, however, considerable variation from this national mean in individual states.

In 1952, India became the first developing country to introduce a government-backed family planning programme designed to reduce the fertility rate and aid development. As a result, the birth rate has fallen from 45 per 1000 people in 1951–1961 (calculated from census data) to 21 per 1000 today.

Mortality has also fallen considerably.

- The infant mortality rate, which was about 129 per 1000 live births in the early 1970s, fell to 40 per 1000 in 2013. The rate of improvement has been particularly high in recent years.

- The maternal mortality rate, estimated at 560 per 100,000 live births in 1990, dropped steadily to 167 per 100,000 live births by 2013. This is a very significant fall in a fairly short period of time.

- Life expectancy at birth has improved from 50 years in 1970–1975 to 68 years today. Within India, however, there is wide variation from the average, from 63 years in Assam to 75 years in Kerala. These wide regional variations are due to a big gap in education and access to health services.

Urbanisation

Economic development is the major cause of **urbanisation**. An increasing proportion of India's population is living in urban areas, where most of the better paid jobs are located. The country's towns and cities are growing because of a combination of **rural–urban migration** and **natural population increase**. However, the level of urbanisation in India remains a long way behind the global average (Table 9).

Table 9 Urbanisation in India

	2000 (% urban)	2015 (% urban)
India	30.9	32.7
China	49.2	55.6
World	51.6	54.0

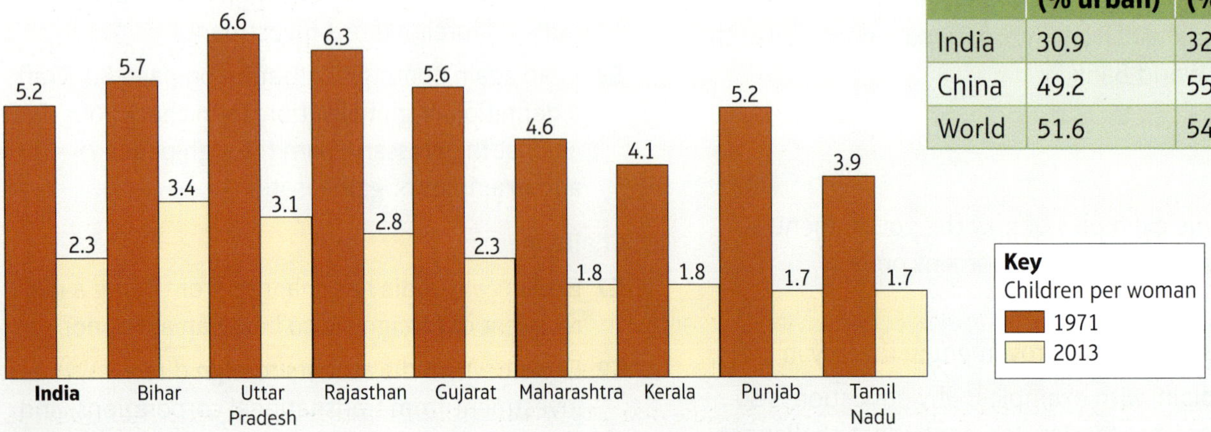

Figure 16 The total fertility rate for India and selected states, 1971 and 2013

Data (1971, 2013):
- India: 5.2, 2.3
- Bihar: 5.7, 3.4
- Uttar Pradesh: 6.6, 3.1
- Rajasthan: 6.3, 2.8
- Gujarat: 5.6, 2.3
- Maharashtra: 4.6, 1.8
- Kerala: 4.1, 1.8
- Punjab: 5.2, 1.7
- Tamil Nadu: 3.9, 1.7

Key — Children per woman: 1971, 2013

Age and gender

The impact of development has varied according to different age and gender groups. Gender inequality is still high, but the gap has narrowed with development.

- **Education** – between 2001 and 2011 the female literacy rate improved from 53.7% to 65.5% – a higher rate of improvement than for males.
- **Health** – research had shown that girls tend to receive less food and medical care than boys.
- **Economic participation** – only one-third of working-age women in India have jobs compared with two-thirds in Brazil.
- **Political representation** – in 2015, women accounted for only 12% of the Indian parliament.
- **Access to finance** – this has risen sharply for men and women, but the gender gap remains.

Table 10 The percentage of people using a bank account or other financial account

Gender	2011 (%)	2014 (%)
Women	26	42
Men	44	62

Although change is occurring, the generally low status of women in Indian society remains a disappointing aspect of life and a considerable hindrance to development.

Gender inequality is particularly high among marginalised groups such as tribal populations and low castes. In terms of age, many older people feel left out of the benefits of progress. This is mainly because they have not benefited from the more recent improvements in education and health. They are also more likely to remain in rural areas rather than migrate to the more dynamic urban areas where living standards are generally higher.

Regional contrasts

GDP per capita varies greatly between Indian states (Table 11). The mean for India is US$1627. The most important economic areas (the core regions) have GDP figures well above the mean, while the less developed regions (periphery regions) have figures below the mean. For example, Goa, the highest ranking state, is US$3276 above the mean; Bihar, the lowest ranking state, is US$945 below the mean. There is considerable variation in all other socio-economic indicators as well. For example:

- in 2011, literacy in India was highest in Kerala at 94% and lowest in Bihar at 64%. For females the highest literacy was also in Kerala and the lowest in Rajasthan, at 53%
- life expectancy at birth ranges from 63 years in Assam to 75 years in Kerala, reflecting the gap in education and access to health services.

Table 11 GDP per capita by state and territory, 2014

Rank	State	US$	Rank	State	US$	Rank	State	US$
1	Goa	4903	8	Tamil Nadu	2464	15	Madhya Pradesh	1133
2	Delhi	4642	9	A. & N. Islands	2350	16	Jharkhand	1009
3	Sikkim	3861	10	Gujarat	2337	17	Assam	968
4	Chandigarh	3433	11	Meghalaya	1346	18	Manipur	909
5	Puducherry	3143	12	Jammu & Kashmir	1297	19	Uttar Pradesh	793
6	Haryana	2919	13	Chhattisgarh	1281	20	Bihar	682
7	Maharashtra	2561	14	Odisha	1150		India	1627

Activity

1. Study the text and Figure 16.
    a. What is the change in India's total fertility rate between 1971 and 2013?
    b. Name two states with above average fertility rates, and two states with lower than average fertility rates.
2. Study Table 11. You will need an outline map of India and an atlas. Identify two states which are richer than the average for India, and two which are poorer. Use graphics to show these data on your outline map.
3. Calculate the difference from the mean GDP per capita for India for the two richest and two poorest states.

2 Development Dynamics

What impact has economic growth had on the natural environment?

India has 2.4% of the world's land area but is home to almost 18% of the world's population. This fact alone sets the scene for a difficult balance between people and the natural environment. Rapid economic development in recent decades has placed increasing pressure on India's natural environment. In many parts of the country the limits of sustainability have either been reached or exceeded. Economic activity has polluted the nation's land, water and air, and contributed significantly to global greenhouse gas emissions. The scale of pollution has had a big impact on the health of the population and has contributed to global climate change. A World Bank report in 2013 concluded that environmental degradation was costing India US$80 billion a year – nearly 6% of GDP!

Air pollution

A recent study by the World Health Organisation (WHO) found that 13 of the world's top 20 polluted cities are in India. Delhi topped the list, with **air pollution** at 153 micrograms per cubic metre (μg/m^3; in comparison, London is 16 μg/m^3). A major problem in India's urban areas is low standards for vehicle emissions and fuel (Figure 17). Air pollution reduces life expectancy by 3.2 years for the 660 million Indians who live in cities, and is the fifth biggest cause of death in India as a whole. In rural areas indoor pollution inhaled from dung-fuelled fires and paraffin stoves and lights may kill more than one million people a year. The WHO states that most Indians breathe unsafe air. Air pollution affects the productivity of labour, with many workers suffering from heart and lung disease and chronic bronchitis. The poorer population who live on the streets are at greatest risk. There are concerns that tourism will be affected. It is also causing crop yields to fall.

The National Capital Region (NCR) of Delhi has grown rapidly in recent decades and now covers approximately 900 km^2. The population of the NCR, which was estimated at 17.8 million in 2014, is expected to reach 22.5 million in 2025. Such a rapid rate of expansion will increase the environmental impacts of transportation, industrial activity, power generation, construction, domestic activities and waste generation. Thus, Delhi's pollution problems have a wide variety of causes.

Figure 17 Traffic congestion and air pollution in Delhi

Water pollution

India's water supply is under enormous pressure in terms of both quantity and quality. The number of rivers defined as 'polluted' in India rose from 121 to 275 between 2010 and 2015. Increased levels of sewage are the main cause. Less than one-third of sewage generated in urban areas is treated, the rest flows directly into water bodies. The Ganges and Yamuna are ranked among the world's ten most polluted rivers. The other causes of water pollution are industrial waste and agricultural runoff.

Deforestation and desertification

Deforestation has become a major problem, with the ever-rising demand for forest-based products. The causes are commercial logging, the conversion of forests to agriculture, urban and industrial expansion, mining, overgrazing, the construction of reservoirs behind dams, and forest fires. Deforestation causes a range of serious problems which include flooding, loss of biodiversity, soil erosion and climate change.

A 2014 Indian government report stated that 25% of India's land is experiencing **desertification** while 32% is facing degradation that has affected its productivity. This is affecting the livelihood and food security of millions across India. The report concluded that 68% of the country is prone to drought. The largest areas affected by desertification are in Rajasthan, Gujarat, Maharashtra, and Jammu and Kashmir. Vapi in Gujarat and Sukinda in Odisha are among the ten most environmentally degraded zones in the world. Half of India's lakes and wetlands disappeared between 1911 and 2014.

Greenhouse gases

India is the world's third largest emitter of carbon dioxide (CO_2) after China and the USA (Table 12). The main reason is India's heavy reliance on coal as a source of energy – a result of the country's large deposits of coal as opposed to other forms of energy. Four-fifths of electricity in India is produced from coal. India wants to reduce its emissions, but there are still about 400 million people in the country without access to electricity. India therefore needs to generate more power and plans to increase solar, wind and hydroelectric capacity in the future. To meet its targets for lower emissions, India will also need to increase its forest cover to create an additional **carbon sink** of 2.5–3 billion tonnes of CO_2 equivalent.

India emits considerable amounts of the other greenhouse gases as well. However, on a per capita basis, it is well behind developed countries such as the USA, Australia and the UK.

Table 12 Carbon dioxide emissions, 2014

Country	Total (million tonnes)	Per capita (tonnes)
China	8320	7.60
USA	5610	16.50
India	5164	1.80

Climate change

In 2015, a government minister stated that climate change was the biggest threat to India's economy. At the time, India was facing its driest monsoon since 2009. More than 60% of Indian farming relies on monsoon rain. The increasingly erratic monsoon rain patterns pose a threat to a farming sector worth almost US$370 billion, and hundreds of millions of jobs.

Activity

1. Give **two** or more examples to show how serious water pollution is in India.
2. Explain why economic growth has led to an increase in deforestation and desertification.

Checkpoint

Now it is time to review your understanding of the impacts of rapid economic growth on people and the environment.

Strengthen

S1 Suggest why fertility and mortality rates have fallen considerably in India in recent decades.
S2 Describe how the status of women has changed in India since 2000.
S3 Why is India concerned about climate change?

Challenge

C1 What is the extent of regional economic and social contrasts in India?
C2 Describe and explain the extent of air pollution in Delhi.
C3 Explain why economic growth is putting India's water supply under enormous pressure.

2 Development Dynamics

How has India's international role changed?

Learning objectives
- To know that rapid economic development has changed India's international role
- To know the importance of India in global climate negotiations
- To understand that rapid economic change brings both costs and benefits

As India's economy has developed it has become the second largest market in the world, and many countries are anxious to establish good trading relationships. India is on track to become an upper middle-income country by 2025 and the third largest economy in the world by 2050. One measure of India's increasing economic strength is the level of its **foreign exchange reserves**, which have grown to over US$300 billion from just US$2 billion in 1950. As India has developed, its **geopolitical influence** has increased – it is now a major international player.

The BRICS

India is one of a group of five emerging countries called the **BRICS** (Brazil, Russia, India and China plus South Africa). Together they account for almost 42% of the world's population and one-quarter of global GDP. Figure 18 compares the average annual growth rates of the BRICS with three major developed countries. As the graph shows, India's growth is second to China, although per capita income in India is the lowest of all these countries.

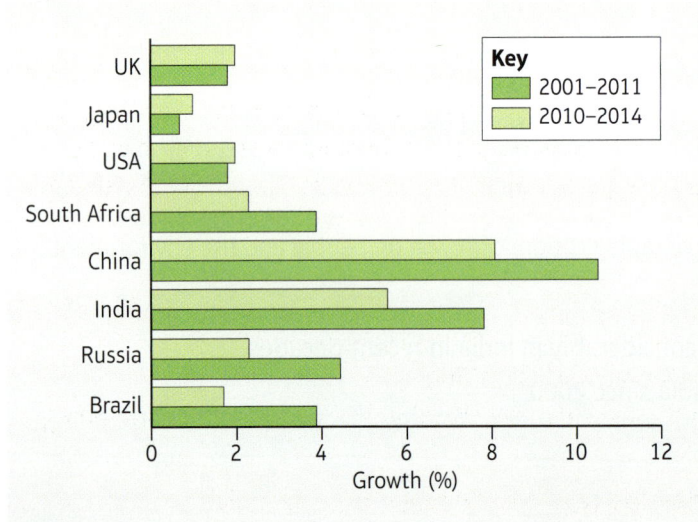

Figure 18 Average annual growth rates for the BRICS and three major developed economies, 2001–2011 and 2010–2014

The economic power of the BRICS has recently increased considerably. A high demand for goods and services in these countries provides business opportunities for the rest of the world. One sign of their importance is that the BRICS nations act together as a group. For example, in 2015 the BRICS set up the New Development Bank to provide resources for infrastructure and sustainable development projects in BRICS and other emerging developing countries.

The G-20

India is a member of the influential G-20, the group of 20 major developed and emerging economies (Table 13). This group formed because these countries realised that globalisation had changed the world economic order in a big way and major global problems required a much greater level of international cooperation.

Table 13 G-20 nations

USA, North America	Brazil, South America
Canada, North America	Mexico, North America
Japan, Asia	China, Asia
UK, Europe	South Korea, Asia
Germany, Europe	India, Asia
France, Europe	Indonesia, Asia
Italy, Europe	Saudi Arabia, Asia
Russia, Europe	Turkey, Asia
South Africa, Africa	Australia, Oceania
Argentina, South America	European Union

India's relations with the USA and EU

India cooperates with the EU and the USA, including in education and science, technology and global issues like climate change. India's trade with the EU is balanced – in 2014 India exported goods worth 35,500 million Euros there, with imports worth 37,100 million Euros. Exports to the USA were worth US$45,200 million, compared with imports of $21,600 million.

Political ambitions

India's growing economic strength means it wants to play a more important role on the world stage. Its relations with the USA and the EU have improved in recent years. India has become a leader in key global initiatives, particularly speaking up for emerging and developing countries. India wants:

- a permanent seat in the United Nations Security Council. The Security Council has only five permanent members – China, France, Russia, the UK and the USA
- more influence in big global organisations such as the World Bank, the International Monetary Fund and the World Trade Organization.

International climate negotiations

India plays a major role in international climate negotiations because of the high level of its emissions and its rapid pace of economic growth. Negotiations are always tough because emerging countries such as India have added to emissions rapidly in recent decades, while developed countries have been responsible for most of the problem since their industrial revolutions. So far India has stressed its need for economic growth, but it also recognises the increasing impact of climate change. It is now looking towards developing renewable energy on a larger scale to limit its emissions of greenhouse gases (Figure 19). At the COP21 Climate Summit in 2015, India's Environment Minister said:

'We have opened a new chapter of hope in the lives of 7 billion people on the planet. We have the planet on loan from future generations. We have today reassured these future generations that we will all together give them a better earth.'

Figure 19 Wind farm, Cape Comorin, Tamil Nadu, India

Exam-style question
Explain the changing international role of an emerging country you have studied. **(4 marks)**

Exam tip
A good answer will briefly state why the emerging economy has become more important on the world stage, and will also describe how its role has changed.

Activity

1. Give **three** facts and figures which show India's growing economic strength.
2. Explain why India's growing economy gives it more influence with other developed, emerging and developing countries.
3. Read the text about the BRICS and G-20 again. How does belonging to these groups help India?
4. Explain why India has difficult choices to make about tackling climate change.

2 Development Dynamics

What are the conflicting views about development?

People in India have conflicting views of the costs and benefits of changing international relations and the role of foreign investment. There is also much concern, in common with other emerging countries, that despite rapid growth, high levels of poverty and inequality remain. The government has stated that more inclusive and sustainable growth is central to future development.

> **Did you know?**
>
> The improvements from India's development are not equally shared amongst its people. For example, India's HDI figure loses 29% of its value when adjusted for inequality, down to 0.435.

Foreign investment

Although the benefits of foreign investment are clear to see, there are also concerns about the process overall and the actions of some TNCs in particular. Some people are worried about the economic and political influence of large foreign companies. TNCs can move out of a country as quickly as they move into it, taking investment and jobs with them. TNCs can also exploit workers, sometimes they do not pay their taxes, and they compete with India's many small businesses.

Changing international relations

While most people in India favour the country playing a bigger role on the international stage, there are those who advocate a more cautious approach. Some want the government to place more emphasis on solving India's internal problems as opposed to international issues. International politics may mean forging alliances with countries who do not appear to be natural friends.

Poverty remains a big concern

The percentage of the population below the national poverty line fell from 37% in 2005 to 22% in 2012 (Figure 20). For the first time there was also a large decline in the absolute number of poor people. However, one-third of the population still live below US$1.25 a day – the international poverty line. This amounts to almost 400 million people, the largest number of poor people in any country. About 68% of the population, over 800 million people, continue to live below the US$2-a-day benchmark. Critics of the 'economic miracle' stress these figures and also point out that:

- income inequality continues to rise
- 40% of the world's malnourished children are in India
- about 62 million children under the age of 5 are stunted because of chronic malnutrition; this condition is accompanied by a range of problems – weak immune systems, risk of sickness and disease, and arrested cognitive and physical development
- many of India's newly non-poor remain vulnerable and minor economic shocks could push them back below the poverty line.

Three out of every five Indians are not classed as poor, but live very close to the poverty line. However, a welcome trend is that a larger share of poverty reduction is now taking place in the low-income states. But, despite progress, 54% of the population still does not have a drinking water source at their home.

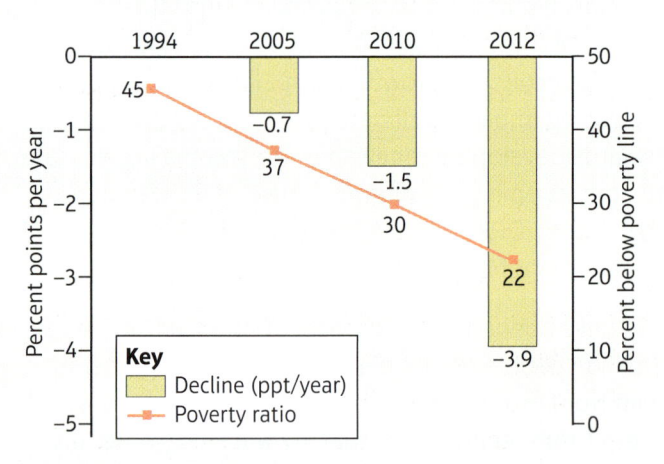

Figure 20 The decline in poverty in India, 1994–2012

Urban and rural lifestyles

Despite the rapid growth of cities such as Dehli, Mumbai, Chennai and Bangalore, India remains an essentially rural country with age-old social and religious traditions. In terms of services and household amenities, there is a big difference between urban and rural areas (Figure 21). In rural areas, bartering of goods and services is still common.

2 Development Dynamics

Did you know?
India's last census was in 2011 – the 15th since 1872. It took 2.7 million officials to visit every household in India's 7933 towns and 600,000 villages. The census is a major source of information which helps the government plan for the future.

India's low level of economic freedom
The 2015 **Index of Economic Freedom** ranked India at 128 in the world – a ranking that many people might find surprising. India's lowly position is due to:

- the state's extensive presence in the economy through state-owned enterprises and subsidies
- a weak rule of law
- corruption in many areas of economic activity.

Development challenges
India faces many challenges over the next decade and beyond. For example, by 2030:

- the population will increase from 1.3 billion in 2015 to 1.5 billion

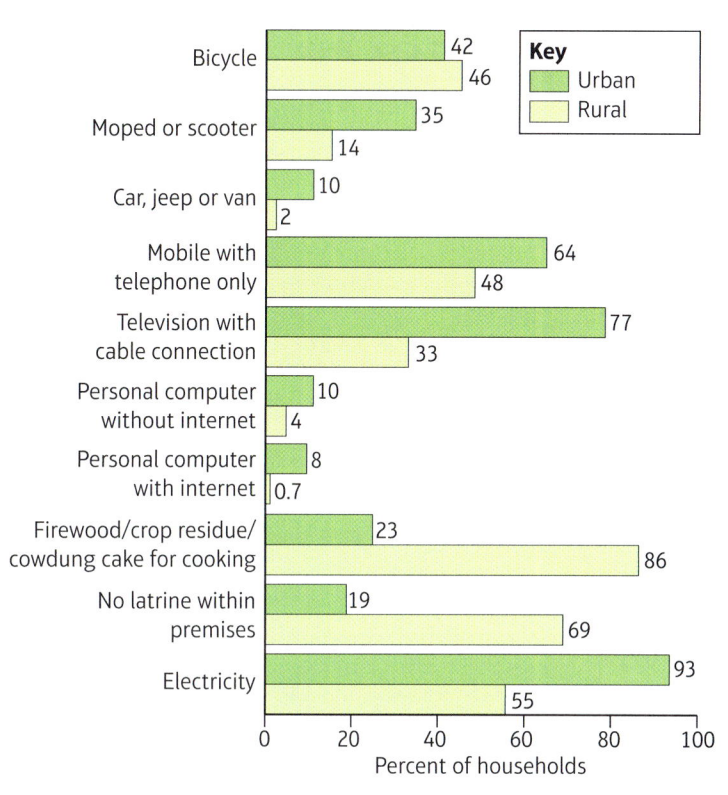

Figure 21 Rural and urban household amenities, 2011

Amenity	Urban (%)	Rural (%)
Bicycle	42	46
Moped or scooter	35	14
Car, jeep or van	10	2
Mobile with telephone only	64	48
Television with cable connection	77	33
Personal computer without internet	10	4
Personal computer with internet	8	0.7
Firewood/crop residue/cowdung cake for cooking	23	86
No latrine within premises	19	69
Electricity	93	55

- the urban population will rise from 377 million in 2011 to 609 million
- the demand for electricity will increase from 776 TWh (terawatt-hours) in 2012 to 2499 TWh.

Activity
1. Create a table to review India's rapid economic development. Use the headings Economic, Social, Environmental and Political for the rows, and Benefits and Costs for the columns.
   a. Start to fill in the table by looking at pages 88–89 again.
   b. Add detail by looking back through the section on India.
2. Look back at your learning in this topic. Examine how India is managing to develop, the problems associated with its development and how these are being reduced.

Checkpoint
Now it is time to review your understanding of how rapid economic development has changed India and its place in the world.

Strengthen
S1 Why are some people in India concerned about the rapid increase in inward foreign direct investment?
S2 To what extent does poverty remain a big problem in India?
S3 Give two reasons why India had such a low position on the 2015 Index of Economic Freedom.

Challenge
C1 What are India's main political ambitions?
C2 What do you think is the main development challenge for India in the next decade? Justify your answer.

Preparing for your exams

Development Dynamics

Definitions of development vary along with attempts to measure it. There is significant global inequality in development which is reflected in demographic data. Global inequality has a range of causes and consequences. Efforts to explain such inequality include modernisation theory and dependency theory. Different strategies have been used to try to tackle the problems of uneven development. Emerging countries show that development can occur successfully although the costs and benefits of change in such countries are unequally shared.

Checklist

You should know:

- [ ] there are different ways of defining and measuring development
- [ ] the extent of the development gap globally
- [ ] how countries at different levels of development have differences in their demographic data
- [ ] the causes and consequences of global inequalities
- [ ] how Rostow's modernisation theory and Frank's dependency theory can be used to explain development
- [ ] the characteristics of top-down and bottom-up development strategies
- [ ] the processes and players contributing to globalisation and why some countries have benefited more than others
- [ ] the advantages and disadvantages of different approaches to development
- [ ] how the development of an emerging country is influenced by its location and context in the world
- [ ] how globalisation has caused rapid economic change in the emerging country
- [ ] the positive and negative impacts of rapid development on people and the environment in the emerging country
- [ ] how rapid economic development has changed the international role of the emerging country.

Which key terms match the following definitions?

a The economic or social progress a country or people makes.

b The average number of children born per woman in a country.

c The total value of goods and services produced by a country in a year.

d Acquiring control over another country, occupying it with settlers, and exploiting it economically.

e The long-term movement of people within or between countries.

f The increasing interconnectedness and interdependence of the world economically, culturally and politically.

g Money owed by a country to another country, to private creditors (for example, commercial banks) or to international agencies such as the World Bank or IMF.

h Money sent back by migrants to their families in the home community or country.

i A firm that owns or controls productive operations in more than one country through foreign direct investment.

j Overseas investment in physical capital by transnational corporations.

k A global system of interconnected computer networks.

To check your answers, look at the Glossary on pages 302–311.

Preparing for your exams

Development Dynamics

Question 1 Explain why the fertility rate declines as the economies of countries develop.   (3 marks)

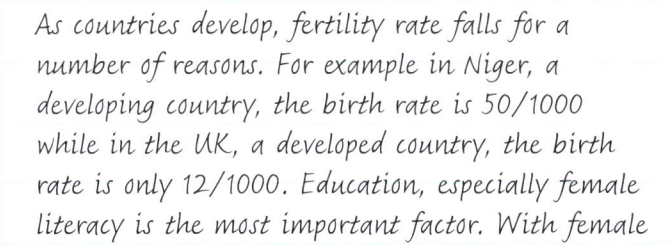

Student answer

As countries develop, fertility rate falls for a number of reasons. For example in Niger, a developing country, the birth rate is 50/1000 while in the UK, a developed country, the birth rate is only 12/1000. Education, especially female literacy is the most important factor. With female education comes more knowledge of birth control and greater opportunities for employment. These factors improve the status of women in society. Government-directed birth control programmes have helped to lower the fertility rate in many countries.

Verdict

The opening sentence recognises that there are a number of reasons for the fall in fertility with economic development. Good examples of differences in fertility are then provided. The importance of education and national family planning programmes are clearly explained.

Exam tip

Your revision should always include learning some basic data to back up statements that you make.

Question 2 Explain the changes in employment structure that have occurred in emerging countries.   (4 marks)

Student answer

In emerging countries such as India, China and Brazil, employment in the primary sector has fallen considerably in recent decades. At the same time, the secondary and tertiary sectors have become much more important. Emerging countries have attracted high levels of foreign direct investment from transnational corporations. This has not just been in manufacturing, but in the service sector in some countries such as India. The increasing wealth of emerging economies allows for greater investment in agriculture. This includes mechanisation, which results in falling demand for labour on the land. So, as employment in the secondary and tertiary sectors rises, employment in the primary sector falls.

Verdict

This answer shows clear knowledge and understanding of employment changes in the different sectors of emerging economies. Relevant use of examples adds to the depth of the answer.

Exam tip

Although the command word in this question is 'explain', some basic description is required first to justify the points made in terms of explanation.

Pearson Education Ltd accepts no responsibility whatsoever for the accuracy or method of working in the answers given.

THINKING GEOGRAPHICALLY

Working with trend lines and scatter graphs

Trend lines

What you need to know about trend lines

Sometimes we want to predict or summarise what is happening with data or we have missing data. That is when we can use graphs to help us think about the overall trend in the data and estimate data we do not have.

- A **trend** is the general direction of change. On a graph you can draw a **trend line** to show the overall change in the data.
- You can also use graphs to estimate or **interpolate** missing values inside a dataset.
- You can also estimate or **extrapolate** extra values outside the range of a dataset.

Example

Some students drew a line graph to show changes in a country's exports over several years (Figure 1). Even though the results went up and down a lot, they were able to identify the trend. They drew a trend line through the middle of the points on the graph, with roughly an equal number of values on each side of the trend line.

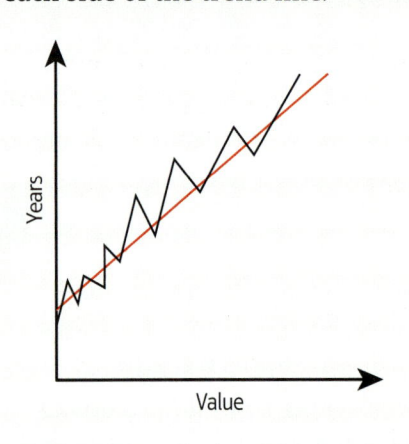

Figure 1 Trend line showing increasing trend

Figure 2 Pedestrian numbers in Compston Road, Ambleside

The students were investigating pedestrian movements in Ambleside, a small town in Cumbria. At five sites they counted the number of passing pedestrians in 15-minute time intervals. At one site they had to take a break at 10:00am but decided they could estimate the missing data. To do so they drew a graph (Figure 2) and interpolated the missing data.

THINKING GEOGRAPHICALLY

Apply your knowledge

1. Describe the trend in pedestrian numbers on Compston Road that morning.
2. Use the graph to interpolate the missing figure for 10:00–10:15 and explain your working.

It started raining so the students stopped counting at 11:15. But they wanted a data set for two hours so they decided to estimate the figure for 11:15–11:30.

3. Use the graph to extrapolate the figure for 11:15–11:30 and explain your working.
4. Which do you think was most likely to be accurate – interpolating or extrapolating values?

Scatter graphs

What you need to know about scatter graphs

Scatter graphs are a way to plot data with two sets of values (or **variables**) on the same graph, to see if there is a relationship (or **correlation**) between them.

Example

- **Correlation** is when the two variables in the data are linked. In Figure 3 scatter graphs (a) and (b) show there is a link between the variables. In scatter graph (c) there is no link between the variables.
- You can draw a **line of best fit** through the middle of the data points, like a trend line. If most data points are close to the line, there is a strong correlation (Figure 3b). If the data points are far apart, the correlation is weak (Figure 3a)

(a) Positive correlation (b) Negative correlation (c) No correlation

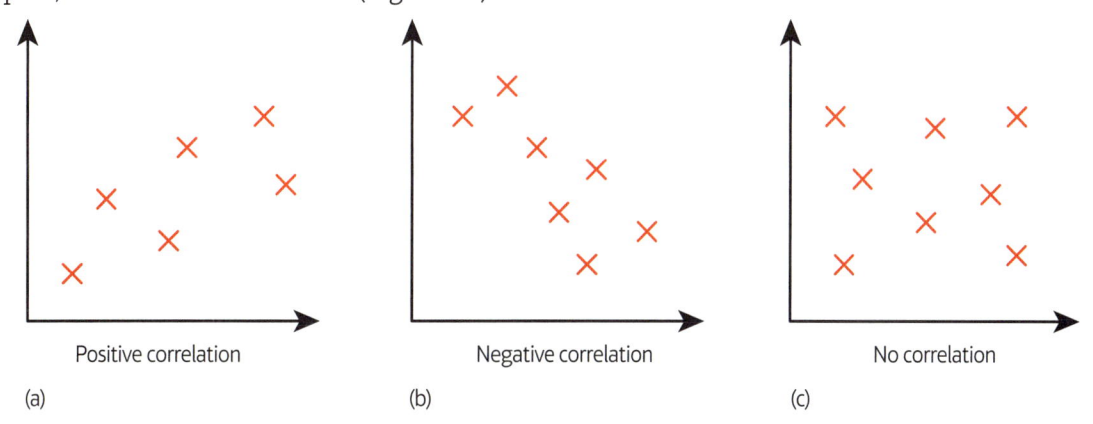

Figure 3 Different types of correlation: (a) Positive correlation (b) Negative correlation (c) No correlation

Apply your knowledge

1. Use Figure 3 to draw sketches of the three types of scatter graph in your notes.
2. Draw and label lines of best fit through the middle of the data points on graphs (a) and (b).
3. Write this sentence under the correct graph, then write similar sentences under the other two: 'On this scatter graph, as one variable increases, the other variable decreases'.

THINKING GEOGRAPHICALLY

Example

Some students were investigating data about development. They wanted to find out:

- if improving people's access to clean water would affect life expectancy
- if better access to clean water would lead to fewer child deaths.

They found data on 12 countries from the World Bank and plotted two scatter graphs (Figure 4).

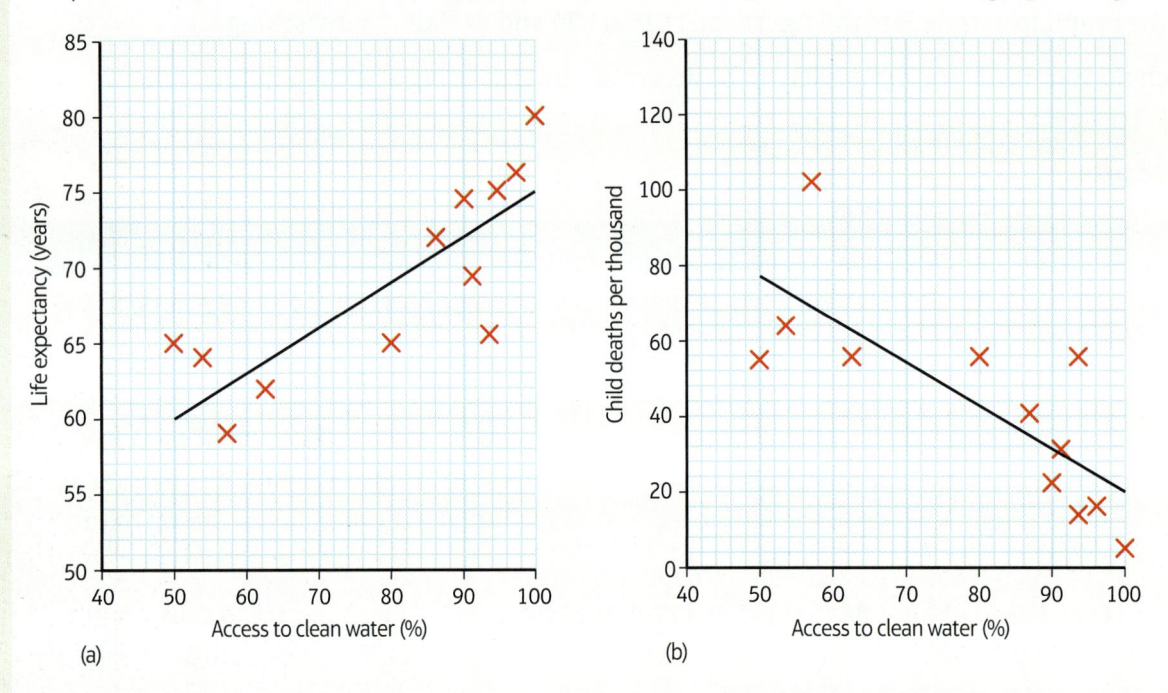

Figure 4 Scatter graphs of development data: (a) Water supply and life expectancy, 2013 (b) Water supply and child mortality, 2013

Apply your knowledge

1. As more people have access to clean water, what happens to life expectancy and child deaths? Use evidence from the scatter graphs to describe these two relationships and include some of the key words in bold from page 93 to make your writing more precise.
2. Which scatter graph seems to have the strongest correlation between the variables?
3. From your understanding of development, explain your findings.

Data with two sets of values (or variables) is called **bivariate data**. For example: in 2013, 93% of people in India had access to a safe water supply (value or variable 1) and life expectancy was 66 years (value or variable 2).

3 | Challenges of an Urbanising World

Today, more people live in urban areas (towns and cities) than in rural areas. In 2007, for the first time in history, the number of people living in urban areas exceeded the number living in the countryside. The most urbanised regions are in North America, Latin America and the Caribbean, and Europe. Africa and Asia still have more people living in rural areas, but this is changing. Africa and Asia are now urbanising faster than the other global regions.

Urbanisation is a global process that has gathered speed since the last part of the 20th century and its effects are becoming more complex. In 1980, 40% of the global population lived in urban areas. By 2015, this had increased to 54%, and by 2050 it is expected that 66% of the world's population will be living in cities.

In this section, you will investigate the causes and challenges of rapid urban change, and in particular how such challenges have affected the quality of life of people in Mumbai, India.

Your learning

In this section you will investigate the following key questions:
- Why is the world becoming increasingly urbanised?
- How do social and economic changes lead to urbanisation?
- Why are urban economies different in developing, emerging and developed countries?
- Why and how do cities change over time?
- What makes Mumbai a megacity?
- How has Mumbai's structure developed?
- Why has Mumbai grown so rapidly?
- What are the opportunities of living in Mumbai?
- What are the challenges of living in Mumbai?
- Why are there differences in quality of life in Mumbai?
- Can top-down strategies make Mumbai more sustainable?
- Can bottom-up strategies make Mumbai more sustainable?

3 | Challenges of an Urbanising World

Why is the world becoming increasingly urbanised?

> **Learning outcomes**
> - To know past and current global trends in urbanisation
> - To understand how the rate of urbanisation varies between global regions
> - To evaluate the pattern of megacities and understand how some urban areas have disproportionate economic and political influence

Urbanisation is the process by which an increasing percentage of people live in towns and cities. It is largely caused by **migration** from rural areas. By 2007, the majority of the world's population lived in cities and this number is expected to increase from 3.8 billion to 5.1 billion by 2030. Nearly all of this growth will take place in **emerging countries** or **developing countries** – from 2.9 billion in 2014 to 4.1 billion in 2030. By contrast, the urban population of **developed countries** will grow far less – from 1 billion to 1.05 billion. Figure 1 shows how the population living in urban areas has increased from 1980 with a **projection** to 2030.

Urbanisation in developed countries

The growth of urban areas in developed countries resulted from the agricultural and industrial revolutions of the 18th and 19th centuries. During this time, workers gradually moved from the countryside to work in factories in the towns. Urbanisation took place slowly over a long period of time. Urbanisation has been steady in developed countries since 1980 (see Figure 2).

Urbanisation in developing and emerging countries

The growth of towns and cities in emerging and developing countries has been rapid and has largely taken place within the last 50 years. People are moving into cities at a faster rate than houses can be built for them. Africa is expected to become the region with the fastest urban growth between 2020 and 2050 (see Figure 2).

One reason why urbanisation is much slower in developed countries is that most people there already live in urban areas – 81% in 2014. Another reason is that in developed countries the rate of natural increase of the population is low, or even negative. By contrast, in many emerging and developing countries, urban areas are growing rapidly, through both **rural–urban migration** and higher rates of natural increase.

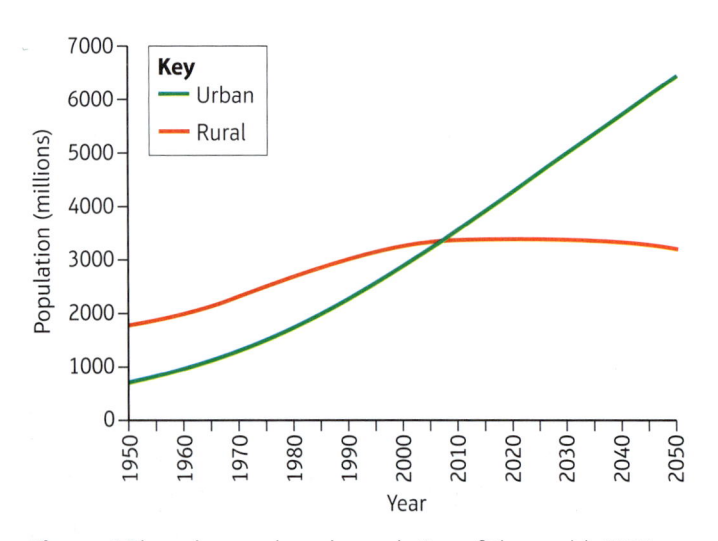

Figure 1 The urban and rural population of the world, 1950–2050

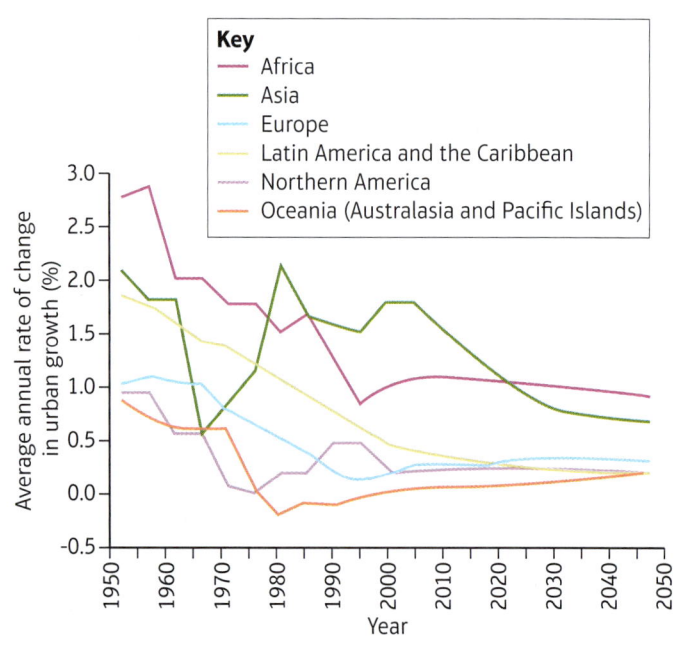

Figure 2 Average annual rate of change in urban growth in major urban areas, 1950–2050

3 Challenges of an Urbanising World

Activity

1. What was the rate of urban growth in Africa in 2015?
2. Where in the world do urban areas have the highest and lowest growth rates today and why?
3. Describe the trend in urban growth in different parts of the world, using examples of data from Figure 2.
4. Explain what primate cities are, why they have grown so big and what challenges this has created.

Megacities

Major cities have populations of more than 200,000, while **megacities** have populations of more than 10 million. A megacity is one continuous urban area. Examples include Jakarta and Los Angeles.

The first megacities were in developed countries. They included London, Paris and New York. Today, the fastest growing megacities are in emerging and developing countries. They are often poor cities with a young population attracted from the surrounding rural areas. By 2015, most megacities were found in Africa and Asia.

Only eight of the world's megacities are in developed countries. Figure 3 shows the world's top megacities.

Primate cities

Some cities are so important within a country that they dominate its economic, financial and political systems. Large numbers of people want to live and work in these **primate cities** because of the opportunities they offer. Primate cities usually have at least twice the population of the country's next largest city. Today, primate cities often have the best infrastructure in the country. Their growth is fuelled by rural–urban migration and industrial development.

Primate cities often suffer from traffic congestion, pollution, housing shortages, unemployment and crime.

Did you know?

Bangkok, the capital of Thailand and an example of a primate city, has over 14 million inhabitants, more than twice the size of its nearest rival. It produces 60% of Thailand's gross domestic product, has 45% of all doctors and 72% of all registered cars.

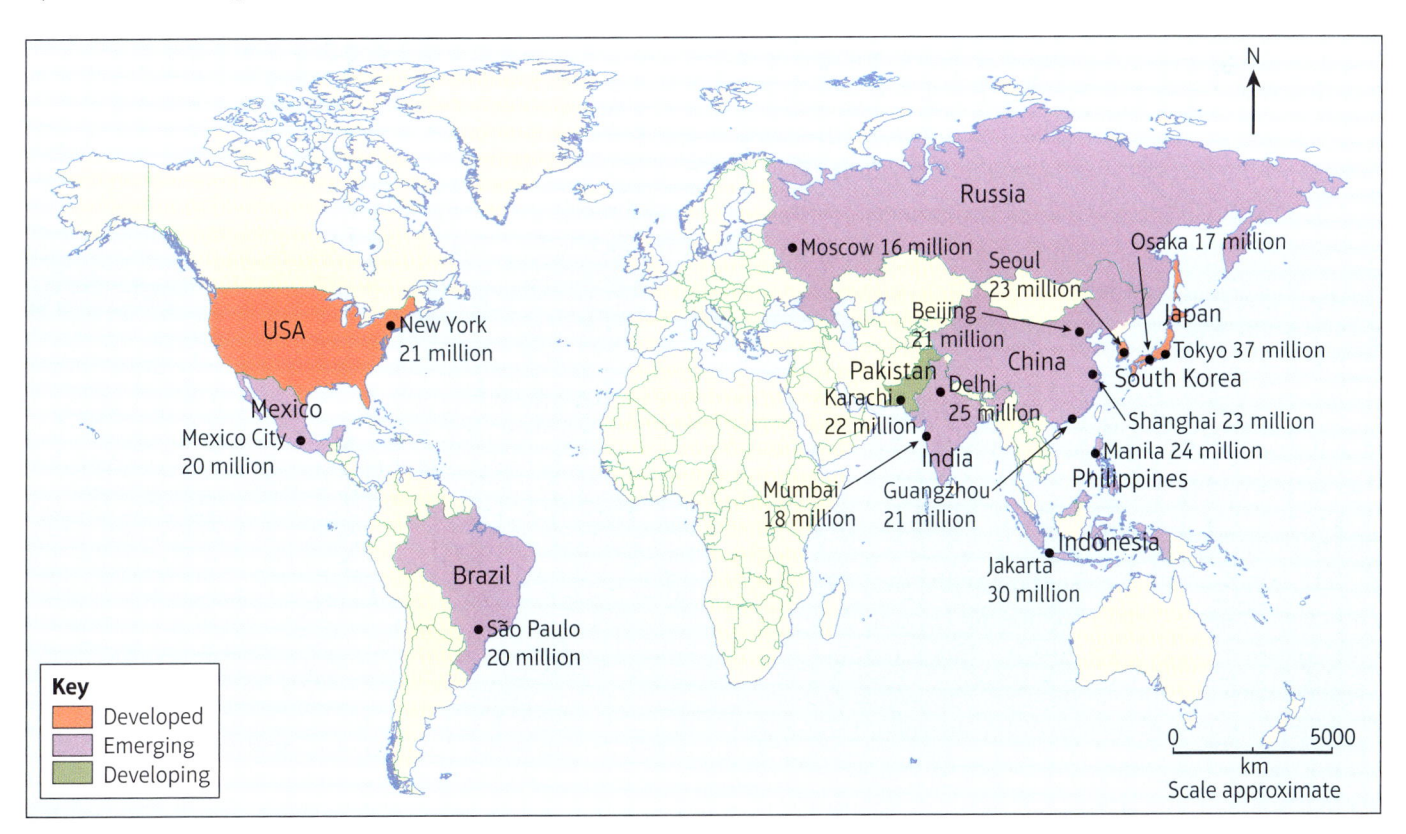

Figure 3 The world's 15 largest megacities, 2014

3 Challenges of an Urbanising World

How do social and economic changes lead to urbanisation?

Learning outcomes

- To know how national and international migration contributes to the growth and/or decline of cities in developed, developing and emerging countries
- To understand how economic change contributes to the growth and/or decline of cities in developed, developing and emerging countries

The impact of migration on urbanisation

Urbanisation results from a number of **socio-economic processes**, in particular national and international migration. Large numbers of people migrating from an urban area can also lead to its decline.

National migration

In 1990, the city of Chongqing in central China had a population of 2 million. Since 2001, there has been a large-scale internal movement of people from rural parts of China into cities. By 2014, Chongqing's population reached 12.9 million, although its rapid growth makes this figure uncertain. What caused this migration?

- Major economic reform in China, following a long period of stagnation, led to the rapid growth of new manufacturing industries after 2001. In Chongqing, this created a demand for labour and incomes began to rise. People were attracted to Chongqing from rural areas where incomes were low and rising only slowly.
- Urbanisation led to the loss of farmland, which was needed for industrial, commercial and residential use. This also meant less work for local people in rural areas and led to further migration from the countryside.
- Migrants were attracted to the cities, which offered better services such as health, education and entertainment.

International migration

In 2001, London had a population of just over 7 million. Until then, more people were leaving London than were coming to live there. By 2011, this situation had changed, with London's population increasing by 14% to 8.1 million, largely as a result of the arrival of thousands of international migrants (see Figure 4). People born in India made up the largest non-UK-born group in London, followed by people born in Poland, Ireland, Nigeria and Pakistan.

What were the **pull factors** that attracted people from other countries to migrate to London? The capital is a major centre for:

- **employment** – it offers a wide range of service jobs at relatively high rates of pay
- **entertainment and culture** – attractions such as shopping, restaurants, theatres and clubs
- **services** – from transport and health to education and social services
- **the UK and international transport network** – with excellent access to all parts of the country and the world.

As well as these pull factors, **push factors** such as lack of job opportunities, services and entertainment where the migrants had been living may also have played a part.

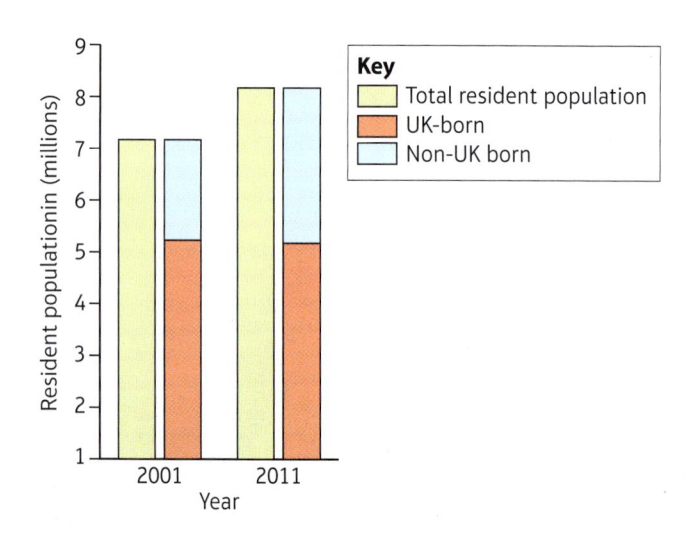

Figure 4 Population of London, 2001 and 2011

> **Activity**
>
> 1. What were the 'push factors' that drove migrants to London?
> 2. To what extent are the 'pull factors' that attracted migrants to Chongqing similar to those attracting migrants to London?
> 3. To what extent are the 'pull factors' that attracted migrants to Chongqing different from those encouraging migrants to London?

The impact of economic change on urbanisation

Growth of cities

Economic change can also lead to urbanisation, as in São Paulo in Brazil. In 1960, the city had a population of 6 million; by 1991, this had doubled to 12 million; in 2014, there were over 20 million living there. What were the reasons for this rapid growth?

- The modernisation of agriculture led to redundancies in the rural workforce. Agricultural workers were forced to migrate to São Paulo to look for employment.
- The closure of local craft industries such as textiles and metal working led to redundancies in the workforce who migrated to São Paulo to find work.
- The city experienced a rapid population growth resulting from a high birth rate and a low death rate.
- Migrants were attracted to São Paulo because it offered better services such as in health and education.

Decline of cities

When a city is dependent on one major industry for its economic prosperity, it becomes vulnerable to changes in the markets for that industry. In the USA, Detroit was the home of a successful car industry and centre of the Motown music industry. At its peak in 1950, 1.8 million people lived in Detroit, but by 2013 this had fallen to 700,000. Competition from cars made abroad in countries such as Japan, Germany and South Korea affected the Detroit car industry. Sales of US-made cars and trucks declined, costs rose and the industry failed to introduce new technology quickly enough. Because the industry failed to compete, Detroit's car factories closed, employees lost their jobs and, because Detroit had no other industries to absorb these workers, the population moved away.

> **Did you know?**
>
> It is estimated that 25% of Detroit's built-up area has been abandoned. In places prairie grass, part of the Mid-West's natural vegetation, is growing again in the city.

> **Activity**
>
> 1. What are the attractions of cities for people in the rural areas of Brazil?
> 2. Suggest some ways in which Detroit might attract more people to live there.
> 3. Do you think the attractions of cities are more or less important than things that force people to leave? Give reasons for your answers.

> **Exam-style question**
>
> Explain why international and national migration have contributed to the growth or decline of a major city in the developed world. **(4 marks)**

> **Exam tip**
>
> Read the question carefully and make sure you know if it is asking for a city in a developing, emerging or developed country.

Figure 5 Detroit – a city affected by economic decline

3 Challenges of an Urbanising World

Why are urban economies different in developing, emerging and developed countries?

> **Learning objectives**
> - To know the differences between formal and informal employment
> - To understand the nature of different economic sectors and working conditions in developed, developing and emerging countries
> - To understand the reasons for the differences in urban economies between developed, developing and emerging countries

Formal and informal employment

People who work in **formal employment** usually receive a regular wage and may pay tax on their income. In some countries they may have certain employment rights, such as sick leave or paid holidays. The formal employment sector includes people working in factories, offices, shops and government offices. By contrast, **informal employment** activities are not officially recognised by the government. Informal workers often work for themselves on the streets, for example as roadside hairdressers or water sellers. They do not pay taxes and have no employment protection. The differences between formal and informal employment are shown in Table 1.

Differences in urban economies

The developed, emerging and developing countries are at different stages in their economic development, and this is reflected in their **urban economies** (see Table 2).

Table 1 Differences between formal and informal employment

Features	Formal employment e.g. traditional industry such as car manufacture	Informal employment e.g. street seller
Scale of activity	Large scale – usually in a factory	Small scale – may be on street corners
Level of skill	Some high-level skill work	Mostly low level of skills
Ease of entry	Needs sizeable funding and often a lot of equipment to get started	Needs little funding or equipment to start
Need for capital	Needs a lot of capital to get started, often financed by the government	Needs little capital to start
Number of workers	Often more than 100 workers	Usually just a few workers or self-employed
Working conditions	Workers usually have some protection to ensure the environment in which they work is safe, e.g. to prevent accidents or stop pollution There may also be set hours of work. Some have trades unions to ensure good working conditions	No protection for workers. No set hours of work, so hours may be long. May have to pay protection to gangs. There are no trades unions to support the workers
Location	Factory	May be at home or on the street
Taxes	Pay taxes to the government	Pay no taxes

3 Challenges of an Urbanising World

Table 2 Main features of urban economies in developed, emerging and developing countries

Developed e.g. London, Paris	Emerging e.g. Mexico City, Mumbai	Developing e.g. Lagos
Usually have a broad range of different industries and jobs: • Little, if any, primary industry • Secondary (manufacturing) industries such as engineering, printing • Many tertiary industries such as tourism, education, finance, health and other services • Quaternary industries such as IT, media, consultation and culture, as well as top-level decision-making	Often have: • Little primary industry • Manufacturing that processes primary products, such as sugar refining and flour milling. Some, for example in China and India, have heavy industry and engineering • Very large tertiary industries, including government administration, and service industries such as tourism, transport and entertainment • Smaller quaternary sector, which is growing rapidly	Usually have: • Little primary industry • Secondary industry that often processes primary products, such as textiles, sugar refining and flour milling • Very large tertiary industries, including large government administration and finance, and service industries such as tourism, transport and entertainment • A small initial quaternary sector, which is growing

The Clark-Fisher model of changing employment helps us to determine the stage of economic development of a country (Figure 6). The stages are:

- **pre-industrial** – most jobs are in farming, mining and fishing
- **industrial** – manufacturing industry and towns grow rapidly. Some tertiary employment provides services such as transport, water and electricity
- **post-industrial** – tertiary sector becomes most important. Demand for services, especially in towns, fuels an increase in health and financial services
- **later stage** – quaternary sector develops, especially research and development.

Exam-style question

Describe the main differences between the economies of cities in developing and emerging countries and economies in developed countries.
(4 marks)

Exam tip

If the question asks for 'differences between' two things, make sure you talk about the differences between them and not simply describe each in turn.

Activity

1. How are working conditions in the informal sector different from those of people working in the formal sector?
2. Which countries are at the later stage of the Clark-Fisher Model?
3. Study Table 2 and Figure 6. List the **four** main types of employment, then give **three** examples of jobs in each.

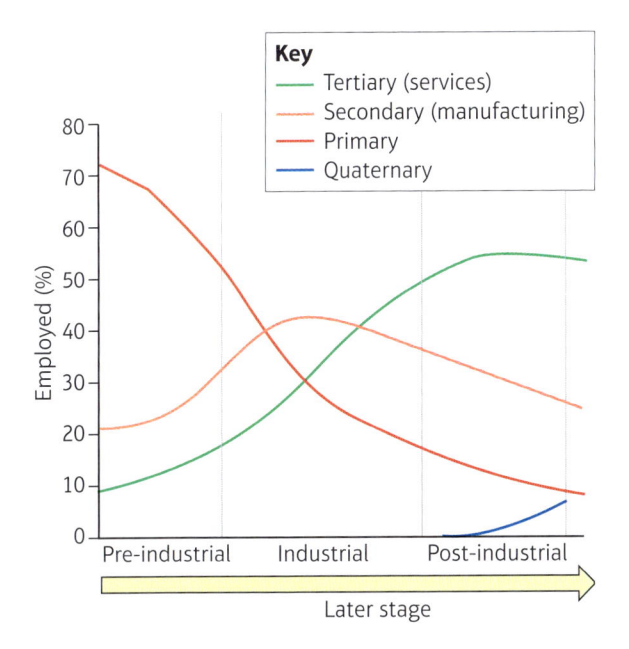

Figure 6 The Clark-Fisher model

3 Challenges of an Urbanising World

Why and how do cities change over time?

> **Learning objectives**
> - To know how urban populations change over time
> - To identify the characteristics of different urban land uses
> - To understand the factors affecting urban land uses

From urbanisation to regeneration

The number of people living in a city, where they live within the city and how the city shapes itself all change over time. A city may move through each of the following stages.

1. **Urbanisation** – In most developed countries, such as the UK or the USA, urbanisation was linked to industrialisation. The industrial revolution and services such as railways, roads and a safe water supply attracted workers to the growing towns. As cities became increasingly urbanised, more factories were built and growing numbers of rural migrants arrived to fill the jobs that were created.

2. **Suburbanisation** – By the early 20th century in developed countries, city centres had become noisy, crowded, polluted places. People who could afford to moved out of the city centre to the new 'suburbs' on the edge of the city where land was cheaper and the air was cleaner.

3. **De-industrialisation** – The industry in the city begins to decline. Often this is the result of technological change, failure to invest or competition from other countries. Detroit is an extreme example.

4. **Counter-urbanisation** – In the 1970s and 1980s, in the UK, Europe, USA and Japan, people chose to leave larger towns and cities to move to more rural areas. This led to a pattern of population decline in inner-city areas and population growth in small towns and villages. Counter-urbanisation was made possible by rising car ownership and motorway construction, which allowed people to live in the countryside and still work in cities. Progress in telecommunications and information technology also meant that people could work from home in remote villages.

5. **Regeneration** – Some older cities have started to redevelop their run-down inner-city areas in order to attract people to live close to the amenities of the city centre. New shopping centres, flats, houses and leisure facilities are built to give the city centre a facelift and attract businesses. In Birmingham, this regeneration process has included developments such as the Mailbox, a development of offices, shops, flats and television studios (see Figure 7).

Figure 7 The Mailbox, Birmingham

Cities in developing, emerging and developed countries share some characteristics but there are also differences

Similarities

Cities in both developed and developing countries:

- have a **Central Business District (CBD)** usually recognisable by tall office blocks
- have areas that are mainly industrial and zones that are mainly residential
- are spread over a wide area
- have extensive suburbs
- have issues of traffic congestion and air pollution.

Differences

- The zones of industry and housing are more distinct and separate in cities in developed countries.
- In developing and emerging countries affluent areas are sometimes very close to industrial zones or areas of squatter settlements; this is not the case in cities in developed countries.
- Most cities in developed countries do not have squatter settlements.
- Cities in developing and emerging countries have not yet experienced counter-urbanisation.

Exam-style question

Identify which of the following is the best description of urbanisation.

- ☐ A The process by which cities shrink, caused by people migrating from them to rural areas.
- ☐ B The process by which people move back to a growing city from rural areas.
- ☐ C The process by which more people live in growing cities, caused by migration from rural areas.
- ☐ D The process by which people leave city centres and move to areas further from the centre. **(1 mark)**

Exam tip

Beware of choices in a question because many may be similar but not quite correct.

Activity

1. Explain what is meant by counter-urbanisation.
2. Why do cities want to regenerate their centres?
3. Devise a simple diagram to show the stages a city may go through from urbanisation to regeneration, including all the stages along the way.

Urban land uses

A visit to any city soon confirms that there are variations in the way land is used. Some land is used for housing, some for factories, some for leisure. Although each city has its own unique pattern of land use, there are some basic similarities in land use patterns. For example, city centres are often dominated by shops and offices. As towns grow, different functions tend to group together in various parts of the town, forming functional zones. These functional zones are generally easy to recognise from aerial images.

Why functional zones form in cities

The centre of a city is the most accessible part of the city. Most land uses that need access to lots of people, such as shops and offices, must locate near the most accessible part of the city. So there is competition between land uses for the most accessible site. This means that the rents charged for sites close to the city centre are usually the highest in the city, therefore only those uses which can pay the high rents can afford to locate there. Shops and offices can afford the high rents and so are found in city centres. Other land uses, such as public administration, markets, warehousing and industry are found at sites further away from the city centre.

Land-use zones

The CBD has a range of high-end shops and tall office blocks, together with multi-storey car parks.

Close to the CBD are usually the rail and bus terminals, as well as markets (wholesale and retail) and public buildings (town hall, civic hall). These zones can be recognised by the area's warehouses.

Industrial areas are usually further away from the CBD and can be recognised by low factory buildings together with old canals and newer dual carriageways.

3 Challenges of an Urbanising World

Residential areas have extensive zones of houses with gardens and some blocks of flats, and are usually further from the CBD.

Activity

Think about a UK city centre you know well, or study the aerial photo of Birmingham city centre on page 198.

1. Write a short description of the land uses found in the CBD, then write a brief explanation of why these land uses are located in this zone. The text on pages 103–104 will help you.
2. Write similar descriptions for land uses in the zone just outside the CBD, and residential zones.

3 Factors influencing urban land use

Urban land use is influenced by a range of factors.

- **Accessibility** – Shops (retail) and offices need to be accessible to as many people as possible and so are usually found in city centres, which have good transport links. In some cities the edge of the city is the most accessible, often by motorway, and this has led to the growth of out-of-town shopping centres, with a mix of shops, offices and leisure facilities.
- **Availability** – City centres tend to be heavily built up. The availability of land may also affect how land is used. When factories and warehouses close, the brownfield sites may be used for housing, shops and offices.
- **Cost** – Land in the city centre is often the most expensive because of its lack of availability. Some land uses, such as shops and offices, can afford to pay high rents in order to be in the city centre.
- **Planning regulations** – Planning also affects land use patterns. Planners try to balance different, often competing, uses for land. The city's authorities often decide how they want a city to look and develop, and have plans that show which land uses will be permitted in different parts of the city.

Checkpoint

Now it is time to review your understanding of the growing urbanisation of the world.

Strengthen

S1 What are the differences between a major city, a megacity and a primate city?

S2 Where is the growth of megacities concentrated? Why is this?

S3 Compare the processes of urbanisation, suburbanisation and counter-urbanisation.

S4 Summarise the main differences between formal and informal industry.

Challenge

C1 Describe how urbanisation in emerging and developing countries differs from that in developed countries.

C2 Compare the reasons for the growth of São Paulo and the decline of Detroit.

C3 Explain the Clark-Fisher model of changing employment.

C4 Explain how accessibility influences urban land use and the development of different functional zones.

Exam-style question

Explain some of the main factors that influence land use in a city. **(4 marks)**

Exam tip

To get full marks, make sure that you include all the factors that might affect an issue.

Activity

1. What benefits do the SPARC toilet blocks bring to Mumbai's residents?
2. In what ways does the project contribute to making Mumbai a more sustainable city?
3. Explain why the Hamara Foundation's strategy for helping Mumbai's street children is a bottom-up strategy.
4. Copy Table 4, which shows advantages and disadvantages of the three bottom-up projects. Add one more advantage or disadvantage (or both) to each project.

Improving quality of life in Dharavi

Dharavi is located on land worth an estimated US$10 billion, close to the Bandra-Kurla Complex – a new business district – and within easy reach of the main railway lines. The city government is keen to re-develop Dharavi through its top-down strategy of selling the cleared land to developers, on the understanding that free housing is provided for slum residents who can prove they have lived in Dharavi since 2000. Through the redevelopment scheme:

- 1.1 million new low-cost, affordable housing units will be built (as tower blocks, leaving space for higher-value apartments on the rest of the cleared site)
- water supplies and sanitation services will be provided for all residents
- education and health care services will also be built into the new developments, along with shopping malls, restaurants and leisure services.

However, Dharavi residents were strongly opposed to the plan. They were concerned that it would not be possible for Dharavi's many small businesses and micro-industries to continue in tower blocks, that the new housing would destroy the strong community of Dharavi and instead there would be social problems – more crime, for example.

A group of Mumbai urban designers suggested a different approach – to give the people of Dharavi the ownership rights to the land on which Dharavi is built, and then involve them in finding ways to improve living conditions in each neighbourhood of Dharavi.

Activity

1. Describe **one** advantage and **one** disadvantage of the government's top-down strategy for improving quality of life in Dharavi.
2. Suggest what are the advantages and disadvantages of giving local Dharavi communities ownership of the land and a role in deciding how best to improve Dharavi's quality of life.
3. Which do you think has more advantages than disadvantages – top-down or bottom-up?

Exam-style question

For a named megacity in a developing or emerging country, evaluate whether bottom-up solutions can improve the quality of life for residents. **(8 marks)**

Checkpoint

Now it is time to review your understanding of top-down and bottom-up strategies for improving quality of life in Mumbai.

Strengthen

S1 Explain the difference between a top-down strategy and a bottom-up strategy
S2 Why might some residents of Mumbai support top-down and bottom-up solutions to slums?

Challenge

C1 Which do you think would be the best approach for improving water supply, transport services or air quality in Mumbai – top-down or bottom-up? Explain your answer.
C2 Which do you think would be the best approach for improving city housing or health services – top-down or bottom-up? Explain your answer.

Preparing for your exams

Challenges of an Urbanising World

Urbanisation is taking place across the world and the process is gathering speed. Cities are struggling to cope with the effects of this rapid growth and at the same time to become more sustainable. Different countries have tried a range of strategies to make their cities more sustainable and small steps have been taken in terms of recycling in cities and attempts to cut down air pollution. However, much remains to be done.

Checklist

You should know:

- [ ] the causes of urbanisation in emerging, developing and developed cities
- [ ] the growth of primate and megacities
- [ ] the impact of economic change on cities
- [ ] the impact of national and international changes on cities
- [ ] the key processes of urbanisation, suburbanisation, counter-urbanisation and regeneration
- [ ] variations in urban land use
- [ ] the site and situation of Mumbai
- [ ] the urban structure of Mumbai
- [ ] factors in the growth of Mumbai
- [ ] population growth and changing functions in Mumbai
- [ ] opportunities for people living in Mumbai
- [ ] challenges facing people living in Mumbai
- [ ] reasons for variations in the quality of life in Mumbai
- [ ] the advantages and disadvantages of bottom-up and top-down approaches to solving Mumbai's problems.

Which key terms match the following definitions?

a   The central area of a city, where land use is dominated by department stores, specialist and variety goods stores, offices, cinemas, theatres and hotels.

b   The increase in the percentage of people living in towns and cities, causing them to grow.

c   Development which meets the needs of the present without compromising (limiting) the ability of future generations to meet their own needs.

d   The movement of people and employment from major cities to smaller settlements and rural areas located beyond the city, or to more distant towns and cities.

e   Reviving the economy or environment of a run-down area.

f   The decline of industrial activity in a region or in an economy.

g   The movement of people, factories, offices and shops away from city centres to suburban and edge of city locations.

h   The area around the edge of a city where urban and rural land uses mix.

To check your answers, look at the Glossary on pages 302–311.

Preparing for your exams

Challenges of an Urbanising World

Question 1 Compare the main differences between the formal and the informal economy in very large cities in developing or emerging countries. **(4 marks)**

Student answer

In large cities like Mumbai there are lots of people who are poor and they have to make a living by working on the street. They sell water or cigarettes or they give haircuts. They work all hours and do not pay taxes. This is called the informal economy. Other people are lucky and find jobs in factories and offices and are paid a wage. This is the formal economy.

Verdict

The first part on the informal economy is correct, but this answer does not actually compare the two and it does not talk about factors other than where the people work, and whether they pay taxes. A good answer would make comparisons about level of skill, ease of entry, need for capital, number of workers. This student shows some level of understanding but does not provide a complete answer.

Exam tip

Make sure that you check the key command words so that you answer the question that was set. If the command word asks you to compare, be sure to make comparisons.

Question 2 Explain how the growth of a major city in a developing or emerging country affected its urban functions? **(4 marks)**

Student answer

Mumbai grew very rapidly in the period after the 1970s because thousands of people moved there from the countryside. This growth led to the expansion of the city into the surrounding area as new suburbs were built along railway lines and as new squatter settlements grew up on areas of waste ground. As Mumbai grew it developed new industries such as chemical and car manufacture, with squatter settlements developing near these and in the port area. Mumbai also further developed its banking sector, becoming India's leading centre of finance, and has become India's foremost centre for information technology.

Verdict

The first part is correct but not really relevant to the question because it does not talk about the urban functions. It does not say what the urban functions were before the city grew so big nor how the current functions are different (or the same). The parts about industrial change, the development as a financial centre are fine, but there is little about its function as a cultural centre (Bollywood), as a population centre (India's largest city), nor its importance in terms of FDI (foreign direct investment). Not all of the information is relevant, and the answer lacks some detail.

Exam tip

When answering a question, make sure that as far as possible you use the key terms from the question. This question specifically mentions economic change so there should be explanation of what that economic change consisted of, and then detail of how it increased the inequality in the city. There was a lot of useful information in the answer above but it needed shaping to answer the question that was asked. This is an important part of exam technique.

Pearson Education Ltd accepts no responsibility whatsoever for the accuracy or method of working in the answers given.

WRITING GEOGRAPHICALLY

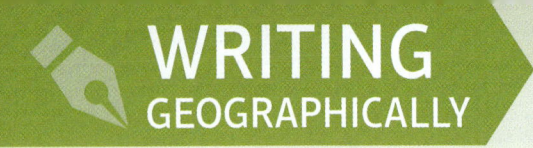

Writing geographically: developing your answer

When you are asked to write an explanation, discussion, assessment or evaluation, you need to support, explain and develop your ideas.

Learning objectives

- To understand how to link and develop ideas using subordinate clauses and non-finite clauses

Definitions

Main clause: the most important clause in a sentence to which other clauses may be linked.

Subordinate clause: a clause which adds detail to or develops the main clause, linked with a subordinating conjunction such as *because*, *if*, *although*, etc.

Non-finite clause: a clause beginning with a non-finite verb. These can be:

- **a present participle:** a verb form ending in *–ing*, e.g. *running*, *building*, *forming*, *falling*, etc.
- **a past participle:** a verb form often ending in *–ed*, e.g. *formed*, *happened*, *etc*, although there are several exceptions, e.g. *ran*, *built*, *fell*, etc.

How can I link and develop my ideas?

Look at this exam-style question

> For a named megacity, assess how far rapid population growth has affected attempts to make it more sustainable.
> **(8 marks)**

Now look at a sentence from one student's response to it:

> Mumbai, India, has experienced significant problems because its population has grown so dramatically in the last 50 years.

This is the main clause in this sentence. This is a subordinate clause which develops the information in the main clause. This subordinating conjunction links the subordinate clause to the main clause.

Now look at these four sentences taken from the same student's response:

> The Mumbai Metropolitan Regional Development Authority was set up in 1975. It has struggled to provide adequate housing, water supply and sewerage systems to support the population. There is great pressure on urban managers and government to find solutions. A large proportion of the population are very poor and live in slums such as Dharavi.

1. How could you use subordinating conjunctions to clearly express the connection between these pieces of information? Experiment with expressing them in two or three sentences, using subordinating conjunctions to link them in a variety of different ways.

Conjunctions bank

| when | because | whereas | if | although | since | as | until | unless |

2. Look closely at your answer to question 1, and compare it to the original version above. Which do you prefer, your version or the original? Write a sentence or two explaining your choice.

WRITING GEOGRAPHICALLY

How can I link and develop my ideas in different ways?

You can also connect two related pieces of information in one sentence using a non-finite clause. Compare these two extracts:

> **Extract A** *The government and urban managers of Mumbai are tackling the poor environment better with the removal of the poorest slum housing. They aim to reduce them to half a million units by 2020.*

In Extract A, the two pieces of related information are expressed in two separate sentences.

> **Extract B** *The government and urban managers of Mumbai are tackling socio-economic issues with the removal of the poorest slum housing, aiming to reduce them to half a million units by 2020.*

In Extract B, the writer clearly expresses the link between these two pieces of information using this **present participles** to form a **non-finite clause**.

3. How could you use non-finite clauses to link these **five** pieces of information in just **one** or **two** sentences?

> *(1) The Dharavi Redevelopment Project plans to move people into large free homes. (2) This will release land for luxury high rise apartment blocks. (3) However it will also increase population density in the area. (4) It will also 'kill off' micro-economic enterprises (worth $650m a year). (5) It could also destroy the social community that has developed.*

Did you notice?

The sentences you wrote in questions 2 and 3 are much longer than the sentences in the original student's answer. But are they too long? Sometimes you can link too many ideas together in a sentence so that it becomes difficult for the reader to understand it.

4. Look carefully at your response to questions 2 or 3. Is its meaning clear or is it too long? Would it be clearer if you re-wrote it using more sentences? Try rewriting your sentence in two or more different ways. Which version expresses the information most clearly?

Improving an answer

Look at these six sentences taken from one student's response to the exam-style question on page 124:

> *The population in Mumbai has doubled in the last twenty years. The local government has helped by improving public transport. A metro system with 9 lines has been built. Only one of those nine lines was running by 2015. Other improvements include better sewage disposal. This cost $500m. The improved sewage system allows more vertical development.*

5. Rewrite the sentences above to link and develop each point as clearly as possible. You could:

   - use subordinating conjunctions to link ideas
   - use non-finite verbs to link ideas
   - link the points into one, two, three or more sentences, checking that each one is clearly expressed and not too long.

6. Rewrite the sentences again, experimenting with different ways of linking them. Which version do you prefer? Which version is the most clearly expressed? Write a sentence or two explaining your choice.

Component 2
UK Geographical Issues

Content overview

In this component you will investigate some of the key geographical issues in the UK today, and the physical and human processes that cause change. You will also investigate physical and human environments through fieldwork.

- Topic 4 The UK's Evolving Physical Landscape starts with an overview of why the UK's natural landscapes are so varied, before you investigate change in coastal and river landscapes in more depth.
- Topic 5 The UK's Evolving Human Landscape investigates why the UK's human landscapes are changing, before you focus on a case study of a dynamic UK city, Birmingham.
- Topic 6 Geographical Investigations will help you to develop your fieldwork and research skills by investigating one physical and one human environment in more depth. You may choose **either** coastal change and conflict (pages 150–155) **or** river processes and pressures (pages 176–181), and **either** dynamic urban areas (pages 214–219) **or** changing rural areas (pages 226–231).

Your assessment

You will sit a 1 hour and 30 minute exam, with three sections.

- **Section A** has questions about The UK's Evolving Physical Landscape: you must answer **all** the questions in this section.
- **Section B** has questions about The UK's Evolving Human Landscape: you must answer **all** the questions in this section.
- **Section C1** has questions about physical fieldwork investigations; you must answer **one** question about **either** coastal change and conflict **or** river processes and pressures.
- **Section C2** has questions about human fieldwork investigations; you must answer **one** question about **either** dynamic urban areas **or** changing rural areas.
- You may be assessed on geographical skills in any section, and can use a calculator.
- Each section is worth 30 marks; in addition, up to four marks will be awarded for spelling, punctuation, grammar and use of geographical language (SPAG).
- There will be a variety of different question types, including multiple-choice, calculations and open questions.
- Open questions require you to write a longer answer, from a few sentences to extended writing worth up to eight marks. Eight-mark questions are where you get marks for SPAG.

4 | The UK's Evolving Physical Landscape

The physical geography of the UK varies greatly due to its complex and diverse geology, a result of it being subject to a variety of plate tectonic processes over an extended period of time. Over time the combination of these past processes, and subsequent continual physical processes, means that the UK has a rich variety of distinctive landscapes.

Your learning

In this section you will investigate the following key questions:

Overview
- How have geology and past processes influenced the physical landscape of the UK?
- How have physical processes helped create distinctive UK landscapes?
- How has human activity helped create distinctive UK landscapes?

4A Coastal change and conflict
- How do geology and physical processes influence the coastline?
- What landforms are created due to coastal erosion?
- What are the influences of transportation and deposition on the coast?
- How do geographers investigate coastal landscapes using OS maps?
- How do human activities influence coastal landscapes?
- What challenges do coastal landscapes create and how are they managed?

4B River processes and pressures
- Why is there a variety of river landscapes in the UK?
- How do river processes form distinctive landforms?
- How do climate, geology and slope processes affect different river landscapes?
- How do OS maps help geographers investigate river landscapes?
- How do physical factors and human activities affect storm hydrographs?
- How do physical and human processes interact to cause flooding on the River Severn?
- Why is the flood risk in the UK increasing and how can it be managed?

4 The UK's Evolving Physical Landscape: Overview

How have geology and past processes influenced the physical landscape of the UK?

Learning objectives
- To outline the distribution of the UK's main rock types: sedimentary, igneous and metamorphic
- To know the characteristics of the UK's main rock types: sedimentary, igneous and metamorphic
- To understand the role of geology and past tectonic processes in the development of upland and lowland landscapes

Exam-style question
Describe the differences between igneous and sedimentary rocks. **(2 marks)**

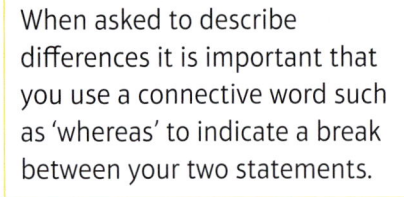

Exam tip
When asked to describe differences it is important that you use a connective word such as 'whereas' to indicate a break between your two statements.

Command word
If you are asked to **describe** something, you need only describe the differences, not offer reasons for them. You will not be awarded marks for offering an explanation.

Did you know?
The oldest rock on Earth is believed to be a type of gneiss (metamorphic rock), which was discovered in Canada. It is more than 4000 million years old. The oldest rocks in Britain are only 3000 million years old - they are also gneiss from the Isle of Lewis in Scotland.

Types of rocks
There are three main rock types that make up the Earth's crust. They are characterised by the different processes that formed them.

- **Sedimentary rocks** – are formed of small particles that have been eroded, transported, and deposited in layers, or from the remains of plants and animals – for example, limestone and chalk.
- **Igneous rocks** – are created by volcanic activity when magma or lava cools, forming rocks made of crystals that are usually hard. Granite is one example of an igneous rock.
- **Metamorphic rocks** – are existing rocks that have been changed by extreme pressure or heat. They are usually comprised of layers or bands of crystals and are very hard. Examples of metamorphic rocks include slate, which is compressed shale, or schists, which are formed from mudstone.

The role of geology, plate tectonic processes and glaciers
Millions of years ago, Britain was much closer to plate boundaries than it is today. There were many active volcanoes, and plate movements caused massive folds and **faults** in the rocks. These **tectonic processes** helped shape the geology and landscapes of today.

UK upland landscapes are formed of harder, resistant rocks that have eroded at a much slower rate than the softer, lowland rocks. These include the igneous and metamorphic rocks found in Scotland, North Wales, the Lake District and parts of south-west England (Figure 1). Around 300 million years ago, tectonic processes caused molten **magma**, under intense pressure, to rise through the Earth's crust. Some magma reached the surface as lava, while some cooled and solidified underground. Today, these are areas of high relief, for example the Cairngorm Mountains in Scotland and Dartmoor in Devon.

Many lowland UK landscapes are formed from softer, younger sedimentary rocks, which are less resistant to erosion. Examples include the North and South Downs in south-east England. These hills are formed of chalk, with even softer clay in the valleys between them.

Some upland areas are also formed of harder sedimentary rocks. An example is **carboniferous limestone**, formed 250–350 million years ago when Britain was surrounded by warm tropical seas that were rich in plant and animal life. When the plants and sea creatures died, the calcium in their shells and skeletons built up in layers on the seabed, forming limestone made of calcium carbonate.

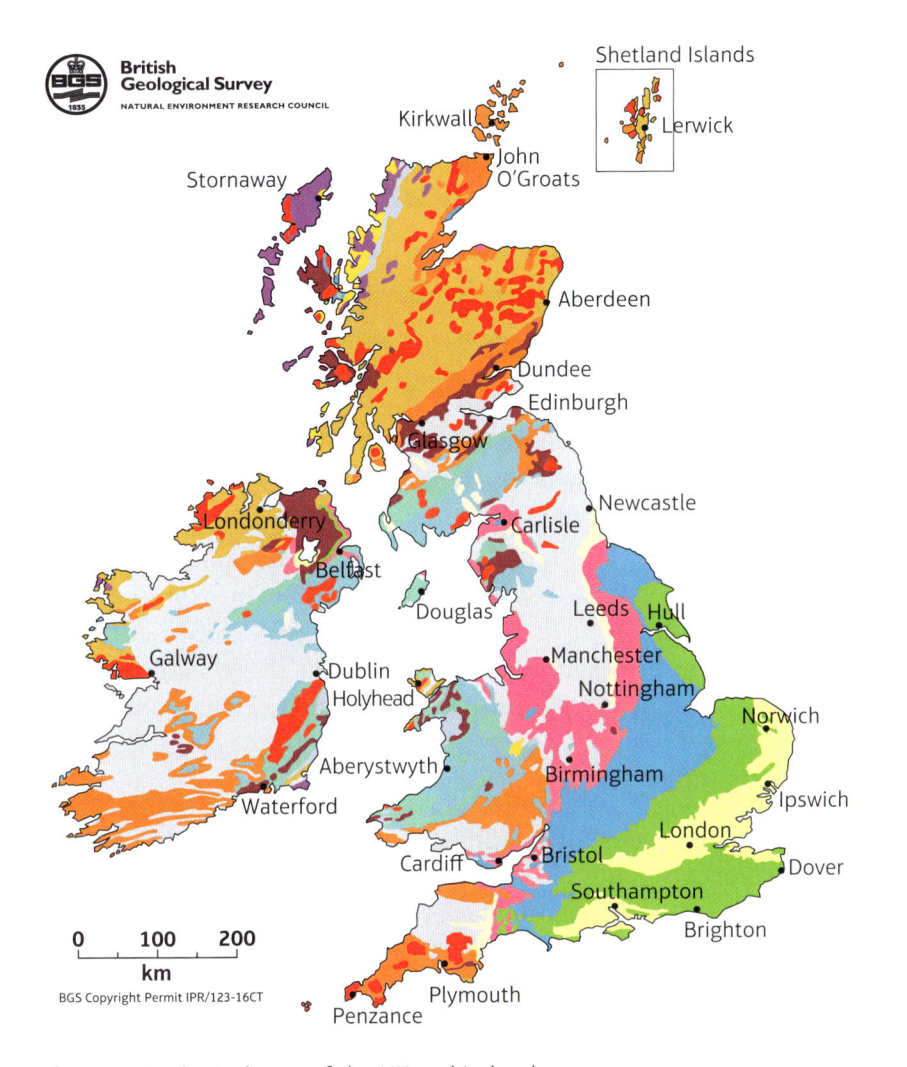

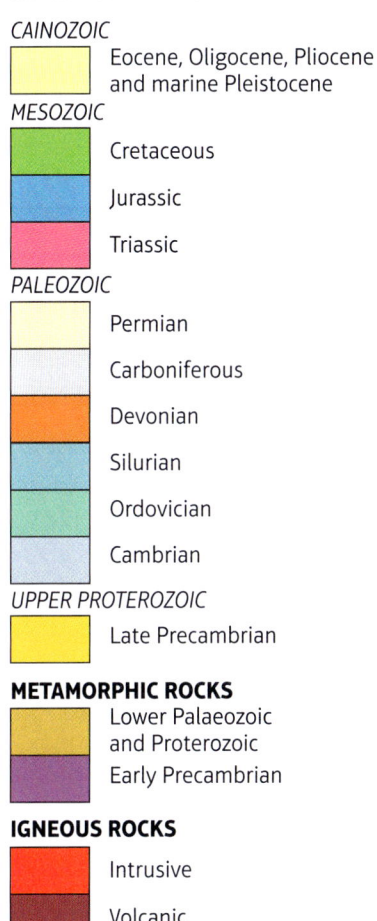

4 The UK's Evolving Physical Landscape: Overview

Figure 1 Geological map of the UK and Ireland

Key
SEDIMENTARY ROCKS
CAINOZOIC
- Eocene, Oligocene, Pliocene and marine Pleistocene

MESOZOIC
- Cretaceous
- Jurassic
- Triassic

PALEOZOIC
- Permian
- Carboniferous
- Devonian
- Silurian
- Ordovician
- Cambrian

UPPER PROTEROZOIC
- Late Precambrian

METAMORPHIC ROCKS
- Lower Palaeozoic and Proterozoic
- Early Precambrian

IGNEOUS ROCKS
- Intrusive
- Volcanic

In this topic you will investigate how weathering, slope processes, erosion and deposition by coasts and rivers shape the UK's landscapes. In the past, the Earth's climate changed constantly (see pages 16–19), including several Ice Ages when Britain was partly covered by ice. Erosion by glaciers was the dominant force in the uplands, and glacial deposition in some lowlands.

Activity

Look at Figure 1.

1. Describe the distribution of the UK's main rock types.

Tip When describing a distribution, remember to use the PQE (general Pattern, Qualifications, Exceptions) technique.

2. Copy and complete the table below.

	Sedimentary	Igneous	Metamorphic
Rock characteristics			
Rock formation			
UK locations			

Did you know?

Britain has had several glacial periods – in the coldest, ice sheets hundreds of metres thick covered the landscape as far south as London. Glaciers eroded deep U-shaped valleys between the mountains of North Wales, the Lake District and the Scottish Highlands, forming today's **relict** upland glacial landscapes. When the last Ice Age ended 11,700 years ago the ice retreated, leaving behind deposits of clay and boulders in lowland areas like East Anglia as well as the uplands.

4 The UK's Evolving Physical Landscape: Overview

How have physical processes helped create distinctive UK landscapes?

Learning objectives

- To know the location of distinctive UK upland and lowland landscapes
- To recognise the key features of distinctive upland and lowland landscapes
- To understand how distinctive upland and lowland landscapes result from the interaction of physical processes

Dartmoor is an example of an upland landscape formed when a massive dome of magma developed underground 290 million years ago. As it cooled and contracted to form granite, cracks known as **joints** developed. The presence of the weaker joints made the rock vulnerable to **freeze thaw weathering**, where the repeated freezing, expanding and thawing of water causes fragments of rocks to become detached. Over time, as the granite became exposed on the surface, erosion and mass movement processes removed the broken-up granite downhill. Blocks of rock with fewer joints are left behind, and the largest blocks are left standing. These landforms are Dartmoor's famous **tors** such as Bowerman's Nose (Figure 2), surrounded by **clitter slopes** covered in smaller rocks. The tors continue to change from the influence of freeze thaw and chemical weathering.

The Yorkshire Dales has one of the largest areas of carboniferous limestone in the UK. The impact of various physical processes on this rock has created cliffs, deep gorges, impressive valleys, beautiful waterfalls and unusual limestone pavements. One distinctive landform is Malham Cove, a high limestone cliff shaped like an amphitheatre. Over millions of years, earth movements caused the the softer rock to slip, forming the large Middle Craven Fault and creating a line of limestone cliffs. About 15,000 years ago, at the end of the last ice age, melting water from glaciers created a massive waterfall which eroded the cliff backwards to its current position. The combination of the water flowing over the cove, as well as erosion, weathering and mass movement processes, have created the curved face seen today. Along the top of Malham Cove the unique structure of the carboniferous limestone has created **limestone pavements**. The rock is made of blocks with horizontal lines (**planes**) and vertical cracks (joints). As rainwater passes through the lines of weaknesses in the rock, it causes a chemical reaction, enlarging the joints and planes. The widening and deepening of the cracks on the surface form **grykes**, exposing blocks of limestone called **clints**, and creating the pavement shown in Figure 3.

Figure 2 Bowerman's Nose

Figure 3 Limestone pavement above Malham Cove

Activity

1. Study Figure 2.
   a. Draw a series of diagrams to show the formation of Bowerman's Nose.
   b. Annotate your diagrams to explain how the tor was formed.
2. Draw a flow diagram to show how Malham Cove was formed.

4 The UK's Evolving Physical Landscape: Overview

During the last Ice Age, almost all the Yorkshire Dales were covered with ice. These glaciers eroded and transported large quantities of rocks, sand and clay. About 11,700 years ago the ice retreated, resulting in deposition and the formation of the boulder clay that covers the floors and sides of many parts of the Dales today. One example can be found near Ingleborough, where **Silurian rock** can be found lying on top of carboniferous limestone, forming an **erratic**.

The North and South Downs

Around 75 million years ago, during the **Cretaceous Period**, Britain was covered by warm, tropical seas; this resulted in the marine deposits that created the chalk foundations for the North and South Downs. Thirty million years ago, large earth movements caused the compacted layers of sediment to be forced upwards, creating a giant, chalk-covered dome (the Weald-Artois Anticline). Over time, the dome experienced erosion, which removed the chalk at the centre of the dome, leaving the two remaining chalk escarpments of the North and South Downs on either side. The South Downs escarpment consists of the **scarp slope**, which is steep, and the **dip slope**, where the slope is gentler. Between the North and South escarpments, where the chalk has been eroded, sandstone ridges (the High Weald) and gentler, clay vales (the Low Weald) have been exposed.

Activity

Study Figure 4.

1. Describe the routes of the minor roads.
2. Identify and describe the possible recreation land use shown on the map.
3. Locate the chalk escarpment.
4. Look at the contour pattern in boxes A and B. These represent the scarp slope and dip slope of the chalk escarpment.
   a. Decide which box represents the scarp slope and which box represents the dip slope. Justify your decision.
   b. Describe the contour patterns for the scarp slope and the dip slope.

Tip When looking at contour patterns, remember that the closer the lines are together, the steeper the slope.

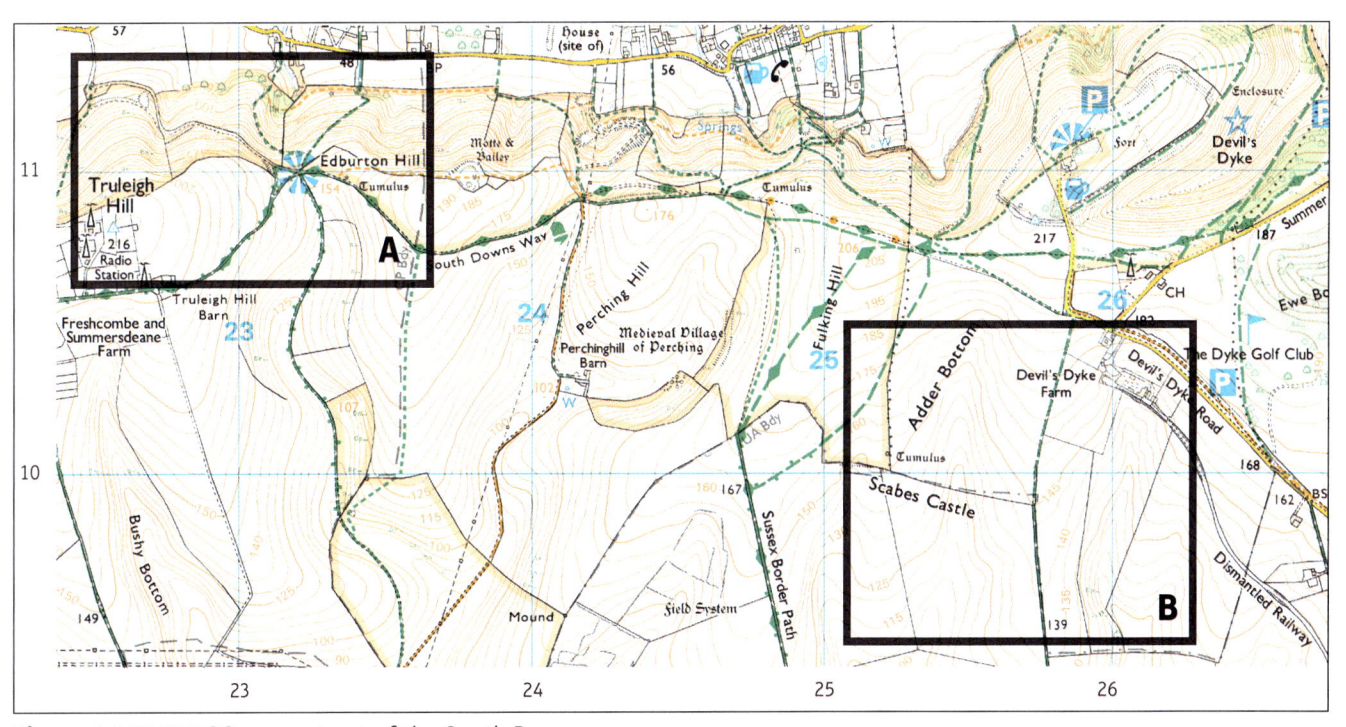

Figure 4 1:25,000 OS map extract of the South Downs

4 The UK's Evolving Physical Landscape: Overview

How has human activity helped create distinctive UK landscapes?

Learning objectives
- To know how the UK's distinctive landscapes provide resources for agricultural, forestry and settlement use
- To understand how human activities shape the UK's distinctive landscapes over time

Did you know?
The South Downs National Park is covered by approximately 5600 hectares of chalk grassland. In recent years, the chalk grassland has suffered significant loss and fragmentation. This may be because only 45% of it is designated as Sites of Special Scientific Interest (SSSI).

Exam-style question
Explain how human activities can have both positive and negative impacts on UK landscapes.
(4 marks)

Exam tip
For this type of question it is important to explain both positive and negative impacts to achieve full marks. Read the question a couple of times to be sure of what you are being asked to do.

Command word
For this question you must **explain** how the chosen human activity can have positive and negative impacts. Use the word 'because' to offer an explanation, which for this question will need to be done twice.

Agriculture
The South Downs **National Park** is an example of how distinctive landscapes result from human activity over time. Around 85% of the National Park is farmed, with approximately 1100 farm businesses operating here. Chalk grassland is ideal for grazing sheep and training racehorses because it is short and rich in nutrients, whereas clay grassland is more suitable for dairy cows because of its longer grass length. On the south-facing lower slopes of the South Downs, the deeper chalk soils are more suitable for **arable** farming, for example wheat, barley and vine **cultivation**. Farming on the South Downs has advantages and disadvantages, some of which are shown in Table 1.

Table 1 Advantages and disadvantages of farming on the South Downs

Advantages	Disadvantages
The income generated from farming supports the local economy; agricultural businesses account for approximately 6% of the employment structure in the park	The decline in arable farming and changes in farming practices have reduced the presence of arable plants, which has damaged wildlife habitats
Arable farming has contributed towards supporting rare bird species on the Downs, which include the corn bunting, grey partridge, skylark and stone curlew	The decline of traditional practices, such as extensive sheep grazing, has led to **scrub encroachment** on the remaining chalk grassland
The formation of hedgerows and field margins has provided **wildlife corridors** for bats	There has been a significant decline in chalk grassland due to the use of chemicals in farming

Figure 5 Farming in the South Downs National Park

Forestry

The South Downs National Park has a widespread mix of deciduous and coniferous woodland that covers a total of 23.8% of the park (38,420 hectares) and is a key feature of the western half of the National Park. The distribution of woodland across the National Park is uneven, with the west being significantly more wooded than the east. Human activity on woodland areas of the UK has increased, resulting in large areas being cleared. Human intervention in woodland landscapes has advantages and disadvantages (see Table 2).

Table 2 Advantages and disadvantages of forestry on the South Downs

Advantages	Disadvantages
A large percentage of the woodland that makes up the South Downs National Park is comprised of ancient trees, which provide habitats for a diverse range of wildlife	The removal of woodland for new developments is threatening some of the ancient large-leaved lime woodland. This woodland may closely resemble the post-glacial 'wildwood' that covered the South Downs some 6000 years ago
The timber harvested from the National Park woodland is a valuable sustainable product, with growing markets in construction and fuel for heating	Many of the hazel and chestnut **coppices** are no longer being managed as they traditionally were. As a result they are becoming overgrown, and this is causing a decline in the quality of the woodland and its **biodiversity**

Settlements

The chalk escarpments that make up the ridge and valley scenery of the South Downs were suitable for the development of **spring-line settlements**. The settlements were built on the naturally formed south slopes, which afforded them shelter.

The South Downs is the most populated National Park in the UK, with around 120,000 people living there. A large proportion of these people live in the major urban areas and villages that surround the National Park. The South Downs has the largest market towns of any UK National Park – Lewes, Petersfield and Midhurst. The character of these and many other settlements throughout the National Park originates from the use of local building materials.

In recent years there have been new developments in many of the settlements in the South Downs, which have not always reflected local character in terms of traditional design and materials. This has resulted in some loss of local distinctiveness. Along with the change in the local character of the buildings, many historic features have been replaced – for example, standard metal signage has taken the place of traditional wooden signage. There has also been a decline in community facilities, such as post offices, general stores, pubs or schools.

Checkpoint

Now it is time to review your understanding of how upland and lowland landscapes result from the interaction of geology, physical processes and human activity over time.

Strengthen

S1 Using Figure 1, shade the main areas of igneous and sedimentary rocks on an outline map of the UK.

S2 On your map of the UK, locate and label Dartmoor, the Yorkshire Dales and the South Downs. Add details of the geology of the three landscapes, including whether they are upland or lowland.

S3 Look at your map. What is the link between geology, tectonic processes and where the upland and lowland landscapes are situated in the UK?

Challenge

C1 Draw a diagram showing how geology and physical processes such as weathering and erosion have created the South Downs landscape.

C2 Assess the costs and benefits of human activity on the South Downs over time.

C3 Consider the possible impact of other human activities on the distinctive landscapes of Dartmoor, the Yorkshire Dales or the South Downs – for example, tourism, mining or quarrying.

4A | Coastal Change and Conflict

How do waves and geology influence the coastline?

> **Learning objectives**
> - To know how different types of waves operate in the coastal zone
> - To understand the influence of geology on coastal landforms
> - To use British Geological Survey (BGS) maps

Wave action

Waves are generated by wind blowing over the sea. Friction with the surface of the water causes ripples to form, which grow into waves. The amount of energy in waves, and therefore their ability to erode, transport or deposit material along the coast, depends on their height. The height and energy of waves are determined by wind strength, duration and the distance over which the wind has been blowing (the **fetch**). The stronger the wind and the longer the fetch, the more powerful the waves will be.

When the wave approaches a beach it starts to lose energy. The water that surges up the beach until it runs out of energy is called the **swash**. The water that then runs back down the beach under gravity is called the **backwash**.

There are two types of wave – destructive and constructive (Figure 1).

Destructive waves are formed by strong winds that have blown over long fetches. These waves are powerful and cause coastal erosion. Destructive waves are tall and steep, they are closely spaced and break frequently – typically between 11 and 15 waves per minute. The backwash is much stronger than the swash, so rocks, pebbles and sand are carried back out to sea. If beaches form, they tend to be narrow and steep and offer cliffs little in the way of protection as they cannot absorb much of the wave energy.

Constructive waves are associated with light winds and short fetches. The waves have less energy and encourage deposition. They are low in height and widely spaced, breaking gently – typically, between six and nine waves break per minute. The swash is stronger than the backwash, so more material is carried up the beach than is removed. The resulting beaches tend to be wide and shallow, and they help to protect the cliffs from erosion as the wave energy is absorbed by the beach.

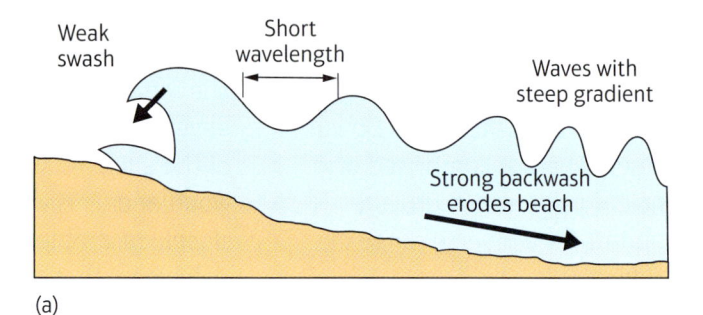

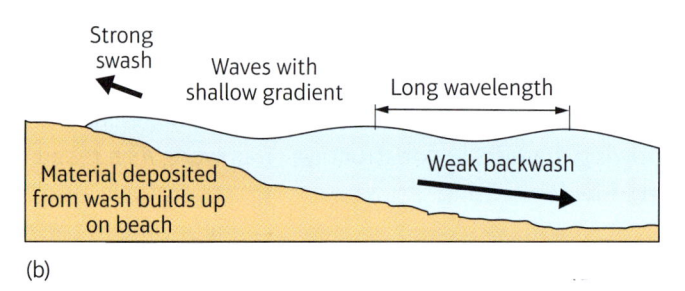

Figure 1 (a) Destructive and (b) constructive waves

> **Activity**
> 1. Create a table to compare the characteristics of destructive and constructive waves. Include formation, energy, shape, breaking characteristics and coastal impact.
> 2. Explain why constructive waves are more likely to deposit material than destructive waves.

Geological structure: concordant and discordant coasts

The UK's coastline includes distinctive landforms that are a result of wave action and physical processes interacting with the local geological structure and rock type.

The coastline around the Isle of Purbeck, part of the Dorset Coast in southern England, has different geological structures (Figure 2). The coastline from Studland to Durlston Head is an example of a

4A Coastal Change and Conflict

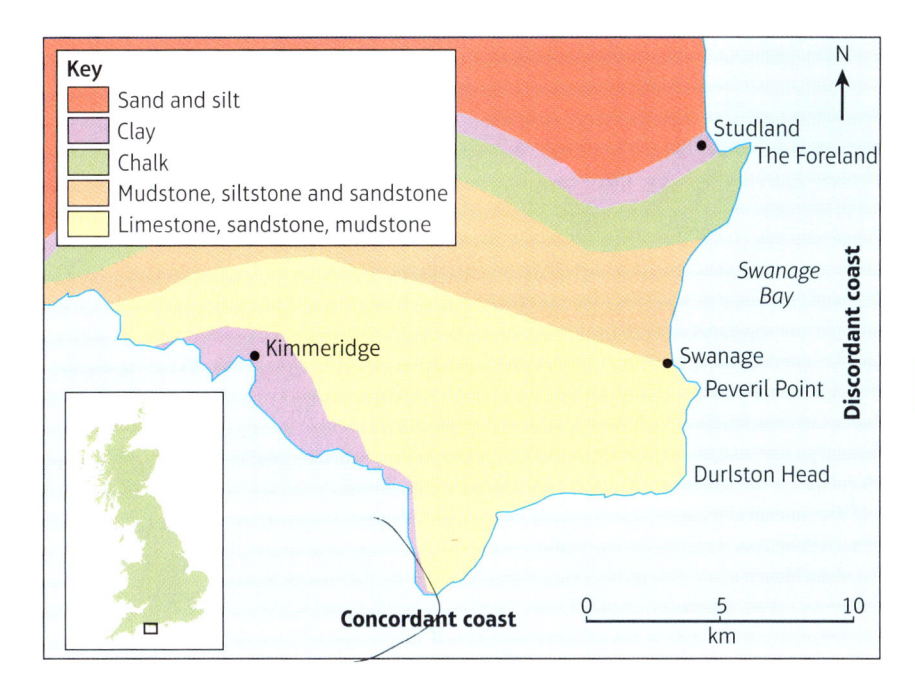

Figure 2 Map to show the geological structure of the Isle of Purbeck, Dorset

Did you know?

You can use interactive geology maps from the British Geological Survey (BGS) to support your work. Use the Geology of Britain viewer on the BGS website to find a map for anywhere in the UK.

discordant coast because bands of resistant and less resistant rocks run at right angles to the coastline. The southern coastline, from Durlston Head to Kimmeridge, is an example of a **concordant coast** because bands of resistant and less resistant rocks run parallel to the coastline.

Headlands and bays

The cliffs along a discordant coast erode at varying rates as rocks of different hardness and resistance meet the sea. The stronger or harder rocks, such as the chalk at Studland and limestone south of Swanage, are able to resist wave attacks and erosion for longer. These sections of cliff stand out as prominent rocky **headlands** – for example, The Foreland to the north (chalk) and Peveril Point to the south (limestone). The softer or weaker rocks, such as the mudstones and siltstones found at Swanage, are eroded back more quickly to form **bays** – Swanage Bay, for example.

Fewer bays and headlands are formed along concordant coastlines where the rock type is the same along its length, and so the rate of erosion is similar. If the outer rock is a more resistant rock, such as limestone, the cliffs are likely to be high and steep. The harder rock acts as a barrier, but if breached through lines of weakness, such as **faults** and **joints**, the sea is able to erode the softer rock behind. This creates a **cove** – a circular area of water with a narrow entrance from the sea (Figure 3).

Activity

1. Explain the difference between a discordant and a concordant coastline.
2. Draw a sketch of Figure 2. Using evidence from the map **and** the text:
   a. add labels to show the concordant and discordant coasts, a headland, a bay, and hard and soft rocks (naming the rock types)
   b. label and name key landscape features, including Studland and Peveril Point.
3. Draw a sketch of Figure 3, Lulworth Cove. Use the text to annotate details of how the Cove was formed, then check the BGS online viewer to add details of the geology to your work.

Figure 3 Lulworth Cove on the Dorset Coast, west of the Isle of Purbeck

135

4A Coastal Change and Conflict

What other landforms are created due to coastal erosion?

> **Learning objectives**
> - To know the different processes of erosion that change coastal landscapes
> - To know the characteristics of landforms of coastal erosion
> - To understand that parts of the UK coastline are retreating and at different rates

When waves hit a coast they can cause **erosion**. There are four erosion processes:

- **Attrition** occurs when pieces of rock material are moved by waves and knock into each other. When this happens any corners sticking out get knocked off. The material gets smaller and rounder, eventually turning into sand. Even sand grains get rounded.
- **Abrasion** occurs on a cliff, or other exposed area of rock, when waves pick up sand and pebbles and throw and scrape them against the rock surface. This wears away the rock in an action similar to sandpaper on wood.
- **Hydraulic action** occurs when large waves break against a cliff. When this happens they compress air into the cracks. When the water falls away the compressed air is suddenly released explosively, shattering the rock around the crack and making it bigger.
- **Solution** (or **corrosion**) occurs when seawater dissolves some of the rock minerals, causing the disintegration of the rock. Limestone rocks are affected the most by this process.

As well as large erosional features such as headlands and bays, there are many smaller features which are created by the combination of these erosion processes.

Caves, arches and stacks

Caves, arches and stacks often form at headlands, where the rocks are relatively hard or resistant. As destructive waves break against the headland, any lines of weakness in the rock such as joints or faults are attacked. Through hydraulic action and abrasion, the waves erode the rock along the joint or fault which will increase in size and may eventually form a **cave**.

Waves continue to erode the cave, in particular through hydraulic action. When a wave breaks, it blocks off the entrance to the cave and traps air within it. The trapped air is compressed, increasing the pressure on the sides, roof and back wall of the cave. Also, pebbles and sand trapped in the cave will be swirled around by waves causing further abrasion. If the cave forms part of a narrow headland, the pressure from the waves may result in the back of the cave being eroded through to the other side. The cave then becomes a natural **arch**, as it is open on both sides.

Continued erosion by the sea widens the arch. As the sea undercuts the base of the arch, more pressure is placed on the top of the arch. Eventually the weakened roof of the arch collapses, leaving a **stack**, a pinnacle of rock, separated from the mainland (Figure 4).

Further erosion and **weathering** over time may cause the stack to collapse to leave a small, flat **stump**, which is often covered by the sea at high tide.

> **Exam-style question**
> Explain how an arch and a stack are formed from a combination of different processes. **(4 marks)**

Figure 4 An arch and a stack in the UK

4A Coastal Change and Conflict

> **Exam tip**
>
> When answering formation questions, always name processes and explain how they operate to create the landform. Using a sketch may help, provided that it is annotated for formation.

Cliffs and wave cut platforms

Sea cliffs are the most widespread landform of coastal erosion. Cliffs begin to form when destructive waves attack the land between the **high and low water marks**. Through hydraulic action and abrasion, the waves undercut the cliff, forming a **wave cut notch**. As the notch gets deeper, the overhanging cliff above becomes increasingly unsupported and eventually collapses. Once the waves have removed the rock debris, they begin to erode and undercut the new cliff face. Through a continual sequence of wave erosion and cliff collapse, the cliff face and coastline gradually retreat inland.

A gently sloping rocky area is left at the bottom of the retreating cliff (Figure 5). This is called a **wave cut platform**. The platform is covered at high tide but exposed at low tide. Its surface is not smooth because differences in rock structure are picked out by abrasion and weathering to create a variety of grooves, rock pools and ridges within the bare rock.

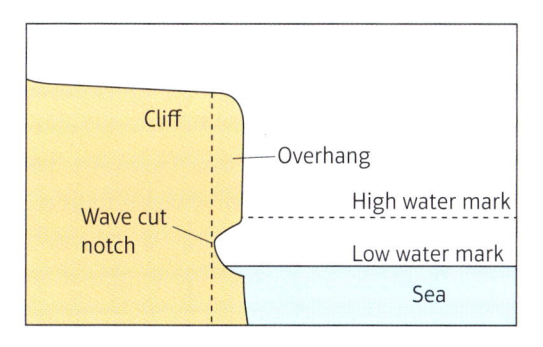

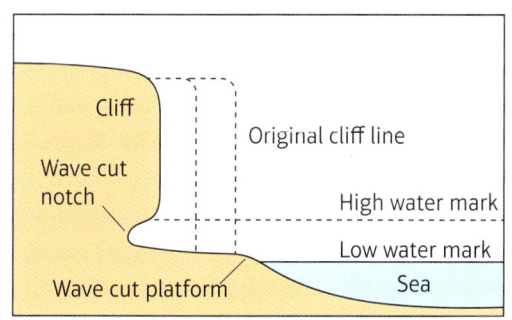

Figure 5 Formation of a wave cut notch and wave cut platform

How fast is the coast changing?

Some parts of the UK coast are eroding at a faster rate than others. Across England and Wales, about 28% of the coastline is eroding by more than 10 cm each year; in some locations, the average is much higher (Table 1). Coastal erosion is not always gradual; many metres of land may be lost in a sudden **landslip** or after a great storm (see Figure 17 on page 147), which may occur just once in five to ten years.

Table 1 Mean rates of coastal erosion

Site (cliff height)	Retreat over 10 years (metres)	Cause
Happisburgh, Norfolk (7–10 metres)	90	Failure of coastal defences
Sidestrand, Norfolk (60 metres)	20	Large, infrequent landslides
Aldbrough, Holderness, Yorkshire (17 metres)	26	Small, frequent landslides; storm damage

Activity

1. Study Figure 5. Explain why wave cut platforms are a good place for children on holiday to fish in rock pools. Why might parents worry about this?
2. Study Table 1.
   a. Calculate the mean rate of erosion per year for each location.
   b. Explain the reasons for the high amount of coastal erosion at each location.

Tip Calculate the mean rate by dividing the amount of retreat by the number of years (in this case, 10). Show your working and remember to include the unit in your result.

4A Coastal Change and Conflict

What sub-aerial processes act on the coastline?

Learning objectives
- To know the different sub-aerial processes that change coastal landscapes
- To know how climate can affect these processes
- To understand how climate and physical processes change the coastline

Different **sub-aerial** processes act on the land after waves have undercut the bottom of the cliff, weakening the cliffs and slopes above the high-water mark. These include weathering and mass movement.

Weathering is the breakdown of rocks at or near to the surface of the ground. The three key weathering processes that can affect rocks exposed at the coast are as follows.

1. **Mechanical (freeze thaw)** – in cold climates, freezing and thawing of water in cracks or holes in the rock may take place. When water freezes, it expands by about 10%, causing stresses within the rock. When the ice melts, water seeps deeper into the rock along the deepened crack. After repeated cycles of freezing and thawing, fragments of rock may break off. In warmer climates, something similar happens when salty seawater gets into cracks in the sea cliffs. As the water dries, crystals of salt form and build up. When they expand, they break up the rock.

2. **Chemical (acid rain)** – rainwater is slightly acidic (carbonic). When rain falls on rocks such as limestone, a chemical reaction takes place, causing the rock to weaken and break down when it is dissolved.

3. **Biological** – the roots of growing plants can widen cracks in cliff rocks. Burrowing animals and nesting birds on cliff faces can also cause the rock to weaken and break up.

All these processes weaken the rocks around the coastline making them vulnerable to attack by the processes of erosion.

Mass movement is the downslope movement of rocks and soil from the cliff top under the influence of gravity. The three key types of mass movement are as follows.

1. **Rock falls** – these happen suddenly when pieces of rock fall from a cliff that has been weathered or undercut (Figure 6). Often this occurs when the rock at the base of the cliff has been undercut by the action of the waves, leaving the rock above unsupported and causing it to collapse.

2. **Slumping** – this often occurs after long periods of rainfall. The rain seeps through soil and **permeable** rocks such as sandstone. At the junction where the permeable rock meets an **impermeable** rock such as clay, the saturated rock slumps and slips, often in a rotational manner along a curved surface.

3. **Sliding** – this is similar to slumping but the movement of material occurs along a flat surface, usually a **bedding plane**. Large amounts of soil and rock move downslope rapidly (Figure 7).

When rocks and soil from rock falls, slumping and sliding reach the bottom of a cliff, they build up on the beach or wave cut platform below where they are eroded by wave action.

Figure 6 Rock fall at Birling Gap, East Sussex, UK

4A Coastal Change and Conflict

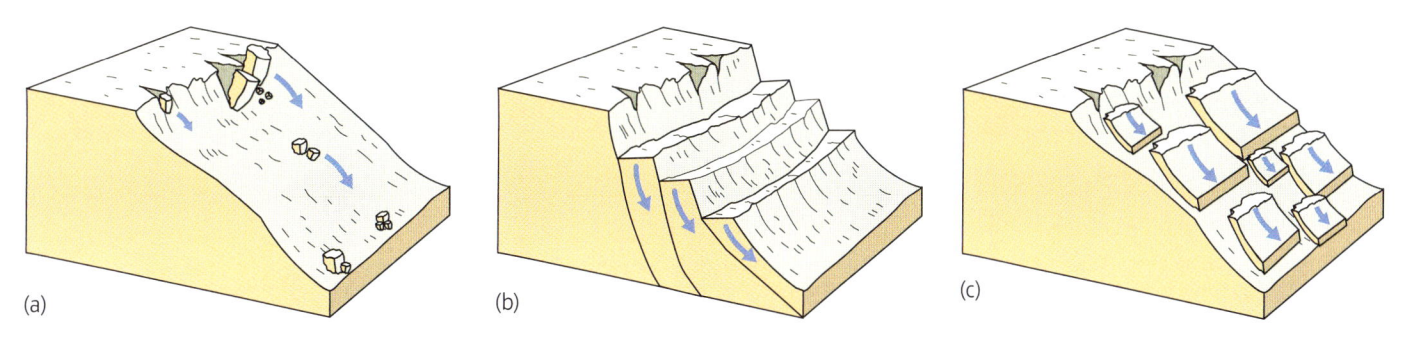

Figure 7 (a) Rock falls (b) Slumping (c) Sliding

> **Exam-style question**
> Describe **one** type of mechanical weathering that might have an impact on coastal landscapes. **(2 marks)**

> **Exam tip**
> A good answer will give the details of the process, explaining how it works.

The impact of the weather

The climate of an area will affect the type of weathering that operates on a slope and will govern the rate of erosion and mass movement. For example, heavy rain will add volume and weight to the soil, making mechanical and chemical weathering, and therefore slumping, more likely along certain parts of the coastline. The coastline of the UK can be affected by the seasons, storm frequency (see page 147) and **prevailing winds**.

The prevailing wind is the direction the wind normally blows from. In the UK, the prevailing winds are from the south-west. Some parts of the coastline are protected by the land so the prevailing wind comes from a different direction. For example, along the coast of southern England, prevailing winds are from the south-west, whereas along the east coast, they are from the north. During the winter months, low-pressure weather systems over the Atlantic Ocean create winds in excess of 150 km per hour and cause high-energy, destructive waves to form. This results in greater rates of coastal erosion in the winter than the summer months.

> **Activity**
>
> 1 There are several key words on these pages that you need to know the meaning of. Work with a partner to test each other. Which were the easiest/ most difficult to learn?
>
> 2 Draw a sketch of Figure 6 and annotate it to describe:
>   a the type of mass movement
>   b the processes acting above and below the cliff that may have assisted this movement
>   c what will happen next, and how this process will affect the coastline in the long term.

> **Checkpoint**
> Now it is time to review your understanding of the processes that change the coastal landscape, and the influence of geology.
>
> **Strengthen**
>
> **S1** Think about erosion, weathering and slope processes. How do waves influence these processes?
>
> **S2** Put these landforms of erosion in order of their formation: stack, cave, headland, arch.
>
> **S3** Why are resistant rocks also eroded?
>
> **Challenge**
>
> **C1** Explain why fewer headlands and bays are formed along concordant, rather than discordant, coastlines.
>
> **C2** Explain why there is likely to be more erosion at the coast in the winter and the type of coast that will be affected the most.
>
> **C3** Which of the processes that you have found out about do you think will have the most dramatic impact on the shape of the coast? Explain why you think this.

4A Coastal Change and Conflict

What are the influences of transportation and deposition on the coast?

Learning objectives
- To know the characteristics of landforms of coastal deposition
- To understand the role of transportation and deposition in the formation of coastal landforms
- To understand the influence of geology and wave action on coastal landforms

Transportation

Methods of transport are similar to those in a river channel (see Figure 2 on page 159): large boulders are rolled along the seabed by waves (**traction**); smaller boulders are bounced (**saltation**); sand grains are carried in **suspension**; and calcium from limestone and chalk rocks dissolves and is carried in **solution**. The transport of sand and pebbles along the coast by waves is called **longshore drift**.

Longshore drift

Waves approaching the coast move sand and pebbles. Longshore drift is the process of **transportation** which moves sand and pebbles along the coast, as waves often approach the coast at an angle. The swash carries the sand and pebbles up the beach at the same angle as the wave approaches. The backwash then draws the sediment back down the beach at right angles to the coastline, as this is the steepest gradient. The process is repeated, resulting in a 'zigzag' movement of sediment along the coast (Figure 8).

The general direction of longshore drift around the coasts of the UK is controlled by the direction of the prevailing wind which causes the most common wave direction. Along the Devon and Dorset coasts in southern England, prevailing south-westerly winds cause longshore drift movements from west to east for most of the time.

Deposition

Beaches

Beaches are formed when eroded material is transported by longshore drift and deposited by constructive waves along the coastline. Sandy beaches are often found in sheltered bays (known as bay head beaches). They are usually wider than pebble beaches and slope gently down to the sea. Pebble beaches are often found in areas where cliffs are being eroded and where there are high-energy waves. They have steep gradients.

The **profile** (cross section) of a beach is rarely smooth. At the top end, it may include a **storm beach** made up of boulders and shingle deposited by the largest waves during storm conditions. Below this, a ridge of shingle and sand, called a **berm**, marks the normal

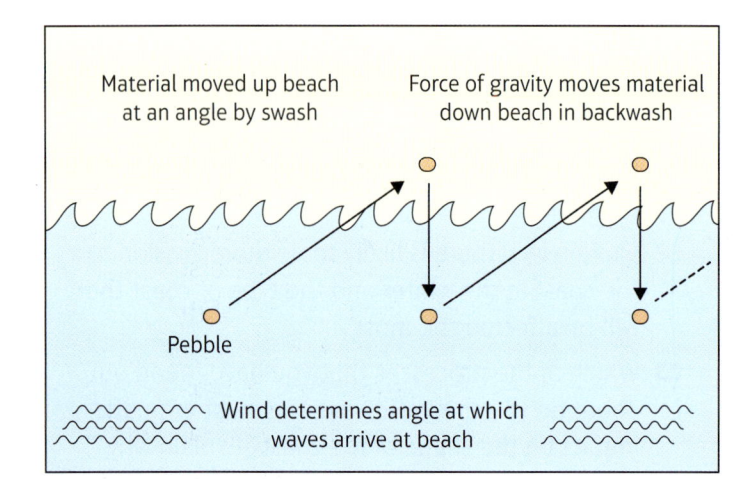

Figure 8 The process of longshore drift

high tide. A series of berms can be left by retreating tides. The smallest material (sand) is deposited near the sea.

Spits

A **spit** is a long and narrow ridge of sand or shingle, one end of which is attached to the land while the other end projects across a gap in the coastline (Figure 9). If the spit is formed of sand, sand dunes are usually found on the highest part of it. The area behind the spit is sheltered, leading to the deposition of silt and mud and the creation of a **saltmarsh**.

The formation of a spit begins in the same way as that of a beach. Material is transported along the coast by longshore drift and is deposited on the seabed where there is a bend in the coastline or a river mouth occurs. Gradually, more and more sediment is deposited, forming a ridge that extends out of the sea. Fresh water and seawater are trapped behind this ridge as it forms. As the ridge extends into deeper and more open water, the tip is affected by the wind and waves approaching from different directions. These cause the end of the spit to curve. A spit will not form completely across the gap in the coastline due to strong river and sea currents which prevent sediments settling in the deepest water.

Figure 9 An aerial photograph of Dawlish Warren sand spit, Devon

Figure 10 The bar and lagoon at Slapton Sands in South Devon

Bars

A **bar** is a ridge of sand or shingle across the entrance to a bay or river mouth. A bar begins to form in the same way as a spit. Material is transported along the coast by longshore drift and deposited where there is a bend in the coastline. Deposition then continues in a line right across the entrance to the bay or river mouth. Fresh or slightly salty water is trapped behind it to form a **lagoon**, such as at Slapton Sands in South Devon (Figure 10). As you can see in Figure 10, a road has been built along the bar to link up the two parts of the coast.

Activity

1. State one similarity and one difference between spits, bars and bay head beaches.
2. Why does longshore drift mainly move sediment from west to east along the coast of Devon and Dorset?
3. Draw a sketch of the landforms shown in Figure 10 and annotate it to:
   a. describe the landforms
   b. explain their formation.

4A Coastal Change and Conflict

How do geographers investigate coastal landscapes using OS maps?

> **Learning objectives**
> - To use four- and six-figure grid references to locate coastal features on OS maps
> - To understand that the same symbol on an OS map can be used for different landforms
> - To recognise coastal landforms and human features on OS maps at different scales.

All OS maps include a numbered grid. We use **grid references** to help locate features and places on maps:

- eastings are the vertical lines with numbers that run eastwards across the top or bottom of the map (numbered 02–06 on Figure 11)
- northings are the horizontal lines with numbers that run northwards up the side of the map (numbered 77–82 on Figure 11).

Four-figure grid references are used to give a general location by referring to the square in which a feature is located. Six-figure grid references are used to give a precise location. Always work first from west to east, before working from south to north ('along the corridor and up the stairs').

For example, in Figure 11, the four-figure grid reference for Ballard Point is 0481. The six-figure grid reference for the same feature is 048813 – it is 8/10s going east and 3/10s going north in the square.

Scale and distance

Maps come in many different **scales**. If a map has a scale of 1:50,000, this means that the map represents things 50,000 times smaller than they really are.

If a map's scale is 1:50,000, then 1 cm on the map represents 500 metres in reality, and 2 cm represents 1 km. On any scale of OS map, a grid square is always 1 km × 1 km, or 1 km².

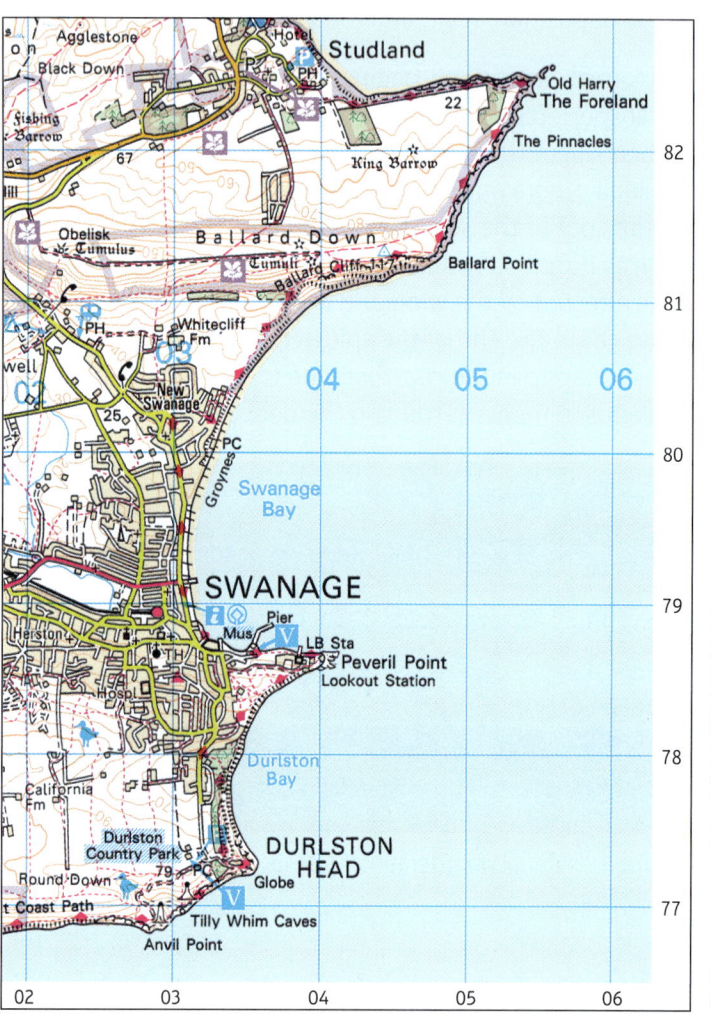

Figure 11 Extract from 1:50,000 OS map of Swanage, Dorset

> **Activity**
>
> Study Figure 11.
> - **a** Give the four-figure grid reference for The Foreland.
> - **b** Give the six-figure grid reference for Old Harry.
> - **c** Locate Swanage Bay. How wide is the entrance to the bay, from Ballard Point to Peveril Point?
>
> **Tip** To give an accurate six-figure grid reference, use a ruler to help you work out the position of the feature within a grid square. On a 1:50,000 scale map, each grid square is 2 × 2 cm, so one increment is 2 mm.

4A Coastal Change and Conflict

Figure 12 Extract from 1:25,000 OS map of Dawlish Warren, Devon

© Crown copyright 2016 OS 100030901

Activity

1. Study Figure 12. How long is the spit? Give the distance between the railway station in square 9778 and the end of the spit in square 9980.

2. Draw a sketch map of the spit in Figure 12 and annotate it to:
   a. describe the key features
   b. explain how different processes interact to produce these key features.

Tip To draw your sketch map, begin by drawing a grid of 4 cm squares to represent the grid squares on the map. You can then copy the spit accurately. Then draw the mean high water line – the bold, blue line marking the outline of the spit. Remember to add a north point, scale and title to your sketch.

3. Use map evidence to list the tourist attractions at Dawlish Warren. Classify these into natural and human.

Coastal OS map symbols

On OS maps of coastal areas, the same symbol can be used for different landforms. For example, the flat rock symbol is used for cliffs and wave cut platforms, and the sand symbol for beaches and sand dunes. To identify a coastal landform on an OS map follow these steps.

1. Find the high water mark: this is shown by a black line on 1:50,000 maps and a blue line (labelled 'Mean High Water Springs' in places) on 1:25,000 maps.

2. On which side of the high water mark is the symbol? Cliffs and sand dunes will be on the landward side; wave cut platforms and beaches will be on the seaward side.

Some landforms such as cliffs are shown using two different symbols. In Figure 11:

- a rock symbol is used to represent the vertical cliffs between The Foreland and Ballard Point
- a steep slope symbol is used to represent Ballard Cliff. This indicates that the cliff is not completely vertical – some slumping or sliding may have occurred.

Checkpoint

Now it is time to review your understanding of the processes of coastal transport and deposition and how we use OS maps to study the coastline.

Strengthen

S1 Describe the process of longshore drift.

S2 Put these landforms of deposition in order of their formation: lagoon, spit, bar, saltmarsh.

S3 What conditions are needed for coastal deposition to occur?

Challenge

C1 Compare the characteristics and profiles of a sandy beach and a pebbly beach.

C2 Study Figures 11 and 12. Identify as many coastal landforms as you can. Note down a four- or six-figure grid reference for each. Then use two different colours to categorise them into landforms of erosion and of deposition.

143

4A Coastal Change and Conflict

How do human activities influence coastal landscapes?

> **Learning objectives**
> - To know how humans use the coastline around the UK
> - To understand how human activities have direct and indirect effects on coastal landscapes and processes
> - To investigate how coastal management helps balance the needs of people and the environment

Human causes of coastal erosion and where it might impact

The coast works as a naturally interconnected and balanced system. Erosion in one place leads to the transport and deposition of sediments in another. Although much of the UK's coastal landscape is natural, large areas are impacted by human activities, often increasing the risk of coastal erosion.

The following activities have an impact on coastal landscapes, and are in turn affected by coastal processes:

- **Settlements** – over 20 million people in the UK live within the coastal zone. At Holderness, for example, over 29 villages have been lost due to coastal erosion in the past 1000 years.
- **Tourism** – coastal tourism plays a major part in local economies. For example, about 13% of jobs in Dawlish are in tourism. Structures like groynes are built to trap sand to protect areas such as tourist beaches. However, removing sediment from the system results in increased erosion further along the coast.
- **Infrastructure** – roads and railways, oil refineries, chemical plants, and ferry and shipping ports are located along the coast. In fact, the Esso oil refinery at Fawley, near Southampton, is the largest in the UK. It handles over 2000 ships a year, transporting 22 million tonnes of crude oil. Large cities and industrial areas have a high economic value leading to coastal management, often in the form of **hard-engineering** techniques. The buildings you can see in Figure 13 are protected from the sea by concrete sea walls, but this also means that the coastline is prevented from changing naturally.
- **Construction** – dredging also removes sand and gravel from the system. In 1897, over 600,000 tonnes of gravel were dredged from the sea bed to build Plymouth Docks in Devon. Soon after, wave action eroded the 5 metre high beach protecting nearby Hallsands village, which was then destroyed by storms in 1917.
- **Agriculture** – sea level rise and increased coastal erosion is already leading to the loss of farmland, and could affect the fishing industry in areas such as the Exe Estuary in Devon. Land that is used for agriculture has a low economic value and is often not protected from the natural coastal processes meaning that the coastline can develop naturally.

Figure 13 Human development along the coast

4A Coastal Change and Conflict

Case Study – The Dorset coast

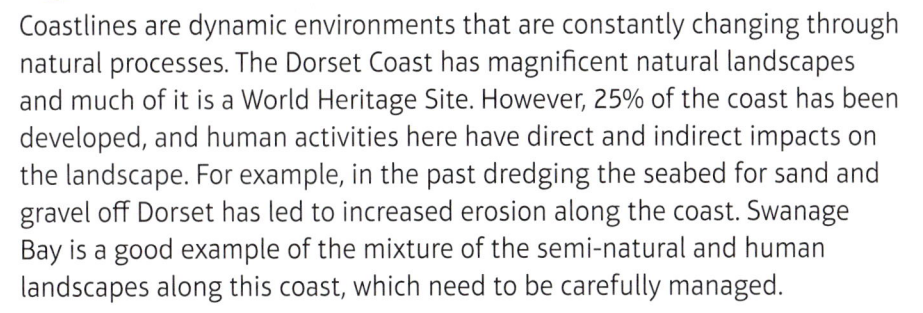

Coastlines are dynamic environments that are constantly changing through natural processes. The Dorset Coast has magnificent natural landscapes and much of it is a World Heritage Site. However, 25% of the coast has been developed, and human activities here have direct and indirect impacts on the landscape. For example, in the past dredging the seabed for sand and gravel off Dorset has led to increased erosion along the coast. Swanage Bay is a good example of the mixture of the semi-natural and human landscapes along this coast, which need to be carefully managed.

- Durston Bay is part of the World Heritage coast. Landslides and rock falls occur on its unstable cliffs, which contain internationally important fossil beds.
- About half of Swanage Bay is built up. Swanage is a residential and employment centre and an important tourist resort, centred on its wide sandy beach. Sea defences, including groynes, and a sea wall (see Figure 11, page 142) have been built to protect the beach and town.
- North of Swanage to Ballard Point and The Foreland, the beach gives way to scenic limestone cliffs, part of the World Heritage coast, which contain a range of important habitats.

Table 2 Natural and human processes in Swanage Bay

	Natural processes	Human actions
Durlston Bay	Mass movement and coastal erosion	Minimal defences
Swanage Bay south	Coastal erosion and deposition	Well defended
Swanage Bay north to Ballard Point	Some erosion of hard limestone cliffs	Unprotected

Activity

1. Draw a sketch of the aerial photo of Swanage Bay (Figure 14).
   a. use the text to annotate details of the human and natural landscapes
   b. use Table 2 to add details of natural processes and human actions.
2. Explain why the southern part of Swanage Bay is defended, but not the northern part near Ballard Point.
3. Read page 144 again. Using examples from Dorset, explain how human activities can affect the coasts directly and indirectly.

Figure 14 Aerial photograph of Swanage Bay looking north-west

4A Coastal Change and Conflict

What challenges do coastal landscapes create and how are they managed?

Learning objectives

- To know how the coast creates challenges for people
- To understand methods of managing coastal landscapes to adapt to these challenges
- To understand how decisions are made about how to management coastlines sustainably

Climate change is leading to rising sea levels and is also resulting in more frequent and more powerful storms (see Topic 1). Together they are having a significant impact on the coastline of the UK through increased marine erosion and deposition.

Many people in the UK choose to live within coastal areas because they provide economic, environmental and recreational opportunities. For some of these people, coastal erosion and the threat of flooding are real concerns. Coastal erosion removes material from the coast by wave action, causing the coastline to retreat inland. This results in loss of land and damage to buildings, roads and railways. It can also increase the risk of coastal flooding. Figure 15 shows places at greatest risk from flooding in England and Wales.

Dawlish on the South Devon coast is a place where protecting people and their properties is becoming increasingly difficult. The impact of the storms in recent years has been substantial: coastal defences breached, people's homes damaged and flooded, businesses closed, roads and railways destroyed or disrupted (Figure 16), farmland flooded, together with the psychological trauma of dealing with flooding.

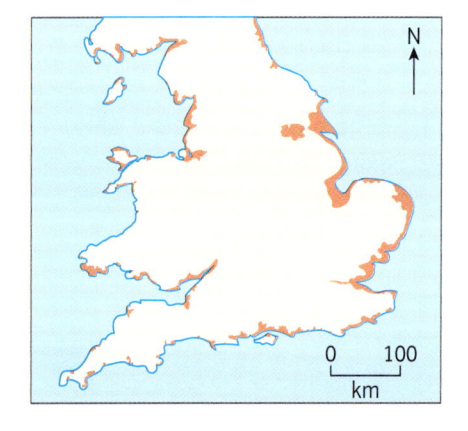

Figure 15 Places in England and Wales most at risk from coastal erosion and flooding

Did you know?

The coastline of England is 5496 km long: about 1800 km is at risk of coastal erosion, of which about 340 km is defended. In 2013, about 200 homes were thought to be at risk of being lost due to coastal erosion, increasing to about 2000 homes by 2029.

Figure 16 Waves erode the coast at Dawlish

146

4A Coastal Change and Conflict

Figure 17 Coastal erosion with active landslips as a result of storm damage at Aldbrough, Holderness, Yorkshire

Exam-style question
Coastal erosion has a number of different impacts on UK coasts. Identify one impact which is **not** the result of coastal erosion

- [ ] A It removes material by wave action.
- [ ] B It causes the coastline to retreat.
- [ ] C It causes the sea level to rise.
- [ ] D It can increase the risk of coastal flooding.

(1 mark)

Rising sea level

Sea level along the English Channel has risen by about 12 cm in the past 100 years. Levels are expected to rise by another 11–16 cm by 2030 due to **global warming**. A warmer climate causes seawater to expand and also causes the ice sheets and glaciers to melt, leading to increased sea levels as a result. The likely effects are as follows.

- Cliffs that are currently being undercut and collapsing will continue to retreat; the position of the wave cut notch and the level of the wave cut platform may change.
- Areas of 'soft' coastline (clays and gravel) may experience more erosion and retreat due to more frequent and stronger storms.

Storms and storm surges

A **storm surge** is a large-scale increase in sea level due to a storm. Onshore gale-force winds drive water towards the coastline while low air pressure allows the level of the sea to rise. In seas around the UK, storm surges can raise sea levels by 3 metres. They can last from hours to days, span hundreds of kilometres and cause significant damage and loss of life.

The North Sea storm surge of 1953 was one of the worst natural disasters to hit the UK. The storm lasted two days, flood defences were breached and coastal towns in Lincolnshire, East Anglia and Kent were devastated as seawater rushed into the streets. In England, 307 people were killed and 24,000 properties and 65,000 hectares were damaged.

In December 2013, a storm generated another major North Sea storm surge which coincided with one of the highest tides of the year and threatened the east coast in a similar manner to the 1953 event. Due to coastal defences and early warnings, major damage and flood-related deaths were avoided. In January and February 2014, a sequence of very deep depressions driven by the **jet stream** towards the UK coincided with very high winds. The resulting storm surges caused widespread coastal damage and flooding along the south coast.

Activity

1. Draw a table with the headings as shown below. Use Figures 16, 17 and the text to complete the table by thinking about the problems caused by climate change and the people it affects.

Problem	Named group of people	Impact on people

2. Explain why the risk of coastal erosion and flooding in the UK is likely to increase in this century.

Can we protect our coastline?

Planners have to find **sustainable** ways of managing the coast and minimising conflicts between people and the environment. By looking at the whole of the coastal area from the shoreline to several kilometres inland, it is easier to balance the interests of all its users and make decisions about which areas to protect, and how. This process is called **Integrated Coastal Zone Management (ICZM)**.

The Environment Agency then publishes detailed **Shoreline Management Plans (SMPs)** for each area, which help decide how coastal erosion and flood risk should be managed. The possible plan policies are as follows.

1. No intervention – no investment in defences against flooding or erosion.
2. Hold the line – maintain the existing shoreline by building defences.
3. Managed realignment – allow the shoreline to change naturally, but manage and direct the process.
4. Advance the line – build new defences on the seaward side.

In most cases the decision is to 'hold the line' – the authorities can then choose soft- or hard-engineering techniques.

Building coastal defences is expensive, so planners use **cost–benefit analysis**. This compares the economic, social and environmental costs of a 'do nothing' strategy with the costs of coastal defences. If the cost of damage and losing land to the sea is too high, then coastal protection methods will be used. However, on some coasts, people have to accept a 'do nothing' policy, because protecting the coast would be more expensive than the value of the benefits any defences would bring.

At Dawlish Warren, the SMP decision was to 'hold the line'. The coast can be protected using expensive hard-engineering techniques because the benefits of protecting the land and businesses there is greater than the cost of defences.

Figure 18 Sea wall and rip rap (rock armour) at Dawlish Warren, Devon

Hard-engineering techniques, as at Dawlish, aim to deflect or absorb the amount of energy that hits the coastline by building a barrier such as a **sea wall** or **rip rap** (Figure 18). The beach material is kept in place with wooden **groynes**. These stretch out into the sea and help to prevent longshore drift moving sediment away.

In other areas of the coast **soft-engineering** techniques are used. **Beach replenishment** at Exmouth (Figure 19) and Torcross aims to hold the line of current sea defences. Following storms, these beaches were replenished with a surplus of material from the other end of the beach. This was relatively cheap – it created a wider beach that absorbs the wave energy as it rolls up the beach, helping to prevent erosion. In some areas where beach replenishment is used, material is either dredged from off shore or is brought in from other areas making it more expensive.

Figure 19 Beach replenishment at Exmouth, Devon

4A Coastal Change and Conflict

Some coasts are undergoing managed retreat or **strategic realignment**, where there is a gradual move inland away from the coast. Here erosional processes will take their natural course and the land will be destroyed. At Man Sands in Devon, the **gabions** (rock-filled wire baskets) that were in place were taken away to allow managed retreat. First a **ley** was formed behind the beach on what used to be grazing land, attracting many birds to the area. This is developing into a saltmarsh ecosystem. This is a relatively cheap option although compensation is often paid to the owners of land or houses.

Slope stabilisation is a technique used to prevent the cliffs from slumping and reduce erosion. Drains are installed at the top of the cliff to remove groundwater, preventing the rocks from becoming saturated. Often wire mesh is placed over the cliff and piles and then long nails are sunk deep into the cliffs to hold them in place.

Table 3 The advantages and disadvantages of coastal defences

Coastal defence	Advantages	Disadvantages
Sea wall	Protects base of cliff. Made of resistant concrete. If 'recurved', reflects energy	Expensive. Restricts beach access. Unsightly
Groynes	Builds a wide beach. Beach attracts tourists	High maintenance, as wood rots. Sand prevented from moving so can cause erosion further along coast
Beach replenishment	Looks natural. Beach attracts tourists. Cheap	Material easily transported away. Replacement sediment needed regularly
Slope stabilisation	Prevents mass movement. Keeps cliff in place. Safer for people on the beach	Difficult to install. Costly

Did you know?
Sea defences are expensive – a sea wall can cost between £5000 and £10,000 per metre. Rip rap is cheaper at a cost from £2000 per metre. A wooden groyne costs £1000 per metre.

Activity
1. Working with a partner, take it in turns to suggest reasons why we should protect our coastline. Try to think of economic, social and environmental reasons. Record these on a concept map.
2. Sketch a diagram based on Figure 18. Use it to describe what is meant by rip rap and explain how it works.

Checkpoint
Now it is time to review your understanding of the risks of coastal erosion and flooding and how it can be managed.

Strengthen
S1 Give two reasons why people in the UK will be at greater risk of coastal flooding in the future.

S2 How are storms contributing to the increasing threat of coastal erosion and flooding in the UK?

S3 Is a 'no intervention' management plan ever appropriate or should all areas at risk of coastal flooding have some protection? Explain your answer.

Challenge
C1 Explain how the UK's weather and climate make it difficult to predict the likelihood of future coastal flood events.

C2 Explain how human activity may be increasing coastal erosion and the impact of coastal flooding on people and the environment.

Investigating Coastal Landscapes

Learning objectives

- To understand how to conduct a geographical investigation of coastal change and conflict
- To know how to choose enquiry questions, fieldwork methods and data sources for an investigation into coastal processes and management
- To know how to present, analyse and evaluate data collected from a coastal investigation

Figure 20 The beach at Dawlish Warren, Devon

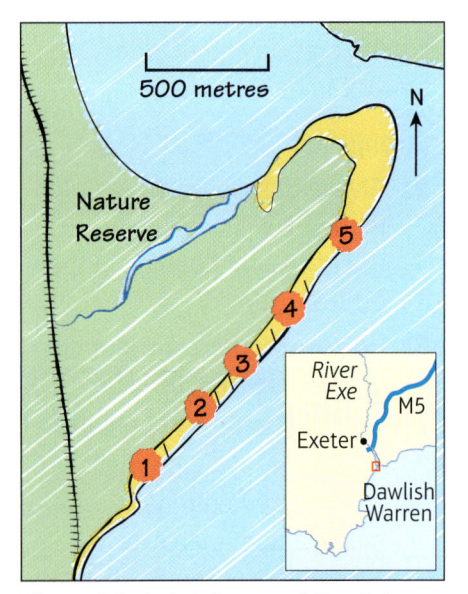

Figure 21 A sketch map of Dawlish Warren in Devon showing the sample sites

The enquiry question

When conducting a geographical enquiry, it is important to have a purpose. One way to do this is to ask a task question.

For this enquiry on coasts, the task question is:

How does management of the beach at Dawlish Warren affect coastal processes and people?

The beach at Dawlish Warren in Devon is about 2 km long and has formed on the seaward side of a spit. Prevailing wind conditions along the south coast of England mean that sediment is transported by longshore drift from the west to the east end of the spit. However, groynes have been built at regular intervals to help manage and stabilise the beach. The aim of this enquiry is to discover if the beach changes from west to east, and if this is linked to the management of the beach or to natural processes.

To help answer the task question, geographers next devise some key questions. These help to provide a focus for the enquiry.

For this task, a key question could be:

Do the groynes at Dawlish Warren affect changes in sediment size and shape further along the beach?

You might expect sediment size to decrease and roundness to increase from west to east on Dawlish Warren beach as it is transported by longshore drift. However, groynes act as sediment traps, interrupting the natural movement of material, so their presence may also influence beach sediment characteristics.

Locating the study

It is important to show the study location. Use maps at different scales, as in Figure 21. The main map shows study sites, while the inset map gives the regional location. This helps to set the scene.

As well as describing your study location, you need to explain your choice of study sites. This may depend on the data collection method(s) you choose. At Dawlish Warren, for example, study sites were chosen at regular intervals at every third groyne along the beach (Figure 21). These five sites were approximately 300 metres apart at the high tide mark. Each one was measured 5 metres to the east of the end of the groyne. This gave a representative sample along the beach and a chance to collect the samples before high tide.

Activity

1. Read the text about Dawlish Warren and study Figure 21. Create another key question that would help answer the main task question.
2. Using Figure 21 and an atlas, write an overview of the location of Dawlish Warren and the fieldwork investigation.

Investigating Coastal Landscapes

F Methodology

Once you have decided on some suitable key questions and located your investigation, the next stage is to choose the methods you will use to collect your data. Geographers use both **primary data** (data that is collected first hand) and **secondary data** (data that has already been published). In your investigation, you need a mixture of **quantitative** methods (using numbers), such as measuring the size and shape of beach sediment, and **qualitative** (descriptive) methods, such as a questionnaire or field sketch.

> **Exam tip**
>
> You need to investigate two secondary sources:
> - a geology map, such as the BGS online Geology of Britain viewer
> - one other secondary source.

For each method, it is important that you decide where and how you will collect the data and why the data collected will help to answer the overall task question. You cannot collect data from every part of the coastal area or measure every pebble on the beach, so you need to sample.

- **Random sampling** – data is collected by chance. An example might be picking up stones from the beach with your eyes closed.
- **Systematic sampling** – the locations of the sites are found at equal intervals from each other. An example might be to measure the dimensions of a pebble every 20 metres along the beach.
- **Stratified sampling** – is used when the study area has significantly different parts. An example might be measuring pebble characteristics at either end of the beach (Figure 22).

An example of how to present your methodology is shown in Table 4.

Table 4 Measuring the size and shape of sediment along a beach

Method	Outline of method	Purpose of method	Recording
Measuring the size and shape of beach sediment. Sample measurements collected at Sites 1–5. Each site is located 5 metres to the east of the end of the groyne (at the high tide mark).	At each site, we placed the quadrat down and randomly selected (eyes closed) 10 particles of sediment. Using the ruler, we measured the longest axis of each piece of sediment. We then decided what shape each piece was by comparing it to the Power's scale of roundness.	We measured sediment size and shape at five points along the beach so we could see if there was a difference between them. We used random sampling to allow an equal chance of each size of particle being selected.	We had drawn up a table in class and entered the data at the beach. We also sketched some of the sediment particles to show the different shapes.

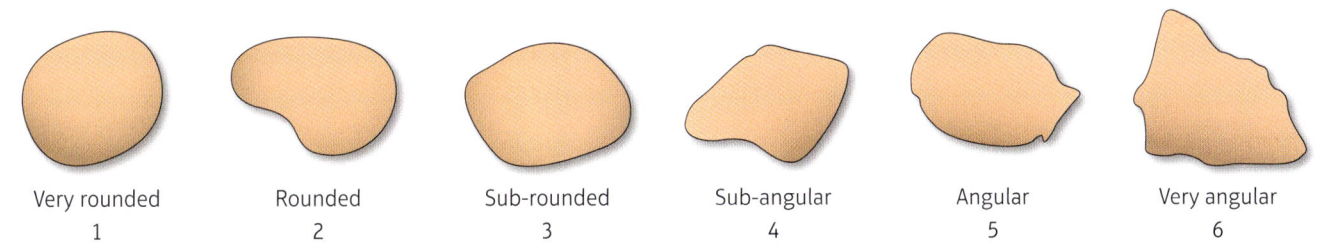

Very rounded 1   Rounded 2   Sub-rounded 3   Sub-angular 4   Angular 5   Very angular 6

Figure 22 Sediment shape using the Power's scale of roundness

F Investigating Coastal Landscapes

Did you know?
You can use interactive geology maps from the British Geological Survey (BGS) to support your fieldwork. Use the Geology of Britain viewer on the BGS website to find a map for anywhere in the UK. For weather and climate data for the UK, visit the Met Office website.

Activity
Find Dawlish Warren on the BGS online Geology of Britain viewer. Using the geology key, draw a sketch map to show the solid geology (bedrock) and superficial deposits.

Exam-style question
Study Table 6. Calculate the mean sediment size at Sites 1–5.
(1 mark)

Exam tip
Calculate the mean by adding the numbers in each column (for size) and dividing by the number of sediment samples (four).

If you are investigating different key questions, you will have to use different methods for collecting your data. These may include:

- drawing beach profiles using distance and angle measurements
- taking measurements either side of the groynes to compare sediment build up
- using field sketches and maps to record the details of coastal landforms
- conducting a questionnaire to survey the thoughts of local people about the impact of coastal processes or the effectiveness of coastal management techniques.

Risk assessment
Now that you have decided on the methods you will use to collect your data, you need to produce a risk assessment with your teacher's guidance before you collect and record your data. In your risk assessment, you should consider: the potential risks, the severity of each risk – on a scale of 0 (low) to 10 (high) – and how the risk can be managed (Table 5).

Table 5 Risk assessment

Risk	Severity rating	Management
Being swept away by waves	6/10	Only conduct fieldwork with a partner, on a falling tide and in fair weather. Stay 5 metres from the sea.

Recording data
Make sure you record the same information for each site – in this case, the site number, and the size and shape of each sediment sample. An extract of a data sheet is shown in Table 6.

Command word
When asked to **calculate** you work with numbers to solve a problem. Show your working and include the unit (for example, millimetres).

Table 6 An extract of sediment data collected by a geography student at Dawlish Warren

Sediment	Site 1 Size (mm)	Shape	Site 2 Size (mm)	Shape	Site 3 Size (mm)	Shape	Site 4 Size (mm)	Shape	Site 5 Size (mm)	Shape
1	46	3	47	2	98	3	52	1	88	4
2	24	2	55	2	56	3	96	1	77	4
3	36	2	53	1	87	4	67	3	94	3
4	63	1	68	3	82	2	106	4	90	3
Mean		2		2		3		2		3.5

Investigating Coastal Landscapes

F Data presentation

Once you have collected your data, you then need to decide how to present it. Geographers use a range of graphical techniques to present their findings. For your investigation, you should aim to produce a number of simple and sophisticated techniques. A sophisticated technique is one that uses at least two variables to represent the data, for example using a scattergraph to investigate if there is a correlation between sediment size and roundness.

Techniques that could be used to present information for the coastline at Dawlish Warren include:

- annotated photographs/field sketches – for example, to show coastal management techniques and the impact on local people
- line graphs to represent continuous data – for example, beach profiles showing a cross section of the beach on each side of a groyne, from the shoreline to the top of the beach
- bar graphs to represent group values – for example, to show the number of pebbles of different sizes along a beach
- pie charts, also to represent group values – for example, to show frequency of roundness of sediment
- GIS maps to present spatial data; these can be used with located photographs and data for different sites – for example, to show coastal conflicts, erosion and flood risk.

Presenting data on sediment characteristics

The students measured sediment size at five sites, then calculated the mean value for each site (see Table 6). Figure 23 shows an example of how the students presented their data for sediment size in a scattergraph.

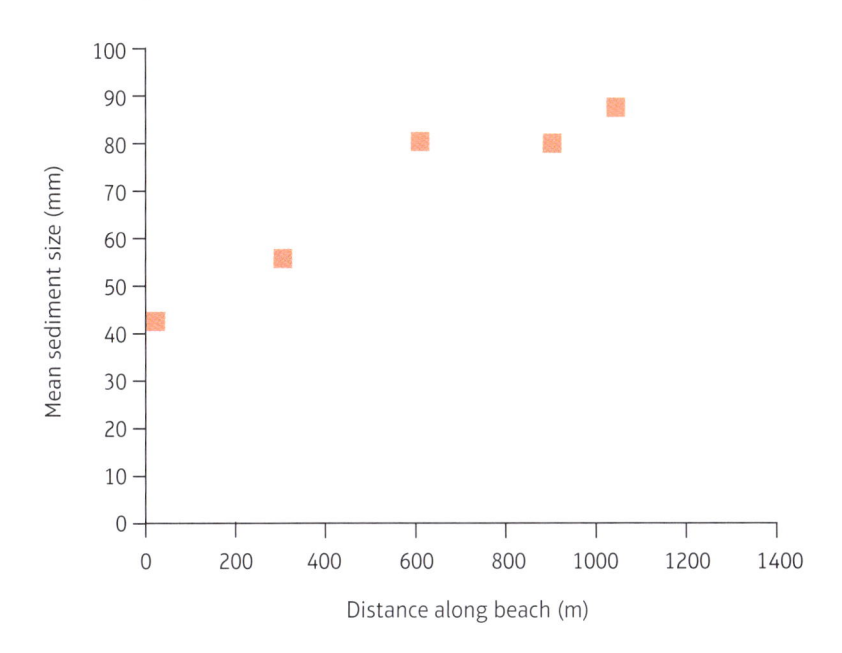

Figure 23 Scattergraph of sediment size with distance along the beach

Activity

The students decided to investigate coastal flooding at Dawlish Warren. They obtained climate data for the past three years from the Met Office and looked at the Environment Agency website for information on coastal management schemes.

a What type of data are these: primary or secondary; qualitative or quantitative?

b The students downloaded a flood map from one site. Describe one simple and one sophisticated way they could use this map in their study.

Investigating Coastal Landscapes

F Analysis and conclusions

The next stage of the enquiry is to analyse the data collected to begin answering your key questions. When analysing your data, it is important to:

- **describe** the general trends from your data – for example, 'The mean sediment size is greatest at Site 5'
- **make comparisons** using data – for example, 'Site 1 has a mean sediment size of 42.25 mm whereas at Site 5 the mean sediment size is 87.25 mm'
- **explain** the patterns of your data with links to geographical theory – for example, 'The sediment has increased in size along the beach and become more angular, which we did not expect as the direction of longshore drift is from west (Site 1) to east (Site 5). We would need to carry out another investigation to see if the groynes are affecting the results'.

Read the extract below from an analysis a student wrote about data collected at Dawlish Warren. The student gave a structured response with:

- reference to the figure and data (red)
- use of geographical terminology and theory (green)
- an explanation of their data and links to geographical theory (yellow).

> The sediment size on Dawlish Warren spit increases from Site 1 to Site 5. The scattergraph shows that this is a positive correlation. The values calculated from Table 6 show that the mean sediment size at Site 1 was 42.3 mm and increased to 87.3 mm at Site 5. This shows an overall increase in mean sediment size of 45.0 mm. This was not what we were expecting as longshore drift would usually result in smaller, rounder sediment being deposited along the beach.

Activity

1. Discuss the two paragraphs showing the student's analysis and conclusion. For **each** paragraph decide: what is good about it, how it might be improved or developed, anything that you think should be added. Justify your decisions.
2. Rewrite the **second** student paragraph with your suggested improvements.

Next you need to write a conclusion for each key question as well as the overall task question. When writing your conclusion, it is important to:

- focus on your task question and key questions: what did your investigation find out?
- summarise your findings from the data you collected and presented and link each finding to the evidence
- point out any anomalies in your data – these are results that are very different from what you expected: you might try to explain them
- refer back to any theory that related to your investigation; for coasts, you should refer to longshore drift, wave types and coastal management.

You then need to write your overall conclusion to the task question, in this case: How does management of the beach at Dawlish Warren affect coastal processes and people? Read the extract below from a conclusion written by a student.

> The purpose of my investigation was to find out if the management of the beach at Dawlish Warren affected coastal processes, such as changes to sediment, and people. I can conclude that with distance along the beach, from west to east, the sediment becomes larger and more angular. This was not the conclusion that I was expecting. It is possible that the groynes are interrupting the process of longshore drift.

F Evaluation

The final part of the enquiry is to evaluate your investigation. Here you think about how well you answered the task question or theory, and how you could improve or develop the process. The key questions below will help you review your data collection methods, results and conclusions.

- How successful and useful were your methods for sampling and collecting data? Could they be improved?
- How accurate were your results? Did your data collection methods affect the results?
- Did missing or inaccurate data make the investigation unreliable or affect your conclusions?

Activity

1. Read the students' reflections in Figure 24. Discuss which ones are about:
   a. strengths and weaknesses in the investigation
   b. the accuracy of the data
   c. missing data or the size of the sample.
2. Suggest how the data collection methods could be improved if other students repeated the study.

> When I was measuring the size of the sediment, I wasn't always sure which was the longest axis. Maybe we should have measured three axes and taken a mean.

> I found it difficult to decide where the sediment fitted on the roundness scale.

> We used 30 cm rulers – they weren't that good for measuring smaller pebbles.

> We worked on five sites on the beach. I think we should have taken samples at more sites between the groynes.

> The results weren't what I was expecting. We can't really explain the results unless we do another investigation.

Figure 24 Students' reflections on their geographical investigation of Dawlish Warren

Checkpoint

Now it is time to review your understanding of how to plan and conduct an investigation into coastal landscapes and processes.

Strengthen

S1 With a partner, note down two things you can remember about each of the following: the enquiry question, locating the study, presenting data and evaluation.

S2 Classify the following into simple and sophisticated presentation techniques: scattergraph, pie chart, bar graph, located photo, located bar graph, and explain why in each case.

S3 Explain why it is important that a student's conclusion is linked to their task question.

Challenge

C1 For random, systematic and stratified sampling, note down an example of how each could be used in a coastal investigation.

C2 Write out example(s) of the methods below, deciding if they are qualitative or quantitative, primary or secondary, and the strengths and limitations of information gained from each of them:
   a. method(s) to measure longshore drift
   b. method(s) to investigate the impact of coastal processes on local people
   c. method(s) to investigate coastal landforms
   d. method(s) to evaluate the effectiveness of coastal defences.

Preparing for your exams

Coastal Change and Conflict

The coastline is constantly changing due to the processes that act upon it. Processes of coastal erosion and deposition create distinctive and dramatic landforms. Human activities can lead to changes in coastal landscapes which affect people and the environment. Efforts to protect the coast from erosion and flooding are challenging, and are not always effective or sustainable.

Checklist

You should know:

- [ ] the physical processes at work on the coast – weathering, mass movement, erosion, transportation and deposition
- [ ] how the physical processes interact to shape coastal landscapes
- [ ] the influence of geological structure and rock type on coastal landforms
- [ ] how constructive and destructive waves shape coastal landforms
- [ ] how the UK's weather and climate affect rates of coastal erosion and retreat, and impact on landforms and landscapes
- [ ] the role of erosional processes on the development of headlands and bays, caves, arches, cliffs, stacks and wave cut platforms
- [ ] the role of depositional processes in the development of bars, beaches and spits
- [ ] how human activities have affected coastal landscapes
- [ ] the effects of coastal erosion and flooding on people and the environment
- [ ] the advantages and disadvantages of different coastal defences used on the coastline of the UK
- [ ] how hard- and soft-engineering techniques can lead to change in coastal landscapes
- [ ] how one area of coastline has been influenced by different processes to create its distinctive landscape.

Which key terms match the following definitions?

a The breakdown and decay of rock by natural processes acting on rocks, on cliffs and valley sides.

b The type of coast where the rock type runs parallel to the coastline.

c Direction in which the wind blows most frequently.

d A ridge of sand or shingle deposited by the sea. It is attached to the land at one end but ends in a bay or river mouth.

e The distance a wave has travelled towards the coastline over open water – the longer the distance, the more powerful the wave.

f A flat area of rock at the bottom of cliffs seen at low tide.

g The movement of material along the beach transported by wave action.

h An isolated column of rock, standing just off the coast that was once attached to the land.

i Flood defences that work with natural processes to reduce the risk and impact of coastal or river flooding.

j A gently breaking wave with a strong swash and weak backwash.

k A wooden barrier built at right angles to the coast, used to break waves and reduce the movement of sediment along the coast.

To check your answers, look at the Glossary on pages 302–311.

Preparing for your exams

Coastal Change and Conflict

Question 1 Beach replenishment is one type of soft engineering. Explain why beach replenishment can have advantages and disadvantages in protecting the coastline. *(4 marks)*

Student answer

Beach replenishment is where sand or shingle is added to a beach which has been eroded by waves. The main advantage is this is a quick way to restore a beach and help protect the coast behind from more erosion. Another advantage is it looks natural so it is popular for tourist beaches. However a major disadvantage is if the beach was already being eroded the new sand will soon be eroded too so it will start all over again.

Verdict

The answer gives a concise definition of what beach replenishment is. It clearly explains two advantages, but gives only one disadvantage so would be unlikely to get full marks.

Exam tip

When you are asked to explain something, try to use geographical language and be concise but accurate. The mark allocation here suggests students' answers should include two advantages and two disadvantages.

Question 2 Explain the coastal processes that lead to the formation of a spit. *(4 marks)*

Student answer

The spit at Dawlish Warren has been formed due to the process of longshore drift. The prevailing wind is from the south-west, which means that the waves hit the south-facing coast at an angle. This pushes the sediment up the beach in the swash. The material then comes back down the beach at right angles in the backwash. This is due to gravity. This zigzag movement of material along the beach will create a spit which has a curved end with a saltmarsh behind it.

Verdict

The student has referred to the prevailing wind and a process (longshore drift), used correct geographical terms and a named example. However, they have mainly focused on longshore drift and have not linked this process to the formation of the spit, which is what the question asks for.

Exam tip

When writing about processes relating to the formation of a feature, link each process back to the feature. To answer this question fully, you need to write about deposition at the point where the coastline changes direction. At Dawlish Warren, this is due to the River Exe estuary, where longshore drift continues along the previous direction of the coast, building up deposited materials in the open sea. You then need to explain why the spit has a curved end and has not progressed all the way across the estuary. Finally, you could explain why there is a saltmarsh behind.

Pearson Education Ltd accepts no responsibility whatsoever for the accuracy or method of working in the answers given.

4B | River Processes and Pressures

Why is there a variety of river landscapes in the UK?

> **Learning objectives**
> - To know the different processes that change river landscapes
> - To understand the main processes operating in river channels
> - To understand how erosion, transport and deposition interact to form a number of distinctive river landforms

Watershed
The boundary of a drainage basin separates one drainage basin from another and is usually high land, such as hills and ridges.

Tributary
A stream or small river that joins a larger stream or river

Figure 1 The drainage basin

Source
The starting point of a stream or river, often a spring or lake

Confluence
A point where two streams or rivers meet

Mouth
The point where a river leaves its drainage basin and flows into the sea

A **drainage basin** is the area of land drained by a river and its **tributaries**. When it rains, much of the water usually finds its way into rivers eventually, either by moving across the surface or by going underground and moving through the soil or the rock beneath.

Figure 1 shows the location and definition of the key features of a drainage basin.

The impact of processes on river landscapes

Different processes in the drainage basin act together to change the river landscape.

Weathering is the breakdown and decay of rock by natural processes, usually acting on the river valley sides. There are the three key weathering processes that can affect river valleys.

1. **Physical (freeze thaw)** – this happens when rainwater enters cracks or gaps in the rock and then freezes if temperatures drop below zero. The water expands as it turns into ice and then exerts pressure on the rock, causing it to break into smaller pieces.

2. **Chemical (acid rain)** – all rain is slightly acidic. If the air is polluted by factories and vehicles, it can become more acidic. When rain falls on rocks, the acid in it can react with weak minerals, causing them to dissolve and the rock to decay.

3. **Biological weathering** – the roots of plants, especially trees, can grow into cracks in a rock and split the rock apart.

Mass movement is the downslope movement of material due to gravity. The extent of the movement will depend on how steep the slope is, the speed at which the rock and sediment move and how much water is present. Here are two of the main types of mass movement that may affect river valleys.

1 **Soil creep** – this is where individual particles of soil move slowly down a slope under the force of gravity and collect at the bottom of the valley sides. The river may then erode this material.
2 **Slumping** – this happens when the bottom of a valley side is eroded by the river. The slope becomes steeper and the material above slides downwards, rotating as it does so. The movement is often triggered by periods of heavy rain, which saturate the overlying rock, making it heavy and liable to slide.

River erosion involves the action of water wearing away the rocks and soils on the valley bottom and sides. Rivers have most energy for eroding and transporting **sediment** when there is a large amount of water and there is a steep **gradient**. There are four key erosion processes that can affect river valleys.

1 **Hydraulic action** – this results from the sheer force of the water hitting the river bed and banks and wearing them away. This action is particularly important during high-**velocity** flows.
2 **Abrasion** – this is caused by material carried in the river rubbing against the bed and banks of the channel, so wearing them away. Overall, abrasion causes most erosion.
3 **Solution** – river water is slightly acidic, so it can dissolve some rocks and minerals in contact with the river. Limestone and chalk are most affected.
4 **Attrition** – sediment particles carried in the river collide with each other, causing the edges to be knocked off. The continued collision of particles in the river causes them to become rounder and smaller downstream.

Transportation of load in a river

A river picks up and carries material as it flows downstream. The four types of **transportation** processes are shown in Figure 2.

Deposition

When a river no longer has enough energy to carry its load, **deposition** occurs. As the river's **discharge** reduces, the heaviest material is deposited first, for example after flooding.

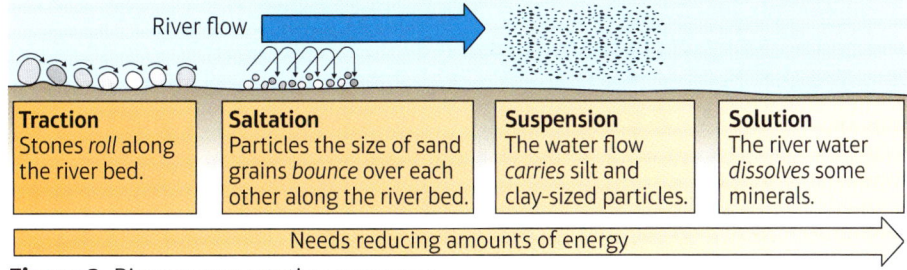

Traction	Saltation	Suspension	Solution
Stones *roll* along the river bed.	Particles the size of sand grains *bounce* over each other along the river bed.	The water flow *carries* silt and clay-sized particles.	The river water *dissolves* some minerals.

Needs reducing amounts of energy →

Figure 2 River transportation processes

Activity

Create a mind map to represent the physical processes that cause changes to river landscapes. On your mind map, include:

a the definition of each physical process with a suitable drawing
b an explanation for how each physical process will cause a river landscape to change.

Tip When creating your mind map, use a colour code to represent erosion, weathering and mass movement processes.

4B River Processes and Pressures

Figure 3 Interlocking spurs in the upper course of a river

Exam-style question

Explain how waterfalls are formed from the interaction of different processes. **(4 marks)**

Exam tip

'Formation' questions (like the one above) ask you to explain how the processes lead to the landform. Including an **annotated** sketch can be a useful way to show the order of processes.

How do river processes form distinctive landforms?

Interlocking spurs

Near their **source**, rivers are small, they do not have a lot of power and they mainly erode downwards. So they tend to flow around valley side slopes, called spurs. The spurs are left interlocking, with those from one side of the valley overlapping with the spurs from the other side. You can see these **interlocking spurs** labelled in Figure 3.

Waterfalls

A waterfall is formed along a river when a band of hard, more resistant rock lies over a band of soft, less resistant rock. The river erodes the less resistant rock at a faster rate, gradually undercutting the more resistant rock. The continued erosion of the soft rock by abrasion and hydraulic action causes an overhang of the hard rock. Eventually, the hard rock cannot support its own weight and collapses under the force of gravity. The force of the falling water and abrasion by large, angular boulders leads to erosion of the river bed and the formation of a **plunge pool**. As the soft rock continues to be eroded and the hard rock collapses, a steep-sided **gorge** is formed as the waterfall retreats upstream. Gorges form in hard rocks, where **vertical erosion** by rivers is dominant.

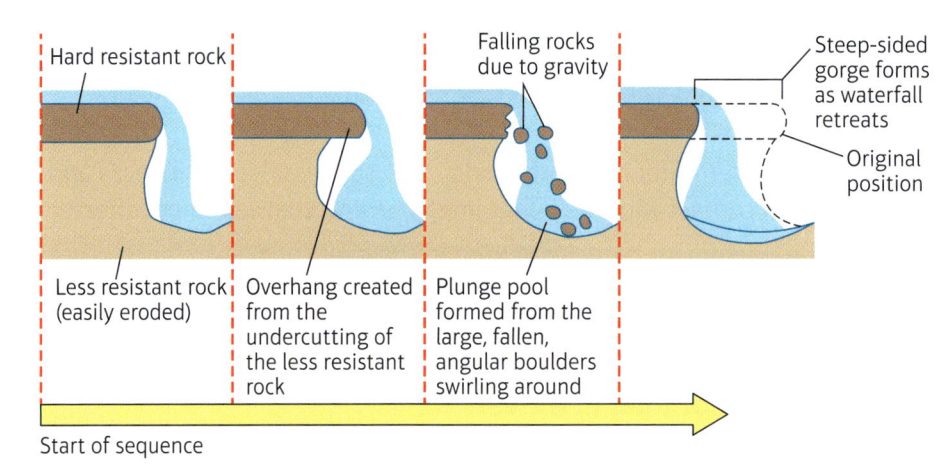

Figure 4 The stages in the formation of a waterfall

Meanders

Meanders are bends in a river's course, commonly found on a river's **flood plain**. The flow of the water swings from side to side, directing the line of maximum velocity and the force of the water towards the outside of the bend. This results in **lateral erosion** by undercutting and an outer, steep bank is formed. This is called a **river cliff**. On the inside of the bend the velocity and force of the water is less, leading to deposition and the formation of a gently sloping bank, known as a **slip-off slope**. The material deposited is called a **point bar** and is characteristically curved in shape. Due to erosion and deposition, the **cross section** of a meander is asymmetrical – steep on the outside of the bend, gentle on the inside.

Figure 5 A meander on the River Severn at Leighton, Shropshire

Oxbow lakes

As a meander bends and develops, its **neck** becomes narrower. Eventually the river may erode right through the neck, especially during a flood. Water then flows through the new, straight channel and the old bend is abandoned by the river. Deposition at the neck seals off the bend, which gradually begins to dry up, leaving behind a horseshoe-shaped lake, called an **oxbow lake**, as shown in Figure 6.

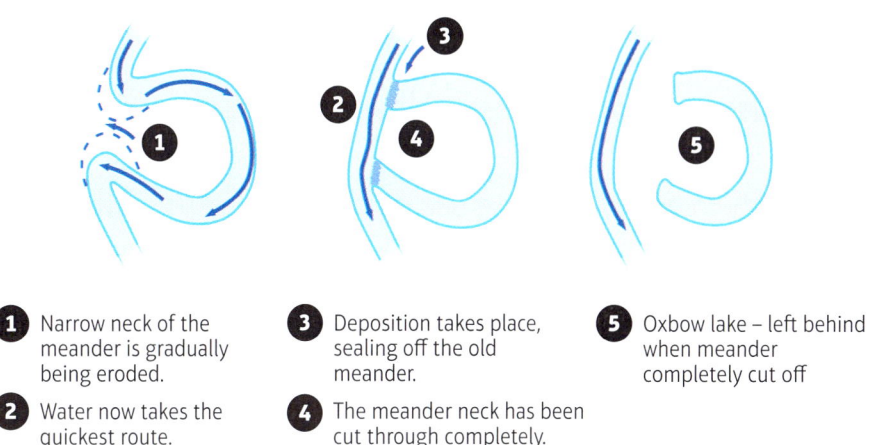

1. Narrow neck of the meander is gradually being eroded.
2. Water now takes the quickest route.
3. Deposition takes place, sealing off the old meander.
4. The meander neck has been cut through completely.
5. Oxbow lake – left behind when meander completely cut off

Figure 6 Formation of an oxbow lake

Flood plains

A flood plain is the flat area of land either side of a river, especially in its lower course. It is formed by erosion and deposition. Lateral erosion on the outside bends of meanders means they **migrate** across the valley floor and can erode the valley sides, so the valley floor becomes wide and flat. During floods, the flood waters spread out across the valley floor. As they slow down, with less energy for transport, the river deposits fine sediments called **alluvium**.

Levees

Levees are natural embankments of sediment formed along the banks of rivers that carry a large load and occasionally flood. In times of flood, water and sediment come out of the channel as the river overflows its banks. As it overflows, the river immediately loses velocity and energy and deposits the larger and heavier sediment first, on its banks. Repeated flooding causes these banks to get higher, forming levees.

Deltas

When a river reaches another body of water, such as an ocean, it loses velocity and deposits sediment. If the river deposits sediment faster than coastal processes erode it, sediment builds up in layers in a fan-shaped **delta**. The river splits into many smaller channels called **distributaries** and creates large areas of wetlands.

Activity

Study Figure 5.

1. Draw a sketch of a meander bend shown in Figure 5. On your sketch label the key geographical features, for example river cliff and slip-off slope.
2. Annotate your sketch to:
   a. describe the key geographical features
   b. explain how different processes interact to produce these key features.

Checkpoint

Now it is time to review your understanding of the physical processes that change river landscapes, and how they interact to create river landforms.

Strengthen

S1 Think about weathering, slope processes and erosion. Which of these involve movement? Which happen mainly on valley sides?

S2 Put these river processes in the right order: deposition, erosion, transportation.

Challenge

C1 Summarise the formation of a flood plain in no more than 125 words. You must include the following: a full sequence describing the formation, key features, named processes and an explanation. Underline in a different colour where you have explained.

C2 Classify the landforms on pages 160–161 into those formed mainly by erosion, mainly by deposition, or by both.

4B River Processes and Pressures

How do climate, geology and slope processes affect different river landscapes?

Learning objectives
- To know the key contrasts between landscapes in different parts of a river valley
- To understand the changes in river processes between its upper, middle and lower course
- To understand how climate, geology and slope processes affect sediment load

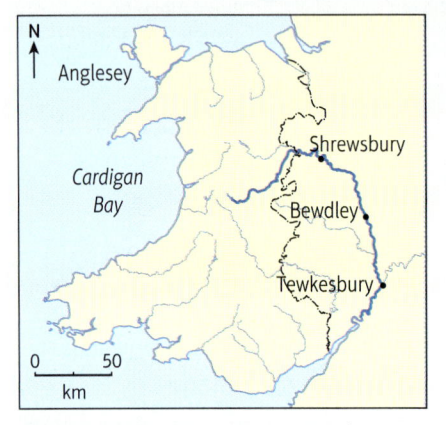

Figure 7 The River Severn catchment

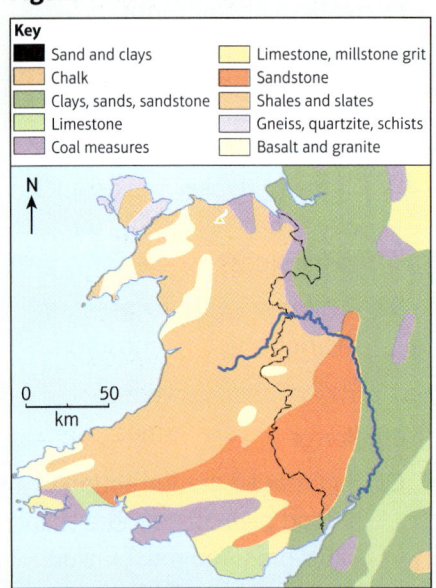

Figure 8 Simplified geology map of the River Severn catchment

Key:
- Sand and clays
- Chalk
- Clays, sands, sandstone
- Limestone
- Coal measures
- Limestone, millstone grit
- Sandstone
- Shales and slates
- Gneiss, quartzite, schists
- Basalt and granite

Did you know?
The River Severn is the longest UK river, at 354 km long, including its **estuary**. With its large drainage basin and many tributaries, the Severn has the biggest UK discharge, reaching 107 cumecs near Gloucester.

Geographers divide a river and its valley into the upper, middle and lower course. A river's **long profile** shows the height and distance downstream from the river's source to its **mouth**. It is a curved shape, steeper near the source and flatter near the mouth.

The upper course
The source of the River Severn is on the slopes of Plynlimon, 610 metres above sea level. Here in the Welsh Mountains the average annual rainfall exceeds 2500 mm and **runoff** is high from the steep upland slopes. The geology is mainly hard, impermeable shales and grits. Near the source, the channel is narrow, shallow and full of angular stones, so friction with the bed and banks slows the river down. In the upper course the river mainly erodes vertically, cutting down into the landscape and forming a **V-shaped valley** with steep slopes, where processes such as soil creep and mass movement are active.

The middle course
As the Severn leaves its upland area and flows downstream towards Shrewsbury, the climate changes, with average annual rainfall under 700 mm in the rest of the catchment. The rocks are softer and more permeable including sandstones, conglomerates and marls covered in sands and gravels. The river channel is wider and deeper. As well as eroding downwards, the river erodes sideways through lateral erosion, so the valley becomes wider and flatter, creating areas of flood plain. There is also deposition by the river, for example on the inside bends of meanders and on the flood plain during flooding. Sooner or later the sediments will be eroded by the river again, so they become smaller and more rounded, and transported further downstream. As more tributaries join the River Severn, its discharge increases.

The lower course
In the lower Severn valley the geology is mainly soft mudstones and lias, covered with alluvium, sands and gravels. The river channel widens: by the time it reaches Tewkesbury it is 70 metres wide. Because the channel is wide, deep and smooth, there is less friction with the river bed and banks, and so the river's velocity is greatest. Major tributaries increase the river's discharge still more. Lateral erosion and transportation continue, and the muddy river water shows its **sediment load** is high. This encourages deposition, for example at the river mouth where the flow is checked by the sea.

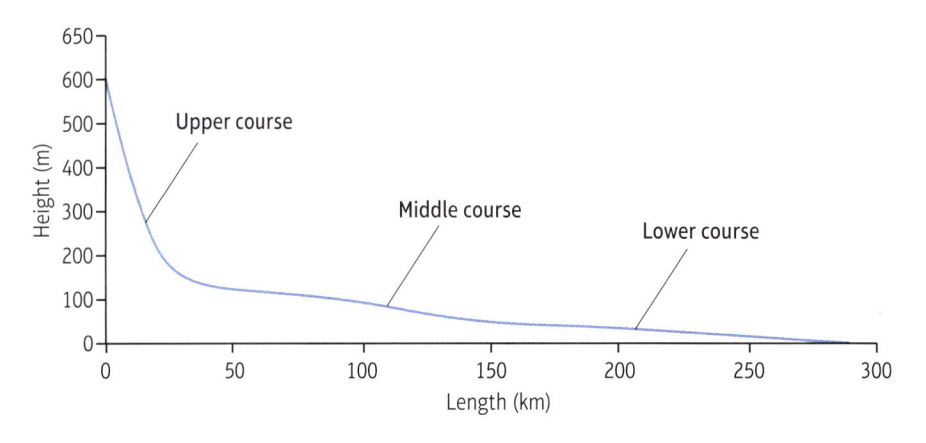

Figure 9 The long profile of the River Severn

Most rivers change in a similar way as they flow from source to mouth. Table 1 shows how different characteristics of a typical river change downstream: we can use this as a model to compare with rivers in real life.

Table 1 Changes in the long profile of a river: Bradshaw's Model

Characteristic	Definition	Change from source to mouth
Width	The distance from one bank to the other	Increases
Depth	The distance from the surface of the water to the river bed	Increases
Velocity	How fast the water is flowing	Increases
Discharge	The volume and speed at which water flows through the river channel	Increases
Gradient	The steepness of the river bed	Decreases
Channel roughness	How rough the river's bed and banks are	Becomes smoother, so less friction
Sediment size and shape	The material (sediment, debris) carried by the river	Becomes smaller and rounder

Activity

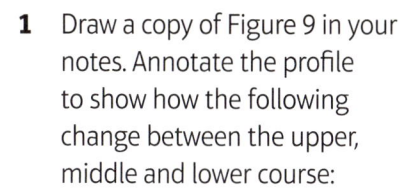

1 Draw a copy of Figure 9 in your notes. Annotate the profile to show how the following change between the upper, middle and lower course:
   a the gradient of the river channel and valley
   b the width and depth of the river channel
   c the shape and width of the river valley
   d erosion and deposition.

2 Read the text on pages 160–161. Add details of the river landforms you would expect to find in each part of a river valley.

3 Draw a sketch map of the River Severn catchment (Figure 7). Annotate your sketch map with details of:
   a differences in geology in the River Severn valley
   b differences in climate: you could check your atlas for more detail
   c where valley slopes are steepest, and slope processes are most active.

4 Study Table 1 and the text. **Explain** why the River Severn's velocity and discharge increase downstream from the source to the mouth.

Command word

When asked to **explain** a pattern or process you should give the reasons why something occurs. Here you should give details from the text and diagrams, for example about the geology.

4B River Processes and Pressures

How do OS maps help geographers investigate river landscapes?

Learning objectives

- To recognise river landforms on OS maps at different scales
- To understand that contour patterns show heights and slopes in the landscape
- To be able to draw contour cross sections from OS maps

Activity

Study Figures 10 and 11.

Choose one grid square from **each** map that includes the river. Draw squares with sides 50 mm in your notes, then sketch the course of the river channel across each.

a Decide whether the maps are of the upper, middle or lower course. Write a title for each sketch map including this information and its location.

b Annotate details about the river channel, for example its width and shape as it flows through the river valley.

c Look back to pages 160–161, then use map evidence to identify landforms in each part of the Severn Valley. List these with grid references, or label them on your sketch maps.

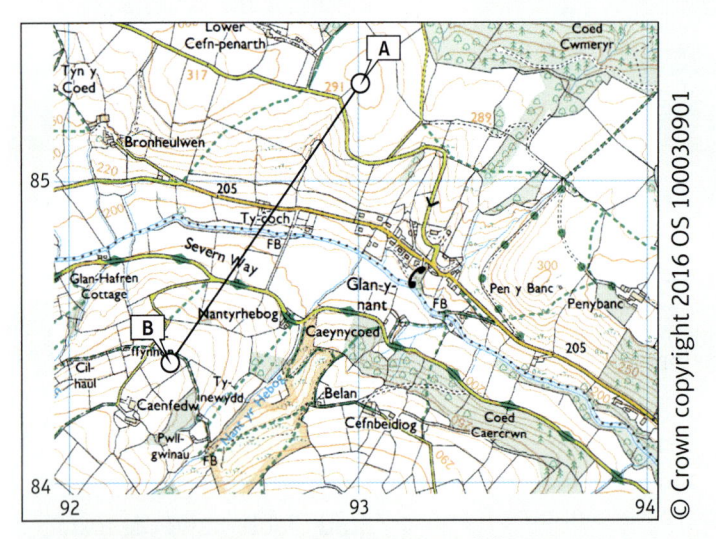

Figure 10 Extract from 1:25,000 OS map of the River Severn west of Llanidloes, Powys

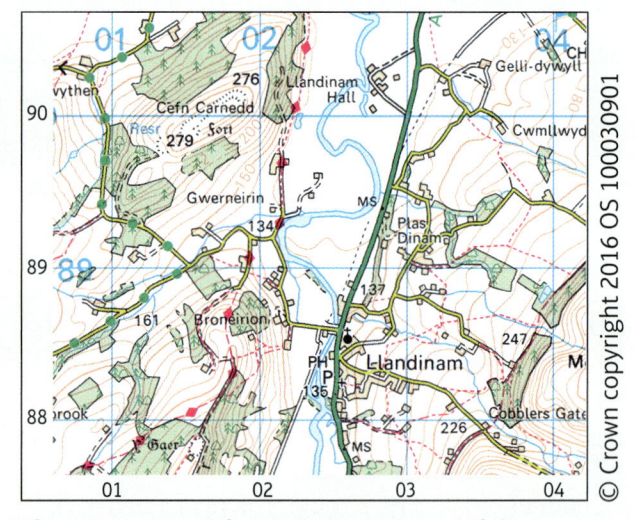

Figure 11 Extract from 1:50,000 OS map of the River Severn near Newtown, Powys

Exam tip

If you check the maps carefully, this type of question is usually straightforward, but watch out for choices which are nearly correct, but not quite right.

Exam-style question

Study Figures 10 and 11. Which of the following is the best description of the River Severn on **each** map?

- ☐ A   A mountain stream near its source
- ☐ B   A river meandering across its flood plain
- ☐ C   A river flowing through a steep-sided valley
- ☐ D   A lowland river close to its mouth

(2 marks)

4B River Processes and Pressures

How to draw a contour cross section

Contours are lines on a map joining places of equal height above sea level. They also tell us how much the land slopes:

- contours that are close together on the map show where the land slopes steeply
- contours further apart on the map show gentle slopes
- areas with few contours, or none at all, are flat: there is little or no gradient.

Drawing a cross section through the contour lines shows what the landscape looks like.

1. Choose where you are going to make your cross section. Place a strip of paper across the contour lines on the map.
2. Mark on the strip of paper each place where a contour line crosses it. Label the heights of the contours on your paper.
3. Make the horizontal axis the same length as your strip of paper.
4. The vertical axis is the height of the land from the lowest point to the highest point on the cross section.
5. Use the information on your strip of paper to plot the heights on the graph paper.
6. Join the dots and label some of the landscape features.

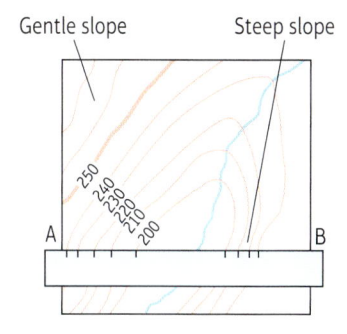

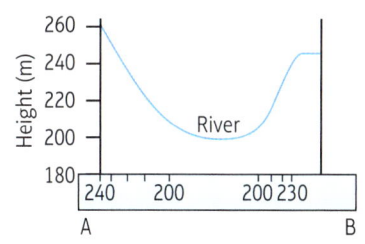

Figure 12 How to draw a contour cross section

Activity

1. Read the information about contours and then look again at Figures 10 and 11.
   a. Find areas of flat land, gentle slopes and steep slopes on the two maps.
   b. Find areas of steep slopes, gentle slopes and flatter land on the two maps.
2. Read how to draw a cross section.
   a. Draw a contour cross section between points A and B on Figure 10. Annotate details of the valley height and slopes, and the river channel.
   b. Choose and draw a cross section of a contrasting part of the river valley from Figure 11, and add similar details.
   c. Write a paragraph **comparing** the two contour cross sections, and what they show about different parts of the Severn Valley.

Command word

When asked to **compare** two things you need to identify what is similar and different about both of them in two statements.

Checkpoint

Now it is time to review your understanding of landscapes and processes in different places along the long profile of the river.

Strengthen

S1 Describe the shape of a typical long profile of a river.

S2 Describe the differences in contour patterns you would expect to see on an OS map of the upper and middle course of a river.

Challenge

C1 Match these river landforms with the section(s) of a river's course where they are most likely to appear: delta, levee, flood plain, interlocking spurs, meander, oxbow lake.

C2 Think about the geology of the Severn catchment, river and valley processes, and the idea of sediment load. Explain why the river is usually clear near the source but muddy near the mouth.

4B River Processes and Pressures

How do physical factors and human activities affect storm hydrographs?

Learning objectives
- To know the features of different types of storm hydrograph and be able to interpret them
- To know how to construct a hydrograph and calculate the lag time
- To understand how a range of physical factors and human activities affect storm hydrographs

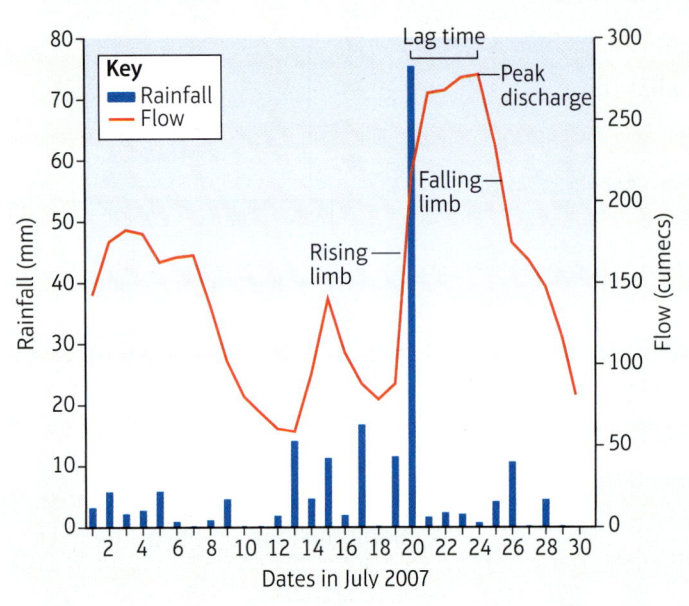

Figure 13 A flood hydrograph of the River Severn at Bewdley, July 2007

When it rains, how much rainfall reaches a river, and how quickly, depends on the amount and type of rainfall and what the catchment is like. A **hydrograph** is a way of showing how a river responds to a rainfall event. Figure 13 shows the relationship between rainfall (as a bar graph) and the river discharge (as a line graph) for the River Severn. The discharge of a river is measured in cumecs (cubic metres per second).

A hydrograph has a number of key features including:

- the **rising limb**, which shows the rising water after rainfall
- the **lag time**, which is the difference between the time of the heaviest rainfall and the point at which the river contains the largest amount of water
- the **falling limb**, which shows discharge falling as less water reaches the channel.

The shape of a storm hydrograph varies due to a number of factors, including physical factors and human activities (see Table 2).

Exam-style question
Explain how drainage basin shape can affect the shape of a storm hydrograph. **(4 marks)**

Exam tip
You will need to explain the two main drainage basin shapes and how these will influence the lag time, rising limb, peak discharge and falling limb of a storm hydrograph.

Activity
Study Figure 13.
1. What were the peak rainfall, peak discharge and lag time for this event?

Study Table 2.

2. Draw a quick sketch of the two types of hydrograph. Choose some key points from the Summary to add as labels, then add captions to show which hydrograph is less or more likely to show a river in flood.
3. Identify three or more human activities that may alter flood hydrographs, then describe and explain the impacts.
4. Read Table 2 again. Write a 140 character summary of the main difference(s) between what causes a steep hydrograph compared with a flatter one.

Table 2 The processes affecting the shape of storm hydrographs

	Processes that result in quick flows and a steeper hydrograph	Processes that result in slow flows and a flatter hydrograph
Precipitation	Large amounts of rainfall, often in winter; sudden snow melt; or heavy rainstorms, often in summer	Small amounts of gentle rainfall or gradual snow melt
Geology	**Impermeable** rocks such as granite cannot absorb water	**Permeable** rocks such as sandstone can absorb and store water
Drainage basin size and shape	In a small drainage basin, rainfall reaches the river channel quickly; a large drainage basin can create high river discharges over time	If the drainage basin has a more circular than elongated shape, the water reaches the main channel more slowly as some has further to travel
Soil	Frozen soil and soil saturated by previous rainfall holds little water; clay soils have small pore spaces, so less water **infiltrates** and more runs off	Dry soil can absorb and store much more water; sandy soils have large pores so more water can infiltrate and be stored
Slopes and soil depth	Steep slopes and thin soils cause rapid surface runoff	Gentle slopes and deep soils lead to slower surface runoff
Vegetation	Little vegetation cover results in more surface runoff, so deforestation and overgrazing by animals increase the flood risk	Woodland **intercepts** rainfall, and tree roots encourage water to infiltrate into the soil; **afforestation** helps reduce the flood risk
Towns and cities	Many urban surfaces such as roads and roofs are impermeable, so water quickly runs off into drains and rivers	Rural land uses have mainly permeable surfaces, so water permeates the soil and runoff is reduced
Antecedent conditions	If recent high rainfall has already saturated the ground, infiltration is reduced, so any new rainfall causes rapid surface runoff	When there has been little recent rainfall, the ground can absorb and store more water so there is less surface runoff
Summary	These processes cause greater or faster surface runoff. The hydrograph has a steeper rising limb, shorter lag time and higher peak discharge. These conditions usually result in greater erosion, so the river's sediment load is greater.	These processes cause less or slower surface runoff. The hydrograph has a gentler rising limb, a longer lag time and lower peak discharge. These conditions usually result in little erosion, so less sediment is carried by the river.

4B River Processes and Pressures

How do physical and human processes interact to cause flooding on the River Severn?

Learning objectives

- To know about the causes and impacts of recent flooding of the River Severn
- To understand how the interaction of physical and human processes causes a flood risk along the River Severn
- To understand the significance for flood risk of the location of the River Severn and places along it

The River Severn is the UK's largest river. Flooding is a natural event which has happened throughout history; the River Severn has also burst its banks many times in recent years. On page 162 you learned about some of the physical causes of floods along the Severn, including the large catchment size and the influence of its geology and climate, particularly in the upper Severn Valley.

In the past the River Severn was a major waterway and trade route. Important settlements grew up along it, including at bridging points such as Shrewsbury, Bewdley and Gloucester. Some of these riverside settlements are regularly affected by flooding, particularly as their populations have grown and they have expanded in size.

The UK floods of 2007

The summer of 2007 saw very high rainfalls in the UK, resulting in widespread flooding in June and July, especially in Yorkshire and the South Midlands. Flows in some rivers were the highest for over 100 years. Here are the causes of the flooding.

Rainfall in England and Wales was double the average for June and July, with four times the average in parts of Worcestershire. Some extremely heavy downfalls were recorded, especially on 20 July. In one event, 140 mm fell in just a few hours.

The rainfall was caused by a series of depressions tracking across the UK brought by a strong **jet stream**, which lingered further south than normal.

Figure 14 Flood waters in Tewkesbury, 2007

The period May to July was the wettest since records began in 1766. Towards the end of this period rain fell on saturated soils, leading to immediate runoff into already swollen rivers.

In urban areas such as the West Midlands runoff from hard surfaces was immediate. Flash flooding overwhelmed drainage systems in some cities.

Along the Severn and Avon, the large catchments and large volumes of runoff contributed to the flooding. Tewkesbury, located at the confluence of these two rivers, was badly hit. Flood water got into Tewkesbury Abbey for the first time in 250 years (Figure 14).

Figure 15 Map of the River Severn and its tributaries

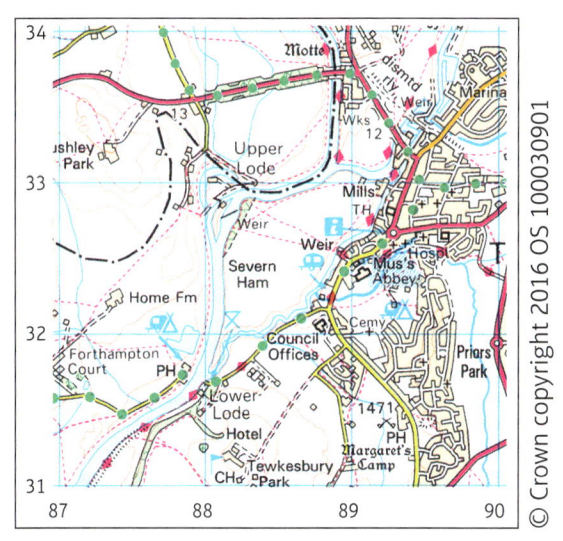

Figure 16 Extract from 1:50,000 OS map of the River Severn at Tewkesbury, Gloucester

Activity

1. Study Figures 14, 15 and 16.
   a. Which tributary meets the River Severn at Tewkesbury?
   b. Using map evidence, discuss why Tewkesbury's location puts it at risk of flooding.

2. Check you understand what **antecedent conditions** means. Read the text again about the causes of the River Severn floods in late July 2007, then list:
   a. the immediate causes of flooding
   b. the antecedent conditions which caused the flooding.

3. Draw an outline sketch map of Figure 16:
   a. draw the course of the River Severn, and the River Avon north of the town
   b. label the site of Tewkesbury and two or more areas that were flooded
   c. for an extra challenge, find the 10 metre contour, then use it to help identify the flooded area.

Did you know?

You can download flood maps from the Environment Agency website. The Environment Agency uses probability to talk about how likely it is that a flood of a particular size will happen. A **1% flood event** has a 1 in 100 chance or greater of happening each year, or a probability of 0.01.

Checkpoint

Now it is time to review your understanding of the influence of the physical and human causes of flooding, and how to interpret storm hydrographs.

Strengthen

S1 What was the peak discharge at Bewdley in July 2007, and on what day?

S2 Using geographical language, describe what the shape of a hydrograph tells us about a rainfall and flood event.

Challenge

C1 Describe how human activities in towns and in rural areas can change the shape of storm hydrographs.

C2 Look back at your learning from pages 168–169. Summarise why the River Severn is prone to flooding, the causes of the 2007 floods and their impact on places in the Severn Valley.

4B River Processes and Pressures

Why is the flood risk in the UK increasing?

Learning objectives

- To understand why the risk of flooding in the UK is increasing
- To know some effects of flooding on people and the environment
- To understand how flood risk management can reduce the chances of flooding and its impact

River flooding is a natural hazard that has affected people and the environment in the UK for centuries. However, the risk of flooding does seem to be increasing. Since 1998, significant flooding has occurred somewhere in the UK every year, and sometimes twice in a year. The following are the main reasons.

- An increasing population, so more people are affected by flooding. For example, building on flood plains has put over 2.3 million properties at risk of flooding.
- Changes to land use. In particular, urban development creates more impermeable surfaces and increases surface runoff rates. Even small-scale changes within settlements can have an impact, for example paving over suburban front gardens.
- Changes to weather patterns, particularly linked to **climate change**. Although no specific flood event can be linked to climate change, most scientists think that a warmer climate is making extreme weather more likely.

Activity

Study Figure 17.

1. Classify the effects of flooding in the UK into social, environmental and economic impacts: you could make three lists, or draw up a table including the three flood events.
2. Summarise the similarities and differences between the three flood events.

Did you know?

Major floods were recorded on the River Severn in 1740, 1947, 2000 and 2007. In 1947, the discharge at Bewdley reached a record 671 cumecs.

Boscastle 2004
On 16 August 2004, a month's worth of rain fell in one day, leaving the small village of Boscastle in ruins. Around 100 homes and businesses were destroyed and 75 cars were washed into the sea. The tourist industry was significantly affected, with the Wellington Hotel's lower floor unrecognisable and many local businesses destroyed. The devastation caused by the floods left many local residents struggling to deal with what they had experienced during that day.

Tewkesbury 2007
During July 2007, heavy rainfall caused the rivers Severn and Avon to flood, leaving approximately 48,000 homes affected and estimated repair costs for each home of between £20,000 and £30,000. For the local council's economy the floods cost £140,000 and for the British economy an estimated £3.2 billion. The floods left many local schools and businesses closed.

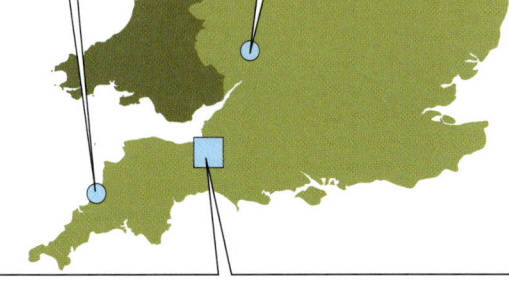

Somerset 2014
During January and February 2014 in Somerset, persistent heavy rainfall resulted in disruption to transport (road and railway) because the flood waters took around 12 weeks to reduce. A total of 1000 hectares of farmland were left under water and six farms, including their animals, had to be evacuated. In the villages of Moorland and Fordgate homes were destroyed and local residents were evacuated because of fear for their safety.

Figure 17 Flood events in England

Floods can have wide-ranging social, economic and environmental effects, which can have both short- and long-term impacts on the affected areas. Figure 17 shows some recent flooding events across the UK and their impacts.

Climate change

Scientists believe that one reason for the increasing risk of flooding in the UK is changes to weather patterns caused by climate change. One factor in a number of recent events is a change in the behaviour of the jet stream, which has brought more intense storms across the UK. In turn, this change in the jet stream may be linked to rising Arctic temperatures.

Scientists believe these intense storm events, which would have previously occurred once in 100 years, are now more likely to happen once every 80 years in the southern UK. This will mean people living close to rivers and the sea are increasingly vulnerable to flooding.

How does the Environment Agency manage flood risk?

The Environment Agency is responsible for managing the risk of flooding in England and Wales. It does this by:

- reducing the chances of a flood happening by managing rivers and land use, controlling development in flood plains and building flood defences
- reducing the impact of flooding by helping people prepare for flooding and giving flood warnings.

Reducing the chances of flooding: catchment management

First, the Environment Agency works out the chances of a flood happening. In the Severn catchment, a 1% annual probability flood would put 60,000 people and 29,000 businesses and homes at risk, as well as farmland and **infrastructure**, including roads and power supplies. Peak river flows are likely to increase by 20%. By 2100, therefore, 68,000 people and 33,000 properties will be at risk. Most of those at risk are in towns along the Severn and Avon.

Then the Agency makes Catchment Management Plans. These look at the flood risk across the whole catchment, then decide the best way to manage it sustainably. The plan for the Severn includes the following actions.

- **In rural parts of the catchment**: work with landowners to reduce runoff by improving land use, and restore flood plains to increase floodwater storage.
- **In the middle and lower catchment**: prevent unsuitable development on flood plains.
- **In urban areas**: reduce surface water flooding, improve some flood defences and encourage owners to protect vulnerable buildings.
- **Where few people are at risk of flooding**: work with natural flood processes.

Did you know?

A total of 4.6 million people and 1 in 6 properties in the UK are at risk from river or coastal flooding. Climate change, population growth and development will increase the flood hazard in future.

Activity

1. Read about how the Environment Agency manages flood risk. Which of these activities are short term, and which are long term?
2. Explain why climate change makes managing flood risk more difficult.

Reducing the chances of flooding: hard and soft engineering

One way to reduce the risk of flooding is to improve flood defences to control the flow of water. However, these can be expensive.

In the past people used hard-engineering methods, often building permanent concrete defences. Some, like the Thames Barrier in London, only operate when a flood is forecast. However, they do not reduce the risk of flooding in other parts of the catchment, and some may even increase it.

Table 3 Advantages and disadvantages of hard-engineering techniques

Advantages	Disadvantages
Embankments (levees) – high banks built on or near riverbanks £	
They stop water from spreading into areas where it could cause problems, such as in settlements. They can be earth and grass banks, which blend in with the environment.	Flood water may go over the top, then get trapped behind them. They can burst under pressure, possibly causing even greater damage.
Flood walls – artificial barriers designed to raise the height of the river banks to hold more water ££	
They prevent water from spreading into areas where it would have a high impact, such as housing.	Expensive to build. They help flood water flow quickly past, but this may cause flooding downstream. They do not look natural, and can spoil the view of the river.
Demountable flood barriers – a temporary structure that is only installed when needed £	
They are put up when a flood is forecast, then taken down afterwards. They are used in places like Bewdley on the River Severn, where a permanent flood wall would look ugly.	Can only be used in the specific location that it has been set to be deployed. There is a risk that the defence may not be installed in time.
Flood barriers, or storm surge barriers – floodgates built near the river mouth to prevent a storm surge or spring tide from flooding the area behind the barrier ££–£££	
The gates can be closed when a high tide or surge is forecast. They are able to protect large areas from storm surge conditions.	Construction costs are high and they need regular maintenance.

£ cheapest
£££ most expensive

4B River Processes and Pressures

Longer term, **soft engineering** may be the answer, using a more natural approach to managing floodwater. This approach aims to create space for floodwater in the landscape to reduce the risk of flooding in other areas. Soft defences are usually cheaper, need little maintenance and provide habitats for wildlife.

Table 4 Advantages and disadvantages of soft-engineering techniques

Advantages	Disadvantages
Flood-plain retention – strategies to maintain and restore the river's original flood plain £	
Allowing rivers to flood helps slow flood waters down and recover a river's natural sedimentation processes. This helps restore the soil structure in the flood plain, making it more efficient at storing water.	Allowing land to flood may mean a change of land use, for example a change in farmland.
River restoration – using a variety of strategies to restore the river's original course £	
The aim is to restore rivers to a more natural course by taking away embankments and restoring meanders: this allows rivers to flood but slows them down. Natural rivers are more attractive for recreation and create natural habitats which benefit wildlife.	Some flood banks are often still needed, and like flood-plain retention, changes in land use may bring some disadvantages.

£ cheapest
£££ most expensive

Activity

Draw the following table.

Management technique	Advantages	Disadvantages
Hard engineering		
Soft engineering		

a   Summarise the main advantages and disadvantages of hard and soft engineering, adding examples of different techniques.

b   Using three shades, colour code your notes to show which costs and benefits are economic, environmental and social.

Exam-style question

Describe the differences between soft and hard engineering.
(2 marks)

Exam tip

When you are asked to describe the **differences**, use a connective word such as 'whereas' to form two descriptive sentences.

4B River Processes and Pressures

Building flood defences

Flood defences are often expensive, and sometimes only move the problem further downstream. So the Environment Agency works out where flood defences would be most effective in preventing floods, and would not cause environmental damage. The Agency makes:

- an Environmental Impact Assessment, to see the effects of a scheme on local residents, buildings and transport, as well as wildlife, habitats and water quality
- a **cost-benefit analysis** to check whether a scheme would be good value for money.

In 2000, severe flooding of the River Severn affected 140 properties in Bewdley, so local residents and businesses wanted improved flood defences. The Environment Agency worked out a number of possible options, how much they would cost, and the how much they would benefit the area. The cost-benefit analysis in Table 5 shows how they decided on the best option.

Table 5 Cost-benefit analysis of Bewdley flood defences

Options	Total costs	Value of benefit
1 Do nothing. Flooding would continue and get worse. River banks would collapse, perhaps blocking the river flow, and some properties may have to be abandoned.	£0	£0
2 Continue river maintenance. Present flooding would continue and worsen, although maintenance of river banks and structures would prevent collapse and blockages.	£0.2 million	£0.3 million
3 Upstream storage dam. A flood storage dam could be built 1 km upstream of Bewdley, but the volume of storage would not be enough to hold back a 1 in 100 year flood.	£15 million	£0.5 million
4 Demountable defences. With a height of 2.7 m these defences would protect 150 properties from a 1 in 100 year event. When a high flow is forecast, the Agency Flood Warning gives 24 hours to put up the barriers.	£6.9 million	£7.5 million

Demountable aluminium flood barriers were chosen for Bewdley (Figure 18). Most of the time they are kept in storage. There needs to be at least a 24-hour flood warning for the barriers to be put up in time to protect the town. They were completed in 2005, in time to prevent flooding there in 2007.

Activity

1. Study Table 5, the cost-benefit analysis for the flood defences at Bewdley, then **calculate** the cost-benefit ratio for each option. To do this you need to:
   a. make a copy of the table, with an extra column for your calculations
   b. calculate each cost-benefit ratio by dividing the benefits by the costs
   c. write a sentence or two describing which was the best option, and why.
2. Look at Figure 18 showing the flood defences, and the other options in Table 5. Why do you think Option 4 did well on the Environmental Impact Assessment and was popular with local residents?

Command word

When asked to **calculate** you work with numbers to answer a problem. Don't forget to show your working. Here, show your results as a number, to two decimal places.

4B River Processes and Pressures

Figure 18 Demountable flood barriers at Bewdley

Reducing the impact of flooding

Sometimes flooding is inevitable, as in 2007. At these times, the Environment Agency tries to reduce the impact on people, land and property. Through its website and the news, the Agency provides flood warning feeds, a live flood warning map and a three-day flood risk forecast of areas at risk. There are three warning levels: flood alert, flood warning and severe flood warning.

The Environment Agency and local government work together to educate people about the hazards of living in flood risk areas. They use television, the internet, leaflets, helplines and training exercises to make people aware of what they should do before, during and after a flood. Advice for homeowners includes the following:

- use tiles or rugs instead of carpets on ground floors
- fit plastic window frames and doors instead of wooden
- fit stainless steel or plastic units and cupboards in the kitchen, not wooden ones
- electrical sockets should be fitted 1.5 metres above ground floor level
- install boilers for heating systems on the first floor
- fit non-return valves to drains and water inlet pipes
- install flood door barriers.

Local government will only give planning permission to build properties near a river if a full flood risk assessment has been completed. The new laws set out by the government in 2010 state that all new properties built near rivers need to be flood resistant.

Activity

Look back at your learning in this topic. **Examine** why the River Severn valley is prone to flooding, give an example of its impact and how it can be managed.

Checkpoint

Now it is time to review your understanding of how flood risk management can reduce the chances of flooding and reduce its impact.

Strengthen

S1 Give **two** reasons why people will be at greater risk of flooding in future.

S2 Summarise the advice for homeowners living in a flood risk area.

S3 Explain why planners have strict rules about development in flood plains.

Challenge

C1 Describe the environmental benefits of soft-engineering techniques.

C2 Explain how cost-benefit analysis helps choose between flood defences.

C3 Summarise the approaches to flood risk management in different parts of the Severn catchment: why are there different approaches in urban and rural areas?

Command word

Examine questions ask you to break something down into its different parts or processes. Here you can structure your answer by first drawing a mind map of the physical and human causes of Severn flooding, how each part contributes to the flood risk and then link these to an example and ways to manage the floods.

F Investigating River Processes and Pressures

Learning objectives

- To understand how to conduct a geographical investigation of change in river valleys and channels
- To know how to choose enquiry questions, fieldwork methods and data sources for a river investigation
- To know how to present, analyse and evaluate data collected from a river investigation

Activity

1. Using your knowledge of the changes in the long profile of the River Severn (see pages 162–163), create another two key questions that would help you to answer the main task question.

2. Using your wider geographical knowledge, suggest the results you would expect for your chosen key questions based on a typical river profile. Refer to Bradshaw's Model on page 163.

F The enquiry question

When conducting a geographical enquiry, it is important to have a purpose. One way to do this is to ask a task question.

For this enquiry on rivers, the task question is:

How and why do the drainage basin and channel characteristics of the River Severn influence the flood risk for people and property?

To help answer the task question, geographers next devise some key questions. These help to provide a focus for the enquiry.

For this task, one of the key questions is:

Does the width and depth of the river channel increase as the river flows downstream?

F Locating the study

It is important to provide maps showing where the investigation is located. You should include maps at a local and a national scale, plus detailed maps showing your survey or data collection sites. You can then use your location and survey site maps to give a detailed overview of the place in which your investigation will take place. This part of your enquiry helps set the scene.

Figure 19 River Severn, Hafren Forest, near site 1

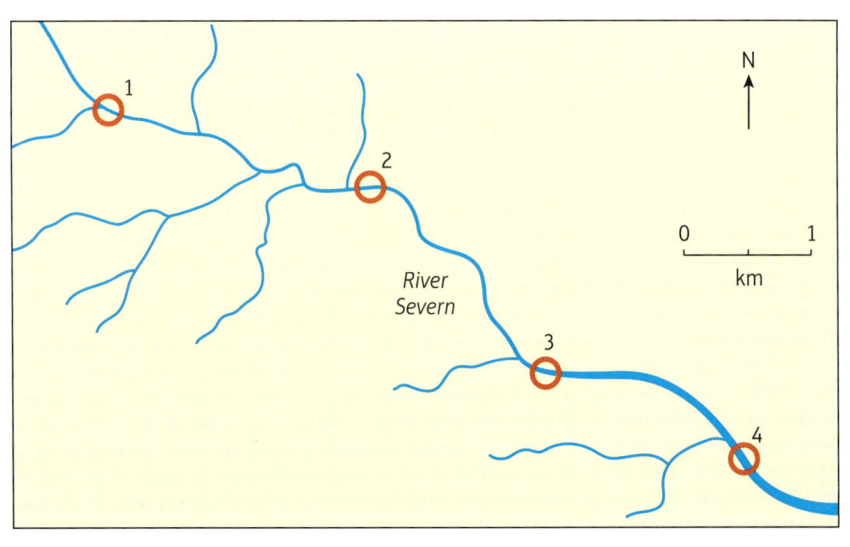

Figure 20 A student's sketch map of survey sites on the upper River Severn

176

Investigating River Processes and Pressures

F Methodology

Once you have decided on some suitable key questions and located your investigation, the next stage is to choose the methods you will use to collect your data. Geographers use both **primary data** (data that is collected first hand) and **secondary data** (data that has already been published). In your investigation, you should choose at least three **quantitative** (using numbers) methods, for example measuring the width and depth of a river, and one **qualitative** (descriptive) method, for example a field sketch.

For each method, it is important that you decide where and how you will collect the data and why the data collected will help to answer the overall task question. You cannot collect data from every part of the river or measure every pebble in its bed, so you need to sample.

- **Random sampling** – data is collected by chance. An example might be picking up stones from the river bed at random with your eyes closed.
- **Systematic sampling** – the locations of the sites are found at equal intervals from each other. An example might be to measure the depth of the river every 0.25 metres across its width.
- **Stratified sampling** – is used when the study area has significantly different parts. An example might be measuring the discharge just below every confluence.

> **Did you know?**
> You can use the interactive Environment Agency Flood Map to support your fieldwork. Use the viewer to zoom in on any stream or river in England to see flood zones and any flood defences.

An example of how to present your methodology is shown in Table 6.

Table 6 Measuring the width and depth of a river (quantitative method)

Method	Outline of method	Purpose of method	Recording
Measuring the width and depth of the river. Sample measurements collected at Sites 1–4. Each site is located where a tributary joins the River Severn.	We found a suitable representative point at each site. We measured the width from one bank to the other with a tape measure. To measure the depth, at 0.25 metres intervals I placed a metre ruler into the water until it reached the river bed.	We chose this method to investigate how the width and depth of the river changes as it flows downstream – so we are trying to prove Bradshaw's theory.	On a tablet, we set up a simple spreadsheet for the width and depth at each of the four sites. We entered the data directly in the field.

When you investigate the changing river processes, it is also important to find out how people and rivers interact, for example in an area at risk of flooding. One method you could try to survey the thoughts of local people is to conduct a questionnaire. When deciding on a questionnaire, you should consider the following.

- What questions will allow you to collect the information that you need for your investigation?
- Will the questions be open (allowing people to offer opinions) or closed (for example, yes or no)?

F Investigating River Processes and Pressures

Exam-style question

Is a questionnaire about people's opinions a qualitative or quantitative method? **(1 mark)**

Did you know?

Timing how long an orange takes to float for 5 or 10 metres downstream is an easy way to measure river velocity. However, rivers flow faster near the surface, so the results need to be multiplied by 0.85 to allow for the friction along the river bed and banks.

Activity

1. What do you think are the advantages and disadvantages of recording river channel data directly into a spreadsheet on a tablet?
2. Make a blank copy of Table 6.
   a. Choose **two** investigations from the following: land use in the river valley, velocity and discharge, gradient or bedload. Discuss what you could find out about them, how you could do so and why they will help with answering the main task question.
   b. For each investigation, describe the methods and explain how and why you would conduct and record them. Use a highlighter to identify where you have explained *how* you would carry out the methods.
3. You have been asked the following key question, 'How does the risk of flooding affect people living in the catchment?' Create a questionnaire that would enable you to gather the information you need to answer this key question.

Now that you have decided on the methods you will use to collect your data, you need to produce a risk assessment with your teacher's guidance before you collect and record your data. In your risk assessment, you should consider: the potential risks, the severity of each risk – on a scale of 0 (low) to 10 (high) – and how the risk can be managed. An example is shown in Table 7.

Exam-style question

Study Table 8. **Calculate** the cross-sectional area of the River Severn at Sites 1–4. **(2 marks)**

Exam tip

Calculate the cross-sectional area by multiplying channel width by mean depth.

Command word

When asked to **calculate** you work with numbers to answer a problem. You must show your working and do not forget to include the unit (e.g. m^2) in your result.

Table 7 Risk assessment

Risk	Severity rating	Management
Slipping on rocks	6/10	Take care before entering the river and listen to the teacher

Table 8 River Severn channel data collected by a geography student

Channel variable	Site 1	Site 2	Site 3	Site 4
Width (metres, m)	3.20	6.40	8.40	15.20
Mean depth (m)	0.16	0.30	0.25	0.27
Cross-sectional area (m^2)				
Velocity (m/s)	0.07	0.11	0.12	0.12
Discharge (m^3/s)	0.03	0.18	0.21	0.42

Investigating River Processes and Pressures

(F) Data presentation

Once you have collected your data, you then need to decide how to present it. Geographers use a range of graphical techniques to present their findings. For your investigation, you should aim to produce a number of simple and sophisticated techniques. A sophisticated technique is one that uses at least two variables to represent the data. An example of this would be located graphs of data for the river at different sites. Techniques that could be used to present information for the River Severn include:

- flow-line maps to show velocity or discharge (see Figure 21)
- annotated photographs/field sketches of the river landforms
- maps of land use in flood risk zones
- located proportional circles of mean sediment size
- a GIS map with located photographs and channel data for different sites.

Presenting data on river velocity and discharge

The students measured river velocity at four sites, then calculated the discharge. Figure 21 shows an example of how the students presented their discharge data for the River Severn in a flow-line map.

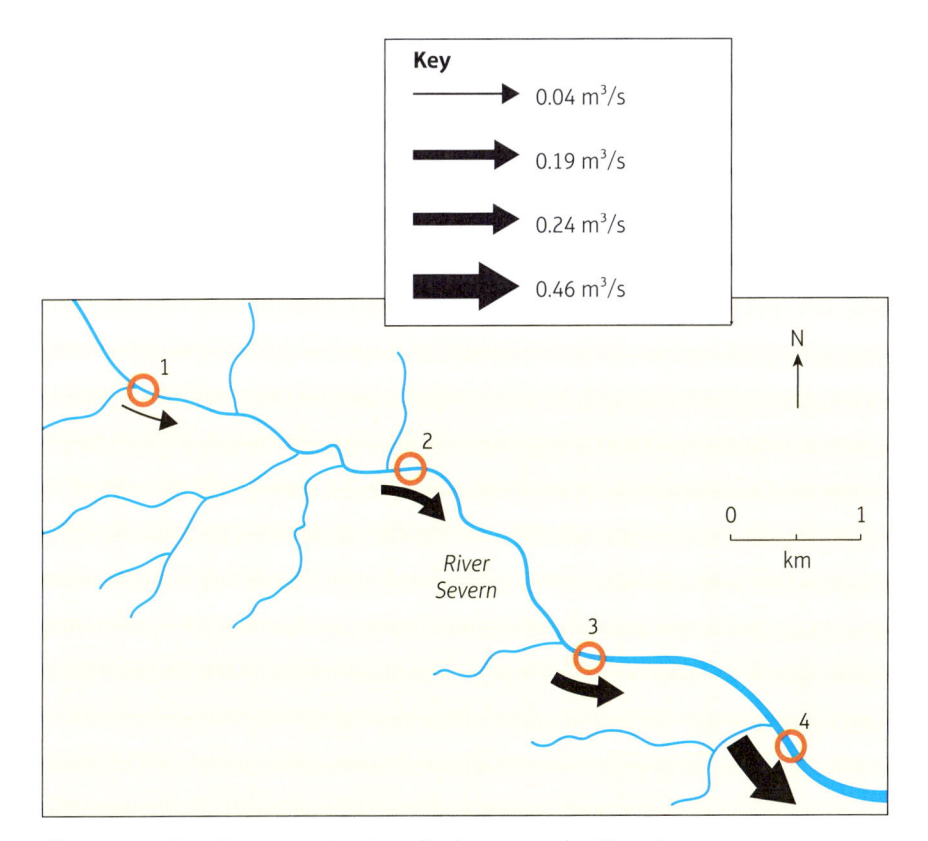

Figure 21 Flow-line map showing discharge on the River Severn

Activity

1 Study Table 8. Describe the changes in the velocity and discharge of the River Severn from Site 1 to Site 4, and give reasons for them.

Tip Remember to make reference to the map as well as the data, use geographical terminology and explain how the data links to geographical theory.

2 The students decided to investigate four more sites on the River Severn, downstream of Shrewsbury. They obtained depth and discharge figures from two web pages: 'Environment Agency – River and sea levels' and 'National River Flow Archive'.

  a What type of data is this: primary or secondary; qualitative or quantitative?

  b The students downloaded a catchment map from one site. Describe one simple and one sophisticated way they could use this map in their study.

179

F Investigating River Processes and Pressures

(F) Analysis and conclusions

The next stage of the enquiry is to analyse the data collected to begin answering your key questions. When analysing the data, it is important to:

- **describe** the general trends from your data – for example, 'The discharge of the river increases travelling downstream'
- **make comparisons** using data – for example, 'The discharge of the river is greatest at Site 4, measuring 0.49 m^3/sec, a difference of 0.45 m^3/sec from Site 1'
- **explain** the patterns of your data with links to geographical theory – for example, 'The width of the river has increased because of lateral erosion of the banks due to attrition, hydraulic action and other processes'.

Read the extract below from an analysis a student wrote about data collected along the River Severn. The student gave a structured response with:

- reference to the figure and data (red)
- use of geographical terminology and theory (green)
- an explanation of their data and links to geographical theory (yellow).

> The velocity of the River Severn increases from Site 1 to Site 4 as predicted by Bradshaw's Model. As you can see in Table 8, the mean velocity at Site 1 was 0.07 m/s and increased to 0.12 m/s at Site 4. This shows an overall mean velocity increase of 0.05 cm/s. The reason the mean velocity increases is that as the width and depth of the river increases there is less friction against the bank.

Activity

1. Discuss the two paragraphs showing the student's analysis and conclusion. For **each** paragraph decide: what is good about it, how it might be improved or developed, anything that you think should be added. Justify your decisions.

2. Rewrite the **second** student paragraph with your suggested improvements.

Once you have analysed your data using the structure above, you need to write a conclusion for each key question as well as the overall task question. When writing your conclusion, it is important to:

- focus on your task question and key questions: what did your investigation find out?
- summarise your findings from the data you collected and presented and link each finding to the evidence
- point out any anomalies in your data – these are results that are very different from what you expected: you might try to explain them
- refer back to any theory that related to your investigation; for rivers, you should refer to the Bradshaw Model.

You then need to write your overall conclusion to the task question, in this case: 'How and why do the drainage basin and channel characteristics of the River Severn influence the flood risk for people and property?'

Read the extract below from a conclusion written by a student.

> The purpose of my investigation was to find out if my chosen valley and channel characteristics vary along the River Severn. I can conclude that as the River Severn flows downstream, the width and depth of the river increases, the bedload alters in size and roundness, and the discharge increases. My data generally supports the Bradshaw Model with only a few anomalies identified.

Investigating River Processes and Pressures F

F Evaluation

The final part of the enquiry is to evaluate your investigation. Here you think about how well you answered the task question or theory, and how you could improve or develop the process. The key questions below will help you review your data collection methods, results and conclusions.

- How successful and useful were your methods for sampling and collecting data? Could they be improved?
- How accurate were your results? Did your data collection methods affect the results?
- Did missing or inaccurate data make the study unreliable or affect your conclusions?

Activity

1. Read the students' reflections. Discuss which ones are about:
   a strengths and weaknesses in the study
   b the accuracy of the data
   c missing data or the size of the sample.
2. Suggest how the data collection methods could be improved if other students repeated the study.

> When I was measuring the depth of the river I found it difficult to know if I was touching the bottom of the river bed because there were a lot of rocks.

> We chose four sites just below where tributaries joined the Severn. This way of sampling was useful – you could see how the discharge increased.

> I found it difficult to decide where the sediment fitted on the scale.

> We worked on four sites in the upper Severn. Downstream of Site 4, we couldn't get safe access to the river.

> I found that a lot of bedload acted as a barrier to the float, especially at Sites 1 and 2. As the float kept stopping, it took a long time to travel 10 metres. This meant my velocity measurements were slower than the actual velocity of the river.

Figure 22 Students' reflections on their geographical investigation on the River Severn

Checklist

Now it is time to review your understanding of how to plan and conduct an investigation into change in river valleys and channels.

Strengthen

S1 With a partner, note down **two** things you can remember about each of the following: the enquiry question, locating the study, presenting data and evaluation.

S2 Classify the following into simple and sophisticated presentation techniques: flow-line map, bar graph, located pie graph, multiple-line graph, pie graph.

S3 Explain why it is important that a student's conclusion is linked to their task question.

Extend

C1 Think about what you know about random, systematic and stratified sampling. Note down an example of how each could be used in a river investigation.

C2 Write out example(s) of the methods below, deciding if they are qualitative or quantitative, primary or secondary, and the strengths and limitations of information gained from each of them:
   a method(s) to measure river velocity and discharge
   b method(s) to record river landforms and landscapes
   c method(s) to investigate the impact of river flooding on local people.

Preparing for your exams

River Processes and Pressures

Rivers shape the world. The majority of people live on or close to major rivers and we all depend on the food grown on their flood plains. We use rivers for transport, power, water, food and recreation. Rivers are also dangerous – more people are killed by river flooding than by any other natural disaster.

Checklist

You should know:

- [ ] the drainage basin terms – watershed, confluence, tributary, source and mouth
- [ ] the physical processes of weathering, mass movement and erosion
- [ ] the characteristics of a river profile and how these change from the source to the mouth
- [ ] how the UK's climate, geology and slope processes affect river landscapes and sediment load
- [ ] how storm hydrographs and lag-times can be explained by physical factors
- [ ] how erosion processes and geology influence the development of river landforms such as interlocking spurs, waterfalls and river cliffs
- [ ] how depositional processes cause the formation of flood plains, levees and deltas
- [ ] how the interaction of deposition and erosion cause the development of river landforms such as meanders and oxbow lakes
- [ ] why human activities and changes in land use affect river processes and impact on river landscapes
- [ ] the physical and human causes of river flooding
- [ ] how river flooding affects people and the environment
- [ ] the advantages and disadvantages of different defences used on UK rivers
- [ ] how one named distinctive river landscape has been formed and the most influential factors in its change.

Which key terms match the following definitions?

a The area of land drained by a river and its tributaries.

b A graph showing changes in a river's discharge and rainfall over time.

c The naturally raised bank of sediment along a river bank, which may be artificially strengthened or heightened.

d The speed at which a river flows, often measured in metres per second.

e A type of erosion where particles carried by rivers or waves are worn down as they collide with each other, becoming smaller and rounded.

f The flat land in the valley floor each side of a river channel, which is sometimes flooded.

g Using artificial structures to prevent river or coastal flooding.

h A bend formed in a river as it winds across the landscape.

i The starting point of a stream or river, often a spring or a lake.

j The movement of material down a slope due to gravity.

k Conditions in a drainage basin in the period before a rainfall event, such as saturated or frozen ground.

To check your answers, look at the Glossary on pages 302–311.

Preparing for your exams

River Processes and Pressures

Question 1   Explain **one** physical and **one** human cause of flooding.   (4 marks)

Student answer

One cause of flooding is deforestation. This causes flooding because removing the trees reduces interception, causing more rainwater to reach the river channel faster.

A second cause of flooding is urbanisation. This is where humans build near rivers, using hard, impermeable materials. This causes flooding because the rainwater will not infiltrate into the concrete, causing the rainwater to run-off into the river channel at a quicker rate.

Verdict

Part 1 is correct – the answer has identified a correct cause, 'deforestation', and explained the reason why this causes flooding – 'reduces interception'.

Part 2 is incorrect. Whilst the human cause is correct, the question asks for **one** physical and **one** human cause of flooding. The student should have explained a physical cause of flooding, such as intensity or duration of rainfall and types of rocks.

Exam tip

The student has not answered the question being asked. Reading the question through at least a couple of times can help avoid this sort of mistake. Underlining key words can also help you to focus. Finally, if at all possible, leave time to check back on your answers to make sure you really have answered the questions being asked in each case.

Question 2   Explain how different river processes work together in the formation of a meander.   (4 marks)

Student answer

A meander is a bend in a river's course, which is often found in the lower course of a river. The formation of a meander results from a combination of erosion and deposition processes. On the outside of the bend the water is deeper and the current is flowing with greater speed. The force of the water causes undercutting of the bank through abrasion, which is where material carried in the river rubs against the bed and banks of the channel, causing a river cliff to form. On the inside of the bend the water is flowing at a much slower velocity. More friction and therefore less energy means that deposition occurs on the inside of the river bend. Over time sediments are deposited, forming a point bar and slip-off slope and eventually a floodplain.

Verdict

This answer precisely answers the question, by examining the physical processes that work together to form a meander. It includes key geographical features relating to meanders.

Exam tip

Once again it is important to answer precisely the question being asked – in this case you need to explain the interaction of physical processes to form a meander. You will need to learn the key features of landforms, the physical processes and how these cause the formation. Good answers will also include accurate use of geographical terms.

Pearson Education Ltd accepts no responsibility whatsoever for the accuracy or method of working in the answers given.

THINKING GEOGRAPHICALLY

Using the mean, median and mode

What you need to know about mean, median and mode

In geography we use them to give us an overall summary of a set of values and to compare different sets of data with each other.

- The **mean** is the sum of the data values divided by their number, often called the average.
- The **median** is the middle value when a set of values in a data set is written in order.
- The **mode** is the most frequent value in a data set.
- To calculate the mean, add up all the values then divide by the number of values.
- To calculate the median, arrange the data in rank order (lowest to highest): the median is the middle value. If there are two middle values, add them together and divide by two.
- To find the mode, you can make a tally chart to see which value occurs most often.

Sample question

Some students were investigating whether a river's discharge increased downstream. At five sites they drew cross sections of the river. At each site they measured the width and sampled the depth by measuring every 50 cm across the river. The results for one site are in Figure 1.

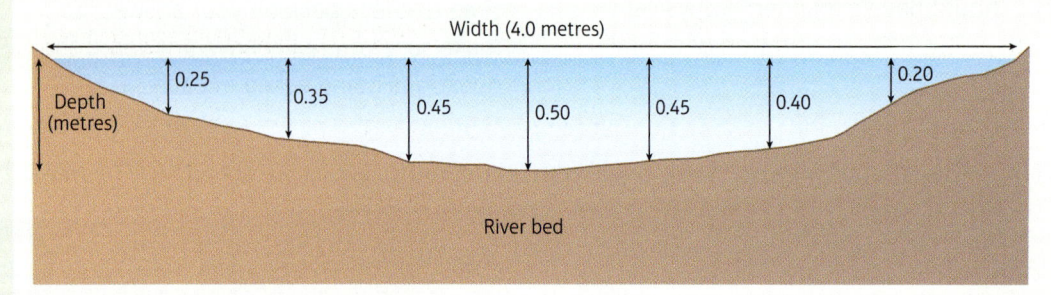

Figure 1 River investigation: channel cross section

Calculate the mean depth of the river.

The mean depth
= (0.25 + 0.35 + 0.45 + 0.50 + 0.45 + 0.40 + 0.20) ÷ 7
= 2.60 ÷ 7
= 0.37 metres (to 2 decimal places).

Apply your knowledge

1. The students measured river velocity by timing how long an orange took to float 10 metres. They did this ten times to try to eliminate error. Their results are shown below, in metres per second.

   | 0.2 | 0.3 | 0.5 | 0.5 | 0.3 | 0.6 | 0.6 | 0.5 | 0.4 | 0.1 |

   Calculate the mean of the students' ten results to give an average for the river's velocity.

2. One student argued that using the mode would be better. What do you think?

THINKING GEOGRAPHICALLY

Command word

When asked to **calculate**, you must show your working and remember to include the unit(s) (e.g. m/sec or cumecs) in your result.

What you need to know about modal classes

- In geography we sometimes organise data into classes (groups) to help make sense of it.
- The **modal class** is the most frequent class in a data set.
- The **range** is the difference between the smallest and biggest values.

Example

Some students were investigating a beach to see if the sediments were bigger in some places than others.

They sampled 40 pebbles at Sites A and B and measured the longest axis (side) of each. They recorded their results on a tally chart for each site, divided into five classes and started drawing a graph to show the data for Site A (Figure 2).

The students went to Site C but they only had time to measure nine pebbles. They quickly recorded the pebble sizes as shown in Figure 3.

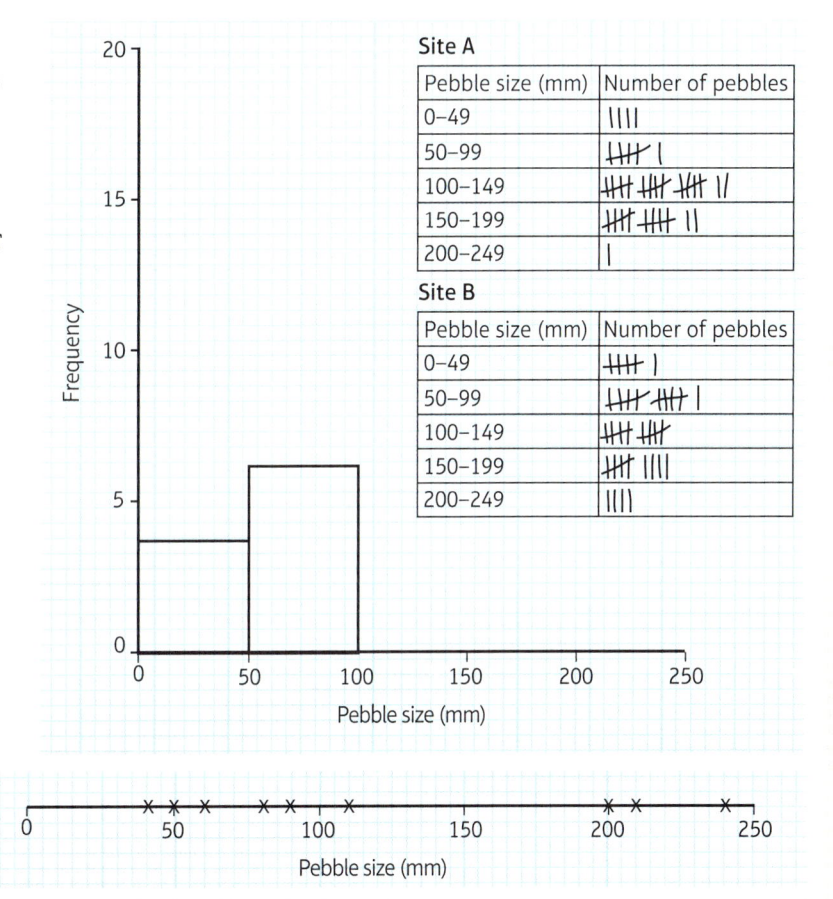

Site A

Pebble size (mm)	Number of pebbles
0–49	IIII
50–99	HHT I
100–149	HHT HHT HHT II
150–199	HHT HHT II
200–249	I

Site B

Pebble size (mm)	Number of pebbles
0–49	HHT I
50–99	HHT HHT I
100–149	HHT HHT
150–199	HHT IIII
200–249	IIII

Figure 2 Pebble sizes at Sites A, B and C: tally for Sites A and B; pebble distribution for Site A

Figure 3 Pebble distribution for Site C

Apply your knowledge

1. Copy and finish the graph in Figure 2, then draw a similar one showing the data for Site B.
2. Label the modal class on each graph.
3. The mean pebble size at Site A is 125 mm, and 118 mm at Site B. Discuss why drawing graphs and finding the modal class may be better than using the mean for this data.
4. Use Figure 3 to identify the median pebble size, and the range of values for the pebbles at Site C.
5. If the mean pebble size at Site C is 120 mm, discuss whether you think using the median or the mean pebble size would be better for this data.

THINKING GEOGRAPHICALLY

Using quartiles and the inter-quartile range

What you need to know about the inter-quartile range

In geography we sometimes need to know about how spread out are the values in a dataset around the median (The median is the middle value: it divides a set of data into two halves.). One advanced method is to find out the **inter-quartile range**.

Example

Some students measured the size of pebbles on the outside and inside of a meander bend to see if there was a difference. The students plotted diagrams of the pebble sizes, from smallest to largest, on graph paper. Their results for the outside of the meander bend are below.

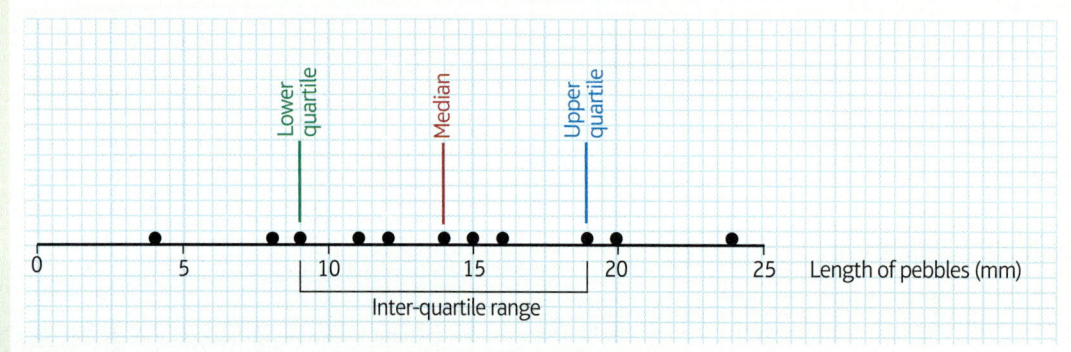

Figure 4 River investigation: pebble sizes on the outside of a meander

The students found the **median** pebble size and marked it on their diagram = 14 mm.

They now had a set of values divided into two halves. Next they split each half in half again and marked these on their diagram. These are called the **lower quartile** and **upper quartile**.

- The **lower quartile** divides the bottom half of the data in two halves = 9 mm.
- The **upper quartile** divides the top half of the data in two halves = 19 mm.
- The **inter-quartile range** is the difference between the two quartiles = 10 mm.

Apply your knowledge

1. Study the record of pebble sizes on the inside of a meander below.

| 5 | 3 | 2 | 16 | 12 | 10 | 8 | 11 | 6 | 14 | 7 |

2. On graph paper, draw a scale from 0 to 25 mm. Mark on the values of the pebbles on the inside of the meander, in size order.

    (a) Mark on the median, lower quartile and upper quartile.

    (b) Mark on and calculate the inter-quartile range.

    (c) Use your findings about the median and inter-quartile range to write a comparison of the pebbles on the outside and inside of this meander bend.

5 | The UK's Evolving Human Landscape

The human landscape of the UK has been changing for thousands of years; however, it is doubtful that it has ever changed as much as it has in the last 50 years. This topic will highlight some of the ways in which the UK's different human landscapes, rural and urban, are changing. It will also investigate why some of these changes are taking place and what the effects of these changes have been. In particular, the topic will look at the growing impact of the wider world on people and places in the UK, with particular reference to two contrasting regions and one major city – Birmingham.

Your learning

In this section you will investigate the following key questions:

- Why are population, economic activity and settlements key elements of the human landscape?
- How is the UK economy and society linked to and shaped by the wider world?
- What is the impact of globalisation, trade and investment, and migration?
- How is Birmingham, a major UK city, changing?
- What are the causes and impacts of changes in its structure, economy and population in different parts of the city?
- How can life in the city be improved?
- How is the city interdependent with its surrounding rural areas?
- What are the challenges and opportunities of change in rural areas?

5 | The UK's Evolving Human Landscape

Why are population, economic activity and settlements key elements of the human landscape?

Learning objectives
- To recognise how urban core areas differ from rural areas, and how UK regions differ
- To know how government policies and approaches assist areas in decline

The urban core and rural areas of the UK
Urban core areas of the UK are very different places to rural areas, as Figures 1 and 2, and Table 1 show.

Activity
Identify **five** elements of the urban landscape found in Figure 1 that are not found in Figure 2.

Figure 1 Birmingham city centre

Figure 2 The Yorkshire Dales

Table 1 Comparison of UK urban core and rural areas

	Urban core	**Rural areas**
Population density	High and staying high, over 200 people per km^2	Low, 1–100 people per km^2
Age structure	Many young adults, many single people	Many older people, some single people
Economic activities	Retailing, large shops Offices and corporate headquarters Many jobs – shops, offices, factories Cultural centre – library, museum, theatre	Farming, fishing, forestry, mining Working from home – IT Tourism Renewable energies
Settlement	Metropolis, conurbation, city, large town Mix of low- and high-rise buildings Property often more expensive	Market towns, villages and isolated farms Low-rise building Property generally cheaper

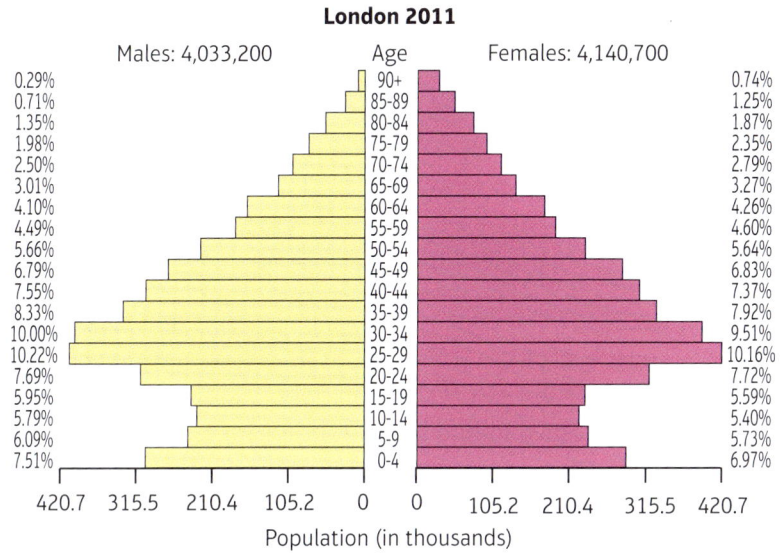

5 The UK's Evolving Human Landscape

Figure 3 Population pyramid for London

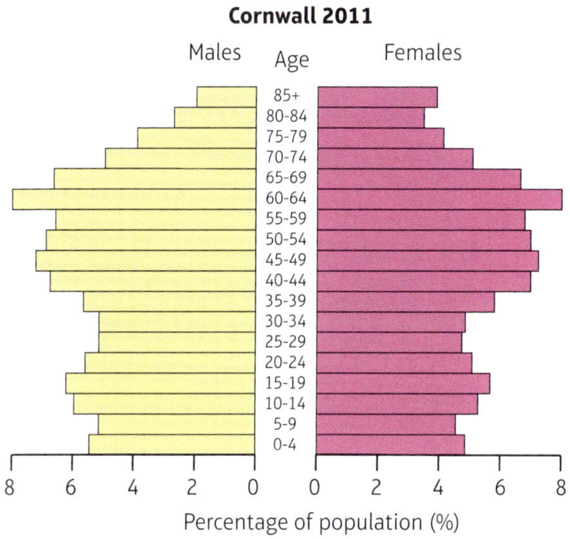

London 2011
Males: 4,033,200 — Females: 4,140,700
Total population: 8,173,900

Males %	Age	Females %
0.29%	90+	0.74%
0.71%	85-89	1.25%
1.35%	80-84	1.87%
1.98%	75-79	2.35%
2.50%	70-74	2.79%
3.01%	65-69	3.27%
4.10%	60-64	4.26%
4.49%	55-59	4.60%
5.66%	50-54	5.64%
6.79%	45-49	6.83%
7.55%	40-44	7.37%
8.33%	35-39	7.92%
10.00%	30-34	9.51%
10.22%	25-29	10.16%
7.69%	20-24	7.72%
5.95%	15-19	5.59%
5.79%	10-14	5.40%
6.09%	5-9	5.73%
7.51%	0-4	6.97%

Population (in thousands): 420.7, 315.5, 210.4, 105.2

Figure 4 Population pyramid for Cornwall

Cornwall 2011 — Percentage of population (%)

Activity

The city of London attracts many people (Figure 3). Cornwall, an area in the south-west of England, attracts many retired people (Figure 4).

Use data to compare the population pyramids of London and Cornwall and explain the differences and similarities.

Reducing regional disparities

Figure 5 shows the UK areas that qualify for assistance from the government and the European Union. Assisted Areas in north Wales, northwest Scotland and Cornwall are largely rural, and face isolation and a lack of jobs. In general, people are poorer here than in other parts of the UK. Other Assisted Areas include more urbanised, former industrial areas, such as South Wales and north-east England, where the decline of the coal, steel and shipbuilding industries have left a legacy of unemployment and poverty.

Regional development

The EU's European Regional Development Fund supports UK regions by economic regeneration, improved communications and safeguarding jobs. Cornwall gets ERDF support because its GDP is below 75% of the EU average – this has funded a project to connect businesses to fast broadband, allowing people to live in Cornwall and work from home or local offices.

Transport infrastructure

Investment in transport for people and goods promotes growth, for example improvements to the rail routes linking Manchester with Sheffield.

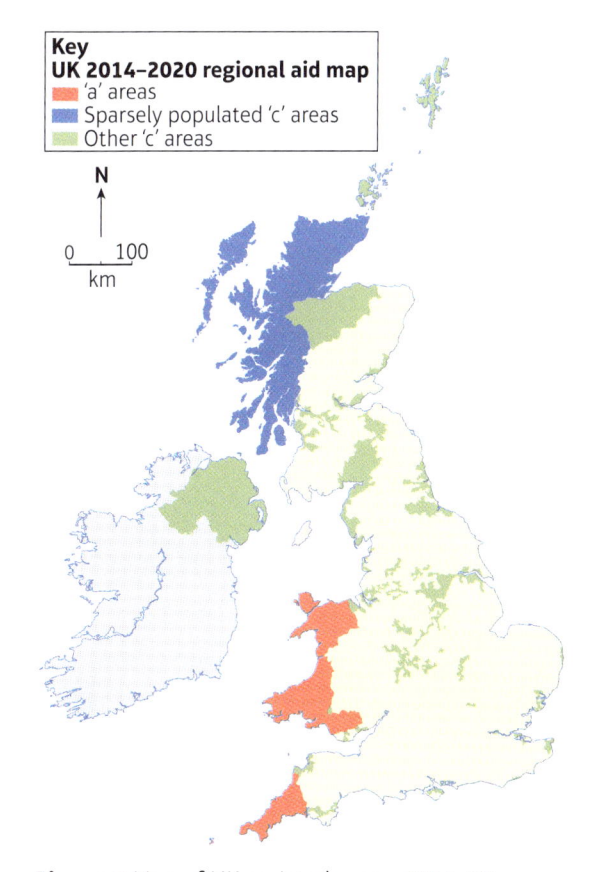

Key
UK 2014–2020 regional aid map
- 'a' areas
- Sparsely populated 'c' areas
- Other 'c' areas

Figure 5 Map of UK assisted areas, 2014–20

5 The UK's Evolving Human Landscape

How does migration shape the UK economy and society?

Learning objectives

- To know how migration over the last 50 years has altered the population geography of the UK
- To recognise these changes in the number, distribution and age structure of the population
- To understand the effects of EU and UK immigration policies

The population geography of the UK has changed significantly in the last 50 years as a result of internal national migration and international migration.

National migration

There are different types of national migration, which have all had an impact on UK population geography.

Retirement migration

This involves older people who decide to retire to a different part of the UK. The south-west of England (Cornwall, Devon and Dorset) is one area that attracts many retirement migrants, because it has the perceived attractions of beautiful scenery, a slower pace of life, lower crime rates and a sense of community. The impacts on the host area are to add large numbers of older people (so increasing pressure on health services) and to increase house prices. Higher house prices mean that more young adults have to move away as they are unable to afford a home, so the population structure shows a shortage of young adults and eventually children. However, older people also create a demand for services, such as chiropodists, specialist shops and social activities, and this can create jobs locally.

Rural to urban migration

This takes place when there are few job opportunities for people (often young adults) in their local area, for example in isolated areas of central and north Wales. In these areas farming is difficult (**marginal**) because of steep slopes, high mountains and thin soils. Apart from some jobs in fishing or quarrying, there are few alternative job opportunities, so young people leave to find better jobs in cities. As a result, the population geography of areas such as Mid Wales shows a concentration of older people who have decided not to move or who are tied to their primary-sector jobs.

Other factors

These include the general north-to-south drift (following jobs), urban–urban migration and counter-urbanisation

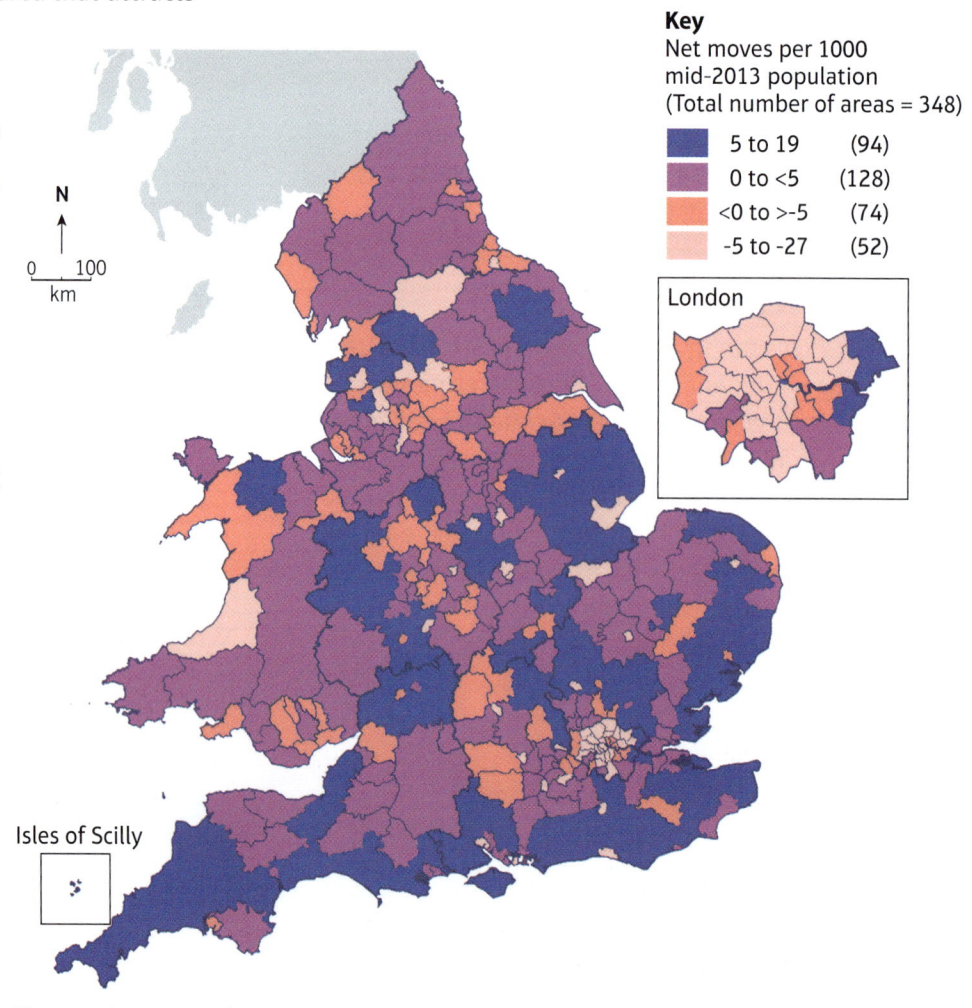

Figure 6 Net internal migration, 2014

Key
Net moves per 1000 mid-2013 population
(Total number of areas = 348)

- 5 to 19 (94)
- 0 to <5 (128)
- <0 to >-5 (74)
- -5 to -27 (52)

(when people move away from cities to more rural areas). For example, 68,000 more people left London in 2014 than moved to the capital.

Activity

Study Figure 6.

1. What factors explain the concentrations of high net migration (dark blue) in London?
2. Explain why there are areas of negative net migration (pink) in mid and north Wales.

International migration

- In the 1950s, responding to a shortage of workers, the UK government encouraged immigration from former colonies in the Caribbean, India, Pakistan and Bangladesh to fill jobs in transport and industries such as textiles and steel. By 1971, about 1 million people had moved to the UK, including 250,000 from the Caribbean and another 250,000 from India, Pakistan and Bangladesh. These were mostly young adults with young children, or single men.
- In the 1970s, there was no longer a shortage of labour and so immigration came under government control. The numbers arriving reduced. Many of the immigrants went to cities such as Bradford, London and Birmingham, where more jobs were to be found.
- A period of economic growth and enlargement of the European Union around 2004 meant that immigrants began to arrive from Eastern Europe, especially Poland, Latvia and Estonia. The majority of the immigrants were young, 80% were aged 18 to 34 years. Many of these immigrants went to cities such as London and Birmingham where they found jobs in industries or services, and to rural areas for farming jobs (fruit farming). In 2014, 560,000 immigrants arrived and 317,000 people emigrated from the UK. Most arrivals were from Poland, China and India.
- In the 2012–15 period many people fled from fighting in Syria and Afghanistan and migrated to Birmingham and other UK cities.

Exam-style question

Compare the reasons for national migration and international migration to the UK. **(4 marks)**

Exam tip

When asked to compare two things, you need to find the similarities and differences between them – here it is reasons why people migrate within and into the UK. You need to discuss both elements, and how they are similar/different.

Impacts of international migration

- Generally, international migrants settle in and around cities, providing a new source of both cheap or unskilled (e.g. construction) and skilled (e.g. nurses and doctors) labour.
- Migration to cities increases population density and puts pressure on services.
- As many migrants are young and have families, this increases the number of children in an area and affects population demographics. In ageing populations, such as the UK, this can also bring benefits.
- Migrants introduce their home culture, for example, cuisine and religious practices.

Checkpoint

Now it is time to review your understanding of UK regional differences and population movements.

Strengthen

S1 Choose one urban core and one rural area of the UK and summarise the differences in their population, economy and settlement characteristics.

S2 Now explain the differences between these urban and rural areas.

Challenge

C1 Classify the impacts of national and international migration to the UK into positive and negative impacts (some may be both or neither).

C2 Describe three examples of support for reasons with high unemployment.

5 The UK's Evolving Human Landscape

How is the UK economy changing?

Learning objectives

- To understand the decline of primary and secondary industries and the rise of tertiary and quaternary sectors
- To recognise the impacts of industrial decline in north-east England
- To understand the impacts of industrial growth in south-east England

Two contrasting regions of the UK

There have been big changes in the UK economy in the last 50 years, including in the primary, secondary, tertiary and quaternary sectors. These have changed the UK's economic structure and employment pattern. These changes are best seen in two contrasting regions of the country, north-east England and south-east England.

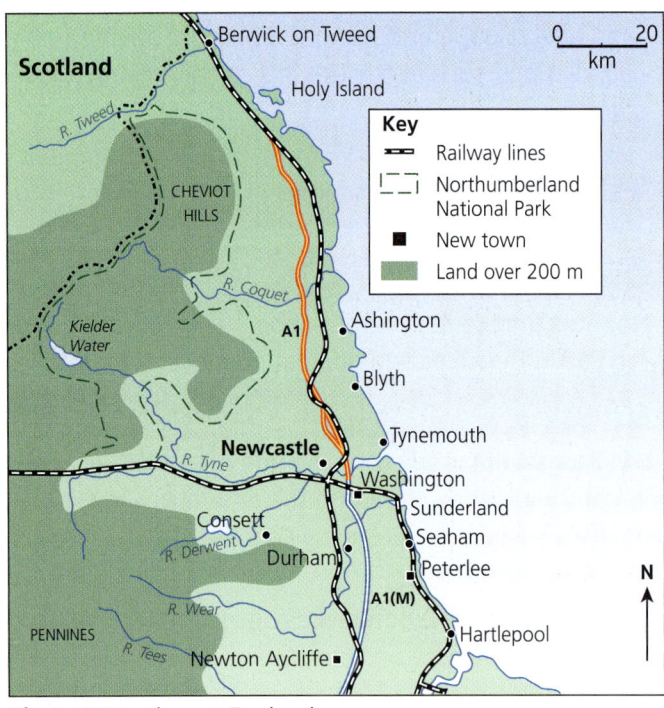

Figure 7 North-east England

The North East

The economy of the North East used to be dominated by heavy industry, especially coal mining, shipbuilding, iron and steel production, and chemicals. In the last 50 years these industries have declined because of foreign competition, high land and labour costs, and the exhaustion of the coal seams. In 1947, there were 108,000 coal miners working in 127 pits but the last mine closed in 1994 and employment fell to 55 people. In 1971, manufacturing industry accounted for 40% of employment in the area, but by 2011 this had fallen to 10.2% (Table 2).

Did you know

In 2014, the *Guardian* newspaper compared the North East to Detroit in the USA, a city scarred by industrial decline, which prompted a vigorous defence, particularly on social media.

The North East continues to be an area of industrial change and decline in manufacturing (secondary) industries. Between 2007 and 2013, unemployment here rose faster than in any other UK region, to over 8%. The contribution of the region to national economic growth, as measured by value added, has shrunk from a weak 3% to barely 2%. Between 2011 and 2012, child poverty rates in Middlesbrough and Newcastle Central rose to 40% and 38%, respectively.

Table 2 A profile of three English regions in 2013

	% of UK population	Median age in years	Unemployment (%)	Manufacturing employment 2011 census (%)
North East	4	41.5	8.2	10.2
South East	14	40.8	6.0	7.2
South West	8	42.9	6.0	9.1

5 The UK's Evolving Human Landscape

The current economic and employment structure shows that primary industry remains largely based on agriculture in the rural parts of the region. Mining and quarrying remain but are very small scale, as is the fishing industry. Manufacturing industry, especially chemicals, is urban-based and still important, but employs fewer people than in the past because of automation and improved technology. Car production at the Nissan factory started in 1986 and now employs 4000 people.

However, it has been the growth of tertiary activities which has led to some improvement in the unemployment figures. In 2013, the public sector employed 257,000 people in the region, which accounted for 22% of all employment.

The South East

Primary industries in south-east England are mainly located in rural areas and centre on farming. Some of the most prosperous farms in Britain are found here – for example, fruit farming in Kent and wheat and barley farming in Essex.

South-east England is one area where manufacturing industry is growing rapidly, mainly in urban areas. There are important oil refineries at Southampton, and the M4 corridor has become a centre for light industries including electronics and engineering. Oxford, too, is an important manufacturing area for cars.

However, the region is also a very important centre for tertiary and quaternary industries. There are a wide range of financial and business service firms located in the region and more are looking to move in. Unemployment here is low at 6% (2013) and prosperity is high in comparison with the North East. Many of the new tertiary and quaternary firms are located in towns such as Basildon and Newbury, which are surrounded by green, open countryside that makes them attractive places to live.

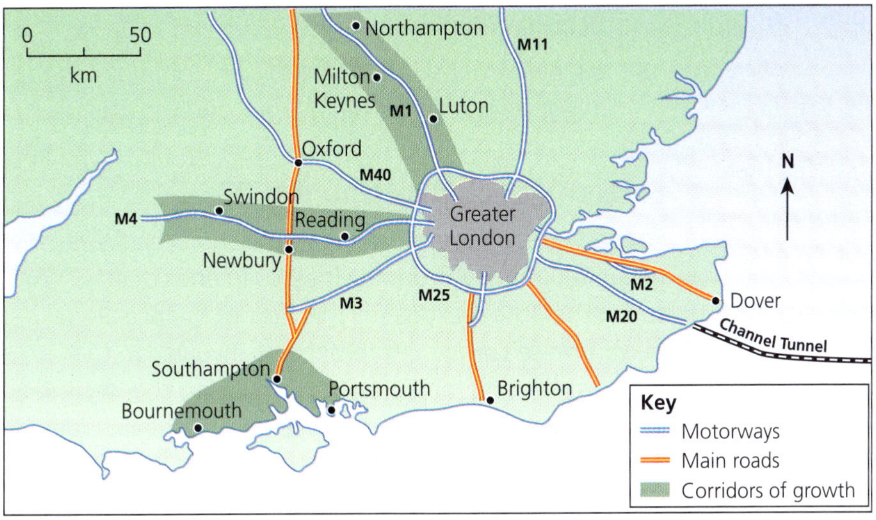

Why is the South East so attractive to industries?

- **Transport** – it has a network of motorways (M25) and railways. In 2013, 72% of UK freight was carried on roads in the South East. Four major airports (Gatwick, Heathrow, Luton and Stansted) give excellent access to other countries. Ports such as Southampton and Tilbury are important for the movement of heavy, bulky goods.
- **Markets and labour** – as the wealthiest UK region, it provides a large market of 19 million people for goods and services. There is also a skilled local labour force (Oxbridge and London universities).
- **Political** – it is close to the decision-making centre of London (national government and corporate headquarters). Also, previous governments encouraged firms to leave London and relocate in the South East at places such as Basildon and Newbury.
- **Geographical** – the rail and road networks centre on and radiate out from London. The region is close to the Channel Tunnel, giving access to Europe.

> **Exam-style question**
>
> Compare the main differences in the economic and employment structures of two contrasting UK regions. **(4 marks)**

> **Exam tip**
>
> To score well on this type of question you need to describe both the economic and the employment structure of the two regions and then compare the two, explaining similarities and differences.

Figure 8 The South East

5 The UK's Evolving Human Landscape

What are the effects of globalisation, trade and investment?

Learning objectives
- To know the importance of globalisation
- To understand the role of privatisation and free trade in terms of economic growth
- To understand the part played by foreign direct investment in the economic growth of the UK

Globalisation

Globalisation is the growing importance of international operations for all economic sectors, and for the culture and way of life of people around the world. Manufacturing industries, tertiary and quaternary industries, and people too, are being increasingly affected by decisions and events in other parts of the world. The three key elements of the global economy are:

- **networks** – linking countries together, for example the internet or trading blocs
- **flows** – of goods and services that move through these networks, such as raw materials, manufactured goods, money or migrant workers
- **global players** – the organisations that have a big influence on the working of the global economy. This includes very large companies known as **transnational corporations (TNCs)** and organisations such as the World Trade Organisation.

One of the impacts of globalisation in the UK has been the need for workers to re-skill when jobs in agriculture, mining and manufacturing have declined and been replaced by jobs in the tertiary and quaternary sectors. The workforce (labour) is also becoming more flexible, with more part-time working, more self-employment and more teleworking.

Privatisation

Another trend has been the **privatisation** of many UK industries, such as steel, transport and distribution, computers, airports, docks, petroleum, electricity, water, gas and postal services.

The effects of privatisation on UK firms include:

- increased **foreign direct investment (FDI)** from businesses wanting to invest in the UK
- increased awareness of global markets and increased competition
- increased foreign ownership of UK firms
- dividends and profits from some UK-based firms going abroad
- a drive to be more efficient, with a loss of jobs in the UK.

Free trade

Most firms want, and need, to take part in international trade to increase their profits. Global links can significantly increase the market for a firm. Not all trade is free trade, which is trade without tariffs or import duties. Some countries still have high import duties to protect some of their industries. The UK, as part of the EU, has pursued a policy of promoting free trade within the EU in order to allow the free movement of goods and services, which should make those goods and services cheaper. Figure 9 shows the main flows in the pattern of world trade.

Activity

Study Figure 9.
1. With which part of the world does western Europe do most trade?
2. With which two parts of the world do Asia and Oceania trade the most?
3. Suggest what goods and services (commodities) might be traded between Japan and the EU.

Foreign direct investment (FDI)

Foreign direct investment is composed of the flows of capital (money) from businesses in one country to another. The reasons for this flow of finance are to permit these companies to become involved in the business life and markets of the receiving country – in our case, the UK and EU markets. The companies can vary in size from small businesses to giant TNCs (such as GlaxoSmithKline). In 2014, the largest single investor in the UK was the USA (Figure 10) and over one-half

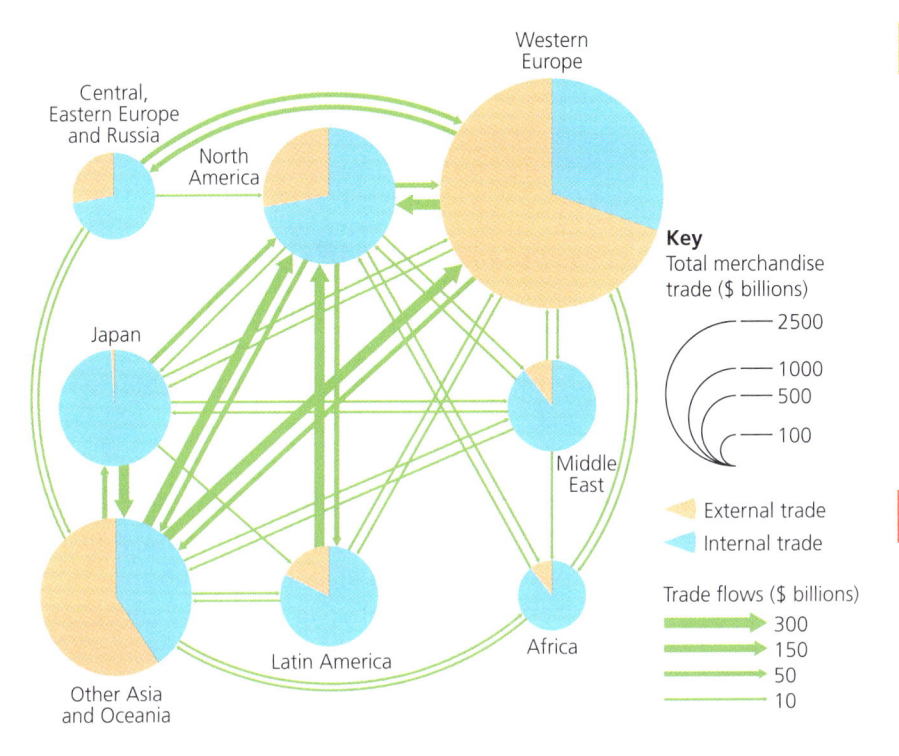

5 The UK's Evolving Human Landscape

Figure 9 The main global flows of trade

Activity

Study the data in Figure 10.

1. Which two countries invested most in the UK in 2014?
2. Estimate the value of FDI from these two countries.
3. Describe the pattern of investment shown in Figure 10, including the sources of FDI and changes over time.

Did you know?

Geographers need good data to keep up to date. Much of the data for the UK in this topic comes from the Office for National Statistics. A good place to find data for the EU is Eurostat.

of all the investment into the UK came from European countries. Most of the investment was in energy projects (wind farms, nuclear power stations) and infrastructure schemes (airports and hotels).

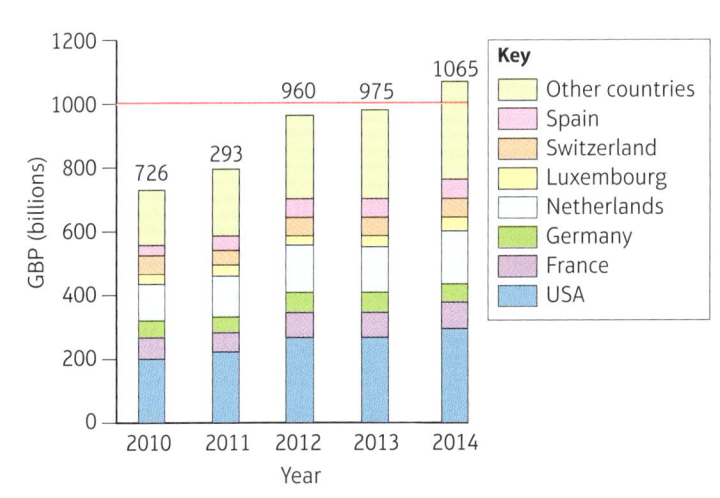

electronics and making motor vehicles. Some TNCs are specialised, such as Nestle (food and beverages) and Rio Tinto (mining), while others are more broadly based, such as Mitsubishi, which has a range of interests from motor vehicles to air transport and food processing.

Figure 10 Inward investment to the UK, 2010–14

Checkpoint

Now it is time to review your understanding of the changing UK economy and globalisation.

Strengthen

S1 Why have industries in north-east England declined in recent years?

S2 Describe one of the impacts of globalisation on the UK.

S3 Explain what foreign direct investment is and how it affects the UK.

Challenge

C1 What are the main contrasts between north-east England and south-east England? Explain the differences you identify.

C2 Compare the impacts of economic change in north-east and south-east England.

C3 Explain how TNCs operate.

Transnational corporations (TNCs)

Transnational corporations (TNCs) are large companies that operate in a range of other countries. They are powerful players in the global economy and they link national economies in different parts of the world. The top TNCs are involved in three main industries – oil,

5 The UK's Evolving Human Landscape

Case Study – How is Birmingham changing?

Learning objectives
- To be able to describe the site of Birmingham
- To recognise the importance of the situation of Birmingham in the region and in the UK
- To understand the global importance of Birmingham

The site of Birmingham

The city of Birmingham grew up on a dry point **site** on a south-facing sandstone ridge overlooking a crossing point of the river Rea. This site gave the original settlers a water supply, and the routes meeting here gave access to nearby resources such as timber, iron and coal. In the 18th century Birmingham was a market town overshadowed by the surrounding county towns of Stafford, Worcester and Warwick. The original main road to London from the north-west crossed the Midlands via Lichfield and Coventry, not Birmingham.

Birmingham developed its own industries of jewellery, gun making and the brass trades. In the time before canals were built to carry bulky goods, these industries needed skilled labour but only small amounts of raw materials to create high-quality goods.

From the 1830s Birmingham began to spread outwards rapidly as workers and industries moved in. This was when its **situation** in the centre of the Birmingham plateau became so important for its growth into a major city.

Situation and connectivity of Birmingham

Birmingham is in a very important strategic economic position in the Midlands region of the UK. The significance of Birmingham's central situation has had an important impact on the growth and development of the city in a variety of ways, particularly enabling manufacturing to source raw materials and reach markets easily.

- It became a centre of the national canal network after the first canal was built in 1768. Soon, more canals were built, connecting it to other Midlands towns, especially the industrial Black Country – a source of coal and iron for its early industries. In the early 19th century, more canals connected Birmingham to other parts of the UK.
- Similarly, after 1833, when railways replaced canals for the transport of heavy bulky raw materials and finished products, Birmingham emerged as a nodal centre for the railway network. The London and Birmingham Railway opened in 1838 and connected London Euston with Birmingham. This was the start of Birmingham's emergence as the central point in the UK rail network.
- 1958 heralded the start of the era of motorways, when the M5 opened. This was followed by the M6 and the M40 in the 1960s and the M42 in 1976. These motorways all met near Birmingham, placing it central to the national network.
- In 1976, as Birmingham grew, its central situation made it the logical choice for the National Exhibition Centre, which hosts 500 events a year and receives 3 million visitors.

In a national context the situation and connectivity of Birmingham is still very important today.

- It is the most central city in the UK.
- It is the Midlands end of routes from London. The first motorway built in the UK, the M1, linked London and Birmingham in 1959. The High Speed 2 train route will also link the two cities.
- It is the key centre linking the North West (Manchester and Liverpool) and the North East (Leeds and Newcastle) with London and the South East.
- It connects routes from the South West (Cornwall, Devon) with those from the North West and North East, as the motorway pattern shown in Figure 11 shows.
- Birmingham Airport has direct connections to around 150 national and international destinations.

5 The UK's Evolving Human Landscape

Activity

1. Using the information in this book and a GIS source, describe the site of Birmingham.
2. Why did Birmingham develop industries such as jewellery, guns and brass?
3. Why can Birmingham be described as well-connected nationally?

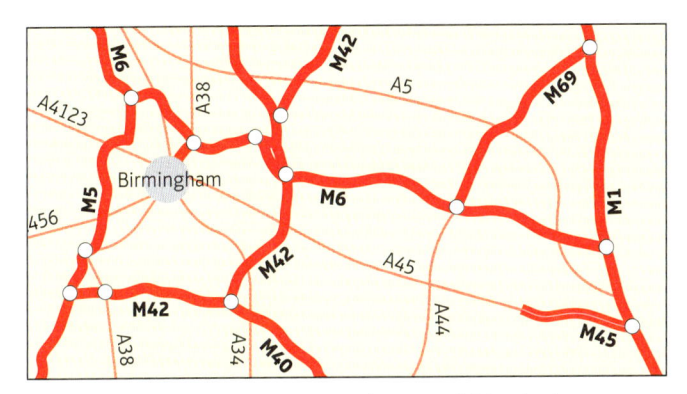

Figure 11 The motorway network around Birmingham

Activity

Study Figure 11 and use an atlas.

1. Which motorways meet at Birmingham?
2. Use your atlas to describe how Birmingham is connected to the rest of the UK by motorway. Include details of distances to well-connected cities, and any areas which are poorly connected.
3. Explain why Birmingham's good communications network is useful for industry, business and leisure.

Global importance

Birmingham's global reputation and importance have been growing and are being increasingly recognised. The city has more canals than Venice, Europe's largest public library, creative hot spots, cultural variety, restaurants and music spots. This illustrates the way in which, since the 1990s, Birmingham has emerged as a globally important city.

- It remains an important industrial and manufacturing centre, and has emerged as an important financial centre.
- The International Conference Centre (ICC) was constructed in 1991 and has hosted exhibitions and conferences from around the world, contributing nearly £1.5 billion to the local economy.
- The concentration of high-quality restaurants in the city centre has an international reputation.
- It has three internationally recognised universities – Birmingham, Birmingham City and Aston.
- Its city centre has been redeveloped to create an important retail centre around the Bull Ring.

5 The UK's Evolving Human Landscape

What is the structure of Birmingham?

Learning objectives

- To know the structure of the city in terms of zones
- To understand the functions of different building types
- To explain the effect of the city's structure, land-use and environmental quality

Figure 12 The centre of Birmingham

Figure 12 shows the centre of Birmingham, in particular the **Central Business District (CBD)**. This area of the city is dominated by department stores, specialist and variety goods shops, offices, banks, theatres and hotels. This is the heart of the city and the centre of local government. Redevelopment projects mean that the buildings in the CBD are new, for example the Bull Ring shopping centre. The quality of the environment in the CBD is quite high with some open green space. Land here is expensive so the building density is high, with buildings both close together and taller than in the rest of the city.

Beyond the CBD are the inner city areas, many originally built in the 19th century, and which were redeveloped in the 1970s through **Comprehensive Development Areas (CDAs)** schemes. Here, the buildings are tower blocks of flats or high density terraces (Figure 13). There are few shops, even fewer factories and a few churches with very little open green space.

The suburbs extend beyond the inner zone and occupy a large part of the city's area. Some of the suburbs were built in the 19th century, but most were built in the 1930s or 1950s and 1960s. Some are centres of council housing (many of which have been privately purchased) and others were built as private estates (owner occupied). Here, the density of buildings is lower, and the land use is mainly housing with a few shops and some good quality green space (Figure 14).

5 The UK's Evolving Human Landscape

Figure 13 Housing in Birmingham inner city

Figure 14 Housing in Birmingham suburbs

The industrial zones of the city stand out clearly, radiating outwards from the city centre – two important ones radiating in an easterly and north-easterly direction. Suburban industrial areas are also significant in the geography of the city, and are usually located close to a main road.

Finally, on the northern and southern edges of Birmingham is the urban–rural fringe, where there is countryside, but it is closely linked to the city.

Activity

1. Study Figures 12–14 and the text about Birmingham's structure. Copy the table below and add details to show the differences between different parts of Birmingham.

	CBD	Inner city	Suburbs
Age of buildings			
Density of buildings			
Functions			
Land use			
Environmental quality			

2. Make a sketch or tracing of Figure 12. On it identify and label different land uses such as offices or hotel buildings, transport and residential.
3. Describe the pattern of land use in Birmingham's central area.

Exam-style question

Describe the variations in the age of buildings and functions in a cross-section from the centre of a major UK city to the outskirts. **(4 marks)**

Checkpoint

Now it is time to review your understanding of Birmingham's site, situation and structure.

Strengthen

S1 Describe the site of Birmingham.

S2 What is the quality of the environment in the CBD and inner city areas of Birmingham?

S3 List three factors that have enhanced Birmingham's global reputation.

Challenge

C1 Describe Birmingham's situation in the West Midlands region.

C2 Why do so many motorways meet near Birmingham?

C3 Explain why inner city parts of Birmingham were redeveloped.

5 The UK's Evolving Human Landscape

How is migration changing Birmingham?

Learning objectives

- To understand the causes of national and international migration
- To know how migration has affected growth in Birmingham
- To recognise the effects of migration on the character of the city

Causes of migration to Birmingham

As with most migration, the pattern in Birmingham is a result of the interplay of 'push' factors, which drive people away from areas (such as a lack of jobs), and 'pull' factors, which attract them to other areas (such as better services). Revisit the reasons for migration for the UK as a whole on pages 190–191 as they are relevant for a city such as Birmingham.

What people said about their move to Birmingham

'I wanted to bring my family from Syria to get away from all the fighting.'

'There was not enough work for me in Poland so I had to move.'

'I wanted somewhere with a better night life.'

'I worked on a farm but the job was poorly paid and I needed to earn more money.'

'Where I lived the nearest shop was 5 miles away, with little choice. I wanted something closer and better.'

'We had family in Birmingham so we could live with them til we got settled.'

Activity

1. List the main factors encouraging people to move to the UK and Birmingham, then colour-code them into push and pull factors.
2. Classify those that are factors for UK migrants, international migrants, or both.
3. Which do you think are more important – push factors or pull factors – in attracting migrants to Birmingham? Explain your reasons.

Influence of migrants on different parts of Birmingham

Many international migrants have moved to the inner city areas of Birmingham such as Sparkbrook, Small Heath, Ladywood, Handsworth, Aston and Soho (Figure 15). Here, they found terraced houses which were cheap to rent and later to buy, and since then communities of people from Pakistan, India and Bangladesh have developed in these areas. There are now many shops and services, including places of worship, in these parts of the city.

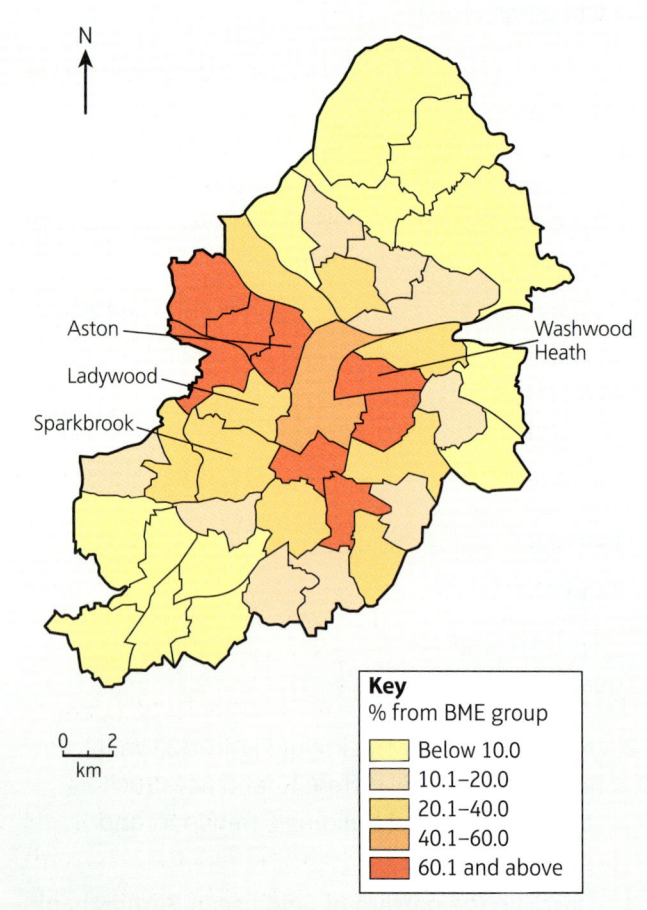

Key
% from BME group
- Below 10.0
- 10.1–20.0
- 20.1–40.0
- 40.1–60.0
- 60.1 and above

Figure 15 Black and minority ethnic (BME) groups by ward in Birmingham, 2010

Many of the more recent immigrants have located towards the eastern side of the city, close to the centre in areas around Bordesley. Here, too, the terraced houses and blocks of flats were relatively cheap to either rent or buy, and community centres have been built to cater for existing and new communities.

Did you know?

A report in 2013 reported that pupils in Birmingham schools speak 108 different languages, including 14,636 pupils who speak English, 3501 Urdu, 3350 Punjabi, 1600 Bengali and 1164 Somali. In some wards nearly 10% of households do not have anyone over 16 years of age whose main language is English.

Immigrants may change the characteristics of the places in which they settle, but they are also initially limited in terms of their choices of location. The increase in numbers may cause a range of impacts on the areas where they locate.

- **Age structure** – the areas of the city where immigrants settle have a young population. They have young children or will soon start families, with consequent demands for more school places.
- **Ethnicity** – these parts of the city generally are the most diverse ethnically.
- **Population** – these areas are forecast to be some of the fastest growing in terms of population in the next 10 years.
- **Housing** – these areas have older housing, with 1970s tower blocks or high density low-rise terraces, which are cheaper and more affordable.
- **Services** – these parts of the city require a lot of services, from health to education and employment, yet they are some of the poorest and most deprived parts of the city.
- **Deprivation** – the **Index of Multiple Deprivation (IMD)** uses statistics of income, employment, health, deprivation, disability, education, housing, crime and environment to produce an index reflecting the quality of life. The pattern for Birmingham is shown in Figure 16 and there are inequalities partly based on ethnicity.

- **Culture** – migrants bring a great cultural mix to the city, making Birmingham one of the most diverse cities in the UK. Although this sometimes brings tensions, it also attracts people and businesses to the city.

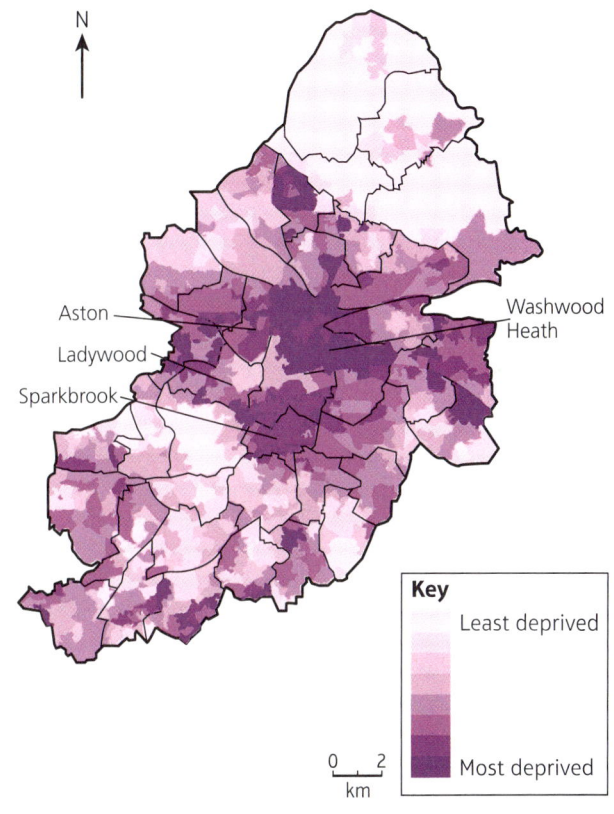

Figure 16 Map of Index of Multiple Deprivation for Birmingham wards

Activity

1. What is multiple deprivation and how is it measured?
2. Describe and explain the pattern of multiple deprivation in Birmingham shown in Figure 16.
3. Why might areas with many new migrants have rapid population growth?

5 The UK's Evolving Human Landscape

What are the patterns of inequality in Birmingham?

Learning objectives
- To understand the link between economic change and inequality in Birmingham
- To know how deprivation is measured and which areas are most affected
- To know the causes of deprivation and inequality

Birmingham, like all UK cities, has patterns of inequality. Some of these were shown in Figure 16; Figure 17 shows the pattern of unemployment and benefit claimants; and Figure 18 is a map of residents with no qualifications.

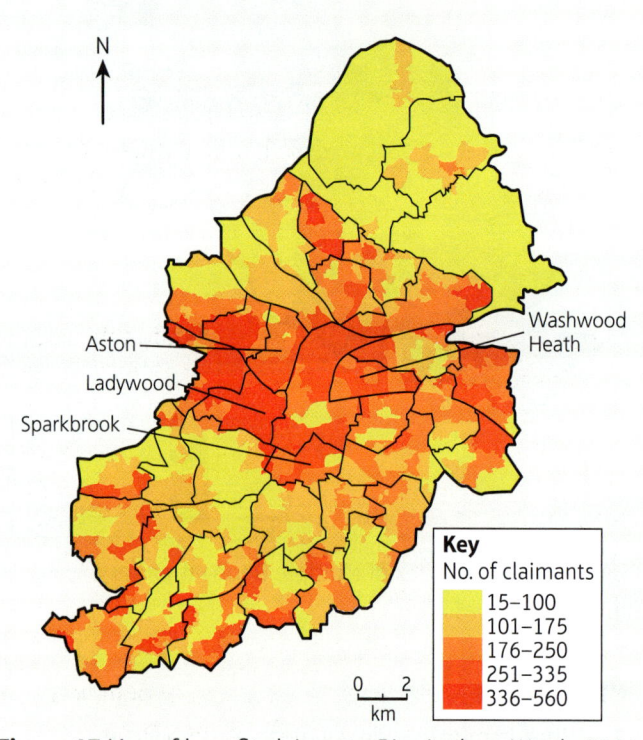

Figure 17 Map of benefit claimants, Birmingham Wards, 2014

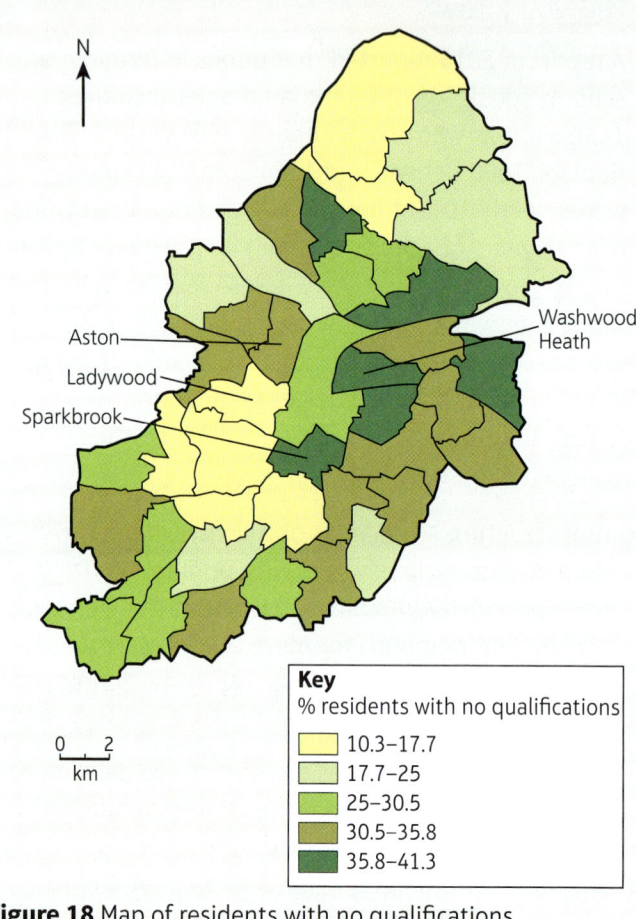

Figure 18 Map of residents with no qualifications, Birmingham wards, 2011

Deprivation in Birmingham

Figures 16, 17 and 18 show clearly some of the issues facing the different parts of the city. The inner city areas are disadvantaged in terms of deprivation, poverty, high unemployment, some poorer health provision and some poorer schools.

However, it would be wrong to think that deprivation is confined to the inner city areas of Birmingham. Some of the suburban areas, particularly towards the south and west, also have issues such as high levels of deprivation, high unemployment, poverty, poor living conditions and poor schools.

Much of the deprivation is the result of the decline in manufacturing industry and the flight of industry away from both inner city and suburban sites in Birmingham. It is often combined with older housing and obsolete buildings which are no longer suitable for newer industry. This, in turn, leads to a lack of investment and hence a spiral of decline.

5 The UK's Evolving Human Landscape

Activity

1. Complete the table below for the area of Aston to summarise some features of this inner city area of Birmingham.
2. Now add the information for Sparkbrook, Ladywood and Washwood Heath to summarise their features.
3. Write a short summary describing and explaining the issues in each area.

	Unemployment % 2013	% With no qualifications	Degree of deprivation	Ethnicity %
Aston	23.5			
Sparkbrook	26.3			
Ladywood	12.2			
Washwood Heath	26.9			

Why is there inequality in Birmingham?

- Economic and population change has been rapid, so cities find it hard to keep pace with providing what the population needs, hence the high deprivation in places.
- Globalisation and **de-industrialisation** have taken jobs out of the city (see page 194). There are fewer factories in central areas and therefore few jobs locally, so people have to travel to find work, which adds to their expenses.
- People with few qualifications find it harder to get jobs; in Birmingham many of the better jobs are taken by people commuting into the city.
- Older houses in deprived areas are often damp and hard to heat, and this can lead to health issues. Central areas of Birmingham tend to have poor air quality.
- There may be some discrimination against newcomers and some racial discrimination, though this is being actively tackled and overcome within communities and through laws.
- Large numbers of people arriving in a short time can put pressure on services, but it can also provide a solution, for example through migrant nurses and doctors.
- Birmingham has not had the money to do all it would wish to reduce these patterns of inequality, especially during an economic recession.

Exam-style question

Explain how economic change in a major UK city has increased inequality. **(4 marks)**

Exam tip

Make sure you define terms such as 'inequality' used in a question at the start of your answer.

Checkpoint

Now it is time to review your understanding of how Birmingham changes through employment and the movement of people.

Strengthen

S1 Explain which pull factors attract national and international migrants to Birmingham.

S2 Give details of two contrasting areas of Birmingham where there is significant deprivation.

Challenge

C1 Summarise the main impacts of migration on Birmingham's age structure and population growth.

C2 Classify the causes of inequality into economic, social and environmental, then write a short summary to explain which parts of Birmingham suffer most deprivation and why.

5 The UK's Evolving Human Landscape

What challenges have been created by the changes in Birmingham?

Learning objectives

- To know which parts of the city have experienced decline
- To recognise the causes – de-industrialisation and decentralisation
- To understand the role of changes in retail and transport in this process

Which parts of Birmingham have experienced decline and why?

The inner city areas of Birmingham have experienced most decline, both in terms of population and economic decline. Inner city Birmingham lost more than 500,000 people in the period 1951–71. The main causes of this were slum clearance and redevelopment schemes, transport and job losses.

- **Slum clearance and redevelopment schemes** – In the 1950s, large parts of inner city Birmingham still consisted of old, decaying, 19th century terraced houses and courtyards. Many houses had no hot water and no inside toilet. Over 70% of the housing was deemed unfit for habitation and by 1951 there were many small factories polluting the area, which had little green space. It was decided to redevelop inner city Birmingham on the basis of Comprehensive Redevelopment Areas (CDAs) (Figure 19). Conditions were so bad that whole areas were flattened and rebuilt from scratch. The new buildings were 'modern' tower blocks of flats, which were centrally heated and had all modern amenities. The redevelopment also aimed to introduce more open green space. But the changes meant that many residents had to move away to estates on the edge of the city and population in the inner city areas declined because they did not move back (Tables 3 and 4).

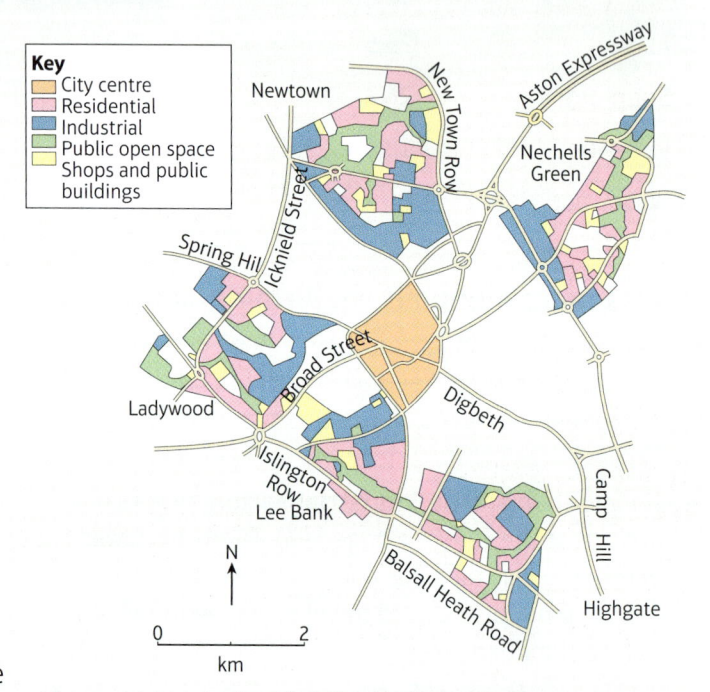

Figure 19 Birmingham's five CDAs

Table 4 Population of CDAs

	1949	1970
Newtown	28,125	15,400
Nechells	19,072	12,537
Ladywood	24,418	12,448
Lee Bank	14,797	6531
Highgate	16,484	10,081

Table 3 Changes in CDAs in Birmingham (%)

Land use	Newtown		Nechells		Ladywood		Lee Bank		Highgate	
	1949	1970	1949	1970	1949	1970	1949	1970	1949	1970
Residential	41	26	44	30	48	30	45	24	43	29
Industrial	30	30	24	24	21	21	24	21	22	21
Open space	2	16	1	16	1	17	0	13	4	17
Others (public buildings, roads)	24	18	28	20	28	23	29	35	28	19

- **Transport** – The construction of an inner ring road formed part of the redevelopment of central Birmingham in the 1970s. In order to build the new road older factories, warehouses and houses had to be demolished. Some of these factories never reopened, while others moved away from Birmingham. Better transport links also mean that workers can live further away from their place of work.

- **Job losses** – De-industrialisation was the result of too many small, inefficient and overcrowded factories struggling in inner city Birmingham, and the job losses that followed were another factor in the city's decline – Birmingham lost 50,000 jobs between 1961 and 1971. Some writers debate whether factory closures and job losses were a cause of people leaving inner city areas, or a result of a process that had already started. It seems clear that it was a combination of the two.

Economic decline

The UK as a whole has experienced a decline in manufacturing industry jobs since the 1960s but inner city areas such as those in Birmingham have experienced the largest decrease. In 1948, manufacturing made up 48% of the UK economy but by 2010 this had fallen to 12%. Many jobs have been lost in manufacturing, and the growth of secondary and tertiary industries has often replaced these with only low-paid part-time jobs.

Activity

Study Tables 3 and 4.
1. Which CDA lost most residential area?
2. Which CDA gained the most roads and public buildings by 1970?
3. By how many did the population of Newtown decline between 1949 and 1970?
4. Which CDA lost the largest percentage of its population between 1949 and 1970?

Decentralisation, e-commerce and transport developments

Decentralisation in Birmingham began when shops and shopping centres began to be built in the suburbs of the city or in rural–urban fringe areas such as the Black Country. From 1984 the Merry Hill centre was built in Dudley on the site of a former steel works. It is 10 km west of Birmingham and, for a time, was the largest indoor shopping centre in Europe. It has 260 shops, including major names such as Marks and Spencer and Debenhams. This centre attracted shoppers away from Birmingham CBD and the shops in the city centre began to close and move away. A further wave of decentralisation was caused by the growth of internet shopping. More people own computers and have discovered the ease of online shopping.

Birmingham's response to this decentralisation was to start a major redevelopment of the city centre shopping, especially the Bull Ring. A major new centre was built by 2003, which is anchored by the Selfridges store. This major new initiative was extremely successful in attracting shops and shoppers back into Birmingham city centre, not least because there is parking for 3000 cars nearby.

More recently, New Street railway station has been rebuilt (reopened September 2015) to create a major transport, shopping and community centre; this will be attached to a large shopping mall anchored by John Lewis.

Reasons for the economic decline of inner city Birmingham

- Lack of space for expansion.
- Out-dated buildings often in a poor state of repair.
- Derelict, unattractive environment, so new firms avoided the inner city in favour of the rural–urban fringe.
- Cramped, overcrowded road network, not designed to accommodate modern vehicles.
- A large number of older 19th century metal-working industries, which were declining nationally.
- Global competition meant that many of Birmingham's traditional industries suffered badly because of cheaper imports.
- As factories closed and unemployment increased there were fewer customers for shops, which closed as trade declined.

5 The UK's Evolving Human Landscape

How have changes in Birmingham caused economic and population growth?

Learning objectives

- To recognise which parts of the city have experienced growth
- To understand the role of financial and business services, and investment in the process
- To know about the effects of gentrification and studentification

The Birmingham rural–urban fringe

On its eastern edge Birmingham gives way to its rural–urban fringe, with a mixture of urban and rural land uses. Parts of the area are still agricultural but it also includes Birmingham International Airport and the National Exhibition Centre. Other land uses in this zone are shopping, housing, golf courses and farming.

Economic growth

Birmingham has experienced recent rapid economic growth. The reasons for this growth are:

- interest in Birmingham's traditional metal manufacturing by TNCs such as Ford and BMW, and investment by large food companies including Kraft
- the city's reputation for producing high-value low-bulk goods such as jewellery
- improved rail communications with south-east England and the growth of Birmingham International airport with links to Asia and the Middle East
- growing importance of finance and business services companies in the city
- a skilled labour force.

Activity

Figure 20 shows part of the Birmingham rural–urban fringe at a scale of 1:50,000. Study the map.

1. List all the different land uses found in this area of green belt.
2. Which of the land uses could create noise, water or air pollution?
3. There is a proposal to build new houses at Meriden in grid square 2382. An advisory group has been set up to consider the proposal and suggest if planning permission should be given. The key members of the group are:
   a. a local builder
   b. a civil servant living in and commuting to Birmingham
   c. a widow who has retired to Meriden.

Give reasons why each person is for or against the building of new houses at this location.

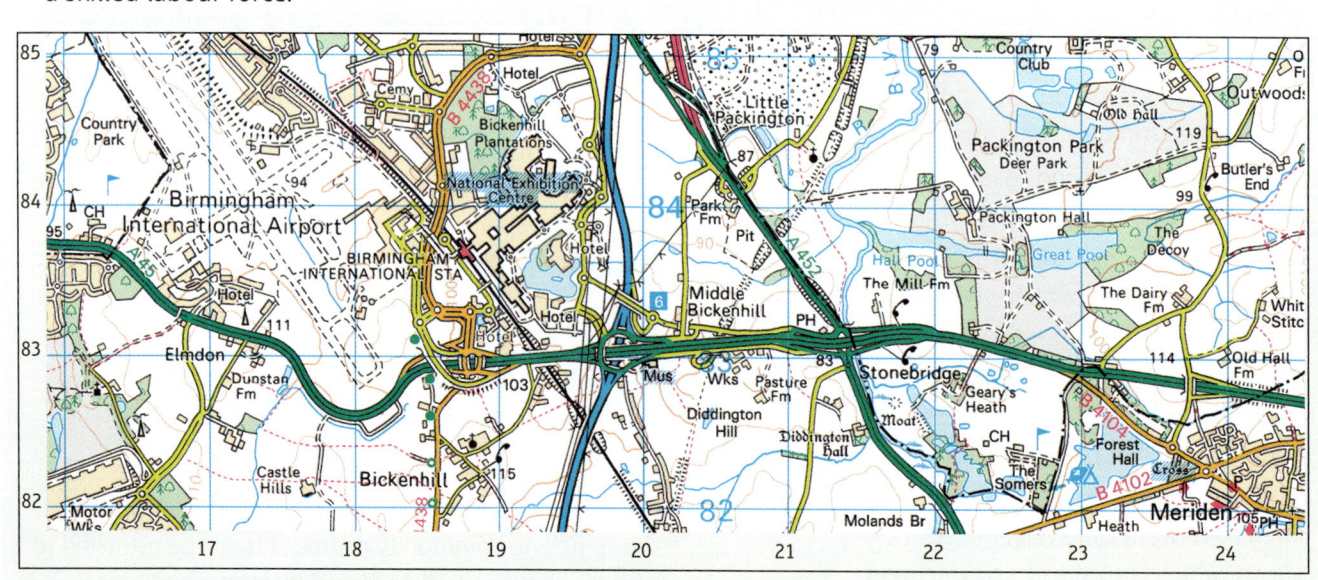

Figure 20 Extract from 1:50,000 OS map near Birmingham airport

> **Why are TNCs interested in investing in Birmingham?**
> - Access to the large EU market.
> - Relatively cheap labour and a highly skilled labour force.
> - Land available from **brownfield sites**, which used to be factories or older houses that have been demolished and cleared for development.
> - Government-backed enterprise zones and other incentives.

Gentrification

Gentrification is the process by which older (often run down) parts of the city, often close to the city centre, become culturally desirable, so wealthier people move in and change the area. An example is Moseley, a 19th century Birmingham suburb, where there are many large houses which were originally built for entrepreneurs and factory owners. After the Second World War many were subdivided into flats and bedsits and the area became run down. However, from the 1980s, the area's leafy streets and Victorian houses again made it a popular place to live and many were renovated. Moseley's location also makes it attractive to a social mix – it is only three miles from the city centre and two miles from the University of Birmingham and the Queen Elizabeth Hospital.

Studentification

Studentification is the gradual change (social and environmental) in an area of a city by the arrival of increasing numbers of students and the conversion of older, often 19th century, houses into student flats by subdividing large properties. Birmingham has three major universities – Birmingham University in Edgbaston, Aston University in Aston, and Birmingham City University in Perry Barr. These institutions have grown rapidly since 2000 and so the demand for this type of accommodation is increasing. Services also begin to change to cater for students' increased spending on arts events, concerts and performances.

There have been a number of impacts from students moving into areas such as Selly Oak:

- social replacement and displacement of older residents with a younger, generally single group of people
- concentration of young people with shared cultures and lifestyles and resulting changes in local shops and services
- physical improvement or degeneration of existing property, depending on the landlord–tenant relationship
- inflation of housing prices, so neighbourhoods become dominated by private rented accommodation and houses in multiple occupation
- increases in low-level anti-social behaviour and reduced owner-occupier levels, which lead to unkempt properties.

Did you know?

Birmingham's 78,000 students (2011), mostly between the ages of 18 and 22 years, have an impact on the city's geography and population structure. In two small areas of Selly Oak near the University of Birmingham more than 80% of residents are students.

Checkpoint

Now it is time to review your understanding of how changes in Birmingham create challenges and opportunities.

Strengthen

S1 Why were large parts of inner city Birmingham redeveloped in the 1970s?

S2 What were the reasons for the economic decline in inner city Birmingham?

S3 What is the rural–urban fringe?

Challenge

C1 Explain the effects of de-industrialisation on inner city Birmingham.

C2 What has been Birmingham's response to decentralisation? How successful do you think this has been?

C3 What has been the impact of studentification on Selly Oak?

5 The UK's Evolving Human Landscape

What has been done to regenerate and rebrand Birmingham and what have been the effects?

Learning objectives
- To investigate examples of regeneration and rebranding
- To recognise the differences between the two
- To understand the positive and negative effects of regeneration and rebranding

Regeneration in Birmingham

The site of the former MG Rover car factory in Longbridge is a good example of a regeneration project in Birmingham. In the 1960s, this site employed more than 25,000 people but declining sales and foreign competition meant that the company was eventually sold in 2005 to SAIC Motor Corporation, a Chinese company. This left a large brownfield site, part of which has been regenerated in a £1 billion programme. Part of the project is the creation of a £70 million town centre in Longbridge, including a new supermarket. Overall there are now over 15,000 square metres of shops, together with new apartments which overlook a new 8 km² park. Currently 200,000 people live within a 10 minute drive of the development and Bournville College, with its 15,000 students, has relocated to a new site in the development.

Activity

1. List four main benefits from the regeneration of the Longbridge site.
2. Identify four costs (problems) of the developments at Longbridge.
3. Considering all the information about Birmingham and its area, explain how important the long-term success of the Longbridge regeneration project will be for Birmingham's economic and cultural future.

Did you know?

The new town centre, with UK favourites including Sainsbury's, Beefeater, Greggs and Costa Coffee, attracts around 30,000 shoppers to Longbridge every week.

The new development has had both costs and benefits.

- Three new green parks have been created to improve the quality of the natural and urban environment.
- The proposals included 10,000 new jobs – in 2013, the new Marks & Spencer store created 350.
- Shop owners in nearby Northfield have lost trade and some shops have closed because of competition.
- Shop keepers in nearby towns such as Bromsgrove are also worried that they may lose trade.
- The growth of housing and shopping has eased the pressure to build new houses on green belt land at the edge of the city.
- House prices are rising as people move into the area, so locals may no longer be able to afford them.
- Unemployment remains high after the closure of the car factory so some young people have been unable to get a job.
- There are concerns over increased traffic on the busy A38 Bristol Road as a result of this development.

5 The UK's Evolving Human Landscape

Rebranding – Eastside Birmingham

Figure 21 Millennium Point, Birmingham

From the time of the Industrial Revolution, Eastside was home to a massive complex of factories and workshops and was accessed by part of the canal network, most notably the Digbeth Branch Canal. However, as the industry in the area reduced, the area fell into decline and many of the original factory buildings became derelict and the canals became dirty and clogged.

Rebranding and redevelopment began in 2002 with the construction of Millennium Point to replace the former Science Museum. This was an area of inner city decline, consisting of closed or demolished 19th century factories, car parks and old railway stations. The 1970s roads, residential and business property were demolished to create space for the redevelopment. The area is undergoing major changes estimated to cost £6–8 billion and should create 12,000 jobs. Another 8000 jobs will be created during the construction period. Rebranding means changing or improving the negative image of the area, and the main focus will be on:

- creating an education centre, based at Aston University and Matthew Boulton College
- Eastside City Park

Did you know?

- Eastside is part of the Birmingham City Centre Enterprise Zone, which aims to create 40,000 digital, finance and creative jobs by 2030. Enterprise zones offer government grants and fewer planning regulations to stimulate business and create more jobs.

- Curzon Park, based around the former railway station
- City Park Gate, a development of apartments
- student housing along the Eastside Locks.

In these ways the aim is to rebrand this key part of the inner city. Positive effects of Eastside are planned to be:

- an improved urban environment
- more homes for people
- employment for people building the new homes
- new jobs in construction of projects
- an improved image of the area and Birmingham as a whole.

Negative effects of the Eastside rebranding may be:

- higher property prices, so local people may no longer be able to afford to buy here
- increased traffic flows
- increased office space may mean that some office blocks stand empty
- the site will need a lot of new infrastructure (roads, schools and health care provision).

5 The UK's Evolving Human Landscape

How has urban living been made more sustainable and improved quality of life?

Learning objectives

- To understand the strategies aimed at making urban living more sustainable
- To understand the strategies aimed at improving the quality of life in Birmingham

The challenge for people in Birmingham is to make their city more sustainable. The definition of sustainable development (1987) says 'Sustainable development is development that meets the needs of the present without compromising (limiting) the ability of future generations to meet their own needs'. So the challenge is how to limit the **ecological footprint** of Birmingham so that people now and in the future benefit.

Recycling

UK households produce over 30 million tonnes of waste each year and much of this still goes to landfill sites.

- One glass bottle recycled saves enough energy to power a computer for 30 minutes.
- Up to 60% of the rubbish in a dustbin could be recycled; 80% of most cars also.
- On average 16% of the money spent on a product is packaging, which ends up as rubbish.
- As much as 50% of the waste in a dustbin could be composted.

The recycling rate for England was 43.5% in 2013; Birmingham achieved 30.1%, so its recycling programme clearly still has a long way to go.

Activity

Study Figure 22

1. Write some key points for a social media site that identify how much more paper and organic matter could be recycled.
2. Write a second set of points for social media to describe what actions each home could take to reduce all waste.
3. Which of the actions to recycle more can be carried out by individuals and which by groups such as governments?

Green transport

Birmingham has a network of bus routes to reduce car transport, and consequently air and noise pollution, in the city. Some buses are powered by gas to reduce pollution, and they offer seat belts and free wifi. The network of bus lanes also helps to persuade more people to use buses for their journey to work as buses can then travel faster than cars. Other initiatives are increasing bicycle lanes and electric car charging points.

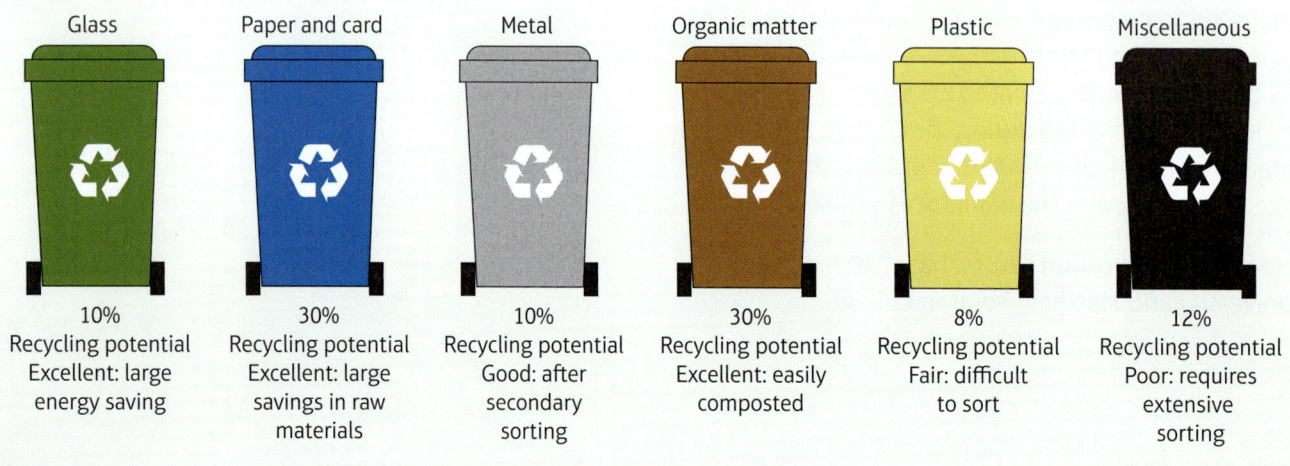

Glass	Paper and card	Metal	Organic matter	Plastic	Miscellaneous
10% Recycling potential Excellent: large energy saving	30% Recycling potential Excellent: large savings in raw materials	10% Recycling potential Good: after secondary sorting	30% Recycling potential Excellent: easily composted	8% Recycling potential Fair: difficult to sort	12% Recycling potential Poor: requires extensive sorting

Figure 22 Recycling household waste

Green spaces

Birmingham has a lot of green spaces – a total of 571 parks (e.g. Cofton Park) covering 3500 hectares, more than any other European city. In addition the city has five local nature reserves, one National Nature Reserve (NNR) and a number of Wildlife Trust Nature Reserves.

Eco-housing

Birmingham is at the forefront of building homes for people. One example is the Birmingham Municipal Housing Trust development in Northfield. This is a development of 400 homes made up of 122 houses and flats to rent and 278 houses for sale outright. The aim is to develop properties for sale alongside affordable housing. The homes are to be built to a high standard in terms of design, space and energy efficiency. The Birmingham Municipal Housing Trust was set up in 2009 by Birmingham Council to build new council homes.

Sustainability in Birmingham

In 2010, Birmingham was ranked 15th in the list of sustainable cities in the UK (Table 5). Some key facts are as follows.

- Birmingham reduced carbon emissions in 2009/2010 by 120,745 tonnes, so the city is on target to reduce its carbon dioxide emissions by 60% by 2016.
- There is continued investment in energy efficiency measures in the city's homes.
- Electric vehicles were used as part of the CABLED project (Coventry and Birmingham Low Emission Demonstrators 2009–10) to help identify where electric vehicles could best be employed and what issues might arise.
- Greener offices are being built for council staff.

Table 5 Birmingham growing greener (rank order)

	2007	2008	2009	2010
Overall rank in sustainability	19	19	17	15
Environmental quality	19	17	5	10
Quality of life	15	14	17	19
Future-proofing	19	18	18	9

Activity

Study Table 5.
1. Give **three** reasons why Birmingham has improved its urban living environment.
2. Suggest why the environmental quality declined between 2009 and 2010?
3. What does future-proofing mean?

Checkpoint

Now it is time to review your understanding of the ways in which Birmingham can be improved by different strategies.

Strengthen

S1 Evaluate the costs and benefits of the new developments at Longbridge.

S2 What are the main aims of the Eastside Project?

S3 How many parks and green spaces does Birmingham have? How are they useful to an urban area?

Challenge

C1 Do you think there are more costs than benefits from the Eastside Project? Justify your answer.

C2 How successful is Birmingham at building homes for people? Justify your answer.

C3 How sustainable is Birmingham overall? Explain.

5 The UK's Evolving Human Landscape

How is Birmingham interdependent with its rural surroundings?

Learning objectives
- To understand that the city is connected to its rural surroundings
- To know the economic, social and environmental costs and benefits to Birmingham and accessible rural areas from their interdependence

Birmingham's interdependence with its rural areas

Birmingham and the area around the city have a close relationship. For example, many people live in nearby villages such as Alvechurch, Belbroughton, Rubery and Tanworth-in-Arden and commute to work in Birmingham using the transport network. People within the city use the surrounding rural areas for recreation and waste disposal. Some of the main links between Birmingham and its accessible rural areas are:

- commuting links between the city and villages in the countryside
- produce links, such as the supply of milk and vegetables from the rural areas into the city
- links of manufactured goods, such as tractors from urban to rural areas
- water supply from the countryside to the city
- urban area supplying services for the rural inhabitants and businesses
- rural areas providing space for urban growth, including transport infrastructure
- rural areas supplying space for solid and liquid waste disposal.

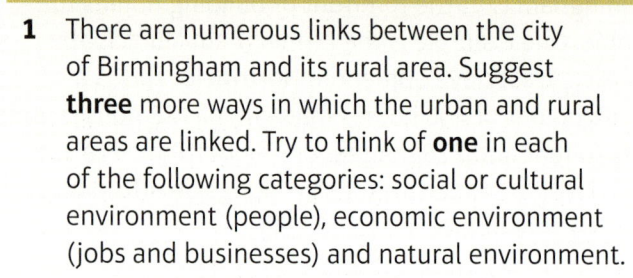

Activity
1. There are numerous links between the city of Birmingham and its rural area. Suggest **three** more ways in which the urban and rural areas are linked. Try to think of **one** in each of the following categories: social or cultural environment (people), economic environment (jobs and businesses) and natural environment.
2. Draw a summary diagram to show all the links between the city and its accessible rural areas. For each link suggest which area benefits most. What does this suggest for managing the Birmingham region?

This pattern of interdependence brings with it both benefits and costs, for both the city and the rural areas. Some of the most important of these costs and benefits are listed below.

- The rising cost of land in the accessible rural area is a problem if people want to buy land, either to build homes or to farm.
- New homes may be built in the countryside (greenfield sites) as this eases the pressure on housing in the city.
- The new homes built in rural areas can provide work for local builders.

5 The UK's Evolving Human Landscape

- Farmers make money from the sale of their land to developers.
- The nearby city provides a market for the milk and vegetables produced in rural areas.
- Farmers who diversify and open farm shops or offer camp sites can make money from being close to the city.
- The cost of houses rises because so many wealthy people from the city want to live in rural areas. This means locals can no longer afford homes in the countryside.
- People who move into the countryside often work in Birmingham. The villages they live in are empty during the day, so local shops may close because of lack of customers.
- People living in villages such as Belbroughton may not use local shops and petrol stations, which may be forced to close.
- There are increasing numbers of children in primary schools in the rural areas so schools can stay open.
- Old houses in rural areas are renovated and lived in.
- There is a loss of fertile agricultural land as more homes are built in accessible rural areas.
- There is a market in rural areas for tractors and machinery produced in the city.
- Firms in the city are able to draw on a supply of workers living in rural areas nearby.
- The people of Birmingham enjoy being able to get out into the countryside for leisure and recreation.
- Some potentially valuable and sensitive natural environments become endangered when the city seeks to expand.
- People in the city may have longer journeys to work from rural areas, adding to pollution from car exhausts.

Activity

Study the list of costs and benefits above.

1. Divide the list into those which are primarily about Birmingham city and those which are about rural areas.
2. Draw a grid, like the one below, for the city of Birmingham and allocate the statements to the correct boxes.

	Economic	Social	Environmental
Costs			
Benefits			

3. Construct a second grid for the rural areas and allocate the remaining statements to the correct boxes in your grid.
4. On balance, is it Birmingham or the rural areas that seem to get more benefits than costs? Give reasons for your answer.

Investigating Dynamic Urban Areas

Learning objectives
- To understand how to conduct a geographical enquiry into the quality of life in urban areas
- To understand how to choose enquiry questions, fieldwork methods and data sources for an urban investigation
- To know how to present, analyse and evaluate data collected from an urban investigation.

Activity
Reread the ideas about the variations in the quality of life from pages 201–207 and then create another **two** or **three** key questions which will help you to answer the main task question.

Tip Think about other factors affecting the quality of city life such as other impacts of traffic and the quality of the built environment.

The enquiry question

The important thing when setting out on a geographical enquiry is to be clear on the purpose. One good way to do this is to ask a question. For this enquiry into urban areas the task question is:

How and why does the quality of life vary in Birmingham's central area?

To help answer the task question, geographers next devise some key questions. These help to provide a focus for the enquiry. For this task one of the key questions is:

Why are there more accidents at some points around a junction in Birmingham city centre than at others?

Locating the study

It is important to provide maps showing where the investigation is located. You should include maps at a local and national scale, plus detailed maps showing your survey or data collection sites. You can then use your location and survey site maps to give a detailed overview of the place in which your investigation will take place. This part of your enquiry helps set the scene.

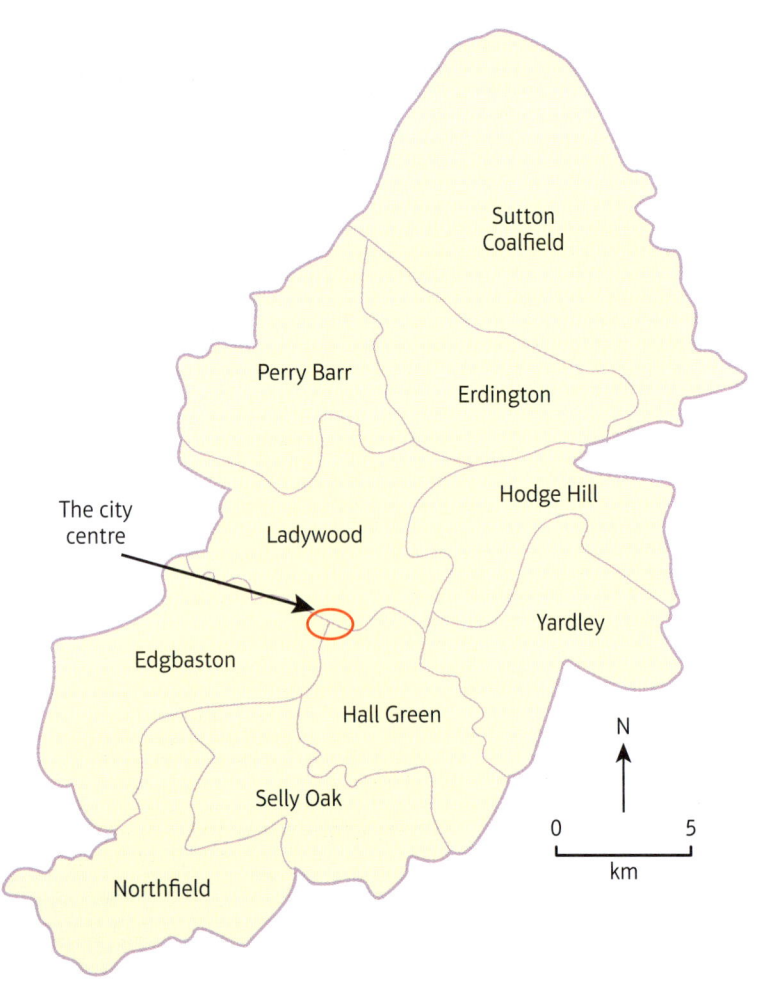

Figure 23 Map of named city areas of Birmingham

Investigating Dynamic Urban Areas F

Background

Road traffic has an important impact on the quality of life in cities. Road accidents, especially those involving children, are an important consideration. In recent years the numbers of road accidents has been declining but their severity has been increasing. Roads are being designed to help reduce accidents but more needs to be done.

In the UK every year about 400 people die from violent crime. By contrast every year over 3000 children die on our roads – nearly nine a day. Although the number killed and injured is falling, it is still too many.

Methodology

Once you have decided on your three key questions and located your study, the next step is to select the methods you will use to collect the data. Geographers use both **primary data** (which is collected first hand) and **secondary data** (which has already been published). In your investigation you should choose at least one **quantitative** method (using numbers), for example a traffic census, and one **qualitative** (descriptive) method, for example photographs or field sketches. It is also important to think about the scale of the fieldwork you will undertake. It would be very difficult to survey all the key roads in a place like the centre of Birmingham. One method is to use a sample, for instance, of the road junctions.

Sampling

Sometimes the most accurate way to investigate an issue is to take a sample; in this case, of roads in central Birmingham. There are three main types of sampling.

- **Random sampling** – is used where the area is the same throughout; for example, a field of crops. It does not matter where in the field you take the samples. Random sampling is achieved by generating random numbers and using them as co-ordinates, such as co-ordinates to generate Ordnance Survey grid references.
- **Systematic sampling** – is used in places where things change in a regular fashion, such as traffic along a road. You could sample at ten equally spaced points along a road to investigate changes in traffic density and flow. Every point should be evenly spaced or distributed.
- **Stratified sampling** – is used in places with several different parts. You need to make sure that the number of samples taken is representative of the total area. An example might be identifying different types of land use in a town (such as retail and residential) and making sure each area is surveyed.

Exam-style question

Some students collected traffic data using a systematic sample of one in five major road junctions in the city centre. Explain **one** reason for using systematic sampling to collect this data. **(3 marks)**

Exam tip

Make sure you say what systematic sampling means, before explaining why it would be useful here.

Exam tip

You need to investigate two secondary sources:
- Census data, such as Neighbourhood Statistics from the Office for National Statistics
- one other secondary source.

F Investigating Dynamic Urban Areas

For each method you select it is important that you decide where, when and how you will collect the data, the size of the sample and why it helps to gather data for the overall investigation. An example of how to present your methodology is shown in Table 6.

Table 6 Counting traffic for one hour on the A38 at the Smallbrook Queensway junction, Birmingham

Method	Outline of method	Purpose of method	Recording
Carry out a traffic census on both sides of the A38 and on the adjoining Smallbrook Queensway and Holloway Head roads in Birmingham.	I chose these sites based on my analysis of the secondary data showing high levels of accidents in this area. I collected data on weather conditions, quality of light and type of vehicle and recorded numbers in each case.	The reason for using this method was to identify what factors affect the possibility of accidents along a busy stretch of main road.	For both northbound and southbound carriageways, record the number of cars, vans and lorries, buses, and motorcycles and cycles passing in one hour.

Risk assessment

Now that you have decided on the methods you will use to collect your data, you will need to produce a risk assessment. In your risk assessment you should consider the following: the potential risks, the severity of each risk – on a scale of 0 (low) to 10 (high) – and how the risk can be managed. An example is shown in Table 7.

Table 7 Risk assessment

Risk	Severity rating	Management
Being injured by traffic	8/10	Choose a place for the survey back from the curb and take care when crossing the road. Wear a high visibility vest.

Activity

1. Copy the table below.

Method	Outline of method	Purpose of method	Recording

   a. Choose **two** investigations from the following: the quality of the built environment or streetscape, air quality, deprivation, access to services.

   b. Discuss what you could find out each of about them, how you could do so and why they will help with answering the main task question, then complete the table.

2. You have been asked the following key question, 'What do local people and visitors think about the quality of life in Birmingham centre?' Create a questionnaire to gather the information you need to answer this key question.

Investigating Dynamic Urban Areas

Data presentation

Having collected your data, you will next need to think about how to present it. Geographers use a range of simple and more sophisticated graphical techniques to present their findings. For your enquiry you should aim to produce a number of both simple and sophisticated techniques. A sophisticated technique is one that uses at least two variables to represent the data: divided bar graphs located either side of the chosen road would be an example of a sophisticated technique using the two elements of location and traffic type. Techniques that could be used to present information for the chosen road or area are:

- annotated photographs/field sketches
- located divided bar graphs for the same area under different weather conditions
- a map of the main danger areas of the site.

When presenting your techniques you should aim to create hand drawn and digitally produced forms of presentation.

Activity

Study Figure 24 and Table 8.

1. At what time of year do most serious accidents happen at this junction?
2. Are there patterns in the weather associated with serious accidents?
3. Why are cyclists at high risk in this type of environment?

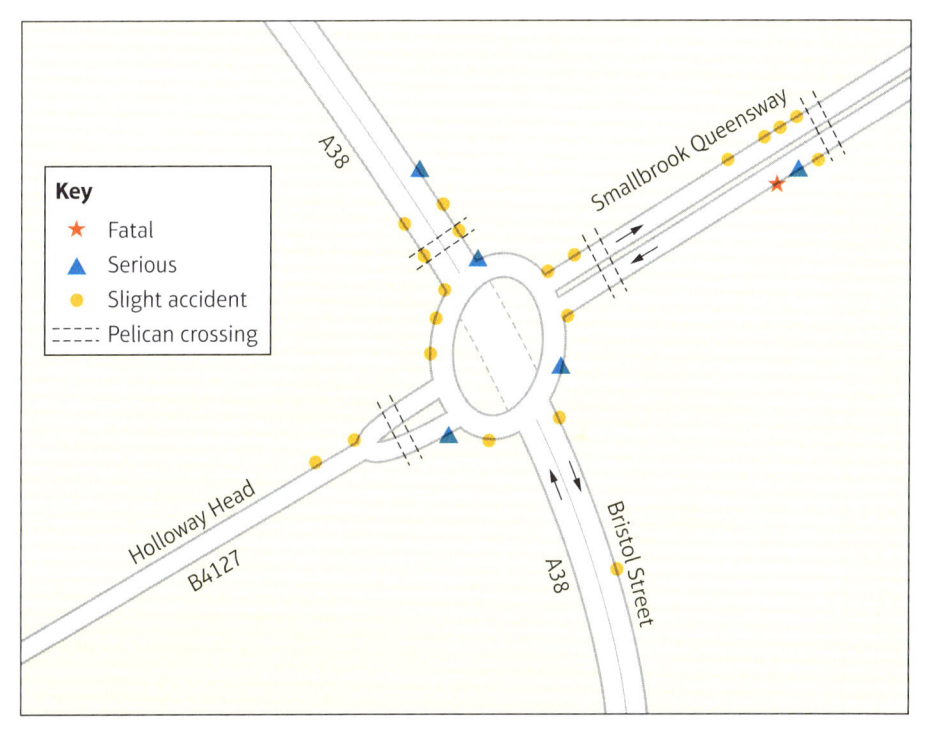

Figure 24 Map showing the location of accidents at the Smallbrook Queensway junction, Birmingham (2012–14)

Table 8 Accidents at the Smallbrook Queensway junction, Birmingham (2012–14)

Accident	1	2	3	4	5	6
Severity	Serious	Serious	Serious	Serious	Serious	Fatal
Month	July	December	November	January	February	March
Time of day	1750	0650	0721	0802	1658	0100
Weather	Dry, windy	Wet, rain and drizzle	Dry	Wet, rain	Dry	Dark, wet, rain
Type	Pedal cycle and taxi	Pedal cycle and van	Pedestrian and car	Pedestrian and car	Two cars	Taxi and pedestrian
Injured party	Cyclist	Cyclist	Pedestrian	Pedestrian	Car driver	Pedestrian

F Investigating Dynamic Urban Areas

(F) Analysis and conclusions

The next stage of the enquiry is to analyse the data collected and to see how far it addresses your key questions and if these are going to help address the task question. When you are analysing your data it is important to:

- **describe** the general trends from the data – for example, 'There were more accidents during the winter months than the summer months'
- **make comparisons** between the two sets of data for the two occasions of the surveys – for example, 'The flow of traffic was not reduced in wet weather'
- **explain** the reasons linked to geographical theory – for example, 'The flow does not seem reduced or slower in poorer weather conditions and this links to theories that accidents are more likely to happen in poor weather conditions'.

Read the extract below from an analysis a student wrote about data collection in Birmingham. This is a structured response by the student with:

- reference to the data and figure (red)
- use of geographical terminology (green)
- explanation of data and links to theory (yellow).

> The flow of traffic along the Smallbrook Queensway was roughly the same (Occasion 1 northbound 237 vehicles per hour, southbound, 198 vehicles per hour, Occasion 2 northbound 218 vehicles per hour, southbound 174 vehicles per hour) on the two occasions of the survey as Figure 24 suggested. However, on the second survey it was raining heavily. This made conditions more slippery and therefore more dangerous. I recorded two cars skidding in the wet at the entry to the tunnel, which suggests the drivers had not changed their speed for the conditions.

Activity

Study Figure 24 and Table 8.

1. Identify the key elements of this location that make it a particularly dangerous location for accidents.
2. Once you have analysed your data using the structure above, you need to write a conclusion for the key questions as well as for the overall task question. When writing your conclusion for the key questions you should summarise the findings from the presentation techniques you used. Then state whether your data has proved your key question to be correct or partly correct or incorrect.

The following is an extract from a conclusion written by a student.

> The purpose of my investigation was to find out why some points at the Smallbrook Queensway junction are particularly dangerous for road accidents. I can conclude that the road junction I selected is generally a danger point and more dangerous in wet weather. My data supports the theory that weather conditions have an impact on the frequency of road accidents at dangerous points along a road. This finding helps towards my overall conclusion about the quality of life here.

F Evaluation

The final part of the enquiry is to evaluate the success of your study. You should review the data collection methods and data presentation techniques, as well as the validity of the overall study.

When writing your evaluation you should follow the structure below for reviewing the data collection methods and data presentation techniques.

- A description of how successful the method/technique was overall.
- The value of the method/technique in providing/presenting appropriate data.
- How the method/technique could have been improved.
- How the method/technique has impacted on the study as a whole.

Below are a student's reflections on their geographical investigation of accidents at the Smallbrook Queensway junction.

> I think overall the methods I used to investigate the traffic flow and danger points worked well. The traffic flow census showed just how much traffic uses this road, but also how it varies with the weather (not much in volume). Presenting the data as divided bar graphs showed the importance of cars, buses and taxis at this junction on the road. The annotated sketches helped to identify the main danger points. I could have improved the study by taking a census at different times of day to see the impact of rush hour, and by suggesting how the junction could be improved.

Activity

1. Discuss the two paragraphs with the student's analysis and conclusion.

   For **each** paragraph decide: what is good about it, how it might be improved or developed, anything that you think should be added.

   Justify your decisions.

2. Rewrite the **second** student paragraph with your suggested improvements.

Checkpoint

Now it is time to review your understanding of how to plan and conduct an investigation into changing urban environments.

Strengthen

S1 With a partner produce a flow diagram of planning an enquiry, starting from the choice of enquiry questions and ending with analysis and evaluation.

S2 Explain the difference between the three methods of sampling and give examples of how they could each be used in a city.

S3 Make a list of the types of qualitative data you might collect on an investigation into traffic in an urban area.

Challenge

C1 Explain where and why hand drawn sketch maps may be very useful in urban areas.

C2 Why is the evaluation part of the study so important?

C3 If the students were going to do this study again what three things do you think they could change?

Exam-style question

Some students used figures from the 2011 census for Birmingham in their investigation. What type of data is this?

- [ ] A Qualitative and primary
- [ ] B Qualitative and secondary
- [ ] C Quantitative and primary
- [ ] D Quantitative and secondary **(1 mark)**

5 The UK's Evolving Human Landscape

What changes have taken place in rural Worcestershire?

Learning objectives
- To know why the rural surroundings of Birmingham have changed
- To understand the causes of counter-urbanisation, pressure on housing, population change and increase leisure and recreation in the rural areas
- To evaluate the impact of changes on Birmingham and the rural area

Part of rural Worcestershire lies south-west of Birmingham. This rural area has experienced many of the changes outlined above, and the associated costs and benefits. Why are these changes, such as the growth of commuter villages, taking place? The answers to this question lie in what changes are taking place in Birmingham and cities like it.

- **The growth of population in Birmingham** – Between 2004 and 2014, the population of Birmingham increased by 100,000 or 9.9% – an average of 0.9% per year. This growth is due to more births, fewer deaths and international immigration (Figure 25). These people need homes, jobs, services such as education and health care, shops and transport links. In trying to provide all these things Birmingham has had an impact on the rural part of Worcestershire close to the city's southern boundary.

- **The demand for housing** – The demand for homes in Birmingham rose by 66% in 2015 – six times the growth in numbers of houses being built. Birmingham is trying to build as many new homes as possible on its brownfield sites, but this is still not enough. Therefore, more homes are being built in the rural area of north Worcestershire. Many of the new homes are for single people because more people are living longer, some are divorced and also many young people choose to live on their own.

Activity

Study Figure 25.

1. In which age groups did Birmingham have more people than the UK average in 2014?
2. In which age groups did Birmingham have fewer people than the UK average in 2014?
3. Assuming those growing population groups will spill out in to surrounding rural areas, analyse which of the following developments are most likely in the rural areas near Birmingham as a result of your answers to questions 1 and 2, and give reasons for your answers:
   a more investments in cafes
   b more investments in boutique clothing stores
   c more investment in cycle shops
   d more investment in crèche facilities
   e more investment in hairdressers.

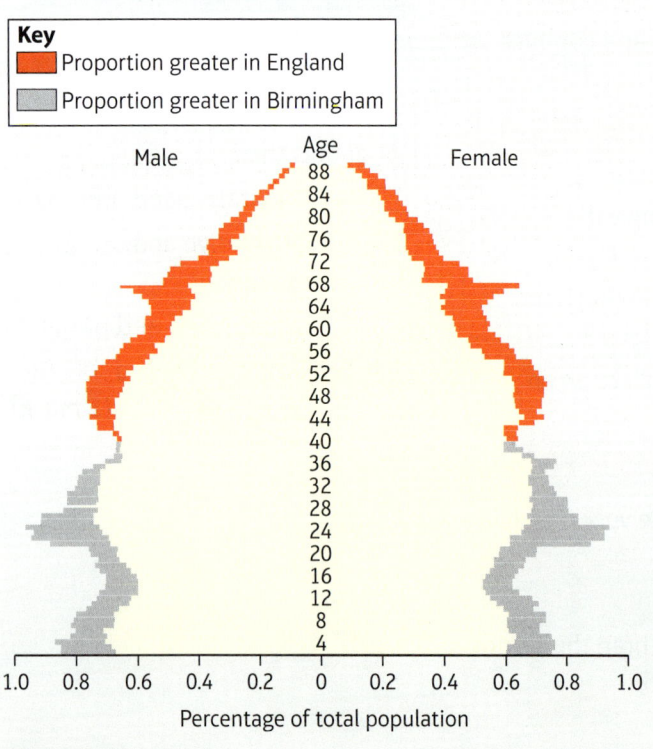

Figure 25 Birmingham's age structure compared with that of England, 2014

- **Employment** – Increasing numbers of people who work in Birmingham are choosing to live in the countryside. For example, Belbroughton has grown from a population of 603 in 1960 to more than 2400 in 2015, because it has become a centre for commuters to Birmingham. More and more people in Birmingham want to live in a pleasant environment in the countryside, away from what they see as the noise, pollution and 'rush' of Birmingham.
- **Redevelopment projects** – The rural areas around the city have been impacted by its industrial heritage and redevelopment projects. Birmingham is actively redeveloping its city centre and inner city areas. This has led to the demolition of older factories and office blocks. Other factories and offices are being moved out of the city and into new premises in rural areas of Worcestershire where land for expansion is available and is relatively cheap.
- **Increased/flexible leisure time** – In the 1970s, it was common for many people to work more than 45 hours a week. This figure has gradually declined and as a result people have more leisure time. People also have more flexibility in their working patterns (such as working from home) and can better choose their leisure hours. More people want to have an active lifestyle and enjoy walking, cycling or mountain biking in rural environments. The combination of these things has meant that areas such as the Lickey Hills, on the southern edge of Birmingham, have become major attractions for many people. The Lickey Hills is an area of 200 hectares of forest, grassland, moorland, streams and lakes, which attract over 500,000 visitors.

Exam-style question

Explain the main costs to rural areas of interdependence with a major city. **(4 marks)**

Exam tip

Look at the marks available – this will give you an indication of how many costs you need to identify.

Activity

As Birmingham grows, more and more people want to visit places such as the Lickey Hills Country Park just south of Birmingham.

1. What sort of problems are likely to be caused as increasing numbers of people visit the Lickey Hills?

Tip Think about traffic, footpath erosion, etc.

2. Why might some people who live near the Lickey Hills be against any growth in the number of visitors to the park?

Checkpoint

Now it is time to review your understanding of the interdependence of Birmingham with rural areas and the changes in those areas.

Strengthen

S1 List five main links between Birmingham and its local rural areas.

S2 Why is the demand for homes in Birmingham so high?

S3 Look back at pages 207 and 220. Explain the shape of Birmingham's age structure at around age 20.

Challenge

C1 Identify the main benefits to Birmingham of its interdependence with its rural areas.

C2 What types of people will be in favour of more people visiting the Lickey Hills?

C3 Explain why people have moved to villages such as Belbroughton, and the benefits and problems this causes.

What are the challenges and opportunities of rural change?

> **Learning objectives**
> - To know the impact in rural areas of affordable housing, declining primary employment, and the provision of health care and education
> - To understand key features of quality of life in rural areas
> - To use Index of Multiple Deprivation data to investigate quality of life

Affordable housing

Property prices are rising in the rural areas around Birmingham. This is because these rural areas are very attractive to different groups of people.

- Older people who want to retire to the countryside are attracted by the idea of a peaceful life in a pleasant, non-polluted environment. Consequently, many choose to retire to places such as Belbroughton in Worcestershire.
- People who work in or near Birmingham also want to move to the countryside, from where they can commute to work. This group tends to be those with young families who want to bring up their children in a pleasant, safer countryside, free from pollution. People are often able to buy a bigger house for their money, with larger outdoor space.

The effect of these two groups seeking homes in rural areas is to push up prices, often beyond the reach of local people. So the challenge is how to provide affordable housing for local people in villages in rural areas.

The answer?

The population profile of the parish of Belbroughton is older than the rest of Worcestershire. This is a result of younger people moving out, either to find work or because they could not afford homes in the village. Worcestershire Rural Housing Enabler Survey found that at least 15 households would genuinely need (not just aspire to) affordable housing – all had strong local connections and were unable to afford a home on the open market in the village. A site was found and new homes built, of which six were rented, two were shared-ownership and seven were fixed-equity-sale (restricted to 57% of their value on the open market).

The challenge of providing services in rural areas

Transport

On average 65% of all households in Britain have the regular use of a car. In rural areas the percentage is higher – for example, in Worcestershire 82% of all households have access to a car. As more people own their own car the demand for bus services declines. Faced with fewer passengers bus companies are forced to raise fares and reduce the frequency of the service. This leads to a vicious circle of higher fares and poorer services resulting in even fewer passengers. In addition, more and longer car journeys increase congestion, air pollution and CO_2 emissions.

Table 10 Methods of transport used in the northern part of Worcestershire (%) by age group

Method	10–14 years	25–60 years	Over 65	Total
Walk	23.2	13.0	20.1	16.9
Car driver	0	59.5	44.7	50.7
Car passenger	48.7	18.2	18.1	19.9
Public transport	13.7	5.2	13.6	6.4
Other	14.4	4.1	3.5	6.1
Total	100%	100%	100%	100%

Activity

Study Table 10.

1. Which age group depends most on public transport?
2. Which age group depends least on public transport? What are the implications of this for the rural area?
3. Describe and explain how dependence on the private car varies between age groups.

Other services

As bus services in the countryside have declined, so too have the numbers of schools, hospitals, doctors' surgeries and shops. A recent survey found that 35% of all villages in rural England and Wales had no food shop, 76% had no doctor's surgery and 85% had no chemist.

Small village schools are expensive to run. People also argue that with only three or four qualified teachers such small schools can only offer a limited curriculum. However, villagers campaigning to keep their school open argue that many schools are the centre of village social life. Villages also lack facilities for teenagers and young adults, with the result that many young people have to travel long distances for their education, entertainment and recreation. Despite the benefits of fresh, clean air in rural areas, many young adults living there complain that their quality of life is poor.

Measuring quality of life with the Index of Multiple Deprivation (IMD)

The Index of Multiple Deprivation (IMD) covers seven main types of deprivation and uses a weighting factor, which is based on what government officials consider to be the most important:

- income deprivation (23%)
- employment deprivation (23%)
- health deprivation and disability (13%)
- education, skills and training (13%)
- barriers to housing and services (9%)
- crime (9%)
- living environment (9%).

Figure 26 shows the IMD for Worcestershire, with a cluster of low scores in the north-east part of the county. These are mainly centred on Redditch, which has challenges of employment and income. However, rural areas do not have such a high IMD because older people there are not seeking employment and have regular pension income, and rates of crime are generally low.

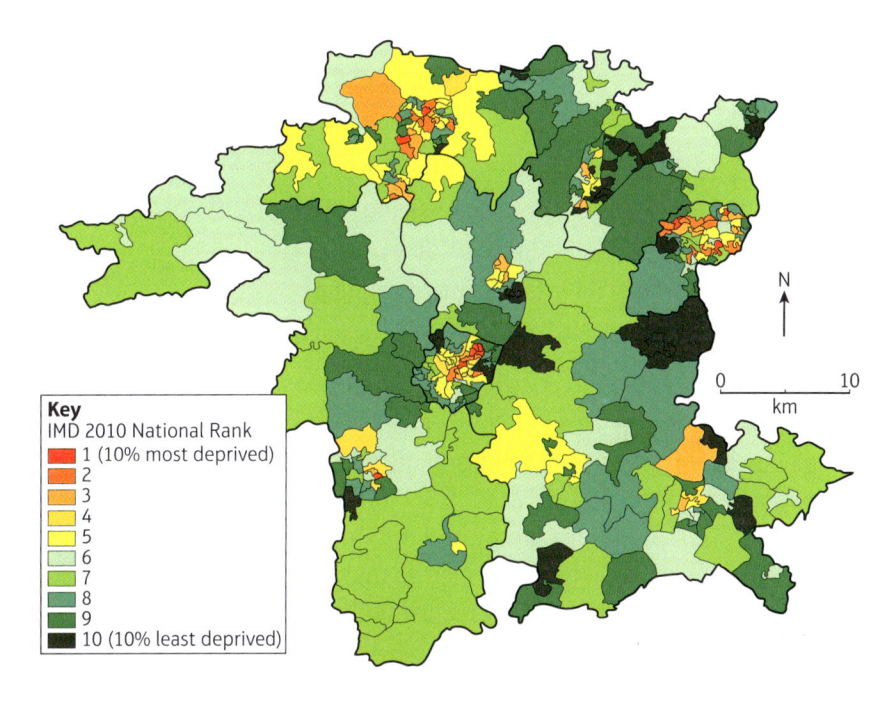

Figure 26 Index of Multiple Deprivation in Worcestershire, 2011

Activity

1. Which two measures of deprivation are the most important in deciding if an area suffers from multiple deprivation? Suggest why these two are rated the highest.
2. Why do rural areas usually have a better IMD than urban areas?
3. Why might old people and teenagers still feel deprived if they live in rural parts of Worcestershire? Which of the IMD criteria would be most important to them and why?

5 The UK's Evolving Human Landscape

What is rural diversification and what are its environmental impacts?

Learning objectives
- To understand the new income and economic opportunities from rural diversification
- To recognise the possible environmental impacts of the new economic activity

Rural diversification

Rural diversification is the development of methods of income generation that are in addition to, or instead of, traditional rural income sources such as farming and quarrying. Farming can no longer support the number of families it did 60 years ago. Many farmers are finding it hard to make a living from traditional food production alone. Supermarkets pay farmers low prices for products such as milk, and cheap food is imported from abroad. Therefore, UK farmers have no choice but to diversify:

- either by finding other ways to make money from their farm, while continuing to farm
- or by transforming their farms into a range of completely different businesses.

The first option is the most common form of diversification. In the second option, farmers usually move into leisure, recreation and tourism, or renewable energies. In other cases the land is sold off, and the farm buildings are turned into micro-businesses or cottage industries such as making crafts (greeting cards, knitwear) or offices (using broadband opportunities) (Table 11).

Advantages of rural diversification

- **Increased revenue** – from different income streams.
- **Adaptability** – branching out shows that farms are able to change to adapt to new circumstances.
- **Security** – farms are able to ensure a longer term future for their farm by diversifying. If the price of one commodity they sell such as milk falls, they have other sources of income they can fall back on.
- **Tradition** – new activities may fund the continuation of traditional farming activities.
- **Develop new skills** – running a new venture gives farmers the chance to develop new skills.

Accommodation

More and more farms are now offering accommodation, usually as bed and breakfast, campsites or sometimes as cottages which are let for short periods. These developments are relatively cheap for farmers and rural people to set up and run, but can bring in substantial amounts of income and give the security of another income source. However, there can be unwanted impacts. For example, if a lot of property in a village is converted to holiday accommodation the village

Table 11 Types of rural diversification

Products	New outlets	Tourism	Leisure and recreation	Development	Energy
• Organic crops • Herbs, cheese, bottled water • Different animals e.g. bees, goats, ducks, ostriches	• Pick-your-own • Farm shop • Farmers' market	• Bed and breakfast • Caravan or camp site • Café or restaurant	• Shooting • Off-road driving • Mountain biking	• Convert barns into housing • Industrial units • Telecentres	• Wind turbines • Solar farms • Energy crops (bio-energy)

may lose its character, as locals can no longer afford to live there and people move away. As a result, the village seems empty at times because so many houses are second homes or holiday homes. Rural land may also look unsightly, and pressures on the natural environment may be increased.

Leisure activities

The Clent Hills Country Park is an area close to Birmingham that attracts many people in search of recreational opportunities. This is an area of forested slopes and moorland hillsides. As a result, many people walk the Hills' footpaths and others ride mountain bikes or horses. Unfortunately, the Clent Hills has become a 'honeypot site' which attracts many people. The result is that some of the footpaths have become so worn by the sheer number of feet using them that they are subject to erosion by rain and wind. As the footpaths become more and more muddy they become wider and vegetation is killed, and so a larger area becomes affected by erosion.

Eventually, the Country Park's Rangers took action to stabilise slopes and footpaths by using rope mats to hold the soil together and planting fast-growing grasses.

Other issues that are caused by becoming a honeypot site such as the Clent Hills are:

- traffic congestion and air pollution at particularly busy times on narrow roads
- congestion and crowding on the footpaths
- people who are unable to find parking in designated areas park on grass verges, which kills the protective grass cover and leads to soil erosion.

In general, park managers deal with these challenges by patrolling the Country Park, helping visitors to find places to park and encouraging them to avoid grass verges. They also monitor air quality in the Country Park and encourage visitors to spread their visits over a period of time to improve the quality of the experience they will get from their visit.

Activity

1. How can the growth of accommodation, housing or campsites, in villages create environmental issues?
2. What are the main causes of footpath erosion on the Clent Hills?
3. How far do the environmental impacts of farm diversification outweigh the benefits?
4. What could be done to solve the issues of tourism and recreation in rural areas?

Checkpoint

Now it is time to review your understanding of the challenges and opportunities arising from change in rural areas.

Strengthen

S1 Why are property prices rising in rural areas near Birmingham?

S2 How did Belbroughton tackle the issue of affordable housing?

S3 What does the IMD cover?

Challenge

C1 What are the main advantages of farm diversification for farmers?

C2 What are some of the challenges arising from leisure in rural areas?

C3 Why is service provision difficult in rural areas near Birmingham?

Investigating Changing Rural Areas

Learning objectives

- To understand how to conduct a geographical investigation of change in rural areas
- To know how to choose enquiry questions, fieldwork methods and data sources for a rural investigation
- To know how to present, analyse and evaluate data collected for an investigation in rural areas

Activity

1. What challenges do you think Ambleside faces in managing the many tourists that visit during the summer months? Suggest how they might affect the quality of the environment.
2. Why do you think that one of the key questions is about how many pedestrians there are and which way they are moving?
3. Suggest **two** more key questions that would help answer this task question.

The enquiry question

When conducting a geographical enquiry, it is important to have a purpose. One way to do this is to ask a task question.

For this enquiry on rural settlements, the task question is:

What impact does tourism have on the quality of life and deprivation in Ambleside, a rural settlement in the Lake District National Park?

To help answer the task question, geographers next devise some key questions. These help to provide a focus for the enquiry.

For this task, one of the key questions is:

What is the impact of pedestrian density and movement in Ambleside?

In 2014, 16.4 million people visited the Lake District, most of them travelling by car. Ambleside is a 'honeypot' location for tourism – it is a place that most tourists want to visit. 2600 people live in Ambleside.

Locating the study

It is important to provide maps showing where the investigation is located. You should include maps at a local and a national scale, plus detailed maps showing your survey or data collection sites. You can then use your location and survey site maps to give a detailed overview of the place in which your investigation will take place. This part of your enquiry helps set out the scene.

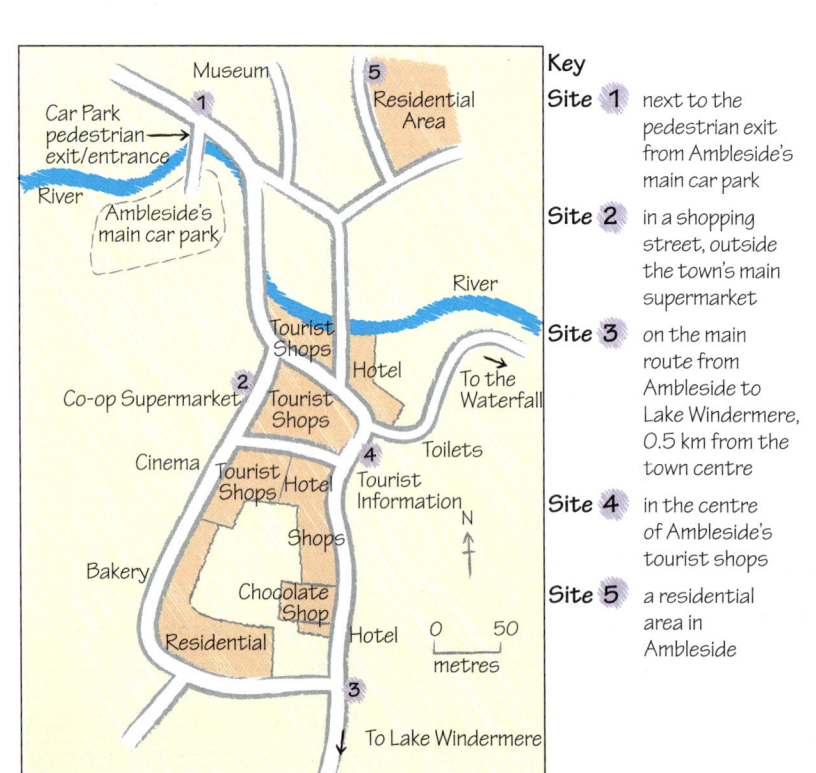

Key

- Site 1: next to the pedestrian exit from Ambleside's main car park
- Site 2: in a shopping street, outside the town's main supermarket
- Site 3: on the main route from Ambleside to Lake Windermere, 0.5 km from the town centre
- Site 4: in the centre of Ambleside's tourist shops
- Site 5: a residential area in Ambleside

Figure 27 A student's sketch map of Ambleside, with the five survey sites marked on it

Figure 28 Ambleside and mountains

226

Investigating Changing Rural Areas F

Ambleside is located 0.5 km north of Lake Windermere, on a small area of flat land between three large mountain groups and at the confluence of two tributaries of the River Rothay.

F Methodology

Once you have decided on some suitable key questions and located your investigation, the next stage is to choose the methods you will use to collect your data. Geographers use both primary data (data which you collect yourself) and secondary data (data that has already been published). In your investigation, you should choose at least three quantitative (using numbers) methods, for example counting pedestrians, and one qualitative (descriptive) method, for example a questionnaire of people's views.

For each method, it is important that you decide where and how you will collect the data, and why the data collected will help to answer the overall task question. You cannot collect data from every part of the area, or count every pedestrian all through the day, so you need to sample.

- **Random sampling** – data is collected by chance. An example might be writing all the street names in Ambleside onto bits of paper, putting them in a bag and selecting the first ten names pulled out. That way every location has the same chance of being selected.
- **Systematic sampling** – the locations of the sites are found at equal intervals from each other. An example might be to measure pedestrian numbers every 100 metres along one road.
- **Stratified sampling** – is used when the study area has significantly different parts. An example might be identifying different areas of land use within the settlement (such as residential or tourism-centred) and making sure each area is surveyed.

An example of how to present your methodology is shown in Table 12.

Activity

1. Some students decided to investigate pedestrian density and movement at five sites in Ambleside, shown in Figure 27.
   a. Explain **one** reason why the students selected more than one site for their investigation.
   b. What reason do you think the students would give for their choice of each of the survey sites?
2. Study Figure 28. How might Ambleside's natural landscape features contribute to the quality of the environment here for residents and visitors?

Exam tip

You need to investigate two secondary sources: census data for the local area and one other source, such as the Index of Multiple Deprivation.

Table 12 Measuring the density and direction of pedestrians (quantitative method)

Method	Outline of method	Purpose of method	Recording
Measuring the number of pedestrians and their direction. Sample measurements collected at Sites 1 to 5. Stratified sampling method used for site selection.	Five different groups carried out the investigation. Each group counted the number of pedestrians at each of the five survey sites for 15 minutes. We counted pedestrians going up the road and those going down the road as two separate counts. Then each group moved onto the next site and repeated the survey.	We used this method to see if some areas of Ambleside experienced higher pedestrian densities than other areas, and to see if there was evidence of an impact on the quality of the environment in Ambleside.	Each group had two clickers. One person recorded pedestrian numbers in one direction up the road and another recorded pedestrian numbers in the opposite direction. Then we recorded the total numbers for each direction after 15 minutes onto a table on our clipboards.

F Investigating Changing Rural Areas

Investigations in rural areas often involve a questionnaire – for example, a questionnaire to survey people's opinions about the quality of life in Ambleside.

- what questions will allow you to collect the information that you need for your investigation
- whether the questions should be open (allowing people to offer opinions) or closed (for example, yes or no).

Activity

1. What do you think are the advantages and disadvantages of recording pedestrian numbers using a clicker (each time you click it, it records the next number) rather than making a tally on a sheet of paper?

2. Make a blank copy of Table 12.
   a. Choose **two** investigations from the following: housing, quality of the streetscape, residents' experiences of Ambleside and job opportunities there. Discuss what you could find out about them, how you could do so, and why they will help with answering the main task question.
   b. Then complete the table. For each investigation, describe the methods and explain how and why you would conduct and record them. Use a highlighter to identify where you have explained how you would carry out the methods.

3. You have been asked the following key question, 'How do high visitor numbers affect the economy and environment in Ambleside?' Create a questionnaire that would enable you to gather the information you need to answer this key question.

Exam-style question

State whether an annotated photo of the quality of the environment, in local streets or green spaces, is a qualitative or quantitative method. **(1 mark)**

Exam tip

Remember the difference by thinking of quantity (something you can measure in numbers) for quantitative and quality (about your experience of things) for qualitative.

Now that you have decided on the methods you will use to collect your data, you need to produce a risk assessment with your teacher's guidance before you collect and record your data. In your risk assessment, you should consider: the potential risks, the severity of each risk – on a scale of 0 (low) to 10 (high) – and how the risk can be managed. An example is shown in Table 13.

Table 13 Risk assessment

Risk	Severity rating	Management
Traffic accidents	8/10	Take care crossing roads and stand well back from the road when at each survey point. Wear a high visibility vest so vehicles can see you.

Investigating Changing Rural Areas

Table 14 Ambleside pedestrian data (collated data from all five student groups)

Times	Site 1		Site 2		Site 3		Site 4		Site 5	
	North	South	North	South	North	South	North	South	North	South
9.30am–9.45am	6	11	5	7	3	4	8	8	0	1
10.00am–10.15am	4	18	6	15	4	7	22	18	1	1
10.30am–10.45am	4	21	9	16	10	12	31	28	2	0
11.00am–11.15am	8	15	21	20	14	18	38	32	0	3
11.30am–11.45am	3	47	8	32	18	8	51	39	4	7
Totals	25	112	49	90	49	49	150	125	7	12

Data presentation

Once you have collected your data, you then need to decide how to present it. Geographers use a range of graphical techniques to present their findings. For your investigation, you should aim to produce a number of simple and sophisticated techniques. A sophisticated technique is one that uses at least two variables to represent the data. An example of this would be a pedestrian flow line map for the different sites. Techniques that could be used to present information for Ambleside include:

- a flow line map showing direction and size of pedestrian flow at each site
- an isoline map, where lines join up places on a map of equal value
- a dispersion graph, plotting the range of data collected from each site
- located proportional circles of pedestrian numbers for each site
- a GIS map with a base map of Ambleside (physical features), with a layer for roads, a layer for shops and tourist attractions and a layer containing the survey information.

Presenting data on pedestrian density and movement

The students measured pedestrian numbers for 15 minutes at each site at five different time slots during one morning. Figure 29 shows an example of how the students presented their data using located bars. A located bar map is a sophisticated data presentation technique because it records two variables: pedestrian numbers and location.

- First a base map is required: remember to mark the precise point where each survey took place.
- A suitable scale needs to be used that will cope with the highest and lowest figures from the data.
- The base of the bar needs to be located at the point where the data was collected.

The students created five located bar maps: one for each survey time slot and one for the totals for each site (all five time slots put together). This allowed them to compare pedestrian numbers through the morning. However, it was also a very time-consuming task.

Exam-style question

Study Table 14. Calculate the median value and the range for the Totals row. **(2 marks)**

Exam tip

When you put a series of numbers in order the median is the middle one (or the mean of the middle two). The range is the difference between the highest and lowest number in the series.

Command word

When asked to **calculate** you work with numbers to answer a problem. Show your working and include the correct unit if one is required.

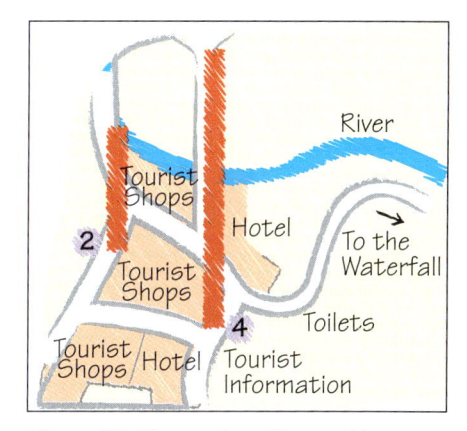

Figure 29 The students' located bar map for 11.30am–11.45am at Sites 2 and 4

F Investigating Changing Rural Areas

F Analysis and conclusions

The next stage of the enquiry is to analyse the data collected to begin answering your key questions. When analysing the data, it is important to:

- **describe** the general trends from your data – for example, 'The number of pedestrians and their impact increased through the morning'
- **make comparisons** using data – for example, 'Pedestrian densities were highest at Site 4 (with a range of 74 throughout the morning) and lowest at Site 5 (with a range of 10)'
- **explain** the patterns of your data with links to geographical theory – for example, 'The flows of pedestrians at Site 1 are consistent with Ambleside being a honeypot location, with large flows from the car park into the town but very small flows northwards up Rydal Road out of town'.

Read the extract below from an analysis a student wrote about data collected in Ambleside. The student gave a structured response with:

- reference to the figure and data (red)
- use of geographical terminology and theory (green)
- an explanation of their data and links to geographical theory (yellow).

> Pedestrian density was highest (275 people) in the main tourist area of Ambleside (Site 4) and at Site 1, leading from the town's main car park into town. Density increased through the morning as more visitors arrived (by 11.45 the cumulative total travelling south from Site 1 was 112 people. Density and flow patterns support Ambleside's honeypot status, in which tourist numbers overwhelm residential pedestrian movements and affect the quality of the environment.

Once you have analysed your data using the structure above, you need to write a conclusion for each key question as well as the overall task question. When writing your conclusion, it is important to:

- focus on your task question and key questions: what did your investigation find out?
- summarise your findings from the data you collected and presented and link each finding to the evidence
- point out any anomalies in your data – these are results that are very different from what you expected: you might try to explain them
- refer back to any theory that related to your investigation (like the concept of honeypots and environmental impact).

You then need to write your overall conclusion to the task question, in this case: 'What impact does tourism have on deprivation in Ambleside?'

Read the extract below from a conclusion written by a student.

> The purpose of my investigation was to investigate the impacts of tourism on the quality of life and deprivation in Ambleside. From looking at pedestrian density and flows, I can conclude that visitors there dominate the numbers of pedestrians, the direction of flows and the locations in which pedestrian density is highest. This is consistent with Ambleside acting as a tourism honeypot.

Investigating Changing Rural Areas

Activity

1. Discuss the two paragraphs with the student's analysis and conclusion. For **each** paragraph decide: what is good about it, how it might be improved or developed, anything that you think should be added. Justify your decisions.
2. Rewrite the **second** student paragraph with your suggested improvements.

(F) Evaluation

The final part of the enquiry is to evaluate your investigation. Here you think about how well you answered the task question or theory, and how you could improve or develop the process. The key questions below will help you review your data collection methods, results and conclusions.

- How successful and useful were your methods for sampling and collecting data? Could they be improved?
- How accurate were your results? Did your data collection methods affect the results?
- Did missing or inaccurate data make the study unreliable or affect your conclusions?

> Pedestrian direction counts at Site 4 were most difficult because people came from three directions and doubled back to visit other shops. The location of Site 4 could have been improved.

> It would have been interesting to have extended the survey to Waterhead (Lake Windermere) to compare pedestrian densities there, but it was too far for us all to walk there in 15 minutes.

> I found Site 5 the most interesting because very few tourists went there. It helped me think about the impacts of tourism.

> Drawing five maps took ages! It was also a shame that we didn't find a way to show the different directions pedestrians were moving in, north and south.

Figure 30 Students' reflections on their geographical investigation in Ambleside

Checkpoint

Now it is time to review your understanding of how to plan and conduct an investigation into changing rural settlements.

Strengthen

S1 Discuss how visitors to rural areas can have positive and negative effects on the quality of life and deprivation there.

S2 Explain one way in which the physical geography of a rural settlement can affect the impact tourists can have on that settlement.

Challenge

C1 Note down examples of how random, systematic and stratified sampling could be used in a rural settlement investigation.

C2 Write out example(s) of the methods below, deciding if they are qualitative or quantitative, primary or secondary, and the strengths and limitations of information gained from each of them:
   a method(s) to measure pedestrian densities
   b method(s) to record the quality of the scenery or streetscape
   c method(s) to investigate people's views on the impact of tourism
   d method(s) to investigate changes in the population or deprivation over time.

Preparing for your exams

The UK's Evolving Human Landscape

The UK's human landscape is changing, with urbanisation, migration, de-industrialisation and decentralisation. There is regional inequality in the UK and there are measures which are put in place by the government and the EU to help address this. Birmingham and the surrounding rural areas have been affected by all these changes in a variety of ways.

Checklist

You should know:

- [ ] why population, economic activity and settlements are key elements of the UK's human landscape
- [ ] how migration shapes the UK economy and society
- [ ] how and why the structure of the UK economy is changing
- [ ] the effects of globalisation, trade and investment on the UK
- [ ] the site, situation and connectivity of Birmingham
- [ ] Birmingham's structure and land uses and function in different parts of the city
- [ ] how national and international migration has influenced Birmingham's growth and character
- [ ] the reasons for different levels of inequality across Birmingham
- [ ] the impact of de-industrialisation and decentralisation on some parts of the city
- [ ] how parts of Birmingham have experienced economic and population growth
- [ ] the effects of regeneration and rebranding on Birmingham
- [ ] how Birmingham is trying to become more sustainable and to improve the quality of life
- [ ] how Birmingham is connected with its rural surroundings and the costs and benefits of their interdependence
- [ ] the causes and impacts of counter-urbanisation on Birmingham's rural surroundings
- [ ] the challenges of rural change and the impact on people's quality of life
- [ ] the opportunities and environmental impacts of rural diversification.

Which key terms match the following definitions?

a The decline of industrial activity in a region or in an economy.

b A measure of the impact of human activities, expressed as the area of productive land and water required to produce the goods consumed and the wastes generated.

c The movement of people, factories, offices and shops away from city centres to suburban and edge-of-city locations.

d A firm that owns or controls productive operations in more than one country through foreign direct investment.

e A term used in urban planning to describe land previously used for industrial purposes or some commercial uses.

f The increasing interconnectedness and interdependence of the world economically, culturally and politically.

g The sale of state-owned assets to the private sector.

h Areas, usually in the inner city, where the whole urban landscape was demolished before being rebuilt on a planned basis.

To check your answers, look at the Glossary on pages 302–311.

Preparing for your exams

The UK's Evolving Human Landscape

Question 1 Urban core areas of the UK are very different to remote rural areas. Describe two differences in the population of urban core and rural areas. (4 marks)

Student answer

Core areas of the UK are big cities like London which have lots of young people in the population. They want to work there because that's where the best jobs are, putting pressure on housing. In the countryside or rural areas the population is not nearly so dense and not many young people want to live there as there's nothing to do.

Verdict

This answer shows some level of understanding. The first part about the age of London's population is correct, and so is the part about low population density in rural areas. However the answer does not describe what is different about the same two aspects, population structure and density, in the urban core and rural areas. Instead it includes things like jobs and housing which aren't relevant.

Exam tip

With questions like this you need to describe differences in two elements – here it is how population age and structure differ in rural and urban areas. Don't get distracted by trying to give reasons.

Question 2 Explain how economic change has increased inequality in a named major UK city. (4 marks)

Student answer

One reason that there is inequality in parts of Birmingham is because a lot of people have no jobs or badly paid jobs. This is places like Sparkbrook and Bordesley Green. A lot of factories have closed in Birmingham lately so there is less work for people. The jobs that people can get are often low paid or part-time. There is also discrimination against people in some parts of Birmingham. Lots of immigrants have arrived in parts of inner Birmingham that has led to problems finding work for some of them. In fact a lot of the immigrants have young children and this is putting a strain on the schools and hospitals so adding to the inequality. The immigrants have come to Birmingham to find a better life and new jobs.

Verdict

The answer implies economic change in terms of factory closures and unemployment, but does not explain why factories have closed or put the changes in context of outdated factories and urban regeneration. It talks about the impacts of immigration to Birmingham, with some reasons migrants move to the city to find a better job and a better life, but more information about the nature and impact of the economic changes is needed.

Exam tip

Make sure when you write an answer that as far as possible you use the key terms in the question. The question above specifically mentions economic change so there should be explanation of what that economic change consisted of, and then detail of how it increased the inequality in the city. There was useful information given but it needed shaping to answer the question.

Pearson Education Ltd accepts no responsibility whatsoever for the accuracy or method of working in the answers given.

WRITING GEOGRAPHICALLY

Writing geographically: building information

When you are asked to write an explanation, discussion, assessment or evaluation, you need to provide as much detailed information as possible.

Learning objectives

- To be able to use relative clauses to add detailed information to your writing, clearly and fluently
- To be able to use nouns in apposition to add detailed information to your writing, clearly and fluently

Definitions

Relative clause: a clause which adds information or **modifies** a noun, linked with a **relative pronoun**, e.g. *who, that, which, where, whose*.

Noun in apposition: two **noun phrases**, positioned side by side, the second adding information to the first, e.g. [1] *Bangalore*, [2] *the second fastest growing city in India*, has benefited greatly from the technology industry.

How can I add detail to my writing?

Look at this exam-style question:

> Assess the causes of variations in house price affordability in the UK. **(8 marks)**

Now look at a sentence from one student's response to it:

> London, which currently has the highest average house price in the UK, is three times more expensive than peripheral areas.

    main clause   relative pronoun   relative clause

In this sentence the noun 'London' is modified by the relative clause: it adds more information about the city.

1. How could you re-structure the sentence above using two separate sentences?
2. Why do you think the writer chose to structure these sentences using a main clause and a relative clause instead of writing them as two separate sentences?

Now look at these four sentences taken from the same student's response:

> London is the capital city of the UK and a World City with many international links. This attracts companies and organisations. These companies employ lots of people. These people require many services.

3. How effectively is this information expressed? Look closely at the first word of each sentence.
4. How could you improve the written expression in the answer above, using relative pronouns?
   (a) Rewrite the sentences, using relative pronouns to link all the information in **one** sentence.
   (b) Now rewrite the sentence using relative pronouns to link the information in **two** sentences.
   (c) Which version do you prefer? Is the information most clearly and fluently expressed in one, two or four sentences? Write a sentence or two explaining your choice.

WRITING GEOGRAPHICALLY

How can I add detail to my writing in different ways?

You can also add detail to a sentence using a **noun in apposition**.

Compare these sentences:

Sentence A

Peripheral areas, like North East England, have lower prices and the core, which is London, has prices three times that of the periphery.

Sentence B

Peripheral areas, like North East England, have lower prices and the core, London, has prices three times that of the periphery.

In **Sentence A**, the writer has used a relative clause to add information clearly and succinctly.

In **Sentence B**, the writer has used a noun phrase in apposition to add the same information clearly and succinctly.

How could you combine the information in these pairs of sentences using a noun in apposition?

Prices are affected by 'supply and demand'. This is an economic idea which means that prices increase when something is in demand.

In London, people have a higher average salary and so can afford to pay more for housing. London is one of the most expensive cities in the world.

Did you notice?

If you remove the relative clause or the noun phrase in apposition from the sentences above, they both still make sense. They are also both separated from the rest of the sentence with commas.

5. Can you explain why? Write a sentence or two explaining your ideas.

Improving an answer

Look at an extract from another student's response to the exam-style question on page 234:

The North East of England and the Highlands of Scotland are two of the more remote, rural areas in the UK. They are isolated and have fewer job opportunities. This means that wages are relatively low and people cannot afford to pay much for their home. These peripheral areas have a smaller population with a relatively low demand for housing, so prices remain lower than the national average. Emigration is also a factor, particularly of young adults. They move from the periphery to core areas of the UK to find work. This further lowers house prices in the periphery and raises them in the cities.

6. Rewrite the information in the answer above, making it as clear and succinct as possible. You could use:
   - relative clauses
   - nouns in apposition.

7. Look carefully at your response to question 5. Are all your sentences easy to read and understand, or are some of them too long and confusing? If so, try rewriting them to make their meaning as clear as possible.

THINKING GEOGRAPHICALLY

Number, area and scale

What you need to know

In geography we use number, area and scale to describe and analyse how data is distributed in space and time to help us understand what has happened and what may happen in the future.

- **Number** is used to describe how much of a measured value there is, e.g. the population of a city.
- **Area** is how much space something occupies and is always written as a unit squared, e.g. the relationship between the number of people in a given area can be described as population density.
- **Scale** is the appropriate system within which we analyse relationships meaningfully, e.g. the speed or rate change in a population is the difference in size on a time scale

Sample question

Students had collected data on population growth after the 2011 census (Table 1) and wanted to investigate the values of different ways of describing demographic trends in London (area: 1583 km^2).

Table 1 Population growth

Year	Population	Population density
2012	8,300,000	5243
2013	8,400,000	
2014	8,500,000	
2015	8,600,000	

How many more people lived in London in 2015 than in 2012?

Population difference

= Population in 2015 (p_2) − Population in 2012 (p_1)

= 8,600,000 − 8,300,000

= 300,000.

In 2012, London's population density was 5243 people per km^2. What was it in 2015?

Population density

= Population ÷ Area

= 8,600,000 ÷ 1583 km^2

= 5433/km^2 (to nearest whole figure).

How much bigger was London's population in 2015 compared with 2012?

The population of London has increased by a scale factor of $p_2 ÷ p_1$

= 8,600,000 ÷ 8,300,000

= 1.04 (to 2 decimal places).

Therefore the approximate percentage increase is:

(1.04 × 100) − 100 = 4%.

THINKING GEOGRAPHICALLY

Calculate how quickly London's population was growing between 2012 and 2015, in terms of the annual percentage growth rate.

Annual percentage growth rate
= $([(p_2 - p_1) \div p_1] \div [\text{Difference in time}, t_2 - t_1]) \times 100$
= $([300{,}000 \div 8{,}300{,}000] \div [2015 - 2012]) \times 100$
= 1.2%.

Apply your knowledge

Students wanting to compare the growth of megacities at a global scale have collected data about the populations of Mumbai in India and London in the UK (Table 2).

Table 2 Comparison of population growth in Mumbai and London

Year	Mumbai	London
1971	6,540,000	7,450,000
1981	9,685,000	6,610,000
1991	12,792,000	6,890,000
2001	16,665,000	7,170,000
2011	18,695,000	8,170.000

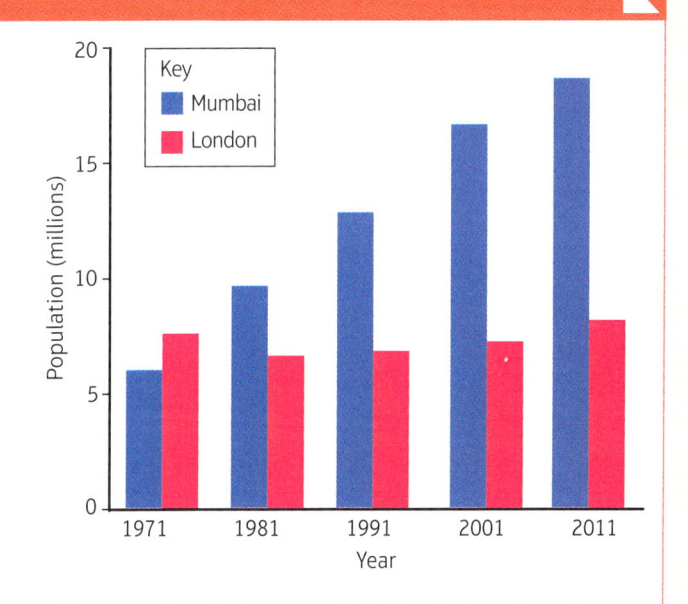

Figure 1 Population growth in Mumbai and London

1. How many more people are there in Mumbai and London in 2011 compared with 1971?

2. Use the following formula to work out the scale of this growth for Mumbai from 1971 to 2011:

   $p_2 \div p_1 =$ Scale factor.

3. If London had grown by the same scale factor as Mumbai over the 40 years from 1971, what would its population have been in 2011?

4. London's population fell between some census dates so the growth rate was not constant. Calculate the average annual percentage population growth rates for Mumbai and London, 2001–2011. Which city had a faster growth rate during this ten-year period? Suggest reasons for this.

Students have been studying patterns of population distribution within Greater London using a sample transect from the City of London to Havering borough.

1. They decided to describe the relationship between a borough's population density (the number of people in an area) and its distance from the City of London. Why couldn't they just use the number of people?

THINKING GEOGRAPHICALLY

Table 3 Comparison of relation between population density and distance from City of London for several London boroughs

	City of London	Tower Hamlets	Newham	Barking and Dagenham	Havering
Distance from the City of London (km)	0	7.6	10.6	15	25.4
Population in 2011	7400	254,100	308,000	185,900	237,200
Area (km²)	2.9	19.8	36.2	36.1	112.3
Population density				5150	2112

Using the formula 'Population density = Population ÷ Area', copy and complete Table 3. Using the table, construct a line graph to show the relationship between the number of people living in an area and the distance from the city of London.

2. The students decided a choropleth map might help them understand the distribution of population more easily. Copy the map they started (Figure 2) and use shading to illustrate your calculations about population density along the transect. Describe what this shows.

3. Do you think the graph or the map gives the best representation of this data? Explain your choice.

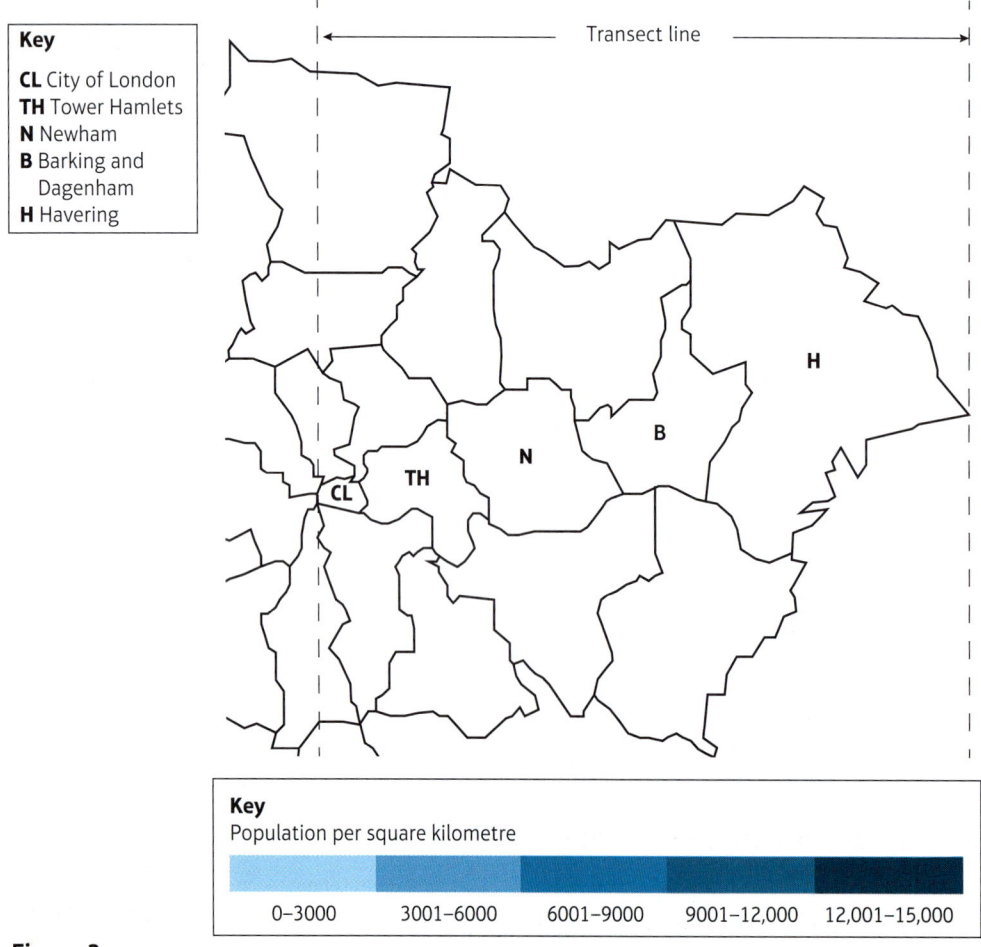

Key
CL City of London
TH Tower Hamlets
N Newham
B Barking and Dagenham
H Havering

Key
Population per square kilometre

0–3000   3001–6000   6001–9000   9001–12,000   12,001–15,000

Figure 2

6 | Geographical Investigations – Fieldwork

Fieldwork investigations help you to understand two different environments in depth, through practical research. You will investigate one physical environment (coastal change and conflict or river processes and pressures) and one human environment (dynamic urban areas or changing rural areas).

Your learning

In this section you will investigate key learning points:
- How can you use enquiry questions to plan your fieldwork investigation?
- How can you develop good questions that focus on your fieldwork location and task?
- What different methods can you use to collect fieldwork data?
- How can you choose qualitative and quantitative methods to collect data?
- How can you measure, record and present the information you find?
- What secondary data sources can you use in your research?
- How can you analyse your data, write a good conclusion and evaluate your fieldwork investigation?

6 Geographical Investigations – Fieldwork

In this book, there are four modelled fieldwork investigations, two physical and two human. Each fieldwork investigation is structured in six parts to help you learn about the enquiry process.

1. The enquiry question
2. Locating the study
3. Methodology
4. Data presentation
5. Analysis and conclusions
6. Evaluation

Investigating Coastal Landscapes

On page 150, you will find an example of an investigation into the impact of coastal management on coastal processes and communities. This sample investigation focuses on the enquiry question 'How does management of the beach at Dawlish Warren affect coastal processes and people?' The investigation looks at the effect the groynes have on the size and shape of the sediment on the beach.

Investigating River Landscapes

On page 176, you will find an example of an investigation into what influences flood risk along a UK river. The sample investigation focuses on the enquiry question 'How and why do the drainage basin and channel characteristics of the River Severn influence the flood risk for people and property?' The investigation looks at the width and depth of the river channel as the river flows downstream.

F Investigating Coastal Landscapes

Learning objectives
- To understand how to conduct a geographical investigation of coastal change and conflict
- To know how to choose enquiry questions, fieldwork methods and data sources for an investigation into coastal processes and management
- To know how to present, analyse and evaluate data collected from a coastal investigation

Figure 20 The beach at Dawlish Warren, Devon

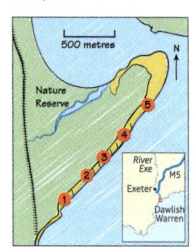

Figure 21 A sketch map of Dawlish Warren in Devon showing the sample sites

F The enquiry question

When conducting a geographical enquiry, it is important to have a purpose. One way to do this is to ask a task question.

For this enquiry on coasts, the task question is:

How does management of the beach at Dawlish Warren affect coastal processes and people?

The beach at Dawlish Warren in Devon is about 2 km long and has formed on the seaward side of a spit. Prevailing wind conditions along the south coast of England mean that sediment is transported by longshore drift from the west to the east end of the spit. However, groynes have been built at regular intervals to help manage and stabilise the beach. The aim of this enquiry is to discover if the beach changes from west to east, and if this is linked to the management of the beach or to natural processes.

To help answer the task question, geographers next devise some key questions. These help to provide a focus for the enquiry.

For this task, a key question could be:

Do the groynes at Dawlish Warren affect changes in sediment size and shape further along the beach?

You might expect sediment size to decrease and roundness to increase from west to east on Dawlish Warren beach as it is transported by longshore drift. However, groynes act as sediment traps, interrupting the natural movement of material, so their presence may also influence beach sediment characteristics.

Activity
1. Read the text about Dawlish Warren and study Figure 21. Create another key question that would help answer the main task question.
2. Using Figure 21 and an atlas, write an overview of the location of Dawlish Warren and the fieldwork investigation.

F Locating the study

It is important to show the study location. Use maps at different scales, as in Figure 21. The main map shows study sites, while the inset map gives the regional location. This helps to set the scene.

As well as describing your study location, you need to explain your choice of study sites. This may depend on the data collection method(s) you choose. At Dawlish Warren, for example, study sites were chosen at regular intervals at every third groyne along the beach (Figure 21). These five sites were approximately 300 metres apart at the high tide mark. Each one was measured 5 metres to the east of the end of the groyne. This gave a representative sample along the beach and a chance to collect the samples before high tide.

150

F Investigating River Processes and Pressures

Learning objectives
- To understand how to conduct a geographical investigation of change in river valleys and channels
- To know how to choose enquiry questions, fieldwork methods and data sources for a river investigation
- To know how to present, analyse and evaluate data collected from a river investigation

Activity
1. Using your knowledge of the changes in the long profile of the River Severn (see pages 162–163), create another two key questions that would help you to answer the main task question.
2. Using your wider geographical knowledge, suggest the results you would expect for your chosen key questions based on a typical river profile. Refer to Bradshaw's Model on page 163.

Figure 19 River Severn, Hafren Forest, near site 1

F The enquiry question

When conducting a geographical enquiry, it is important to have a purpose. One way to do this is to ask a task question.

For this enquiry on rivers, the task question is:

How and why do the drainage basin and channel characteristics of the River Severn influence the flood risk for people and property?

To help answer the task question, geographers next devise some key questions. These help to provide a focus for the enquiry.

For this task, one of the key questions is:

Does the width and depth of the river channel increase as the river flows downstream?

F Locating the study

It is important to provide maps showing where the investigation is located. You should include maps at a local and a national scale, plus detailed maps showing your survey or data collection sites. You can then use your location and survey site maps to give a detailed overview of the place in which your investigation will take place. This part of your enquiry helps set the scene.

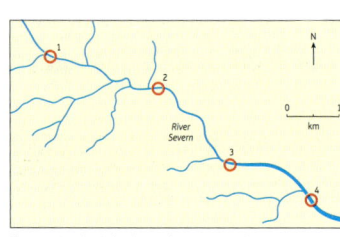

Figure 20 A student's sketch map of survey sites on the upper River Severn

176

240

6 Geographical Investigations – Fieldwork

F Investigating Dynamic Urban Areas

Learning objectives
- To understand how to conduct a geographical enquiry into the quality of life in urban areas
- To understand how to choose enquiry questions, fieldwork methods and data sources for an urban investigation
- To know how to present, analyse and evaluate data collected from an urban investigation.

Activity

Reread the ideas about the variations in the quality of life from pages 201–207 and then create another **two** or **three** key questions which will help you to answer the main task question.

Tip Think about other factors affecting the quality of city life such as other impacts of traffic and the quality of the built environment.

The enquiry question

The important thing when setting out on a geographical enquiry is to be clear on the purpose. One good way to do this is to ask a question. For this enquiry into urban areas the task question is:

How and why does the quality of life vary in Birmingham's central area?

To help answer the task question, geographers next devise some key questions. These help to provide a focus for the enquiry. For this task one of the key questions is:

Why are there more accidents at some points around a junction in Birmingham city centre than at others?

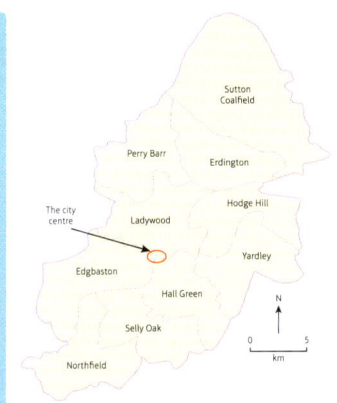

Locating the study

It is important to provide maps showing where the investigation is located. You should include maps at a local and national scale, plus detailed maps showing your survey or data collection sites. You can then use your location and survey site maps to give a detailed overview of the place in which your investigation will take place. This part of your enquiry helps set the scene.

Figure 23 Map of named city areas of Birmingham

214

Investigating Dynamic Urban Areas
On page 214, you will find an example of an investigation into how and why quality of life varies in urban areas. The sample investigation focuses on the enquiry question 'How and why does the quality of life vary in Birmingham's central area?' The investigation looks at the location of the main concentrations of accidents and investigates the causes.

F Investigating Changing Rural Areas

Learning objectives
- To understand how to conduct a geographical investigation of change in rural areas
- To know how to choose enquiry questions, fieldwork methods and data sources for a rural investigation
- To know how to present, analyse and evaluate data collected for an investigation in rural areas

Activity

1. What challenges do you think Ambleside faces in managing the many tourists that visit during the summer months? Suggest how they might affect the quality of the environment.
2. Why do you think that one of the key questions is about how many pedestrians there are and which way they are moving?
3. Suggest **two** more key questions that would help answer this task question.

The enquiry question

When conducting a geographical enquiry, it is important to have a purpose. One way to do this is to ask a task question.

For this enquiry on rural settlements, the task question is:

What impact does tourism have on the quality of life and deprivation in Ambleside, a rural settlement in the Lake District National Park?

To help answer the task question, geographers next devise some key questions. These help to provide a focus for the enquiry.

For this task, one of the key questions is:

What is the impact of pedestrian density and movement in Ambleside?

In 2014, 16.4 million people visited the Lake District, most of them travelling by car. Ambleside is a 'honeypot' location for tourism – it is a place that most tourists want to visit. 2600 people live in Ambleside.

Locating the study

It is important to provide maps showing where the investigation is located. You should include maps at a local and national scale, plus detailed maps showing your survey or data collection sites. You can then use your location and survey site maps to give a detailed overview of the place in which your investigation will take place. This part of your enquiry helps set out the scene.

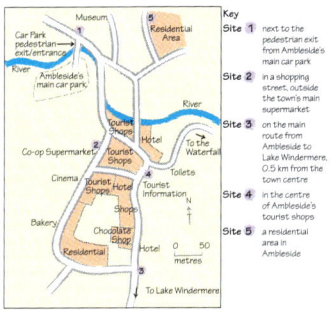

Figure 27 A student's sketch map of Ambleside, with the five survey sites marked on it

Key
- Site 1 next to the pedestrian exit from Ambleside's main car park
- Site 2 in a shopping street, outside the town's main supermarket
- Site 3 on the main route from Ambleside to Lake Windermere, 0.5 km from the town centre
- Site 4 in the centre of Ambleside's tourist shops
- Site 5 a residential area in Ambleside

Figure 28 Ambleside and mountains

226

Investigating Changing Rural Areas
On page 226, you will find an example of an investigation into how and why deprivation varies in rural areas. The sample investigation focuses on the enquiry question 'What impact does tourism have on the quality of life and deprivation in Ambleside, a rural settlement in the Lake District National Park?' The investigation looks at whether pedestrian density and movement vary.

Component 3
People and Environment Issues – Making Geographical Decisions

Content overview

In this component you will develop your understanding of the processes and interactions between people and environments by investigating three important global issues.

- Topic 7 People and the Biosphere is an overview of the world's large-scale ecosystems or biomes, and why the biosphere is important to humans for their wellbeing and for resources.
- Topic 8 Forests Under Threat is a detailed study of how two biomes function – tropical rainforests and the taiga – and how they can be managed sustainably.
- Topic 9 Consuming Energy Resources investigates energy supply, demand and security, and how energy resources can be managed sustainably.

Your assessment

You will sit a 1 hour and 30 minute exam, with questions based on a resource booklet, leading up to a decision-making exercise. You will need to show your understanding of Topics 7, 8 and 9, as well as using your knowledge of physical and human geography from Components 1 and 2.

- There are four sections: you must answer **all** the questions in each section:
- **Section A** has questions about People and the Biosphere.
- **Section B** has questions about Forests Under Threat.
- **Section C** has questions about Consuming Energy Resources, including extended writing worth eight marks.
- **Section D** Making a Geographical Decision is the final question. You will choose **one** out of three decisions, using your knowledge and understanding from the rest of your geography course and evidence from the resource booklet. Then you will justify your decision in extended writing worth twelve marks; in addition, there are four extra marks available for spelling, punctuation, grammar and use of geographical language (SPAG).
- You may be assessed on geographical skills in any section, and can use a calculator.
- The paper is worth 64 marks. There will be a variety of different question types, including multiple-choice, short open, open response and extended writing questions in Sections C and D.

Understanding Making Geographical Decisions

Introduction

Geography is about the real world, focusing on the present and the future. Geography is broken down into physical and human topics to make them easier to study. However, this separation is not as clearly defined in the real world. The Earth is a very complicated planet because everything is linked together, with human processes affecting physical processes and other human processes, as well as physical processes affecting human processes and other physical processes.

By studying the physical and human topics separately, you develop a thorough understanding of geographical processes. However, to become an excellent geographer you need to consider the complex interactions of processes taking place and apply your knowledge to new situations. In the Edexcel GCSE (9–1) Geography B course there are decision-making exercises (DMEs), which take information and data from a real local-scale situation and ask you to apply your knowledge and understanding. In many ways this reflects real life; jobs require research and collection of information, discussion of the benefits and problems (costs), discussion of the possible solutions or ways forward, and then a decision needs to be made on the best course of action to take. Decisions are made in the real world at several scales, such as the problems and solutions linked to climate change (international), increasing immigration (national) and coastal erosion (local).

Activity

Think about the news in the last six months. Identify geographical decision-making situations that have taken place (e.g. in December 2015 the COP21 UN Conference on Climate Change in Paris).

Geographical decision-making

Good geographical decision-makers:

- can research and investigate topics to be up to date with what is happening in the world
- have developed the practical skills needed to investigate and present their ideas
- can interpret a wide range of resources, including graphs, maps, tables of data, photos, GIS images and extracts from news sources
- can write in a style that offers genuine explanation and not just good description
- can make links between pieces of information, including geographical ideas and facts
- can link together pieces of evidence
- have a well-developed understanding of the demands placed on the Earth
- can show how physical and human geographical systems work

Activity

Study Figure 1 and suggest further links that could be added to the diagram.

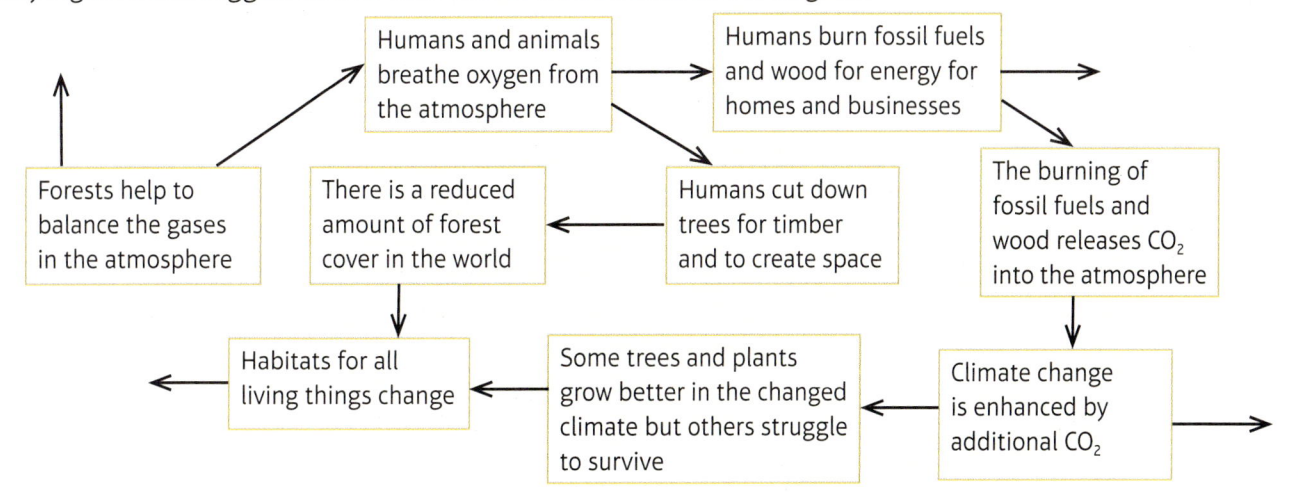

- Forests help to balance the gases in the atmosphere
- Humans and animals breathe oxygen from the atmosphere
- Humans burn fossil fuels and wood for energy for homes and businesses
- There is a reduced amount of forest cover in the world
- Humans cut down trees for timber and to create space
- The burning of fossil fuels and wood releases CO_2 into the atmosphere
- Habitats for all living things change
- Some trees and plants grow better in the changed climate but others struggle to survive
- Climate change is enhanced by additional CO_2

Understanding Making Geographical Decisions

- can appreciate and understand the roles and opinions of different groups of people and organisations, including recognising possible conflicts
- can identify the positives and negatives of plans, options or strategies, and be able to add a weighting to different factors
- can evaluate a range of options, strategies and solutions for an unfamiliar location, and make a judgement on the best choice for the future
- can justify a choice and identify the strengths and weaknesses of the 'best' option, as well as the strengths and weaknesses of 'weaker' options
- have a thorough understanding of sustainability from the social, economic and natural environment perspectives.

'Sustainability' is a term often used in geographical decision-making. It means ensuring that negative impacts are minimised or eliminated and positive impacts are maximised in the long term. Sometimes the word 'costs' is used in geography to indicate problems, disadvantages and issues (negative impacts) as well as financial (money) costs. Social sustainability means ensuring the future well-being of people, economic sustainability means ensuring the future of jobs and businesses, and environmental sustainability means ensuring the future protection and conservation of natural ecosystems and physical processes.

The examination and how to tackle it

Preparation is the key to success in a decision-making examination. Most important is becoming familiar with the situation and resources presented in the Resource Booklet of Paper 3. This means you need to:

- read the information and study the figures provided so that you can use them correctly in your answers to the questions
- make links between different pieces of information in the Resource Booklet and between human and physical geography
- consider the impacts on people and the natural environment
- use your cartographic, graphic, photographic and maths/statistical skills
- make sure that you do not copy text directly from the Resource Booklet, but use your own words
- provide reasoned answers with justification of your thoughts. Show your understanding of the positives and negatives of options or situations. There are short and long decision-making questions in Topics 7, 8 and 9.

Paper 3 of the Geography B specification focuses on people and environment issues and making geographical decisions centred on:

- Topic 7 People and the Biosphere
- Topic 8 Forests under Threat
- Topic 9 Consuming Energy Resources.

These three topics are structured to provide you with information on situations, issues, uncertainties and the contrasting opinions of groups of people. The topics prompt you to explore possible solutions. However, the examiners may include elements from any other topic.

- The exam will be 1 hour and 30 minutes long and is split into four sections (A to D).
- You have to answer all of the questions so there is no choice.
- The exam is worth 25% of your GCSE geography qualification with 64 marks (4 of which are for spelling, punctuation and grammar and use of geographical terminology (SPAG), based on the final long (starred) question).
- There is a Resource Booklet (of about 10 pages) and a question paper with spaces for your answers. You will need a calculator.
- There will be a variety of questions from multiple-choice to extended writing, with a progression of length through the examination (i.e. longest at the end), so you must not spend too long on the early questions and must leave at least 15 minutes for the Section D long answer question.
- Reading time is built into the time allowed for this examination and it is very important that you read through the whole booklet thoroughly before starting any writing. Twenty minutes would be a reasonable amount of time for reading. You will not be wasting your time, as you need a complete understanding of all of the information. Reading will help you become familiar with where pieces of information are and how they link together – both are essential for achieving high marks.

7 | People and the Biosphere

The biosphere is vital to human existence. It regulates the atmosphere, playing a crucial role in absorbing carbon dioxide through photosynthesis. The interaction of rotting vegetation and decomposers, such as bacteria and fungi, releases nutrients that keep soils fertile and encourage the growth of ecosystems and crops. Forests intercept and absorb rainfall, reducing the chance of flooding and helping to regulate water resources. For thousands of years, indigenous (native) people have used the biosphere sustainably, as a source of food, building materials, fuel and medicine – but in such a way that the biosphere is not damaged significantly. However, an increasing world population, and wealth, have led to the large scale commercial exploitation of the biosphere. Will biosphere resources run out and lead to global catastrophe, or will new ways of meeting the needs of society be discovered?

Your learning

In this section you will investigate the following key questions:

- What global factors affect biome distribution and characteristics?
- How can we explain the distribution and characteristics of biomes?
- What local factors affect biomes?
- How do the biotic and abiotic components of biomes interact?
- How does the biosphere act as a life support system?
- How can increasing use of resources lead to over-exploitation?
- Malthus or Boserup: whose theory of population and resources is most convincing?

7 | People and the Biosphere

What global factors affect biome distribution and characteristics?

Learning objectives

- To describe the distribution of different biomes
- To describe the characteristics of different biomes
- To interpret climate graphs for different biomes

The world biome map

A **biome** is a large-scale **ecosystem**, such as the tropical rainforest. Figure 1 shows the distribution of the world's major biomes. Distribution is a key geographical concept which describes where something is found and any patterns in its location. For example, the distribution of the tropical rainforest biome on Figure 1 shows that this biome is found in a zone either side of the. More detail can be added to this description by specifying that it is generally found between about 15°N and 15°S of the Equator. Or key locations can be named, such as South America, West Africa and South East Asia. A really good description of distribution will also point out any areas that do not fit the general pattern. For example, the tropical rainforest spreads further away from the Equator in places, such as in Madagascar (20°S), and there is no tropical rainforest in East Africa, even though it is on the Equator.

Activity

Choose **two** of the other biomes and describe their distribution, as in the text example of the tropical rainforest. Try to:

a outline the general pattern
b add specific detail
c point out any anomalies.

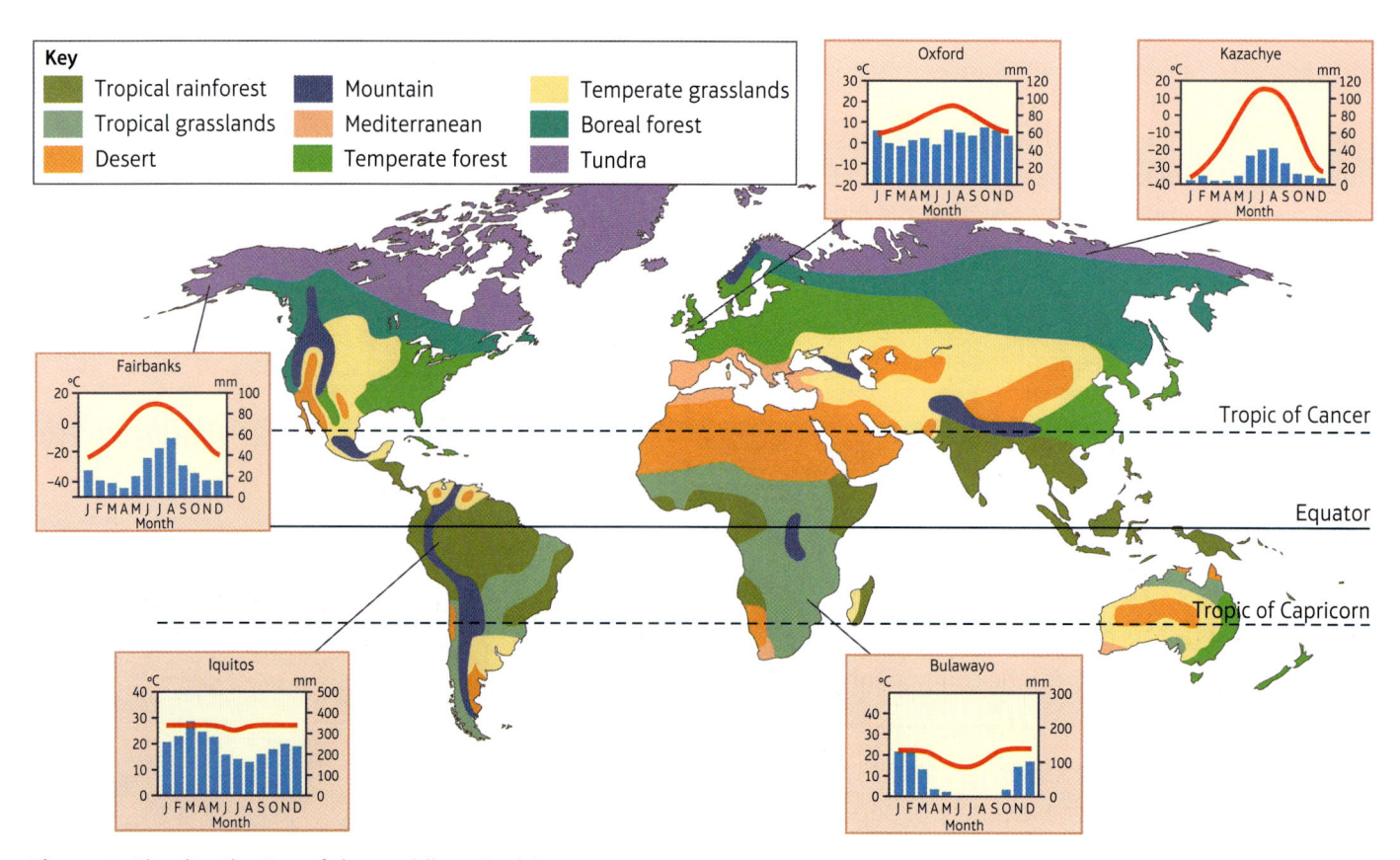

Figure 1 The distribution of the world's major biomes

Characteristics of the world's major biomes

Characteristics are specific features that allow us to identify how one thing differs from another. Table 1 shows how climate differences produce different biome characteristics.

> **Did you know?**
> The boreal represents 29% of the world's forest cover, and is named after Boreas, the Greek god of the north wind.

Table 1 Differences between biomes

Biome	Climate characteristics	Distinctive vegetation
Tropical rainforest	Hot all year (25–30°C). Wet all year (average annual **precipitation** 200–3000 mm)	Dense forests with several layers of trees, with other plants competing for light
Tropical grasslands (**savanna**)	Hot all year (25–35°C). 500–1000 mm of rainfall per year but always with a dry season	Tall grasses, with some drought-adapted shrubs and trees (e.g. baobab)
Deserts	Very hot all year (above 30°C) but with cool nights (large **diurnal temperature range**). Very low rainfall (less than 250 mm per year)	Plants are scarce and have water-storing features, spines instead of leaves and extensive root systems (e.g. cacti)
Temperate grasslands	Hot in summer (25°C), very cold in winter (as low as −40°C). 500–900 mm of rainfall per year, most in late spring and summer	Short grasses with very few trees and bushes
Temperate forest	Warm summers (around 18°C), cool winters (around 5°C). Precipitation all year (around 1000 mm)	**Deciduous** trees such as oak
Boreal forest	Mild summers (generally 10–20°C), very cold winters (well below 0°C). Low precipitation (less than 500 mm) mainly in summer	**Coniferous** trees such as pine
Tundra	Temperatures below 0°C for most of the year, and only reaching around 10°C in summer; Low precipitation, often less than 250 mm. Short daylight hours in winter	Very few plants can live here, mostly lichens and mosses. Trees are rare and stunted

Activity

Figure 1 includes climate graphs from some of the biomes. Climate graphs present average monthly temperatures (shown as a line) and precipitation totals (shown as bars) for a location throughout the year.

1. Construct a climate graph for Zagora from the following data, using graph paper or a spreadsheet.

Climate data for Zagora	J	F	M	A	M	J	J	A	S	O	N	D
Average monthly rainfall (mm)	8	20	12	12	3	6	4	10	9	12	12	20
Average monthly temperature (°C)	16	18	20	25	29	35	38	36	31	25	20	16

2. Using Table 1 to help, which biome do you think Zagora is in? (See page 259 if you need to check the location.)
3. Describe the pattern shown on Zagora's climate graph (refer to data in your answer).
4. The fennec fox is native to the area around Zagora. Research this animal and explain how it is well adapted to the climate of this biome, including cold nights.

7 People and the Biosphere

How can we explain the distribution and characteristics of biomes?

Learning objectives

- To explain the distribution of different biomes
- To recognise the characteristics of different biomes
- To understand the influence of climate on distribution and characteristics

As well as describing distribution, geographers also try to explain patterns. Climate is the key factor influencing the distribution of the world's biomes (see Topic 1). The temperature and the amount of precipitation (such as rainfall) are the main factors affecting what grows in a particular location – though other climate factors like temperature range (annual and diurnal), winds and seasonal variation in precipitation can also be important factors.

The tropical rainforest biome occurs where there are year-round high temperatures and high precipitation. This occurs near the Equator because the Sun is more or less directly overhead all year, and the heat causes air to rise (as warm air is less dense); as it rises it cools, causing water vapour in the air to condense, forming clouds and high rainfall (see Figure 2). This zone is known as the **Inter-tropical Convergence Zone**, where the atmospheric systems of the northern hemisphere meet those of the southern hemisphere.

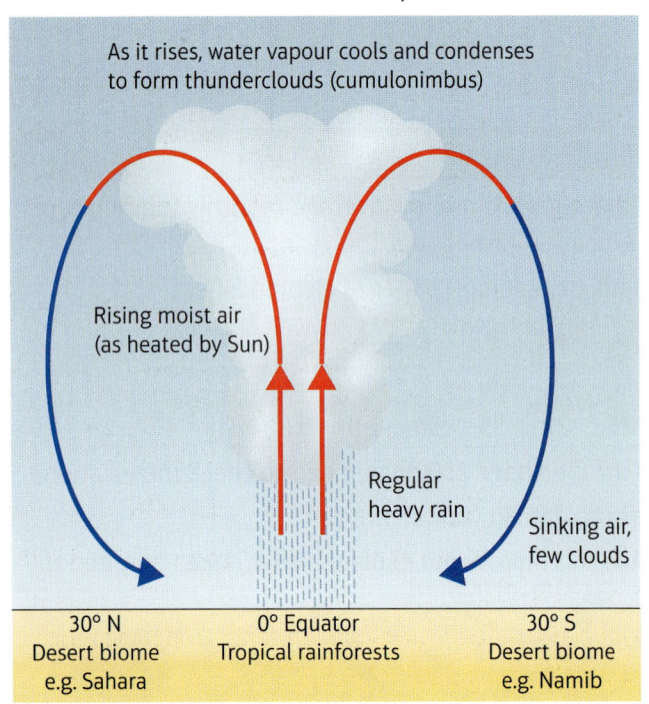

Figure 2 Why rainforests occur at the Equator and deserts around 20–30° N and S

The tropical grassland (**savanna**) biome occurs further from the Equator, where temperatures are still high, but there is a pronounced dry season, preventing dense tree growth. Tall grasses, such as elephant grass, thrive here (Figure 3), growing rapidly in the relatively moist summer, but dying back in the dry winter.

Figure 3 Elephant grass in the tropical grassland biome

The hot desert biome occurs around the Tropics of Cancer and Capricorn, because air is sinking there. Sinking air warms and so can hold more moisture, so there is little condensation or cloud formation. It also creates high air pressure. This leads to high temperatures during the day (the sun is still high in the sky at this latitude), but cooler temperatures at night because there are few clouds to act as a 'blanket', so the heat escapes into the upper atmosphere each night. Clearly, with fewer clouds, rainfall will be low (see Figure 2). This means that the flora and fauna need to adapt to survive with low water availability and hot days, but cool nights.

Temperate forests occur at higher latitudes, for example in the UK (Figure 4). Here the atmosphere consists of many low pressure systems, with rising air creating year-round rainfall. In the winter, the Sun is lower in the sky, so the number of hours of sunshine is reduced, slowing **photosynthesis**. The deciduous trees save energy and protect themselves from colder temperatures by dropping their leaves in the autumn.

Temperate grasslands occur at similar latitudes to temperate forests, but in the interior of continents (such as the prairies of central USA and the steppes of southern Russia). The seasons are more pronounced in these locations away from the moderating effect of the oceans. Grasses thrive in the warm moist summers and are adapted to survive the cold dry winters by slowing their growth rates. There are fewer trees than in the tropical grassland biome because they cannot survive the long, dry winters.

Boreal forests occur further north than the temperate forests, and mostly in the northern hemisphere because there is little land at the same latitude in the southern hemisphere. Boreal forests are found where temperatures are colder, with sinking air which leads to low precipitation. The conifer trees have waxy needle-like leaves; the coating and small surface area protect them from the cold, and allow the trees to start photosynthesising quickly when spring comes. Precipitation is often in the form of snow, so conifers have flexible, sloping branches to allow the snow to slide off.

Figure 4 Deciduous trees in the temperate forest biome dropping their leaves in autumn

The tundra biome occurs further closest to the poles, for example north of 60°N (also on the Antarctic Peninsula and some islands in the Southern Ocean, like the South Sandwich Islands). Here plant growth is limited by the very low temperatures and short sunlight hours in winter (above 66½°N, in the Arctic Circle, the Sun never rises at all for part of the year). The air is sinking here, and therefore precipitation is low. The slow evaporation and frozen subsoil mean that bog plants like mosses and sedges are all that can grow (Figure 5). Due to the lack of trees and shrubs, strong winds blow across the tundra, so plants have tough leaves and grow close to the ground.

Did you know?

On hot days, oceans absorb heat, keeping the air somewhat cooler. When the air gets cool, however, they slowly release heat to the atmosphere, raising air temperatures. This is why temperatures along coastlines are cooler in summer and warmer in winter relative to inland areas.

Figure 5 Mosses growing in the tundra biome

Activity

Locate in an atlas Ulaanbaatar (Mongolia), a temperate grassland biome. Look at the climate data below.

Climate data for Ulaanbaatar	J	F	M	A	M	J	J	A	S	O	N	D
Average monthly rainfall (mm)	2	2	4	10	15	49	67	62	30	8	4	3
Average monthly temperature (°C)	-21	-18	-9	1	10	15	17	16	9	1	-11	-19

a Calculate the mean and mode for the precipitation data. Show your working. What do these suggest about the most usual annual precipitation for this biome (see pages 184–186)?

b Using the temperature data, calculate the range and inter-quartile range. Show your working. What does the result suggest about the variation in temperature during a year?

c Explain **one** possible reason why the rainfall is higher in warmer months and lower in colder months.

7 People and the Biosphere

What local factors affect biomes?

Learning objectives
- To describe how local factors such as altitude, rock and soil type, and drainage, can affect biome distribution
- To explain why these factors affect biomes
- To be able to illustrate these factors with reference to specific examples

Altitude

Temperatures fall at a rate of between 0.5°C and 1°C for every 100 metres climbed in height up a hill or mountain (Figure 6). Mountains are also more exposed to the wind, and precipitation is usually greater at higher altitudes. In addition, slopes usually become steeper and soils thinner. These factors mean that forest biomes will decrease with altitude, becoming stunted, and then replaced by hardier species like grasses. On the slopes of Mount Kilimanjaro, very close to the Equator in Tanzania in East Africa, the biomes change from tropical rainforest on the lower slopes, through scrubland with scattered bushes, to a tundra-like frozen 'desert' with little life other than mosses, lichens and a few tough grasses near the top.

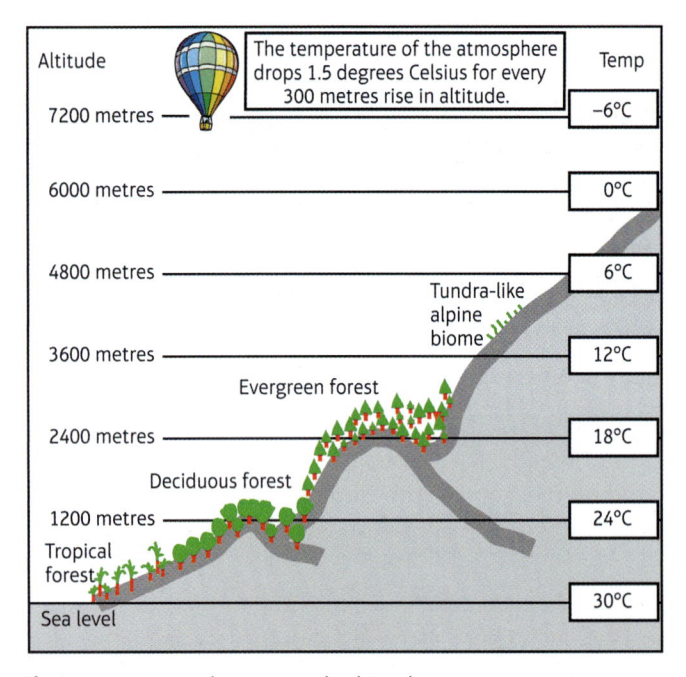

Figure 6 Biome changes with altitude

Rock type

Some rocks are harder than others. For example, granite is a very hard rock, but chalk is a very soft rock and wears away easily.

Some rocks, such as sandstone or chalk, let water soak through them. They are called **permeable** rocks.

Other rocks, such as marble and slate, do not let water soak through them. They are called **impermeable** rocks.

Limestone rocks produce alkaline soils and, due to their permeability, are relatively dry. These factors lead to beech trees replacing oak as the dominant species in some areas, or even prevent tree growth altogether (such as on the **limestone pavements** of Yorkshire).

Soils

Soils are a mixture of tiny particles of rock, dead plants and animals, air and water. Different plants grow better in different types of soil, which affects the biome and the produce humans can derive from it.

- **Sandy soil** is pale coloured with a lot of small air gaps. Water drains through sandy soil easily so it usually feels quite dry. Plants must have some tolerance to drought. Sandy soil supports rye, barley and some root crops.
- **Clay soil** is an orange or blue-ish sticky soil with very few air gaps. Water does not drain through it easily. When it rains, puddles stay on top of clay soil for a long time. It holds nutrients well and supports wheat, beans and grass.
- **Chalky soil** is a light brown soil. Water drains through it quickly. It supports grass and barley.
- **Peat** is different from other soils because it does not contain any rock particles. It is made from very old decayed plants and is dark, crumbly and rich in nutrients (chemicals which plants need to grow). It tends to be acidic and supports rough grazing and forestry.

7 People and the Biosphere

Drainage

Where there are impermeable rocks, the surface may become frequently waterlogged because rain cannot drain away. Where climate would normally form a forest biome, waterlogging can prevent trees from growing, and **peat bogs** or other marshland may form, with only specially adapted plants like bulrushes growing there.

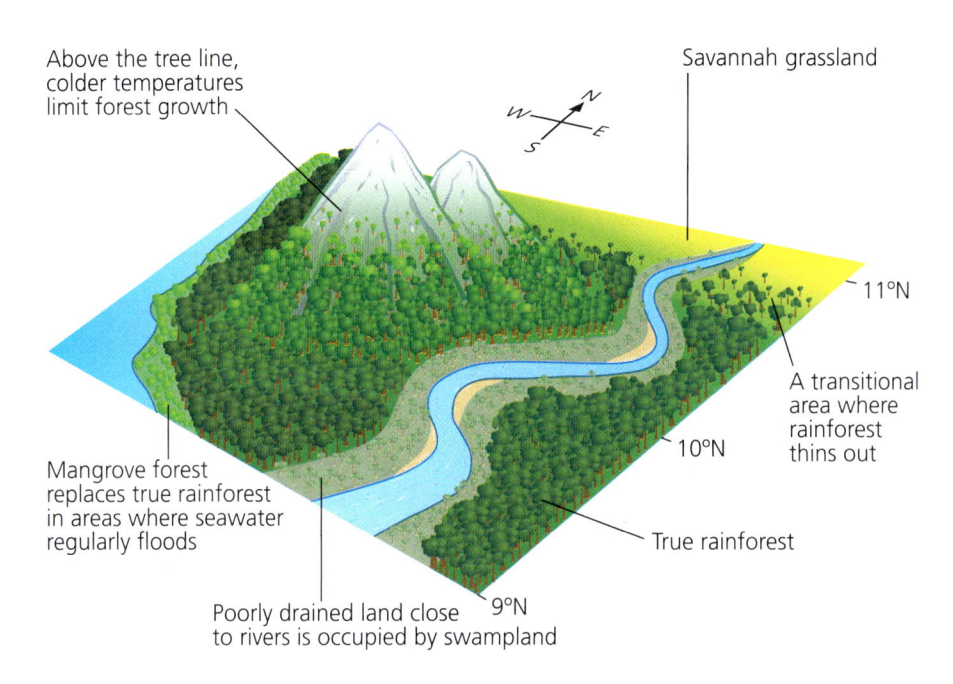

Figure 7 Local factors that can affect tropical rainforest growth

Exam-style question
State **two** local factors affecting biomes. **(2 marks)**

Exam tip
Make sure you are familiar with various factors affecting biomes and be aware that they can also be referred to as biospheres and ecosystems.

Command word
In this **state** question you are being asked to provide two examples. State means simply to clearly provide something.

Did you know?
Humans also affect biomes locally. Woodland coverage in Britain was around 75% about 6000 years ago. This fell to around 5% at the time of the First World War, but had risen back to 13% by 2015.

Checkpoint
Now it is time to review your understanding of the distribution and characteristics of biomes and what affects these.

Strengthen
- **S1** What is a biome? Give three located examples of different biomes.
- **S2** What rainfall would you expect in the tundra?
- **S3** How does altitude affect biomes locally?

Challenge
- **C1** How much colder on average are boreal forests than rainforests in summer?
- **C2** Tropical grasslands have average temperatures similar to rainforests, but little tree growth. Why?
- **C3** Explain what happens in the Inter-tropical Convergence Zone. Draw a diagram if this helps.

7 People and the Biosphere

How do the biotic and abiotic components of biomes interact?

Learning objectives
- To understand the terms biotic and abiotic and know what the different components are
- To describe specific examples of how these components interact
- To explain the importance of these interactions in maintaining balance in ecosystems

The **biotic** components of a biome or ecosystem are the living parts: the **flora** (plants) and **fauna** (animals), plus fungi, bacteria and other forms of life. The **abiotic** components of a biome or ecosystem are the non-living parts, such as soils, rock, water and air. These components interact all the time, in many different ways, and their interaction helps keep ecosystems in **equilibrium** (balance): for example, in a nutrient cycle or hydrological (water) cycle.

Biological weathering

Weathering is when rock gets broken into pieces *in situ* – that is, without being eroded or transported elsewhere. (If rock is worn away and carried elsewhere by rivers, waves, wind or ice, that is **erosion**.) **Biological weathering** is when living things break up the rock. An example of this is when tree roots grow into the joints of a rock and break the rock apart; the rock is physically forced apart, so this is **bio-physical weathering**. Another example is provided by the bivalve mollusc called a piddock. This creature lives in a seashell and has sharp 'teeth' which it uses to grind holes in rock (Figure 8) to create a home.

Sometimes flora or fauna can secrete acids which dissolve rock: **bio-chemical weathering**. Most plants do this when they decompose, producing humic acid.

Seabirds can deposit vast amounts of excrement (**guano**) on cliffs (Figure 9). As guano contains a lot of uric acid, it can dissolve the rocks, especially if the rock is alkaline, like limestone.

Did you know?
Guano is an excellent fertiliser. Fear of guano shortages even led the USA in 1856 to pass the Guano Islands Act allowing citizens to claim unclaimed and uninhabited islands if the island contained guano. Over 50 islands were claimed in the Pacific and Caribbean, many of which are still under US control. One of the most famous is Midway.

Exam-style question
In ecosystems, abiotic and biotic components are interdependent. Define the term 'biotic'. **(1 mark)**

Exam tip
Make sure you know the key terms for all your topics very well. Then you can answer questions like this one quickly and easily.

Figure 8 Holes in rocks produced by piddocks grinding them out (biophysical weathering)

Figure 9 Cliffs covered in acidic guano (causing biochemical weathering)

7 People and the Biosphere

Photosynthesis and respiration

Living organisms interact with the atmosphere in many ways, including producing a lot of methane as a waste product of digestion, or when plants decompose anaerobically (in the absence of oxygen). The main way that they interact is through photosynthesis and respiration (Figure 10). Photosynthesis extracts carbon dioxide from the atmosphere and produces oxygen. Respiration uses oxygen and produces carbon dioxide. As such, these processes **regulate** the atmosphere, keeping these gases in balance.

Nutrient cycle

The nutrient cycle describes how nutrients are transferred around an ecosystem (Figure 11). A scientist called Philip Gersmehl used a model based on nutrient cycles to explain differences between ecosystems. A model is a scientific theory that allows complex systems to be understood more easily.

Gersmehl's model said that all ecosystems have the same three basic compartments: soil, litter and biomass. Each is a store for nutrients. Nutrients are transferred between the stores. The size of these stores is different in different ecosystems, as is the amount of nutrients transferred between stores.

Hydrological cycle regulation

Similarly, plants regulate the hydrological cycle. Trees **intercept** and absorb rainfall, and slow its passage to the ground, reducing **surface runoff** and reducing the flood risk and regulating groundwater and surface water. In tropical rainforests the **transpiration** by plants returns moisture to the atmosphere during the day, and when temperatures cool in the evening condensation takes place and there is heavy precipitation. In the desert biome, **succulent plants** like cacti store water, slowing its evaporation.

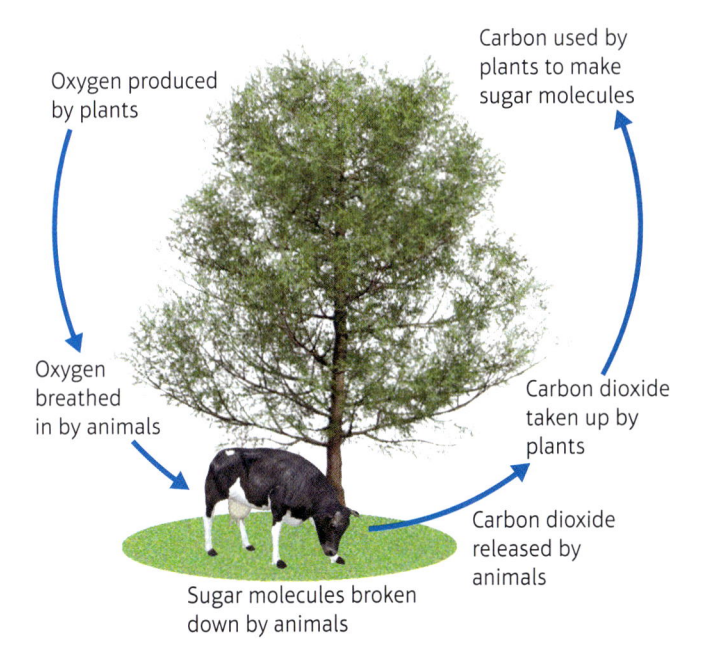

Figure 10 Photosynthesis and respiration

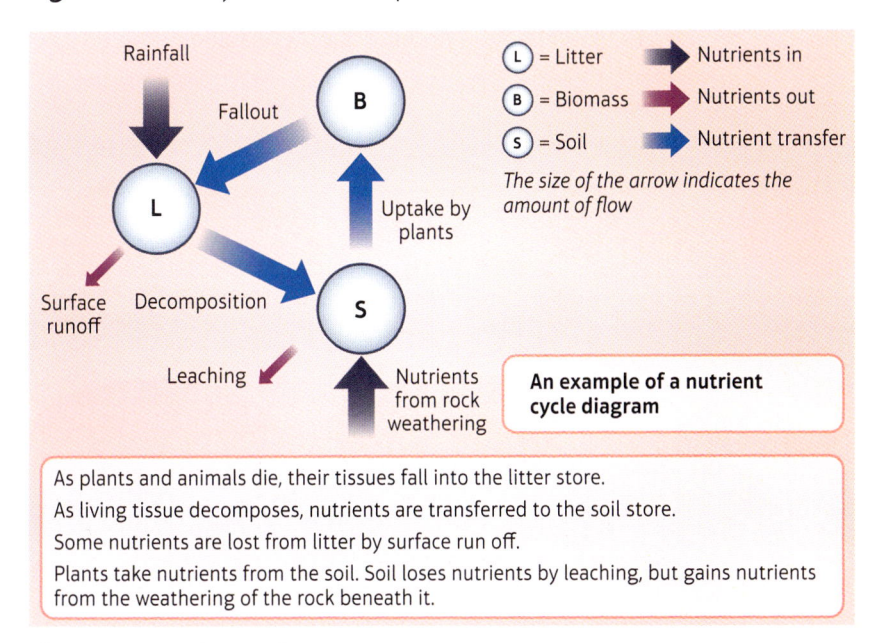

Figure 11 Nutrient cycles

As plants and animals die, their tissues fall into the litter store.
As living tissue decomposes, nutrients are transferred to the soil store.
Some nutrients are lost from litter by surface run off.
Plants take nutrients from the soil. Soil loses nutrients by leaching, but gains nutrients from the weathering of the rock beneath it.

Activity

1. Granite is a hard, impermeable rock which slowly weathers to produce thin, acidic, infertile soils. How does this affect the vegetation likely to grow on it (and therefore the biome)?

2. Explain the difference between biochemical weathering and biophysical weathering.

3. The tropical rainforest ecosystem has a huge biomass store, but only a small store of nutrients in its soil. In desert ecosystems, most nutrients are stored in the soil. What could explain this? Think of possible explanations.

7 People and the Biosphere

How does the biosphere act as a life support system?

> **Learning objectives**
> - To understand the ways in which the biosphere provides vital resources for indigenous people and local groups
> - To recognise the effects of commercial exploitation of resources
> - To be able to outline the ways in which the biosphere provides globally important services

The biosphere provides vital resources

Many people around the world depend on the biosphere for basic goods, such as food, medicine, building materials and fuel (Figure 12). This is especially true for **indigenous** rainforest tribes, desert peoples, like the Tuareg and Berbers of the Sahara, and Arctic peoples like the Inuit of Greenland and Canada.

Of course, all food (except a few things like salt) comes from the biosphere, but developed cultures tend to farm their food rather than using it in its natural state, and then often process it in order to make it more convenient for transporting and storing.

> **Did you know?**
> Insects may become part of our staple diet in the future! Various indigenous groups have, for a long time, eaten insects like grasshoppers and ants as a source of protein. The idea is now spreading to Europe and North America – Noma, a Danish restaurant often ranked the best in the world, has set up a research lab to investigate insects as food.

Commercial exploitation

Modern technologies have reduced our day-to-day dependence on the biosphere, but they have led to an increase in the exploitation.

- The huge demand for water around the world (for rapidly growing cities, for industry and for agriculture) means that other parts of the biosphere are deprived of water. One example is the Hamoun wetlands in Iran. Here a combination of drought, rapid population growth, dam-building in neighbouring Afghanistan and wasteful irrigation practices have caused the wetlands to dry up.
- **Biofuels** are a valuable alternative to fossil fuels because they provide renewable energy. However, commercial production of biofuels means that huge areas of land are devoted to biofuel crops instead of food crops. Forest land has also been cleared for biofuel crops. This makes vital resources from the biosphere – food and fuel – more expensive for local people, and impacts on biodiversity. For example, a sharp decline in the number of orang-utans in Malaysia and Indonesia has been linked to

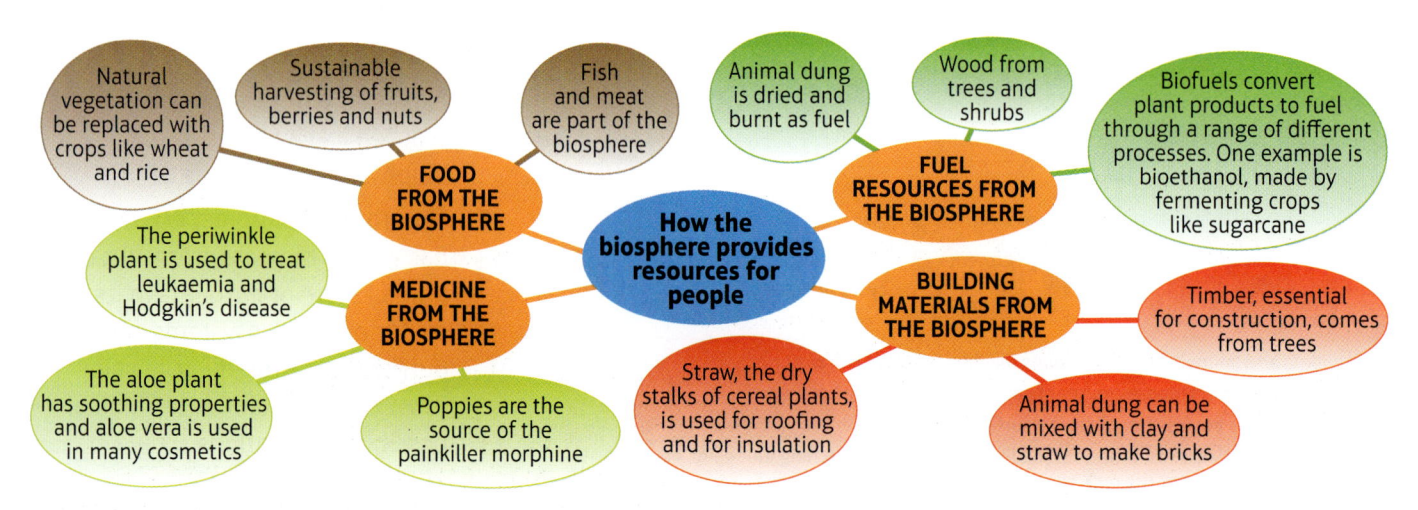

Figure 12 Resources from the biosphere

the increasing number of plantations producing the biofuel palm oil.
- Mineral resources are not part of the biosphere, but increasing demand for minerals has major impacts on the biosphere. An extreme example is mountain-top removal mining, in which coal is mined by removing the tops of mountains to allow easier access to coal seams. This type of mining was developed in the Appalachian mountains in the east of the USA.

The biosphere plays a globally important role

Regulating the atmosphere

The clearest way in which the biosphere supports human existence is through regulation of carbon dioxide and oxygen in the atmosphere (keeping them in balance), mainly through the photosynthesis of plants and the respiration of all living organisms. Although with current concerns over global warming, the extraction of carbon dioxide from the atmosphere via photosynthesis is seen as the most important function. However, without respiration producing carbon dioxide, the Earth would cool down and be plunged into a glacial period, with significant impact on biomes and consequently humans.

Of course, the fact that oxygen is produced by photosynthesis is also vital; forests such as the Amazon rainforest breathe out oxygen during daylight hours. This has sometimes led to tropical rainforests being called 'the lungs of the world' (although lungs actually extract oxygen and produce carbon dioxide, so it is a little bit mis-named).

Soil health

Soils are vital for human existence, and the biosphere plays a key role in maintaining soil health. Most temperate soils, such as brown soils, would be quite infertile if it was not for the leaf litter (dead leaves on the ground) that decomposes in the presence of warm wet conditions, to produce rich **humus**. This decomposition is greatly aided by the biosphere, as earthworms physically churn up humus and other dead organic matter, and fungi and bacteria (decomposers) chemically break it down.

Managing water

The previous spread outlined the role of the biosphere, through regulation of the hydrological cycle, in preventing flooding and in storing water in arid biomes. In 2010, severe flooding in Pakistan (Figure 13) was blamed partly on illegal logging, which reduced **interception** and **absorption**, and increased surface runoff. Mangrove forests line many coasts in tropical and sub-tropical countries, like Bangladesh, and provide a natural defence against coastal flooding.

Figure 13 Pakistan floods, 2010 – partly caused by deforestation

Further to these services, biospheres, and the plants and animals within them, provide an important psychological and aesthetic benefit to people, creating positive feelings and a renewal of energy through the contrasts with daily working lives.

Activity

1. Give **two** examples of commercial exploitation of biospheres.
2. Chose **one** of the indigenous peoples listed on this spread. Looking at Figure 12, list **four** resources they draw from their local biosphere.
3. How does the biosphere ensure soils stay fertile? Draw a rough sketch if this helps you explain.

Decision-making exam-style question

Explain why people in Southern Asia (e.g. Pakistan, India and Bangladesh) are concerned about the changes taking place to their biomes. **(4 marks)**

7 People and the Biosphere

How can increasing use of resources lead to over-exploitation?

> **Learning objectives**
> - To explain the global and regional trends that influence resource use
> - To understand how population growth, rising affluence, urbanisation and industrialisation affect resources
> - To explain how increasing resource demand can lead to exploitation of the biosphere

Global trends

The amount of food, energy and water (and other resources) that people consume has constantly risen over time. Today we extract around 50% more natural resources than 30 years ago to obtain water, food and energy: approximately 60 billion tonnes of raw materials a year. Our natural environment provides us with life resources including cotton (clothing), energy (heat and electricity) and building materials (roads and houses).

People in developed countries are consuming up to ten times more natural resources than those in developing countries. On average, someone who lives in North America consumes around 90 kg of resources each day, whereas someone living in Africa consumes only around 10 kg per day.

The main reason for this is the increasing world population: If there are more people then more resources will be consumed (Figure 14).

However, as significant as the rising numbers of people is the rising **affluence** (wealth) of people. World **Gross Domestic Product (GDP) per capita** has risen steadily from US$6800 in 1993 to US$13,100 in 2013. With the occasional dip due to recession or war, most nations of the world are getting richer, and most people within those countries are getting richer.

> **Did you know?**
> With the world's population expected to rise to 9 billion by 2050 many scientists believe seafood will run out by 2048. The exploitation of fish resources has had an impact on countries that rely on fish as a key food source. In Senegal, barracuda and red carp are no longer available, and instead only much smaller and less appetising fish, such as kobos, are caught.

Regional trends

Previously developing countries are developing into emerging economies. For example, Brazil, Russia, India and China (the BRIC countries) have grown rapidly. Collectively their share of world GDP surpassed that of the USA in 2006 (subsequently Brazil and Russia have fallen back). Mexico, Indonesia, Nigeria and Turkey (the MINT countries) are expected to develop strongly next (Figure 15). As the people gain more wealth, they spend more (**consumerism**), and have more ready access to food, energy and water – meaning that resources get consumed in ever-increasing quantities.

In the next 30 years, rapid urbanisation, industrialisation and growing affluence is going to be significant in Africa. In 2015, ten of the world's 20 fastest growing economies were in the continent of Africa.

Urbanisation and industrialisation

In addition, the rapid **urbanisation** (growth of cities) and **industrialisation** in many developing and emerging countries over the past 50 years has increased resource use, and had a direct impact on biomes. A city requires many resources to support the population, and these are gathered from increasing distances away

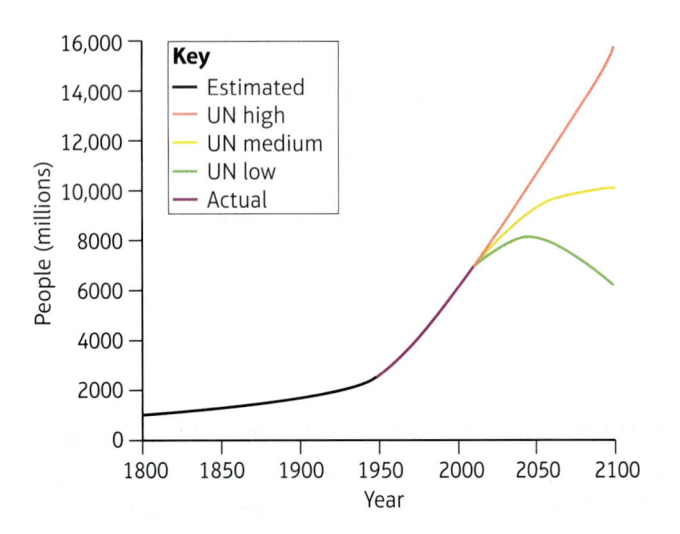

Figure 14 Global population, with different possible future scenarios as predicted by the UN

7 People and the Biosphere

Gross domestic product 2012 (US$ trillions)	Ranking		Estimated GDP in 2050 (US$ trillions)	
16.24	US	1	China	52.62
8.23	China	2	US	34.58
5.96	Japan	3	India	24.98
3.43	Germany	4	Euro area	22.51
2.61	France	5	Brazil	9.71
2.47	UK	6	Russia	8.01
2.25	Brazil	7	Japan	7.37
2.01	Russia	8	Mexico	6.95
2.01	Italy	9	Indonesia	6.04
1.84	India	10	UK	5.69
1.82	Canada	11	France	5.36
1.53	Australia	12	Germany	5.22
1.32	Spain	13	Nigeria	4.91
1.18	Mexico	14	Turkey	4.45
1.13	South Korea	15	Egypt	3.61
0.88	Indonesia	16	Canada	3.47
0.79	Turkey	17	Italy	3.42
0.77	Netherlands	18	Pakistan	3.33
0.71	Saudi Arabia	19	Iran	3.19
0.63	Switzerland	20	Philippines	3.17
0.26	Nigeria	39		

Key: BRIC countries, MINT countries

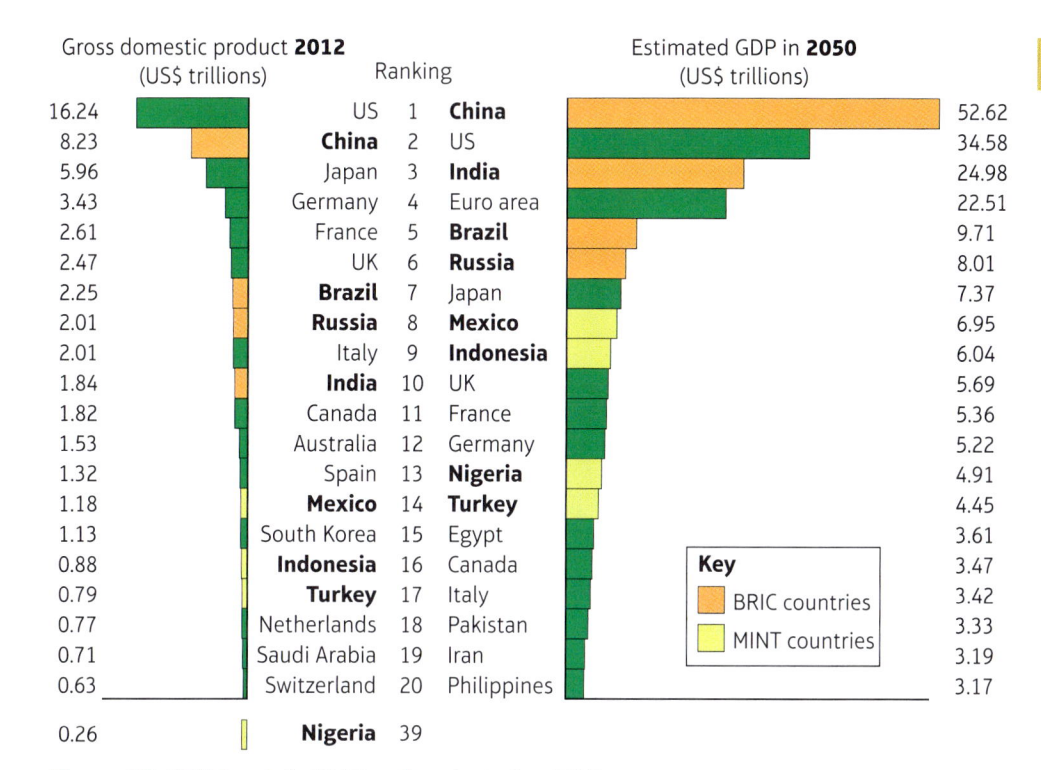

Figure 15 GDP levels in 2012 and projected to 2050

Activity

Create an A4 fact file for each of the ways in which resources are being exploited. For each fact file include the following:

a a location map

b the reason why the resource is being extracted

c the impact of the resource extraction on the environment.

If you can think of an example not mentioned here, add it to your file.

from the central city; for example, people need food and water, factories need raw materials and energy, and waste needs to be disposed of.

The emerging countries of China and India have been the major users of more and more resources. This is because they have grown much richer (6–10% annual growth in GDP since 1990; in 2014, they were the world's second and ninth largest economies, respectively), and also have huge populations (estimated 2.6 billion people in 2015). They have rapidly industrialised and experienced rural-to-urban migrations which have then led to rapid urbanisation.

It is estimated that global energy consumption will increase by 56% in the next 35 years with Asia as one of the leading contributors to the increase. The economic development of China and India will be one of the key factors in the rise as standards of living improve.

Exploitation

The continued increase in the demand for resources such as food, energy and water is leading to a lot of damage to the biosphere.

- Demand for beef (and soya to feed cattle worldwide) has led to massive **deforestation** in the Amazon for growing soya and cattle ranching. (Up to 80% of deforestation is attributed to this.)
- Demand for palm oil (used in many products including ice cream, pizza dough, instant noodles, soap, shampoo and biofuels) has led to massive deforestation in Cameroon.
- Huge water management or hydro-electric power (HEP) projects have led to flooding behind their dams. For example, the Santo Antonio Dam in Brazil flooded about 400 km² of tropical rainforest; the Three Gorges Dam in China is thought to be the major cause of the extinction of the Yangtze river dolphin (baiji).
- Massive swathes of boreal forest have been destroyed through **open-cast mining** of the Alberta tar sands in Canada to extract oil (see Topic 9).

Decision-making exam-style question

Explain the possible impacts of urbanisation on the biospheres surrounding the world's growing cities.

(4 marks)

Exam tip

On longer questions, using geographical terms such as 'boreal', 'open-cast mining', etc. will enhance the quality of your answer – as will the use of specific named locations. Your answer needs to be not only correct but also sophisticated to be awarded the highest marks.

7 People and the Biosphere

Malthus or Boserup: whose theory of population and resources is most convincing?

Learning objectives

- To understand the key difference between Malthus' and Boserup's theories
- To outline some of the evidence supporting both theories
- To evaluate the theories of Malthus and Boserup

Malthusian theory

In the 18th century, the Reverend Thomas Robert Malthus wrote about his beliefs that the human population would grow faster than food (or resource) supply, and a disaster would then take place. As food, water and energy resources began to run out, there would be social unrest and fighting, famine, and **epidemics** (diseases which spread rapidly and affect large numbers of people in an area). The population would then 'crash' until numbers were balanced with the resource supply.

His argument was that population increased geometrically (2 ➡ 4 ➡ 8 ➡ 16 ➡ 32 ➡ 64, etc.), whereas food and resource supplies would only increase arithmetically (2 ➡ 4 ➡ 6 ➡ 8 ➡ 10 ➡ 12, etc.). Clearly, this would lead to a situation where there was not enough food and other resources for the total population, deaths would result, particularly among the poor, and the population would reduce until the point at which there were again enough resources to go around. At this point the population would start increasing geometrically again, until another collapse. Each subsequent adjustment would bring the population closer to balancing the resource supply (Figure 16).

There is evidence for and against this theory. Malthusians will point to wars and civil wars that have taken place and are taking place today, as well as droughts and famines and the spread of disease such as 'bird flu' and Ebola. Others point out that new ways of increasing food and resource production have been discovered, such as the **Green Revolution** (high yielding crop varieties), and that as countries have developed economically birth rates tend to reduce so that a couple tends on average to have two children (replacement level).

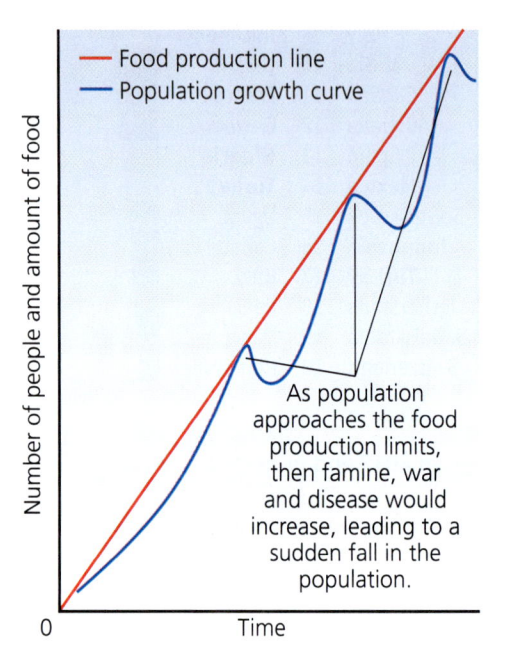

Figure 16 The relationship between food supply and population, according to Malthus

Boserupian theory

In the 1960s, the Danish economist Ester Boserup suggested an alternative view of the population and resource balance. She suggested that as the population size approaches the point when food and resources may run out, then human ingenuity will find ways of increasing food and resource production enough to meet the increased demand. The saying 'necessity is the mother of invention' has been applied to her theory. Therefore, as the **carrying capacity** of a country or the world is approached, i.e. the number of people that can actually be supported by the resources, people will find solutions. There is evidence for and against this theory. In the 20th century, the world's population increased from 1.5 billion to over 6 billion but there has not been a worldwide crash in population. A significant reason has been the improvements in farming and global distribution of food and aid. The Green Revolution, with its use of **selective plant breeding**, **irrigation**, **pesticides**, artificial **fertiliser**, and more efficient farm machinery, has led to large increases in **yields** in many places around the world. In terms of energy use there has been the development of alternative renewable energies, such as solar energy and hybrid and electric cars. Birth control and changes to culture have also lowered birth rates so that now the world's population growth rate is slowing down. However, others will point out the spread of the AIDS pandemic, and the growing number of refugees fleeing fighting and natural disasters.

Activities

1. If the world's population in 2015 was estimated to be 7.26 billion, China's 1.36 billion and India's 1.25 billion, what percentage of the world's population was in China and India combined?
2. Research one of the possible 'Malthusian' situation examples (drought in south-west USA; famine in Ethiopia; refugees from the Middle East) and try to evaluate if it supports Malthus's ideas.
3. Suggest what future inventions and new ideas may be necessary for Boserup's theory to be correct by 2100.

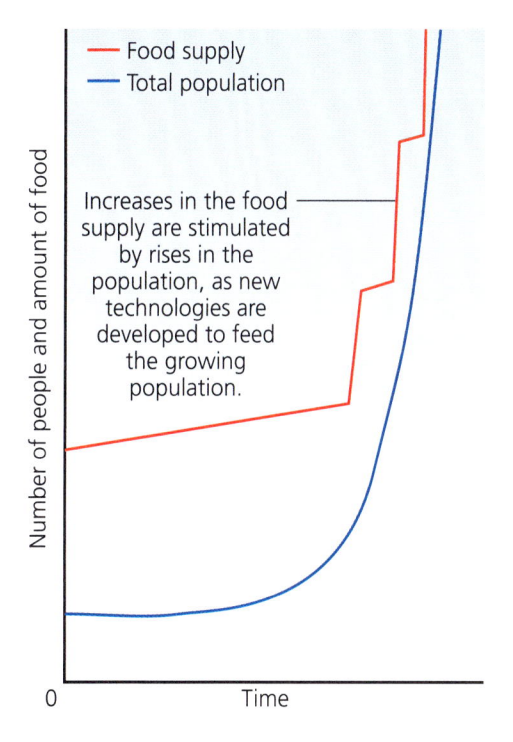

Figure 17 The relationship between food supply and population, according to Boserup

Checkpoint

Now it is time to review your understanding of the relationship between population and resources.

Strengthen

- **S1** Explain how rich people in the USA are likely to use more resources than poor people in Uganda.
- **S2** Explain at least one example of where increased demand for food, water or energy resources has led to large scale destruction of the biosphere.
- **S3** What is, or was, the Green Revolution, and how did it increase crop yields?

Challenge

- **C1** Look at Figure 15. Which current developed nations are expected to remain in the top ten in 2050?
- **C2** Why may economic development be more of a problem for using up resources than the world's growing population?
- **C3** Draw annotated graphs to compare Malthus's and Boserup's ideas about the balance between population and resources.

Did you know?

One of the early successes of the Green Revolution was the development of a variety of rice in the Philippines in the 1960s – IR8. This was one of the first HYVs (high-yield varieties), so called because the amount of crop that could be harvested from a certain area was much higher than for traditional rice varieties. IR8 increased the yield from about 1 tonne to 10 tonnes per hectare.

The location of Zagora (page 247) is Morocco.

Decision-making exercise

People and the Biosphere

Topic 7 explores the interaction between people and the biosphere, examining the characteristics of large-scale ecosystems (biomes) and making links with human activities and their need for the resources provided by the biosphere.

Practise making geographical decisions

Section 1: The background

1. What is the biosphere? **(1 mark)**
2. What is a natural resource? **(1 mark)**
3. The temperate deciduous forest biome is one in which a lot of humans live.
   a. Using Table 1, Figure 4 and the text on page 248, describe the natural characteristics of this biome. **(4 marks)**
   b. Using Table 1 and Figure 12, identify two resources which this biome has provided for humans. **(2 marks)**
4. Using Figures 3 and 4, compare the tropical grassland biome and the temperate forest biome. **(4 marks)**

Section 2: The issues

5. Using Figures 11 and 12, explain the variety of goods and resources that can be provided by the tropical rainforest biome. **(4 marks)**
6. Assess the problems that may be created by human use of tropical rainforests. **(8 marks)**
7. Explain how deforestation may lead to an increase in river flooding. **(4 marks)**
8. Study Figure 16. What does the graph suggest about the relationship between biome resources and population growth? **(4 marks)**

> **Exam tips**
>
> Questions 1 and 2: Definitions need to be accurate and concise.
>
> Question 3: Identify the information from the figures provided and add your basic understanding. Sometimes a question may not directly refer to figures and tables and you may have to search for the information yourself – it is very helpful to take time at the start of the examination to read the Resource Booklet thoroughly.
>
> Question 4: Comparison questions look for geographical similarities and differences.

> **Exam tips**
>
> Question 5: Select detailed features from the information provided. The command word explain means you need to say why there is a variety of resources and how they are useful. Do not simply list resources.
>
> Question 6: Explain can be a tricky question command as you cannot just describe well. There must be statements in the answer that make links – in this case between cause and effect. This is testing your understanding of the situation in a specific biome. In longer questions you will often need to combine pieces of information and ideas from several sources in the booklet.
>
> Question 7: Use correct terminology relating to the water cycle.
>
> Question 8: When presented with graphs that show change over time you need to identify trends and compare different rates of change. For example, does one factor increase faster than another or change as the other changes? Is there a regular (or arithmetic) increase (e.g. 2, 4, 6, 8, 10) or a geometric (logarithmic) increase (e.g. 2, 4, 8, 16, 32)? Are there fluctuations or a random pattern?

Decision-making exercise

People and the Biosphere

Section 3: The options and opinions

9. Explain why indigenous peoples may view resources differently from people living in developed countries. **(4 marks)**

10. Study Figures 16 and 17. Evaluate why some people are concerned about the relationship between biome resources and population growth while other people are not. **(8 marks)**

11. Suggest the extent to which developing alternative food sources from the biosphere could reduce these negative impacts. **(4 marks)**

Exam tips

Question 9: The view of resources may differ by type and quantity, for example.

Question 10: When a question asks you to give opinions, ensure that you identify specific groups in your answer. Remember that the term 'people' will cover international, national and local organisations, businesses and levels of government, as well as local people or citizens of a country. Evaluate means that you must consider the value or success of something using the evidence available, particularly identifying strengths and weaknesses, and conclude which one (or ones) is best. Justify your decision and give reasons for your choice.

Question 11: Consider alternative food sources. Are there negative impacts of their exploitation?

Section 4: The decision

12. Several options exist for improving the relationship between people and the biosphere. Four possibilities are:

    Option 1: Stop deforestation everywhere in the world.

    Option 2: Reduce the amount of resources that people are consuming.

    Option 3: Use technology to make natural resources last longer, or replace them.

    Select the option that you think would be best for improving the relationship between people and the biosphere. Justify your choice. **(12 marks + 4 SPAG)**

Exam tip

Question 12: Leave enough time to complete this question properly as it usually carries the most marks. However, it cannot be done first – as Sections A, B and C (and information in the Resource Booklet) build up to this question. You need to apply the knowledge and understanding from these previous sections. Usually you will be directed to choose **one** best option for solving or reducing the scale of a problem, but there is no one correct answer. Choose the option that you can best justify. Identify the strengths of your choice and state clearly how each would help reduce the problem (or meet the aim). Include facts from the Resource Booklet. You should also identify major weaknesses in the other options and acknowledge that your choice has weaknesses too. Remember that there are four marks for spelling, punctuation, grammar and use of geographical terminology (SPAG), so do **not** use bullet points – a fluent, well-written answer is expected.

8 | Forests under Threat

Two of the world's major biomes are forest biomes: the tropical rainforest (TRF) and the taiga (sometimes called the boreal forest). Like all biomes, the main characteristics of these two biomes result from their climate.

The way the TRF is structured, the processes that go on in this biome and the ways that plants and animals have evolved are all closely related to the equatorial climate: hot all year with rainfall most days.

Although the forest area of the taiga is dominated by trees in the same way as the TRF, the taiga climate makes this forest completely different from the rainforest. The taiga climate has very cold winters, short warm summers and low precipitation. This makes it a much lower-nutrient ecosystem than the TRF, which reduces its biodiversity and means its flora (plants) and fauna (animals) have a very different range of adaptations compared with the TRF.

Both the TRF and the taiga forests are under threat because of commercial development by humans, and because of climate change and air pollution resulting from human industrial development. Action is being taken to protect both biomes, both at an international level and through sustainable management and conservation. Unfortunately, however, not everyone agrees that these forests should be protected – the trees are commercially valuable and so is the land they grow on and, sometimes, the resources lying beneath the forest soils.

Your learning

In this section you will investigate key learning points:
- How does the tropical rainforest reflect the equatorial climate?
- How does the taiga reflect the subarctic climate?
- How different are the climates of the tropical rainforest and the taiga?
- What are the threats to tropical rainforests?
- What are the threats to the taiga?
- How can the tropical rainforest be protected?
- How can the taiga wilderness area be protected?

8 | Forests under Threat

How does the tropical rainforest reflect the equatorial climate?

Learning objectives

- To learn about the non-living (abiotic) and living (biotic) components of the tropical rainforest and how they are interrelated
- To give examples of ways in which plants and animals in tropical rainforests are adapted to the equatorial climate
- To use nutrient cycles to explain the high biodiversity of the tropical rainforest

Most **tropical rainforests** (TRFs) are located in a zone within 20° north or south of the Equator. Their distribution is shown in Figure 1 on page 246 of Topic 7. The climate of this zone is called the **equatorial climate**.

The equatorial climate is hot all year, with an average temperature of between 27°C and 30°C in TRF areas and never falling below 20°C. It is wet all year, too, with an average annual precipitation of 2000–3000 mm (see Figure 6 on page 268). These hot, wet conditions are ideal for plant growth all year round.

The **abiotic** characteristics of the TRF **ecosystem** are made up of its non-living components, such as the atmosphere, water, soils and rocks. These interact closely with all the living things – the **biotic** characteristics – in the TRF, including all the plants, animals and humans. For example, the soil contains **nutrients** which plants use to grow.

The nutrient cycle

The **nutrient cycle** describes how nutrients are transferred around an ecosystem.

- A nutrient cycle diagram has three stores: **soil** (S), **litter** (L) and **biomass** (B). Each is a store for nutrients. Nutrients are transferred between the stores.
- The size of these stores is different in different ecosystems, and so is the amount of nutrients transferred between stores. Figure 1 shows the nutrient cycle for the TRF.

The biggest store in the TRF is biomass, which is made up of all the living things in the TRF (biotic characteristics). When leaves fall or branches drop into the litter store, they decompose very quickly. As soon as the nutrients are released into the soil, the plants of the TRF quickly start to absorb them.

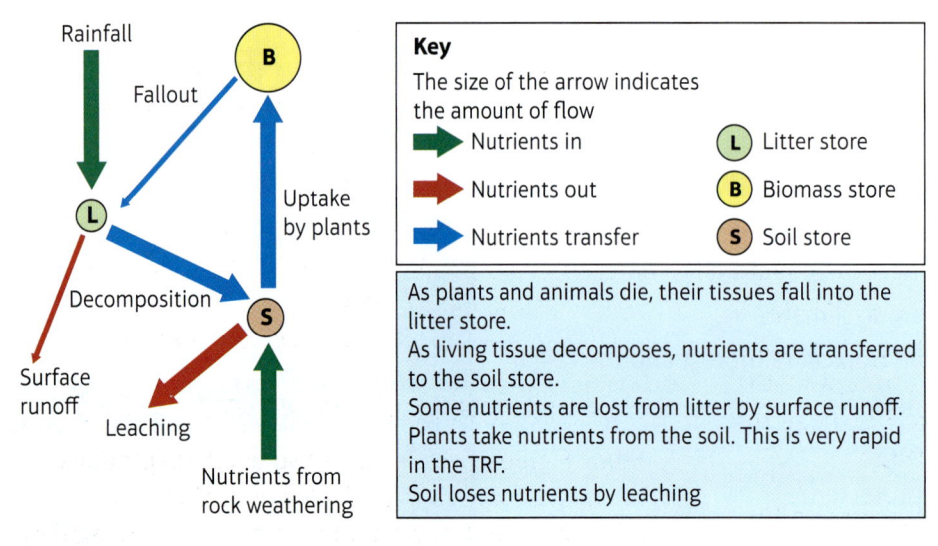

Key
The size of the arrow indicates the amount of flow
- → Nutrients in
- → Nutrients out
- → Nutrients transfer
- (L) Litter store
- (B) Biomass store
- (S) Soil store

As plants and animals die, their tissues fall into the litter store.
As living tissue decomposes, nutrients are transferred to the soil store.
Some nutrients are lost from litter by surface runoff.
Plants take nutrients from the soil. This is very rapid in the TRF.
Soil loses nutrients by leaching

Figure 1 The tropical rainforest nutrient cycle

8 Forests under Threat

(a) The canopy layer is extremely humid: hot and wet. Plants here almost all have 'drip-tip' leaves, which means water runs off them quickly. This is important because otherwise moss and algae would quickly grow over the leaf surface, blocking off its light.

(b) Rainforest trees have 'buttress' structures at their base. As nutrients are concentrated in the top level of the soil only, rainforest trees only need shallow roots and the buttresses have evolved to keep their tall, slender trunks anchored upright.

Figure 2 Adaptations of rainforest trees: (a) drip-tip leaves and (b) buttress roots

The constant rainfall means that a lot of water travels down through TRF soils. As it trickles through the soil, the water takes nutrients and mineral salts with it. This is called **leaching**. Leaching makes TRF soils low in nutrients.

The TRF ecosystem has very high **biodiversity**. This is partly because conditions for plant growth are so good, allowing the ecosystem to support thousands of different species. It is also because TRFs are ancient ecosystems: they have developed over hundreds of thousands of years and many different species have evolved to meet the various challenges of the rainforest.

Plant adaptations

Although the equatorial climate provides ideal conditions for plants, there are also major challenges for plants in the TRF.

The main challenge is light. Some trees have specialised to grow extremely tall (50 metres or more) – they are called **emergents**. The rest of the trees form the rainforest **canopy** at a height of 30–40 metres. When a gap appears in the canopy as an old tree dies and falls over, light reaches the forest floor and tree saplings race upwards to the light. The gap is quickly filled as the winner spreads out its broad leaves to capture the maximum amount of light it can. Figure 7 on page 269 indicates the layered structure of the TRF.

Two other adaptations of rainforest trees are drip-tip leaves and buttress roots (Figure 2).

Animal adaptations

The abundant plant life of the TRF supports huge numbers of animal species. For example, the rainforests on the island of Madagascar have an estimated 14,000 species of plants that support 250,000 known animal species, 75% of which are not found anywhere else in the world. There are also thought to be more than 300 species of frog, 450-plus species of spider and an estimated 700 species of butterfly. Animal species have adapted to the ecological challenges of the TRF in different ways.

- Different tree species produce flowers, leaves and fruit at different times, and some animals travel through the canopy to eat them as they appear. Monkeys, for example, have evolved gripping hands and feet, long **prehensile** tails for balance and colour vision to identify ripe fruit.
- Hundreds of bird species live in the canopy, including birds of prey such as eagles. These have evolved powerful legs with clawed talons that can grab monkeys from the canopy.
- Across the canopy, many species use different forms of camouflage to avoid being eaten. Some insects mimic sticks and leaves, while birds have colouration and barring (stripes) that make them hard to see.

Exam-style question

Study Figure 2, which shows two plant adaptations to an equatorial climate. Explain how each is an adaptation to the equatorial climate. **(2 marks)**

8 Forests under Threat

How does the taiga reflect the subarctic climate?

Learning objectives
- To learn about the abiotic and biotic components of the taiga forest and how they are interrelated
- To give examples of ways in which plants and animals are adapted to the extreme climate of the taiga
- To use nutrient cycles to explain the much lower biodiversity of the taiga forest than the tropical rainforest

The **taiga** is the largest **biome** on the Earth's land surface. As Figure 1 on page 246 shows, it stretches from about 50° to 70° north, and right the way across the north of Asia and America. The climate of this zone is called the **subarctic climate**.

The subarctic climate is dominated by a long, very cold winter: average temperatures of −40°C in taiga areas are not unusual. Summers are short and mild, with average temperatures rarely above 16°C. Snow remains on the ground for many months and average annual precipitation is low, less than 500 mm (see Figure 6 on page 268).

Comparing the taiga and the TRF highlights some big differences in biodiversity and **productivity**. The productivity of an ecosystem is a measure of its biomass (all its biotic components). These differences are due to climate. While the equatorial climate gives year-long warmth, in the taiga the temperature drops below freezing for as many as nine months of the year.

- Taiga plant growth is limited to the short summers. This makes biomass small, so productivity is low.
- Decomposition of the litter layer is slow and even stops during the winter deep freeze, which means the taiga soil has low nutrient levels.
- Only a few specialist plant species can survive the taiga climate. Likewise, only a few animal species can survive its winters. Therefore biodiversity in the taiga is low overall.

The nutrient cycle

In the nutrient cycle for the taiga (Figure 3), the litter store is the biggest store (unlike the TRF, which is biomass). The biomass and soil stores are small and the transfers between the stores are low. The litter store is mostly made up of pine needles from the coniferous trees of the taiga forest. These pine needles are tough and decompose slowly. The litter layer accumulates, or builds up, because decomposition is slow.

As nutrients take a long time to get into the soil, the soil cannot support a large biomass. Pine needles are also acidic and this makes the soil only suitable for plants that can tolerate acidic conditions. These factors, plus the frozen winters, quite low precipitation and short growing seasons, produce extreme conditions that only a small number of plant species can survive. These are species of coniferous trees and simple, low-level plants like mosses and lichens, and fungi.

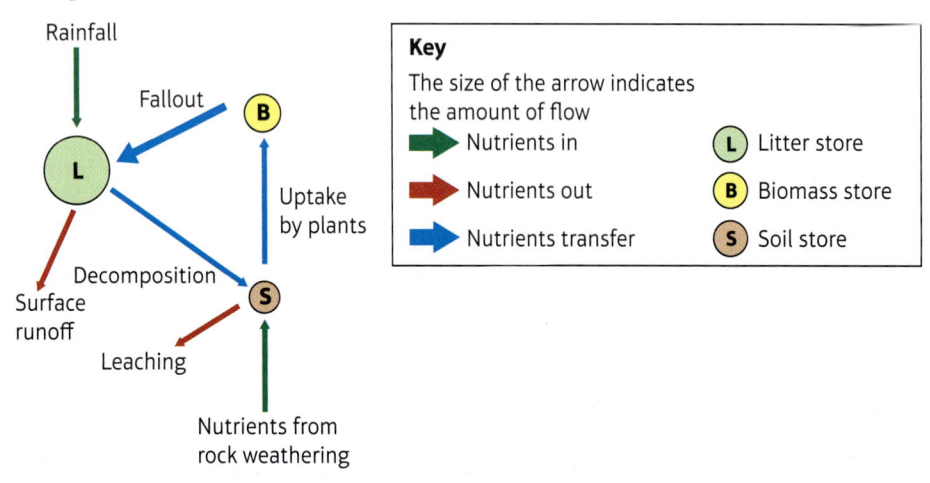

Figure 3 The nutrient cycle of the taiga

As the taiga is a low-nutrient, low-productivity ecosystem, there are far fewer animal species than in the TRF, especially animals that stay in the taiga all year. In the summer months, however, there are a lot of insects in the taiga. These attract **migrating** birds.

Plant adaptations

The taiga forest is made up almost completely of conifer trees. These do not drop their leaves in autumn because leaves take energy to grow each year and energy is in short supply in the taiga. There is also no time to waste once it begins to warm up in spring; the trees need to be ready to photosynthesise straight away.

Taiga trees have specially adapted needle-shaped leaves, often called pine needles (Figure 4), which have the following characteristics.

- The needles have a very small surface area, which means they lose much less water than the broad leaves of TRF plants. They have a waxy coating to help reduce water loss, too.
- The needles are dark green, which helps them to absorb all available sunlight.
- The needles contain very little sap, which means they do not freeze easily and can continue to operate in cold conditions.

The taiga forest has a simple ecosystem structure compared to the TRF (see Figure 8 on page 269). There are only a few different species of conifer in the taiga forest. They grow close together to gain protection from wind damage. Most have a similar conical shape, with downward-facing branches. Heavy snow slides off these branches rather than accumulating and breaking the branches off under its weight.

Animal adaptations

In summer, the taiga has large populations of animal life, especially birds. In winter, however, the number of animal species drops dramatically. For example, the Canadian taiga has more than 300 bird species in summer, but only 30 stay for the winter. The rest migrate south to warmer climatic conditions. These migrating species come to the taiga because the numerous lakes and swamps produce billions of insects during the warm summer months.

Animals that stay in the taiga all year have special adaptations to survive (Figure 5), often including one or more of the following factors.

- Thick fur coats for insulation, smaller ears and short tails to avoid frostbite.
- The ability to hibernate. For example, bears build up fat reserves in the summer and hibernate in a den through much of the winter. At this time, they enter a sleep-like state and allow their body temperature to fall.
- Many animals develop winter camouflage, such as a white coat or plumage, so they do not stand out against the white snow. White fur fibres also provide better insulation than fur with dark pigment.

Activity

1. Identify **three** reasons that help explain why the tropical rainforest is much more productive and biodiverse than the taiga.
2. Explain how the interrelation of abiotic and biotic components leads to taiga soils having low nutrient levels.

Did you know?

The moose, the largest member of the deer family, is one of only a few animals that can eat pine needles. It also eats aquatic plants in the summer, which is unusual for deer.

Figure 4 Needle-shaped leaves are well adapted to cold conditions

Figure 5 Mammals that stay in the taiga all year have thick fur coats and often a white winter coat for camouflage

8 Forests under Threat

How different are the climates of the tropical rainforest and the taiga?

> **Learning objectives**
> - To compare the climates of the tropical rainforest and the taiga
> - To use food webs to explain the high biodiversity of the tropical rainforest and much lower biodiversity of the taiga forest

Climate graphs

Climate graphs are diagrams that provide a visual summary of average monthly precipitation and average monthly temperature for an area or ecosystem. They are very useful for comparing ecosystems. Figure 6 shows climate graphs for rainforest in Manaus (equatorial climate) and for the Siberian taiga (subarctic climate).

Food webs

Food webs are a type of diagram used to show who eats what in an ecosystem. They are useful for comparing ecosystems.

Tropical rainforest
- Food webs for TRFs are highly complex because of the very high biodiversity in TRF ecosystems. There are hundreds of thousands of species.
- TRFs have different layers, from the dark forest floor to the canopy layer and up to the emergent layer. Each layer is like a mini-ecosystem, with plants and animals that have evolved adaptations to that layer. This adds to the complexity of the food webs.

Figure 7 shows a food web for the Madagascan rainforest. It includes a diagram of the different layers found in the TRF. This diagram represents only some of the very complex TRF interactions.

Taiga
- Food webs for taiga ecosystems are much simpler than TRF ecosystems. This is because the climate conditions of the subarctic produce much lower biodiversity.
- Taiga forests are made up of only a few species of slow-growing coniferous tree and they do not have the same layers of forest as in the TRF as the trees are all roughly the same height. The forest floor has very little undergrowth – it is dark because of the conifers' evergreen canopy, with pine needles covering the low-nutrient soil.
- There are few amphibians and reptiles in the taiga as it is too challenging for cold-blooded animals.
- There are big mammals in the taiga. They have very large territories and spend the summer eating as much as possible to help them survive the winter months.

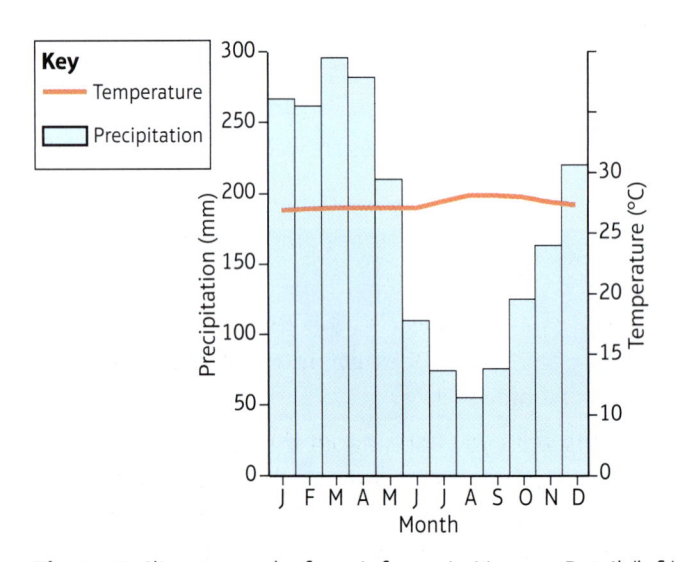

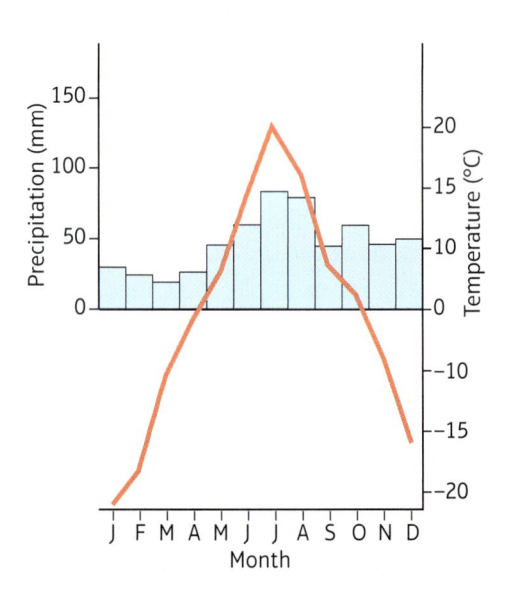

Figure 6 Climate graphs for rainforest in Manaus, Brazil (left) and for the Siberian taiga (right)

8 Forests under Threat

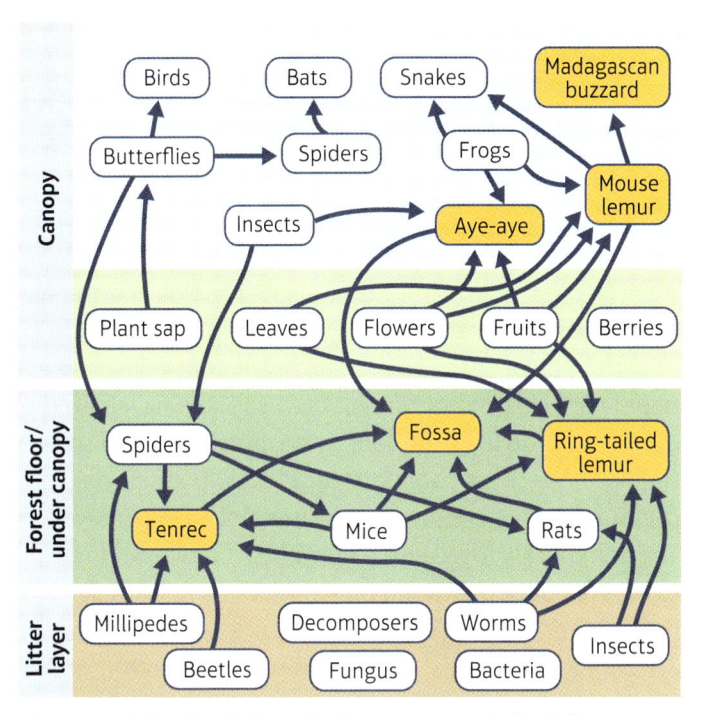

Figure 7 A food web for a Madagascan tropical rainforest ecosystem

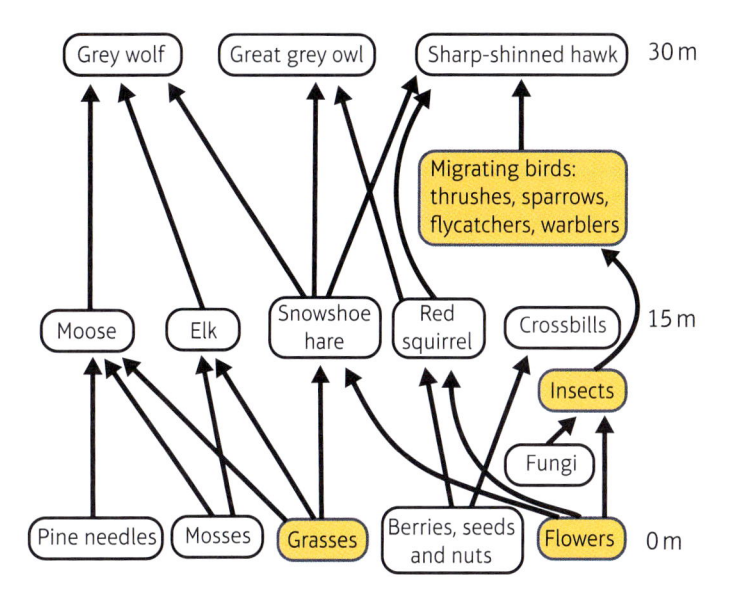

Figure 8 A food web for a Canadian taiga ecosystem

Figure 8 shows a simplified food web for a Canadian taiga ecosystem. The orange boxes indicate food web components that are only available in the short summer months.

Exam-style question

1 Use Figure 6 to answer this question.
   a Identify three differences between the climates of Manaus and Siberia. **(3 marks)**
   b Suggest two ways in which animals may have adapted to the Siberian climate. **(2 marks)**
   c Explain how climate affects the biodiversity of these two forest ecosystems. **(4 marks)**

2 Use Figures 7 and 8 to answer this question.
   a State **one** piece of evidence from Figure 8 that shows that food webs are affected by seasonality in the taiga forest. **(2 marks)**
   b Explain why food webs in the tropical rainforest are more complex than food webs in the taiga forest. **(4 marks)**

Exam tip

On Paper 3 of the exam, questions will always relate to resources. The resources will be in a separate Resource Booklet.

Checkpoint

Now it is time to review your understanding of how the characteristics of the tropical rainforest and the taiga reflect their different climates, including biodiversity.

Strengthen

S1 What types of tree are characteristic of the taiga?
S2 Describe three ways in which plants are adapted to the equatorial climate of the tropical rainforest.
S3 Name the five layers of the tropical rainforest.

Challenge

C1 Imagine you had to survive for a week on your own in either the tropical rainforest or the taiga winter. What would you take with you to deal with abiotic challenges? What biotic challenges might you also have to face?
C2 The taiga ecosystem is described as 'highly seasonal'. What does this mean and how does it affect biodiversity?
C3 Using what you know about the nutrient cycle of the tropical rainforest, predict what might happen to the rainforest if global warming makes droughts more frequent in the equatorial climate.

8 Forests under Threat

What are the threats to tropical rainforests?

> **Learning objectives**
> - To explain the causes of tropical rainforest deforestation
> - To assess the threat to the rainforest from climate change

Deforestation in the tropical rainforest

Deforestation happens as forest is converted to farmland, as trees are cut down to sell as timber or for fuel, and because of mining, especially **open-cast mining**, and hydroelectric power (HEP) schemes where large areas of forest are flooded behind HEP dams.

> **Did you know?**
> - Around half the world's forests have already been cleared.
> - In 2006, the FOA estimated that 7.3 million hectares of forest were cleared: the equivalent of 36 football fields of forest being cleared every minute.
> - If deforestation continues at the current rate, the TRF will all be gone in 100 years.

Clearing forest for farming
Commercial agriculture, when crops are grown to be sold for profit, is the leading cause of TRF deforestation. Most of the rainforest deforestation in Brazil (75%) over the last 20 years was for cattle farming – beef is one of Brazil's key exports.

In recent years, most Brazilian rainforest clearance has been in order to grow sugarcane. In South East Asia, rainforest deforestation has been especially rapid. Much of the forest has been replaced by palm oil plantations. These crops are in high demand as **biofuels**. Many countries have started to use biofuels in order to reduce their reliance on fossil fuels. Biofuels have been called 'deforestation diesel' because so much forest has been cleared to grow these crops.

Subsistence agriculture is when people farm to feed their families. Trees are cut down on a small plot and the undergrowth burned; crops are then planted. The nutrients in the soil are quickly leached out and weed growth takes over. At this point, the farming family often decides to clear another plot. For poor farmers, this 'slash-and-burn' method makes sense as no money is needed to clear the land. However, rapid population growth in developing countries means that many more people are clearing rainforest land. In the past, cleared plots would be left for a long time after each crop so they could recover some nutrients. Now population pressure means people are reusing plots straightaway. The soil quickly loses all its nutrients this way and has to be abandoned. Around one-third of all rainforest deforestation is caused by subsistence farmers.

Commercial hardwood logging
In the 20th century, many countries sold rainforest timber for money, known as commercial logging, to pay interest on international debts. Almost all countries now have strict controls on logging, but a lot of illegal TRF logging still goes on for several reasons.

- **Demand** – there is high demand for tropical hardwood timber, especially rosewood, a very dense, pink-coloured and fragrant hardwood. Chinese buyers will pay very high prices for rosewood.
- **Poverty** – the people who live near rainforests are very poor and illegal logging pays well.
- **Corruption** – police and government officials often let illegal logging happen in return for money.

Other causes of deforestation
- **Mining** – some rainforest areas are on top of valuable minerals. It is often most economic to use open-cast mining to extract the minerals, which affects large areas of rainforest. Roads built to access mines then encourage farmers and loggers to move in. It is estimated that 15% of deforestation is linked to mining and to road-building.
- **Fuelwood** – people living in rainforests, or near them, use them as a source of fuel. Population increase has sped up rates of deforestation. Rainforests are also a major source of charcoal, which is a very important fuel source in many African cities.

Why is climate change a threat to the tropical rainforest?

Agriculture or logging can pose **direct threats** to the rainforest – when someone cuts down a rainforest tree there is a direct connection between their action and damage to the rainforest. An **indirect threat** is when there is no direct cause between one thing and another. Climate change is an indirect threat to the health of the rainforest, although a very serious one.

Warming global temperatures affect the atmospheric systems that bring wet seasons to the equatorial climate. Warmer global temperatures mean these systems shift polewards and do not bring as much rain to the rainforests. Conditions in the rainforest biomes are likely to become hotter and drier, with more droughts.

Figure 9 A tropical rainforest scene from Queensland, Australia

Figure 10 Baobab trees from a seasonally dry forest in western Madagascar; baobab trees store water in their trunks

Many areas that are currently TRF (Figure 9) are likely to slowly become more like seasonal tropical forest (Figure 10). This forest ecosystem is still hot all year but there is a dry season lasting several months.

Temperatures in TRF ecosystems are very similar all year round and species are not adapted to deal with heatwaves. For example, whole colonies of flying fox bats have died as heat levels spiked above the limits they can tolerate. In terms of drier conditions, TRF plant species are not adapted to survive forest fires or long droughts. Climate change would put significant stress on many TRF ecosystems.

As conditions became drier and hotter, other plant species that are adapted to these conditions would spread and out-compete TRF species (like the baobabs in Figure 10). **Ecosystem stress** would also mean that rainforest plants and animals would have lower resistance to new pests and diseases.

Activity

1. The photos in Figures 9 and 10 are taken at ground level rather than being oblique or aerial photos. What are the advantages of ground level photos for showing the characteristics of these two forest ecosystems? Would aerial or oblique photos have had other advantages?

2. An international organisation wants input from geographers about monitoring rates of tropical rainforest deforestation. Which one of the following would you recommend as the best way of monitoring global rates of deforestation:
   - social media reports from observers on the ground
   - satellite monitoring of land use change
   - financial reports submitted by logging companies?

   Explain your choice and how it could be used.

3. If you were a researcher stationed in a tropical rainforest for the next five years, what signs would you look out for to indicate that the forest was being affected by climate change?

8 Forests under Threat

What are the threats to the taiga?

> **Learning objectives**
> - To identify the direct and indirect threats to the taiga from commercial development
> - To identify other factors contributing to a loss of taiga biodiversity

The taiga is under direct threat from commercial development. Commercial development happens when resources in an area are used to make money. Some types of commercial development have bigger impacts than others, and the more commercial development there is, the bigger the impact.

- Threats to the taiga can be divided into direct threats and indirect threats, as follows.
- Logging is a direct threat to the taiga because it removes trees, which are key biotic components of the taiga ecosystem. For example, no trees = no pine needles; no pine needles = lower soil nutrients.
- Mining minerals, oil and gas extraction and HEP are indirect threats. The taiga can be damaged by side-effects of this exploitation, for example oil spills, forest fires and flooding.

Figure 11 A logging yard in the Siberian taiga forest, in Russia's far east

Taiga trees produce softwood and are the world's main source of softwood timber. The most common logging technique in the taiga is clear-cutting. All the trees in an area are cut down and the logs transported to sawmills where they are cut into timber to be used for construction, or to paper mills where the trees are turned into pulp. These mills are often located in the taiga, too, near waterways or railways.

The value of softwood means that large areas of Russia's taiga have been cleared: deforestation is occurring at a rate of 12 million hectares per year (2014). As much as half of the logging in the far east of Siberia is illegal. This illegal logging is a huge threat to the taiga as no efforts are made to replant taiga trees. Logging in Canada is much better controlled as the government ensures that all logging of the taiga forest is accompanied by replanting.

Figure 12 An oil spill in the Samotlor oil field in western Siberia; the Samotlor field is Russia's largest (1700 km^2) and the sixth largest in the world

Russia has 20% of the world's oil and gas, and the majority of those reserves are in the taiga. According to the non-governmental organisation Greenpeace, which campaigns on environmental issues, Russia's oil industry spills 5 million barrels, or 795 million litres, of oil each year through accidents and leaks in the enormous pipelines that transport oil from the remote taiga oilfields to population centres. In Canada, where the government puts much stricter controls on oil companies, oil spills from pipelines still sometimes occur. In 2011, for example, 5 million litres of bitumen (oil from tar sands) mixed with water spilled from a broken pipeline in Alberta. Oil spills are very damaging in the taiga as drainage is often poor, which means that the oil doesn't get washed away. Decomposition occurs very slowly in the taiga, which means that the oil remains in the ecosystem for a long time. Oil seeps down into the soil and is taken up by the shallow root systems of the taiga trees, which often then kills the trees.

> **Exam-style question**
>
> Study Figures 11 and 12 and the text next to them about the commercial development of the taiga in Canada and in Russia.
>
> Describe **one** direct threat and **one** indirect threat to the taiga caused by commercial development. **(2 marks)**

Other threats to taiga biodiversity

Taiga biodiversity is also under threat from **acid precipitation** (acid rain), forest fires and the spread of pests and diseases.

Acid precipitation

- What causes it? When fossil fuels are burnt in industries and power plants, chemicals including sulphur dioxide and nitrogen oxides are released into the atmosphere. (Volcanic eruptions have the same effect.) These react with water and oxygen to form acids, and fall as acid precipitation.
- How does it damage biodiversity? Plants are damaged by the acid, but the biggest problems happen when the acid gets into the taiga's soils, lakes and ponds. The acid kills insects and their eggs, which means fewer insects are present to feed the migrating bird populations in the summer months. The acid also kills soil microbes, which prevents nutrients from entering the soil. This weakens plant species, leaving them less resistant to extreme winters, forest fires and attack from pests and disease.

Forest fires

- What causes them? Lightning strikes are a natural cause of forest fires. Many are also caused by human activity – from hunters lighting camp fires to gas flares in oil fields.
- How do they damage biodiversity? The taiga biome is adapted to forest fires: the ash left after a fire is nutrient-rich and plant species can benefit from this. However, the taiga is adapted to fires every 80–100 years. Forest fires have become much more frequent as global temperatures have risen, and the young saplings are burnt before they can grow to replace the old trees.

Pests and diseases

- What are they? The taiga has fungus and mould species that damage conifers' needles, trunks and roots, and insects also eat their pine cones, needles and young shoots. In addition, new pests and new diseases have also spread into taiga biomes.
- How do they damage biodiversity? One example is the silkworm, which spread into eastern Siberia from Mongolia in the early 2000s. The taiga forest had been affected by forest fires and drought, and the silkworm infestation killed many plants weakened by these stressors. In North America, 'plagues' of spruce-bark beetles have killed large numbers of taiga trees. Over 6 million acres of Alaska's forests showed signs of spruce-bark beetle activity.

> **Decision-making exam-style question**
>
> Assess the severity of the threats to the Taiga biome. **(8 marks)**

> **Checkpoint**
>
> Now it is time to review your understanding of direct and indirect threats to the tropical rainforest and the taiga forest.
>
> **Strengthen**
>
> **S1** Give one example of a direct threat to the tropical rainforest biome and one example of an indirect threat.
>
> **S2** Explain the cause of one direct threat and one indirect threat to taiga biodiversity.
>
> **Challenge**
>
> **C1** 'Even if the tropical rainforest does disappear in 100 years, it won't affect how we live in the UK.' Come up with three reasons that either support this statement or argue against it.
>
> **C2** What is 'ecosystem stress'? Use an example to support your answer.

Activity

1. Why is illegal logging of the taiga more damaging than authorised logging?
2. Climate change is an indirect threat to the tropical rainforest. Which of the threats to the taiga could be made worse by rising global temperatures?
3. The taiga is sometimes called 'the Amazon of the north'. Put this phrase into the design of a poster which explains why the taiga is important and should be protected.

8 Forests under Threat

How can the tropical rainforest be protected?

> **Learning objectives**
> - To examine advantages and disadvantages of global actions to protect tropical rainforest species and areas
> - To consider why tropical rainforest deforestation is increasing in some places but not others
> - To identify reasons why sustainable management of the topical rainforest is challenging

Global actions

International organisations have tried to create international agreements to protect the rainforest. By signing up to these agreements, member countries receive aid and assistance. Two examples are **CITES** and **REDD**.

CITES stands for the Convention on International Trade in Endangered Species of Wild Fauna and Flora. It aims to prevent the international trade in endangered animal and plant species that threatens rainforest biodiversity. Currently, 35,000 different species are under CITES protection, of which there are different levels. Countries sign up to CITES and agree to monitor trade across their borders to catch and punish people exporting or importing products made from endangered species.

REDD stands for Reducing Emissions from Deforestation and forest Degradation. It is a United Nations scheme that advises governments on how to reduce the rate of deforestation and replant forest areas. It uses **remote sensing** to monitor deforestation rates. It arranges very large sums of money to fund these schemes from sources such as the World Bank. For example, a REDD scheme in Brazil has a US$1 billion fund behind it.

Deforestation rates

Tackling deforestation remains very challenging in most rainforest areas of the world. There is too much money to be made from commercial development of rainforest land, or too much pressure from rapidly growing populations requiring farmland, for local people and businesses to stop deforestation unless some other way of making a living is provided for them. However, national and international schemes to reduce the rate of deforestation can work, if enough money and enough political backing for the scheme is provided. One example of an area where deforestation was slowed is in the Amazon rainforest in Brazil, from 2004 (Figure 13).

Table 1 Advantages and disadvantages of CITES and REDD

Advantages	Disadvantages
CITES	
It has a very large international influence – 181 countries have signed up.	The illegal trade in rainforest products is increasing, not decreasing. This is because demand remains high so it is worth the risk to make illegal trades.
CITES is targeting the right problem – most trade in endangered species products is international. For example, rosewood timber from Vietnamese rainforests going to China.	CITES cannot possibly hope to monitor all 181 countries at the same time. It is difficult to check that all countries are doing all they should be doing to halt trade in protected species.
REDD	
Tackling deforestation is very challenging but REDD provides international expertise to develop the best approaches.	Deforestation remains very rapid in South Asia, despite its countries signing up to the REDD scheme.
The funding that REDD can access is very attractive to governments.	REDD is vague about what counts as forest for replanting. In some cases, funding has been given to projects that have replanted deforested areas with oil palm trees.

8 Forests under Threat

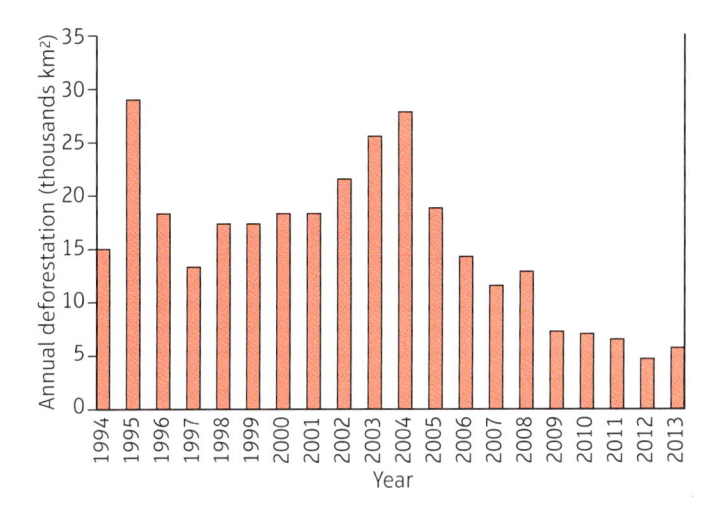

Figure 13 The bar graph shows the rate of deforestation in the Brazilian Amazon, 1994–2013

Brazilian Amazon, 1994–2013

Several different actions explain why the rate of deforestation slowed in Brazil in 1994–2013, which are detailed as follows.

- Deforestation before 2005 was rapid because of rising global demand for soya beans. However, in 2005, the international price for soya crashed.
- Transnational corporations (TNCs) using soya came under pressure from environmental campaigners to only use soya from farmers who protected the rainforest. This led to TNCs changing who they bought soya from.
- The Brazilian government increased its commitment to rainforest protection, helped by a billion dollar REDD fund set up by Norway. Protected areas of rainforest were expanded and laws against deforestation were enforced by government officials and the police.

Decision-making exam-style question

Select the conservation strategy that you think would be best for the tropical rainforest biome. Justify your choice. **(8 marks)**

The challenge of sustainable rainforest management

Unfortunately, deforestation in the Brazilian Amazon started to increase again in 2014 and 2015. The main reason was an expansion of pasture for beef cattle. Protecting the rainforest is particularly challenging because the land is more valuable to farmers and big businesses when it is used for economic activities, such as farming, energy supply and mining.

One alternative is **sustainable rainforest management**. Sustainable management of the rainforest aims to prevent damage to the rainforest in a way that helps benefit local people. This has worked best in areas where **ecotourism** can be combined with sustainable forest management. Ecotourism creates jobs for local people, such as working as forest guides and in hospitality and catering services for tourists. Tourists also spend money in the area on local handicraft products. For those people benefitting from tourism, it makes economic sense to protect the forest from poachers and illegal logging.

Often, sustainable forest management schemes include a sustainable agriculture training programme. This involves teaching local people about farming techniques that keep fields fertile for longer, and types of crops that give higher yields (more food). This means new plots do not need to be cleared from the forest and, instead, land that has already been cleared can support more people.

In the end, however, these sustainable management techniques almost always require financial support from government or international agencies to survive. They also work best in rainforest areas that are already well protected by government, such as national parks and forest reserves.

Exam-style question

Study Figure 13, which shows deforestation rates in the Brazilian Amazon rainforest.

State which of the following is the amount of deforestation recorded in 2004: 28 km^2; 28,000 km^2; 280,000 km^2? **(1 mark)**

Exam tip

Some graphs and charts are more complicated to interpret than others so always take time to check units, scales and axes so that you can be sure you are considering the right thing.

How can the taiga wilderness area be protected?

> **Learning objectives**
> - To identify some of the challenges facing attempts to protect wilderness areas in the taiga
> - To explain why sustainable forestry is sometimes difficult to maintain in the taiga
> - To discuss why people have different views about protecting the taiga or exploiting the forest and natural resources of the taiga

The taiga biome is easily damaged by human activity and needs to be protected from over-exploitation. However, some taiga areas contain valuable resources which can help countries to develop economically. It is difficult to both protect the taiga and allow its resources to be used.

Why does the taiga need protecting?

The taiga is a fragile ecosystem and takes a very long time to recover from damage. Plants grow very slowly because of the long, cold winters and lack of nutrients. If a conifer is cut down, it may take over 50 years for it to be replaced. Decomposition occurs very slowly and pollution remains in the ecosystem for decades. There are very few species in the taiga. A disease that affects one tree species, for example, would have a big impact on the whole ecosystem. Taiga plants and animals are highly specialised. They will struggle to adapt to climate change.

National parks and protected wilderness

These areas prevent commercial development of the taiga within their boundaries. National parks aim to preserve the taiga ecosystems and biodiversity. To do this, national park researchers find out as much as possible about the abiotic and biotic components of the ecosystems in their parks.

Protecting 'wilderness' areas involves active ecosystem management, rather than just leaving the area to 'go wild'. For example, park rangers will sometimes have to cull elk (a type of deer) because there are not enough big predators to keep elk numbers down. Too many elk means that saplings get eaten instead of growing into trees. Vegetation that other species rely on is also over-eaten by elk. So why are there not enough big predators to keep elk numbers down?

Big predators need large territories to survive in the taiga, and often parks and protected wilderness areas are not big enough. Predators that range outside the park are not as protected. Big predators can be a threat to farmers, who may trap or poison them, and they are also a very popular game animal for hunters. Licensed shooting keeps big predator numbers down. National parks want to attract tourists. Although tourists want to see big predators, big predators usually do not want to see tourists and seek more remote areas as a result.

National parks and other kinds of protected wilderness areas are heavily involved in conserving biodiversity, but national parks also are popular tourist destinations. For example, Canada's busiest park is Banff National Park (Figure 14), which has 3 to 4 million tourists visiting each year. This includes winter tourists, who come to ski, sledge and enjoy an Ice Festival. All the visitors to the taiga forest damage the ecosystem they come to enjoy. There are also risks known as 'human–wildlife conflict occurrences', which occasionally involve grizzly bear attacks on tourists.

Other challenges facing national parks and protected areas include the following.

- **Migration** – taiga species often migrate across long distances. Unless parks and reserves are very large, the migrating species cannot be protected once they leave.
- **Money** – where the taiga has oil and gas, governments face huge pressures to develop the area. Exporting oil and gas can lift whole countries out of poverty.
- **Pollution** – taiga is easily damaged by atmospheric pollution. But if parks and reserves are far from cities, no tourists will visit them. Money from tourism helps parks to fund their conservation.

Figure 14 Banff National Park, Canada

Sustainable forestry

In **sustainable forestry**, trees that are cut down are replanted with native taiga species. The whole forest area is carefully managed so that biodiversity is not damaged – habitat areas are preserved and corridors of forest maintained so that species can migrate from one forested area to another. This means that sustainable management is expensive and requires long-term planning. This is usually only possible for large companies or when international organisations provide funding.

Conflicting views on protecting or exploiting the taiga

Many different groups of people have an interest in how the taiga is used.

- **Forestry** – using the forest for timber, sustainably in countries such as Canada with strict controls on logging by the Canadian government, or unsustainably in some areas of Russia.
- **Mining and energy production** – both Canada and Russia, as the two countries with the most taiga, have a lot of mining and energy production in the taiga. Without these industries, Canadian and Russian people would be poorer. For example, 380,000 Canadians work in mining industries.
- **Indigenous peoples** – indigenous taiga people often wish to maintain aspects of their traditional uses of taiga resources, such as hunting.
- **Recreation and tourism** – in both North America and Russia, the taiga forest is where people go to relax.

International tourism also brings new visitors to the taiga, and money to local economies.

- **Consumers of taiga products** – much of the paper we use comes originally from taiga forestry, though it has usually now been recycled since. The energy for many countries comes from taiga oil and gas fields.

Activity

1. Working in groups, prepare for and perform a role play about the creation of a new taiga National Park. Each group member should take on the role of a different type of taiga stakeholder.
2. Which of the following options do you think would be the best way to protect an area of taiga forest: prohibit all commercial exploitation, including tourism; develop tourism and sustainable forestry but no mineral extraction; permit all commercial exploitation but under very strict controls?
3. Many people value the taiga as 'wilderness'. What do you think people would want to experience on a wilderness tour of the taiga? Design a poster to advertise your tour.

Checkpoint

Now it is time to review your understanding of issues about conserving the tropical rainforest and protecting the taiga.

Strengthen

S1 Describe the way one international organisation is working to protect the tropical rainforest.

S2 What is 'remote sensing' and how can it be used to monitor deforestation?

S3 Identify one challenge that makes sustainable forestry difficult and one challenge that makes running a national park difficult.

Challenge

C1 Which do you think is in more need of protection: the taiga forest or the rainforest? Give reasons.

C2 'The rainforest will only be protected when people can't make more money by clearing the forest from the land.' Do you agree with this statement? Come up with one (or more) reasons to agree with it and one (or more) ways it can be challenged.

Decision-making exercise

Forests under Threat

Topic 8 explores the threats to forest biomes and how these threats may be reduced. The topic examines the natural characteristics of tropical rainforests and taiga, the causes of deforestation, climate change threats and other natural and man-made threats. This topic then evaluates ways of managing forests, especially related to the aim of achieving sustainability.

Practise making geographical decisions

Section 1: The background

1. What is meant by the term 'abiotic'? **(1 mark)**
2. Study Figures 2, 4 and 5. Explain what is meant by adaptation when applied to plants and animals. **(3 marks)**
3. Study Figures 1 and 3.
   - **a** Describe how a nutrient cycle operates. **(3 marks)**
   - **b** Explain the importance of the nutrient cycle to maintaining the stability of forest biomes. **(4 marks)**

Exam tips

Question 1: Definitions need to be accurate and concise.

Question 2: As well as a definition, you need to include examples in order to explain adaptation.

Question 3: (a) You should include a detailed description of the stores and transfers.
(b) Notice this is a simple question followed by a more challenging one – remember to focus on the explanation.

Section 2: The issues

4. **a** Identify **three** ways in which the tropical rainforest is being deforested. **(3 marks)**
   - **b** Explain **two** reasons why deforestation is taking place in the tropical rainforest biome. **(4 marks)**
5. Suggest how global climate change may cause problems for the taiga forest biome. **(3 marks)**
6. Study Figures 8, 11 and 12. Suggest how human activities may damage the taiga forest biome. **(4 marks)**
7. Explain the following statement 'Human threats are more severe than natural threats to the taiga forest biome.' **(4 marks)**

Exam tips

Question 4: (a) You need to extract three correct pieces of information; do not include any explanation. (b) Think about the main motives for deforestation.

Question 5: Suggest means that there is a range of possibilities and the exact problems are not known. You must find and give the possibilities in your own words.

Question 6: You need to make specific links between what people do and the damage they cause, such as loss of habitats, loss of biodiversity or damage to soils.

Question 7: This question is testing your understanding of the situation in the taiga biome. Use evidence from the information provided to support your judgement/opinion.

Decision-making exercise

Forests under Threat

Section 3: The options and opinions

8 Study Table 1. Evaluate the obstacles that limit the effectiveness of global strategies aimed at conserving forest biomes. **(8 marks)**

9 Study Figures 3, 6 and 8. Explain why the taiga forest biome may take longer to recover from damage than the tropical rainforest biome. **(4 marks)**

10 a Why do people in the USA, the UK, Japan and China have an important role to play in reducing deforestation? **(3 marks)**

b Why may local people living in forested areas of the world be against establishing national parks? **(4 marks)**

Exam tips

Question 8: You should make it clear how the obstacles 'limit the effectiveness' and then rate them in terms of how obstructive each is. Evaluate means that you must consider the value or success of something using the evidence available, particularly identifying strengths and weaknesses, and conclude which one (or ones) is best. Justify your decision and give reasons for your choice.

Question 9: You need to compare the vulnerability of the two forests linked to the physical geography, for example climate.

Question 10: (a) Think about the links between businesses and consumers in countries such as these with a high demand for resources and the countries where the taiga and tropical rainforest biomes are located. (b) When asked about opinions, try to identify specific groups in your answer, in this case indigenous (native) peoples and their way of life (subsistence farming and hunting). Think about what they need from forests and how this may change if forests are protected.

Section 4: The decision

11 Several options exist for conserving and managing the taiga forest biome in a sustainable way. Three possibilities are:

Option 1: Create a Wilderness Area (such as the Arctic National Wildlife Refuge).

Option 2: Use CITES to protect species within a sustainable forestry strategy.

Option 3: Use remote sensing to closely monitor human activities in forests.

Select the option that you think would be best for conserving and managing the world's taiga forests. Justify your choice. **(12 marks + 4 SPAG)**

Exam tip

Question 11: All the questions in Sections A, B and C (and the information in the Resource Booklet) direct your thoughts towards this decision-making question. Usually you will be directed to choose **one** best option for solving or reducing the scale of a problem, but there is no one correct answer. Choose the option that you can best justify. To justify, you must identify the strengths of your choice and state clearly how each would help reduce the problem (or meet the aim). Include facts from the Resource Booklet. You should also identify major weaknesses in the other options and acknowledge that your choice has weaknesses too. Four marks are for spelling, punctuation, grammar and use of geographical terminology (SPAG), so provide a well-structured, prose answer.

9 | Consuming Energy Resources

Energy is essential for modern life. As the world's population grows and becomes wealthier, the demand for energy is increasing. This is driving the search for new sources of fossil fuels and alternative sources of energy. Energy resources are unevenly distributed across the world, and exploiting them can have significant impacts on landscapes and the environment, including climate change. One of the 21st century's biggest challenges is to manage energy resources and consumption more sustainably.

Your learning

In this section you will investigate the following key questions:

- How can we classify energy resources?
- What are the environment impacts of extracting these resources?
- Why is access to energy resources uneven around the world?
- Can we cope with the rising demand for oil?
- How are oil supplies and prices affected by geopolitics?
- Why are we exploiting ecologically sensitive and isolated areas?
- How can we be more energy efficient?
- What are the costs and benefits of alternatives to fossil fuels?
- How are attitudes to energy and environmental issues changing?

9 | Consuming Energy Resources

Why is access to energy resources uneven around the world?

Learning objectives
- To know that energy resources can be classified as non-renewable, renewable and recyclable
- To understand the uneven global patterns of the energy supply and consumption
- To understand how the extraction and use of energy resources impacts on the environment

Classifying energy resources

Since the industrial revolution, energy – particularly **fossil fuels** – has fuelled economic development, while also causing very significant environmental damage. We can classify energy resources as **non-renewable**, **renewable** and **recyclable**.

- Most of the world's energy (86% in 2014) is from non-renewable sources – fossil fuels like coal, oil and natural gas. These are finite or **stock resources** – no more are being created and eventually they will run out.
- Renewable energy sources (9.3% in 2014) are **flow resources** which can be reused and so will not run out. Examples include wind, **hydro-electric power (HEP)**, solar, tidal and wave, and geothermal.
- Recyclable energy sources (4.4% in 2014) can be reused, so will also last into the future. They include **biofuels** and nuclear power, where the uranium fuel is reprocessed and used again.

Over time, the world's demand for energy has increased, and the balance of different types of energy has changed (Figure 1).

> **Did you know?**
>
> Fossil fuels really are fossils. Coal, for example, is formed from tropical plants that died millions of years ago. It is mostly carbon, so turns into CO_2 when it burns.

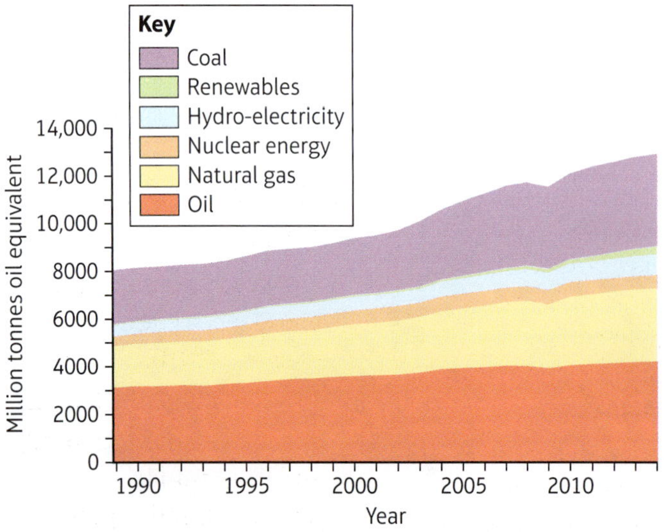

Figure 1 The world's energy consumption, 1989–2014

The distribution of energy resources

Access to energy resources is uneven around the world. Some countries have become wealthy because of their huge **reserves** of fossil fuels – they dominate the map of energy supply (Figure 2). This uneven distribution is caused by a number of factors.

Geology
- Fossil fuels, found in sedimentary rocks, are the world's major source of energy. Countries in the Middle East such as Saudi Arabia and Iran have 48% (2012) of the world's oil and 43% (2012) of gas reserves. Coal is quite widely distributed across the world, with major reserves in the USA, Russia and China.
- Countries located on plate boundaries, such as Iceland and New Zealand, can have access to geothermal energy. Volcanic activity creates heat stored in magma

282

9 Consuming Energy Resources

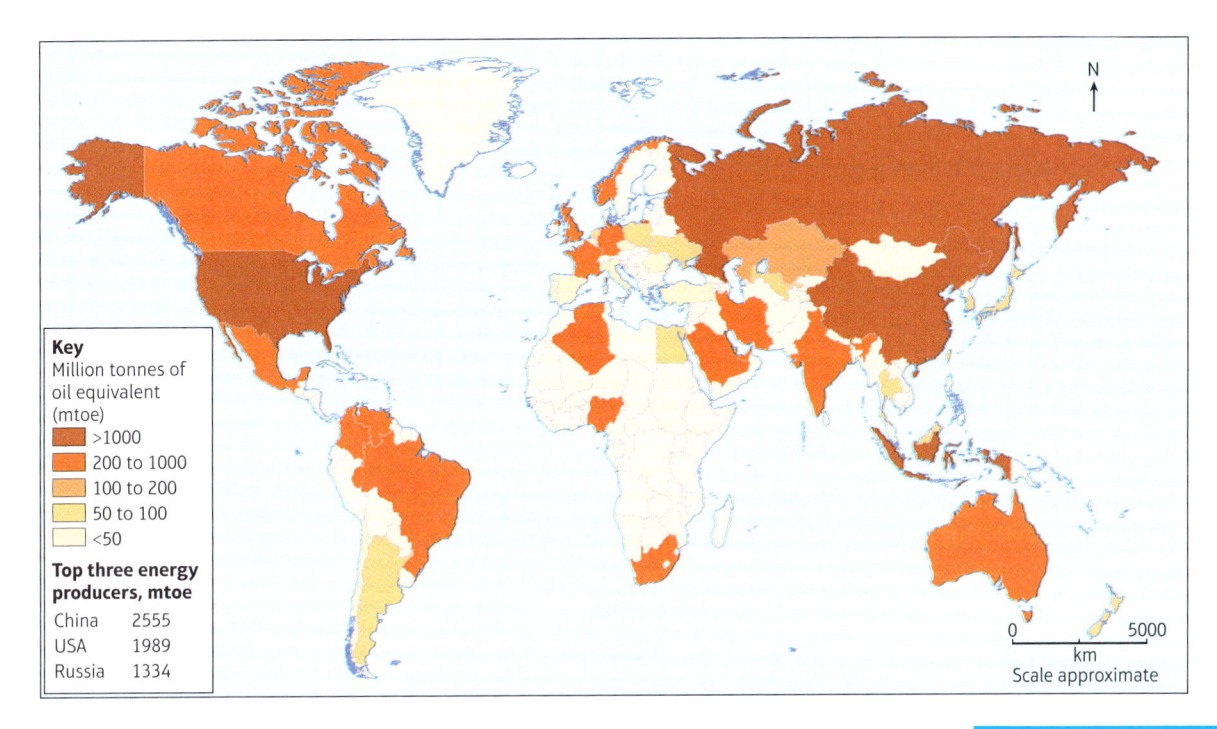

Figure 2 World energy production in million tonnes of oil equivalent, 2014

Key
Million tonnes of oil equivalent (mtoe)
- >1000
- 200 to 1000
- 100 to 200
- 50 to 100
- <50

Top three energy producers, mtoe
China 2555
USA 1989
Russia 1334

beneath the Earth's surface (see Topic 1B), creating a natural geothermal system which can be used to heat water and generate electricity.

Relief and climate
- Regions with high rainfall and suitable relief are often good locations for HEP. Large volumes of water are needed and steep-sided valleys are often chosen for dam construction. The world's largest HEP scheme, the Three Gorges Dam in China, is a good example.
- Climatic conditions are also important to harness the potential of wind and solar power. Exposed areas provide high winds, which is one reason for the location of the UK's largest offshore wind farm, the London Array, in the North Sea. Places that receive longer hours of, and more intense, sunlight provide good locations for solar parks. China, the world leader in generating solar energy, is currently building a giant solar power station in the Gobi desert (page 281), which could potentially produce enough energy to supply 1 million homes.

Accessibility and development
- The economic development of a region can influence its ability to invest in and use new technologies, and explore for and develop energy resources. For example, parts of sub-Saharan Africa have large reserves of oil and gas, but these are largely exported. The region has huge potential to develop renewable HEP, solar, wind and geothermal energy sources, but lacks the funds for investment. Some resources are in remote areas, making them expensive to exploit and bring to consumers – 620 million people, two-thirds of the population, do not have access to the electricity grid. Many rely on **biomass** as a source of energy.

Exam-style question

Study Figure 2, which shows world energy production in mtoe. Identify the world's three major energy-producing regions.

- ☐ A North America, South America and Australia
- ☐ B China, Russia and South Asia
- ☐ C China, North America and Russia
- ☐ D Europe, the Middle East and North Africa **(1 mark)**

Activity

1. What is the difference between stock, flow and recyclable resources?
2. Study Figure 1.
   a. Estimate the consumption of coal and renewable energy in 2010.
   b. Identify **one** type of energy that has increased, and **one** that has decreased, and suggest reasons for the changes.

9 Consuming Energy Resources

Global patterns of energy use

Over the past 100 years, population growth and rising income per person have driven the increased demand for energy. By 2035, an additional 1.6 billion people will require energy, and demand will also grow as people and countries become better off, especially in emerging countries like China. The global distribution of energy consumption (use) per capita (per head) is shown in Figure 3.

> **Did you know?**
>
> Developed countries consume seven times as much energy per capita as emerging countries, and more than 14 times as much as developing countries.

What causes these variations in energy use?

- **Economic development** – energy is vital to growing economies: powering industry, transport, information technology, as well as heating and cooling buildings and household uses. Developed countries have high demands for energy and are able to invest in technology, so increasing national and individual energy consumption (e.g. from electronic goods). Technology also creates new opportunities for energy supply, both for renewables (e.g. solar power) and for mining fossil fuels, such as fracking (see page 290). By contrast, many developing countries have limited access to energy resources and poor distribution systems, which restricts economic growth.

- **Economic sectors** – energy use changes with the economy and technology. In 1970, industry in the UK used 40% of energy and homes used 24%. By 2013, industrial use declined to 21% and energy use in homes increased to 27%, with a growing population, better heating and more technology. By contrast, in rapidly emerging countries like India industry often uses most energy (Table 1).

- **Traditional fuel sources** – in rural areas in many developing countries traditional biomass fuels for domestic use are the main energy use. In Sub-Saharan Africa there is no direct electricity in many rural areas and urban supply is inconsistent. So although Africa is rich in energy resources, 700 million people cook over fires (Figure 4).

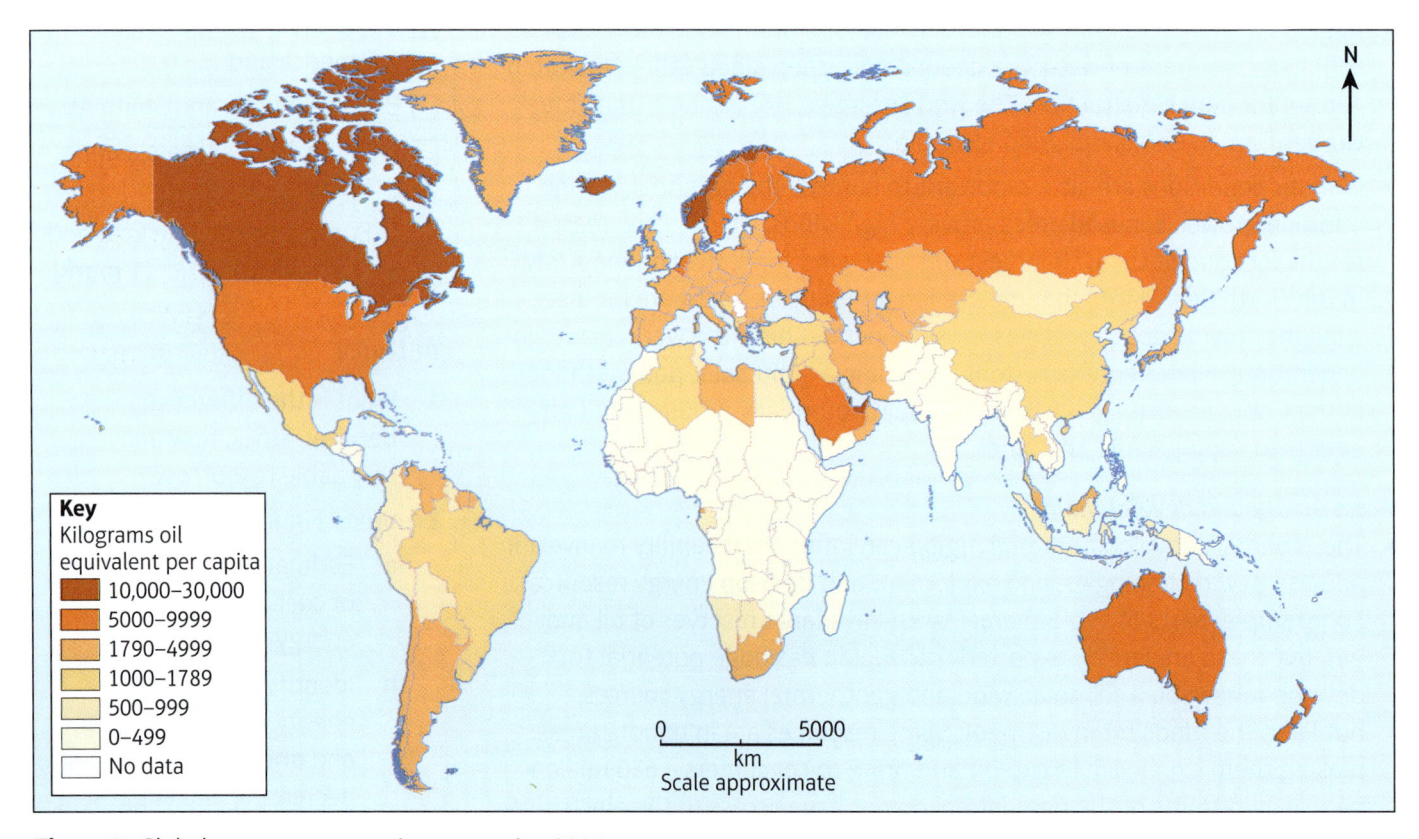

Figure 3 Global energy consumption per capita, 2014

Key
Kilograms oil equivalent per capita
- 10,000–30,000
- 5000–9999
- 1790–4999
- 1000–1789
- 500–999
- 0–499
- No data

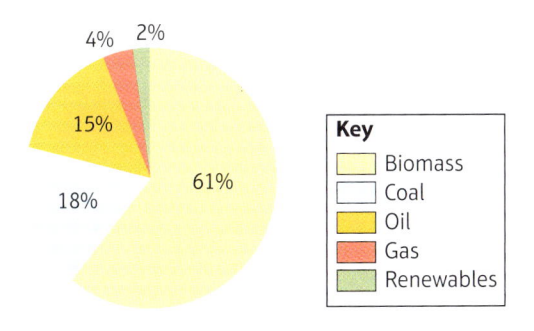

9 Consuming Energy Resources

Figure 4 Primary energy use in Sub-Saharan Africa, 2012

Pie chart values: Biomass 61%, Oil 18%, Coal 15%, Gas 4%, Renewables 2%

Table 1 Energy use in different economic sectors in the UK and India, 2013

	UK (%)	India (%)
Transport	38	14
Industry	21	35
Homes	27	41
Services	13	
Farming/other	1	5/6

What impact does extracting energy have on the environment?

Extracting and using energy is one of humans' most significant impacts on the Earth (Figure 5). The impacts can be local, such as the visual impact of a wind turbine, or regional, for example the impacts of pollution (see page 291). These impacts are far outweighed by the impact of burning fossil fuels on the Earth's atmosphere (see Topic 1A).

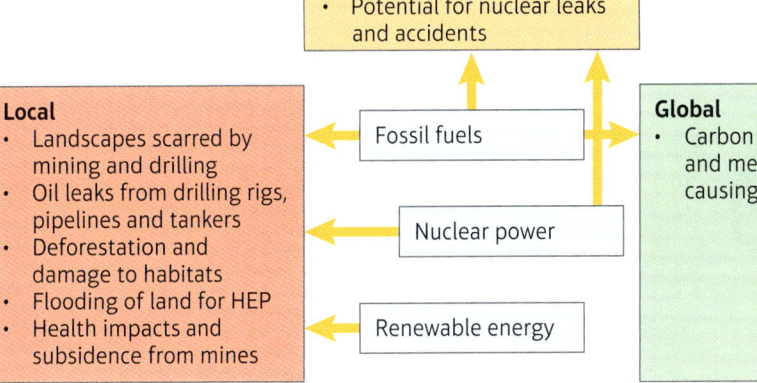

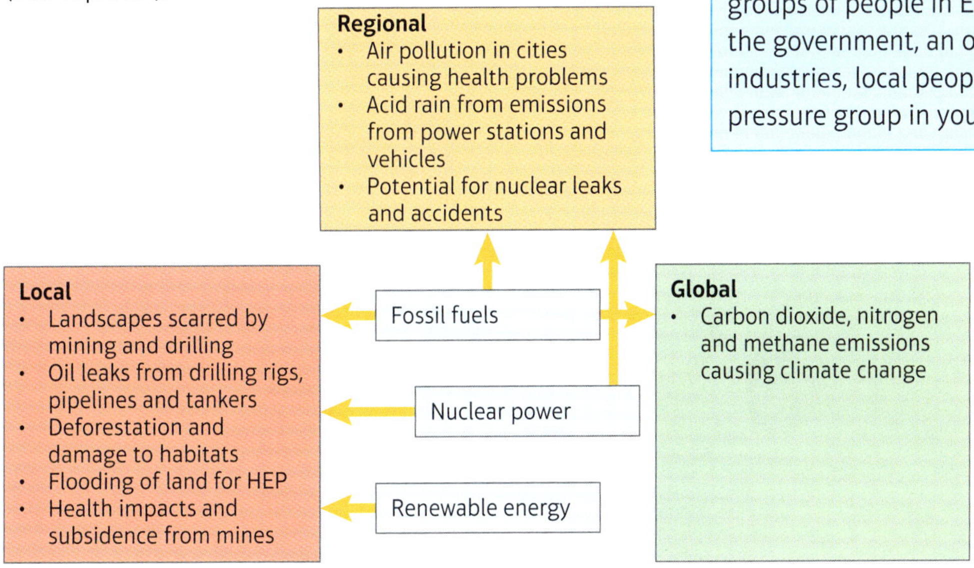

Did you know?

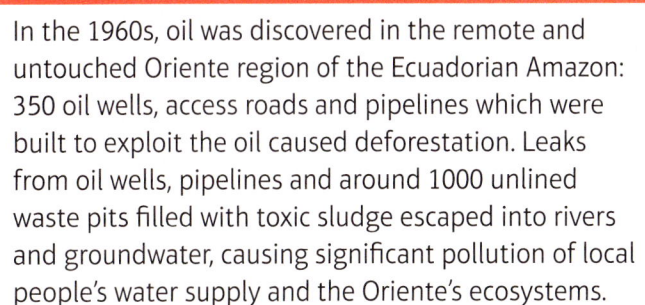

In the 1960s, oil was discovered in the remote and untouched Oriente region of the Ecuadorian Amazon: 350 oil wells, access roads and pipelines which were built to exploit the oil caused deforestation. Leaks from oil wells, pipelines and around 1000 unlined waste pits filled with toxic sludge escaped into rivers and groundwater, causing significant pollution of local people's water supply and the Oriente's ecosystems.

Activity

1. Study the data in Table 1 and Figure 4.
   a. Compare the use of energy in the UK and India, explaining the differences.
   b. Explain the pattern of energy use in Sub-Saharan Africa.
2. Study Figure 5.
   a. Which impacts on the environment are caused by exploiting energy, and by using energy?
   b. Compare the impact of fossil fuels, nuclear power and renewable energy on the environment, giving examples and explanations. **Tip** Look through the images in this topic to add detail.

Decision-making exam-style question

Explain the views on oil extraction of different groups of people in Ecuador. For example, consider the government, an oil company, businesses and industries, local people, and an environmental pressure group in your answer. **(8 marks)**

Figure 5 The impacts of energy production and use on the environment

Regional
- Air pollution in cities causing health problems
- Acid rain from emissions from power stations and vehicles
- Potential for nuclear leaks and accidents

Local
- Landscapes scarred by mining and drilling
- Oil leaks from drilling rigs, pipelines and tankers
- Deforestation and damage to habitats
- Flooding of land for HEP
- Health impacts and subsidence from mines

Global
- Carbon dioxide, nitrogen and methane emissions causing climate change

Sources: Fossil fuels, Nuclear power, Renewable energy

9 Consuming Energy Resources

Can we cope with the rising demand for oil?

Learning objectives

- To know that the global distribution of oil reserves and production is unevenly distributed
- To understand why oil consumption is growing

Distribution of oil reserves and production

The production of oil is the world's largest business – some of the largest TNCs are oil companies. The distribution of oil reserves, like other fossil fuels, is uneven.

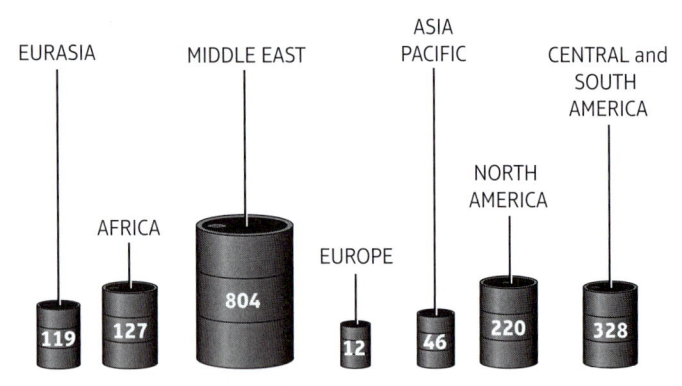

Figure 6 The world's remaining oil reserves (billions of barrels), as of 2014

- EURASIA: 119
- AFRICA: 127
- MIDDLE EAST: 804
- EUROPE: 12
- ASIA PACIFIC: 46
- NORTH AMERICA: 220
- CENTRAL and SOUTH AMERICA: 328

Figure 6 shows the distribution of oil reserves in the world. Currently, the Middle East has the largest reserves, with an estimated 804 billion barrels of oil left, enough for 200 years of production. The USA, Saudi Arabia and Russia are the three biggest producers, all producing over 10 million barrels of oil every day (Figure 7). New oil resources are often found in places that are hostile or far away from world markets, for example in tropical rainforests (Ecuador and Indonesia), the Arctic (Alaska) and under unpredictable seas (North Sea and Gulf of Mexico).

The global consumption of oil has been rising since the 1990s to supply the increasing demands for energy from a growing and wealthier population. One of the key factors in this growth has been rapid industrialisation and development in emerging countries, especially

Figure 7 World oil production levels, millions of barrels per day, 2015

- Canada: 4.4
- USA: 13.7
- Mexico: 2.7
- Iraq: 4
- Iran: 3.4
- Russia: 11
- China: 4.6
- Saudi Arabia: 11.9
- United Arab Emirates: 3.5
- Kuwait: 2.7

China, which has seen oil consumption more than treble since the 1990s. China is now the second highest consumer of oil, accounting for 12.4% of global oil consumption in 2014 in comparison with the USA, the leading consumer at 20%.

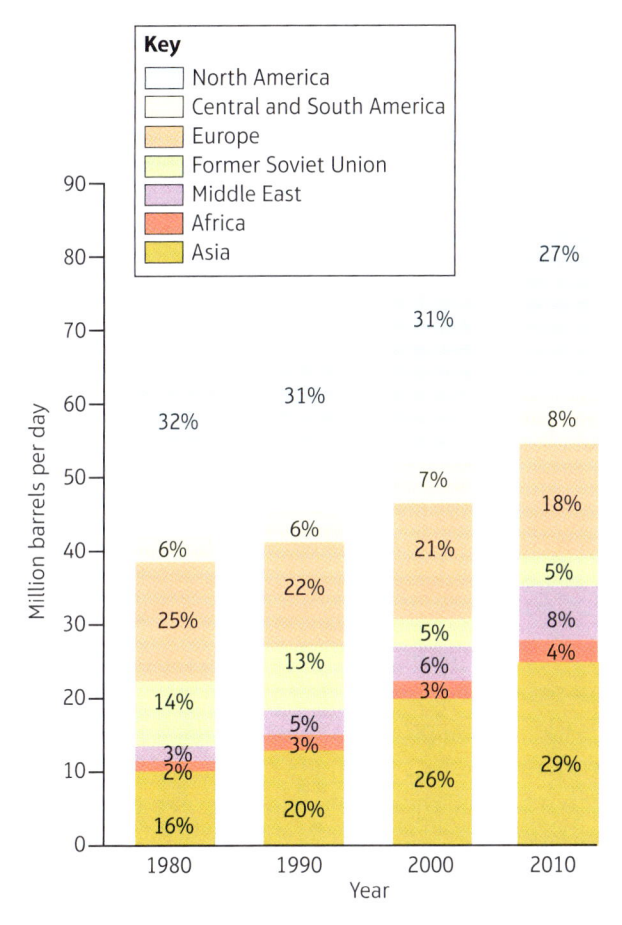

Figure 8 Graph of world oil consumption by region, 1980–2010

Figure 8 shows the per capita consumption of oil by region. Consumption is largely related to the wealth of a country and its dependence on motor vehicles: 70% of oil production is used in transporting people and goods around, both within countries and between them. On average in the world, oil is consumed at the rate of about 1000 barrels (160,000 litres) a second.

Activity

1 Study Figures 7 and 8, looking at which world regions produce oil and which consume oil. Make **three** lists: regions which produce more than they consume, regions which consume more than they produce and regions which are roughly in balance.

2 Discuss what that might mean for future energy supplies in different parts of the world and for the environment.

Checkpoint

Now it is time to review your understanding of how to classify energy resources, energy supply and consumption, and the environmental impacts of energy production and use.

Strengthen

S1 What are the differences between renewable, recyclable and non-renewable energy sources?

S2 Summarise how the energy resources for a country might be influenced by geology, climate and landscape.

S3 Explain the reasons for the increasing world demand for energy, particularly fossil fuels.

Challenge

C1 Study Figures 2 and 3. Compare the distribution of world energy resources and consumption, using examples of continents and regions and data to help structure your writing.

C2 Explain why many scientists consider that most of the remaining fossil fuel reserves should be left in the ground.

C3 Assess whether the benefits of renewable energy outweigh the potential impacts on the landscape.

Exam-style question

Study Figure 8.

1 Describe the pattern of world oil consumption from 1980 to 2010. **(3 marks)**

2 State which region has experienced the lowest change in oil consumption. **(1 mark)**

3 Suggest **one** reason for the change in global oil consumption. **(2 marks)**

9 Consuming Energy Resources

How are oil supplies and prices affected by geopolitics?

Learning objectives
- To know how and why oil prices have changed in the last 20 years
- To understand how oil supply and prices are affected by changing international relations and economic factors

Factors affecting supply and prices

Since 1983, the price of oil per barrel has seen big fluctuations, as shown in Figure 9. Rises and falls in the price of oil are influenced by changes in supply and demand, as well as significant global events.

- Up to 2008, increasing demand caused by growth of the world's economies led to a long-term rise in the price of oil.
- China's rapid industrialisation in the early 21st century further increased the demand for energy which China's own oilfields could not meet, so oil imports filled the gap.
- During periods of recession, such as after 2008, economies slowed down and consumers bought fewer goods. There was less demand for oil and prices fell.
- Short-term spikes in the oil price can be caused by disruptions to supply, such as the 2010 oil spill caused by an explosion on a BP oil rig in the Gulf of Mexico. Political events in the Middle East can also restrict oil supplies.
- Diplomatic relations and conflicts between countries can affect supply and demand. For example, in 2013–14, rivalry between Iran and Saudi Arabia, two of the largest oil-producing countries, meant they failed to agree production targets. Saudi Arabia increased the supply of oil, leading to a fall in prices on world markets.
- The discovery of new sources like shale gas in the USA increased supply, reducing oil and gas imports and leading to lower local and world prices.
- Long-term, rising demands for energy are likely to put pressure on oil supply and on prices.

Did you know?
The Organisation of the Petroleum Exporting Countries (OPEC) is an inter-governmental organisation for oil producers and exporters. When they work together, its members have immense power to influence the supply and price of oil on global markets.

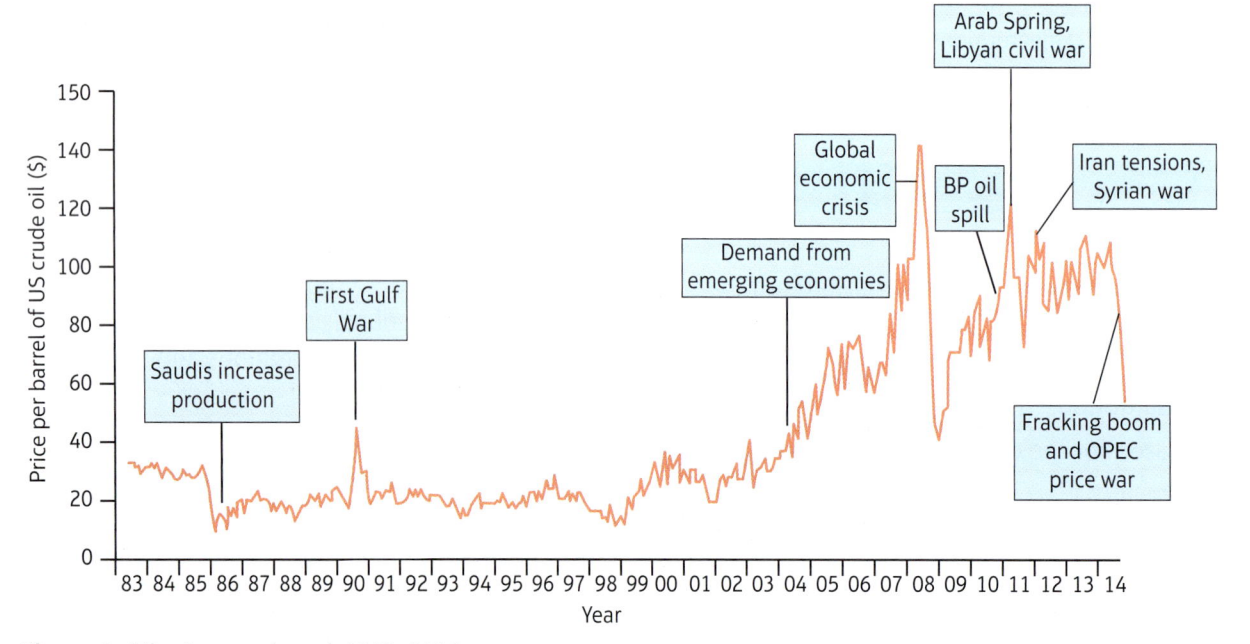

Figure 9 Oil prices per barrel, 1983–2014

The East Siberia–Pacific Ocean (ESPO) geopolitics of oil

- China and Japan are keen to access Russian oil because they want better energy security. Their dependence on Middle Eastern oil makes them vulnerable to price increases.
- A reliable energy supply is essential to China's rapid economic growth. At present 60% of China's oil imports come from the Middle East, transported through the Strait of Malacca (between Indonesia, Sumatra and Malaysia), which is subject to attacks by pirates. China wants to expand its energy supply options – however, the relationship between Russia and China is not smooth. Russia sees China as a potential threat and so is unwilling to commit to supplying large quantities of energy. China is also wary of dealing with Russia because it has a history of switching off energy supplies to countries such as Ukraine when international relationships become strained.
- Japan is also interested in Russia's oil because it has limited oil reserves but is the third largest oil consumer. Japan's major suppliers have been in the Middle East, but access to the ESPO pipeline would mean they could reduce this dependence. This led to the Japanese government offering finance to extend the ESPO pipeline closer to Japan. By 2010, Russia's exports to Japan had increased rapidly. The new pipeline enables delivery in only a few days compared with a few weeks when sourcing supplies from the Middle East.

On a global scale, countries without their own oil supplies do all they can to reduce their vulnerability to oil price shocks.

Exam-style question

Explain how conflict between countries can affect global oil prices. **(4 marks)**

Exam tip

Although this question does not ask for one, including a specific example would help develop your points. In this question start with locating your example and then provide two explained points on the reason for conflict and its impact on global oil prices.

Activity

1. Study Figure 9 and the text.
   a. Make lists of the factors leading to increases and decreases in world oil prices, adding details of events or dates.
   b. Use colour-coding to identify which are short-term changes and which are longer-term trends.
2. Describe the route of the ESPO pipeline, including details of where it starts and ends, and its length.
3. What is meant by 'energy security' for China and Japan?
4. Summarise the advantages and disadvantages of the East Siberia–Pacific Ocean pipeline to China and Japan.

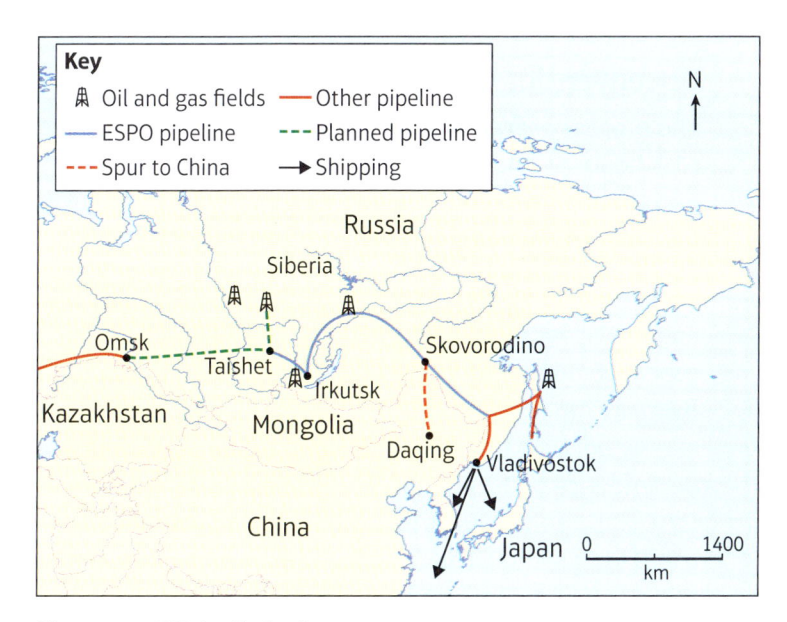

Figure 10 ESPO oil pipeline route

9 Consuming Energy Resources

Why are we exploiting ecologically sensitive and isolated areas?

> **Learning objectives**
> - To know that demand for oil has led to extraction of oil and gas in challenging environments
> - To understand the economic benefits and costs of developing new oil and gas sources in ecologically sensitive and isolated areas
> - To understand the environmental costs of developing new oil and gas sources in ecologically sensitive and isolated areas

New conventional oil and gas source

Exploring and extracting in the Arctic

By the end of the 20th century, many of the most accessible oil and gas fields had already been discovered and exploited. In the 21st century, growing demand for oil has led to searching for new resources from increasingly remote places which are more difficult to exploit and often in fragile environments such as the Arctic.

In an isolated region of the coast along the Beaufort Sea, Exxon Mobile Corporation has been constructing a US$4 billion natural gas extraction facility on flat marshy land. The aim is to move gas 35 km from Point Thompson to the Badami oil field.

The new Point Thompson Facility will have costs and benefits for Alaska.

- Exxon forecasts that the facility will produce 10,000 barrels of gas a day to be exported to Asian countries, earning foreign currency and boosting the US economy.

- There is an estimated 35 billion cubic feet of discovered gas (approximately four times more than the UK's reserves) underneath the North Slope, making this a long-term economic benefit for Exxon and Alaska's government.

- It will provide new employment opportunities for up to 800 workers, with production machinery, offices and living quarters at the facility.

- The cost of constructing the facility is estimated at $4 billion. The remote location makes it more expensive to build and operate, and to export the gas once extracted. The state of Alaska will take a 25% share, investing $5.75 billion in a project worth $45 billion.

- The oil industry's record in the Arctic has been tarnished by accidents and leaks. Any damage to this harsh and ecologically sensitive environment can be long-lasting and difficult to clean up.

Unconventional oil and gas sources

The process of **fracking** involves drilling down into shale rock deposits, then injecting water, sand and chemicals into the rock at high pressure, which frees natural shale gas from the rocks and allows it to flow out to the head of the well where it is collected.

Fracking is most developed in the USA, where it produced 39% of natural gas in 2014. It is supported by many Americans because it has reduced their energy bills, created over 2 million jobs and reduced dependence on oil and gas imports from the Middle East. Gas also produces half the carbon emissions of coal. However, fracking has a number of environmental costs, especially for water quality and ecosystems.

Figure 11 Oil production along the Beaufort Sea

9 Consuming Energy Resources

Case Study – Oil reserves: the Athabasca tar sands, Canada

The area around the Athabasca River in Alberta, Canada, has significant oil reserves in the form of tar sands. There are an estimated 180 billion barrels of **bitumen** within the sand deposits here which can be refined into petroleum. This is an expensive process but dwindling oil supplies elsewhere, the rising cost of oil and the development of new technology made it worthwhile to exploit these resources commercially. However, its exploitation has led to concern about a number of serious environmental impacts.

1. Most tar sand extraction is carried out by surface mining, which means vegetation is cleared and surface oil and rock removed over a large area, resulting in a total loss of local habitats.
2. Large volumes of water are needed to extract the bitumen from the sands. As much as six barrels of water are needed for each barrel of oil produced. This water is extracted from the Athabasca River, threatening local wildlife and wider ecosystems that rely on a clean water supply.
3. To recover and refine oil from tar sands needs large amounts of energy, releasing 15% more CO_2 than refining crude oil.
4. Mining the tar sands has led to leaks into rivers and lakes, in particular an estimated 11 million litres of toxic waste reaches the Athabasca River daily.

Figure 12 The tar reserves of Alberta, Canada

Activity

Describe **two** impacts of extracting oil from tar sands.

- The chemicals pumped in to release shale gas may leak into and contaminate **groundwater** supplies. Some drinking-water wells located near fracturing sites have recorded methane concentrations 17 times higher than normal. Contamination of the groundwater may damage ecosystems and some people report ill health.
- Fracking may be linked with subsidence, as rocks are disturbed deep underground. It has also resulted in gas entering people's homes, including through water taps.
- Although fracking sites are small by comparison with tar sands mining, they lead to some loss or damage to habitats and the industrialisation of rural and wilderness areas. There can be a significant increase in local traffic as trucks bring in water for fracking and take away gas.

Checkpoint

Now it is time to review your understanding of the benefits and costs of developing new oil and gas sources in ecologically sensitive and remote areas.

Strengthen

S1 Describe the factors causing the growth in global oil consumption.

S2 Explain why it is expensive to drill for oil and gas in the Arctic.

S3 What are the economic benefits to Arctic countries of developing oil and gas production?

Challenge

C1 Explain why companies have invested in extracting oil from difficult environments like the Athabasca tar sands.

C2 Explain why there might be opposition to fracking in a UK National Park.

9 Consuming Energy Resources

How can we be more energy efficient?

> **Learning objectives**
> - To know the difference between energy efficiency and energy conservation
> - To understand how energy efficiency and energy conservation can be used in the home
> - To understand how energy efficient transport schemes can be used to reduce carbon emissions and conserve finite energy resources

Using energy wisely

There are two ways of reducing the demand for energy – energy efficiency and energy conservation. Energy efficiency is providing the same service but using less energy: for example, energy-efficient lightbulbs use less energy to produce the same amount of light as non-efficient lightbulbs. Energy conservation is about not using as much energy: for example, switching off lights in your house when you are not using them. Both are important for reducing carbon emissions.

Reducing energy demand

One example of a council promoting the use of energy efficiency and conservation is Woking Borough Council. The council initiated a series of sustainable strategies to become one of the first councils to conserve energy and become more energy-efficient throughout people's daily lives. By 2008, the council had successfully reduced its energy consumption by 52% and CO_2 emissions by 82% compared with the 1990 levels.

One of the ways Woking has achieved its targets is through setting up its own utility company, Thameswey Energy. This council-owned non-profit company is responsible for providing sustainable energy to the council and other organisations within the Woking area, for example through **combined heat and power (CHP) generators** and photovoltaic (PV) solar farms.

Following the introduction of successful strategies the council wanted to encourage local residents to reduce their carbon dioxide emissions and water consumption. The council converted the old police house (Figure 13)

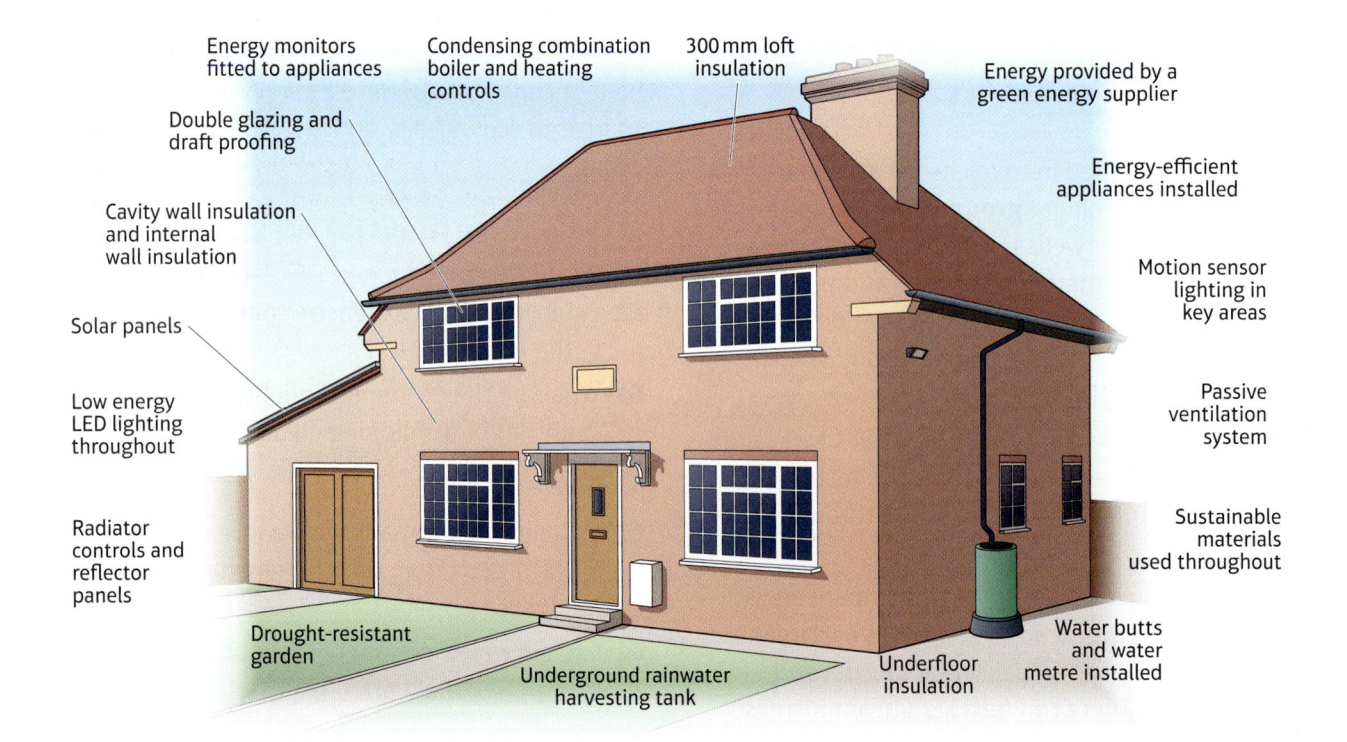

Figure 13 Oak Tree House, low-carbon home

to show homeowners the strategies they could use to conserve energy and lower their carbon footprint.

Energy-efficient transport systems

Transport is responsible for over 20% of worldwide energy consumption, mainly from fossil fuels, and makes a significant contribution to air pollution including greenhouse gas emissions. More sustainable transport uses less energy and improves the quality of life in cities. For example, encouraging low emissions vehicles improves air quality, while public transport such as buses and trains uses less fuel per person than individual cars and reduces air pollution. Congestion charging and cycling schemes are two other examples.

Traffic **congestion** is common in cities, leading to longer journeys, wasted fuel and increased air pollution. In London the congestion charge was introduced to reduce congestion and pollution – since 2003, road users have had to pay to enter central areas of the city. The scheme cost £80 million to set up but generates around £252 million pounds per annum in revenue, which has been invested in public transport. Within the charging zone, the scheme has led to an estimated saving of 19% in traffic-related CO_2 emissions, and 20% in fuel used. There has also been a reduction in average traffic flow of 21% and a 45% increase in the number of bus passengers, while the air pollutants that damage Londoners' health have fallen by 12%.

> ### Activity
> 1. Investigate and explain how your school could conserve more energy.
> 2. Using the example of Oak Tree House, summarise how people can become more energy efficient as well as reduce their energy consumption in the home.
> 3. Compare the benefits of the transport schemes in London and Paris in reducing the demand for finite energy resources and reducing carbon emissions.

> ### Exam-style question
> Explain why urban transport schemes can contribute towards lowering carbon emissions. **(4 marks)**

> ### Exam tip
> Remember when asked to 'explain' you should make a point and then offer a supporting statement. In a four-mark question like this you should aim to provide two points on how urban schemes can help lower carbon emissions.

Figure 14 Paris's Velibs cycling scheme

In 2007, Paris launched its city-wide cycling scheme, Velibs, to reduce the volume of road traffic. The self-service network of 23,500 bikes parked at 1400 stations across Paris has made navigating around the city easier for people who are willing to pay an annual €29 membership fee. The first half hour on the bike is free of charge. After that the hourly rental increases with a price structure designed to push Velib as an alternative to car, bus and metro trips. In the first three months there were 100,000 users daily, traveling an estimated 300,000 km and saving 32,330 tonnes of CO_2 emissions annually. By 2012, Parisians had made 130 million trips using the bike network, an increase of 41% since 2007. During the same period, motor vehicle traffic decreased by 25%.

9 Consuming Energy Resources

What are the costs and benefits of alternatives to fossil fuels?

> **Learning objectives**
> - To know the different types of alternative energy sources and future technologies to fossil fuels
> - To recognise the costs and benefits of using alternative energy sources and future technologies
> - To understand how these sources could help reduce carbon footprints, improve energy security and diversify the energy mix

Wind energy

Wind energy has become one of the fastest-growing renewable energy resources in the world, with a 16.5% rise in wind-generating capacity in 2014, accounting for 3% of global energy production. China is the leading wind energy producer, generating 115 gigawatts (GW) per year. The production of wind energy is through wind turbines, which collect the **kinetic energy** that wind produces and convert it into electricity. In recent years, there has been considerable development in the efficiency and reliability of wind turbines, making them more powerful and cheaper. There are many costs and benefits to the continued use of wind energy, which are summarised below.

Costs	Benefits
Many local residents find wind turbines/ farms spoil their view of the landscape.	Wind energy is a clean fuel source. It does not pollute or emit greenhouse gases.
Offshore wind farms are built far away from where the source is needed, requiring expensive transmission lines to use the power produced.	Large offshore wind farms can create a generating capacity of hundreds of megawatts of electricity.
Turbine blades cause on average about four bird deaths per turbine per year.	Onshore wind is one of the cheapest renewable energy sources for the consumer.

Solar energy

Since 2009, there has been a significant rise in the generation of solar energy. In 2014, the global total of solar power was 178,391 megawatts (MW). The top three leading solar energy producers are Germany, China and Italy, but the USA has the world's largest solar power plants, located in the Mojave Desert. The Solar Energy Generating Systems solar farm produces a total of 354 MW, while the Ivanpah solar farm, currently the world's largest, can produce 392 MW.

Costs	Benefits
Large solar farms can take up land that could be used for growing crops, although the land can often be used for grazing.	Solar energy is a growing industry, creating many hundreds of thousands of jobs around the world.
Manufacturing photovoltaic panels can be harmful to the environment because the panels are made up of silicon and other toxic metals like mercury, lead and cadmium.	Solar energy requires little maintenance once the solar panels are installed and working at maximum efficiency.
Desert habitats are fragile and easily damaged during farm construction.	No noise is created by the solar panels converting sunlight into energy.

> **Did you know?**
> Paraguay and Iceland generate 100% of their electricity from renewable sources.

Hydro-electric power

About 20% of the world's energy supplies comes from HEP, with countries like Norway producing almost all of their electricity from this source of energy.

Costs	Benefits
HEP power plants are expensive to build and can be viewed by many as spoiling the natural landscape.	HEP is a reliable and consistent source of energy with very few fluctuations in the amount produced.
HEP power plants can result in the displacement of farmland and villages to make room for the dam and reservoirs to be built.	HEP power plants' production can easily be altered with changing consumption patterns.
HEP power plants cause changes in river flows leading to impacts on fish and other wildlife that rely on the sources of water.	The construction of HEP power plants can mean the building of dams and reservoirs. This can help with conserving water supplies.

Biofuels

Biofuels like biodiesel are made from plant oils and can be used to power diesel vehicles and generate electricity.

Costs	Benefits
Large quantities of water are required to grow biofuel crops, which can compete with other users, including farming and homes.	The burning of biofuels produces fewer carbon emissions and toxins compared with fossil fuels.
Increasing demand for biofuels increases competition for land, sometimes at the expense of growing food crops.	The growing demand for biofuels could see this alternative energy source become a cheaper option than fossil fuels.
Demand for biofuels and shortage of land is causing an increase in deforestation in some countries.	Biofuels can be manufactured from crop waste, manure and other by-products, reusing materials that would otherwise be wasted.

Hydrogen

Hydrogen energy is a future technology, meaning that the costs are currently much higher than the benefits.

Costs	Benefits
Energy is needed to release hydrogen gas from water. If this is done using fossil fuels then carbon footprints, energy security and the energy mix are all impacted.	Hydrogen energy is clean, producing no greenhouses gases or air pollution.
It is difficult to store hydrogen safely under pressure. This is a research challenge for products like hydrogen-fuelled cars.	Hydrogen energy is made from water, so it does not rely on fuel reserves located in a few countries or in ecologically sensitive areas.
	Hydrogen energy is very efficient so it could be a big part of each country's energy mix.

Activity

1. Summarise the main costs and benefits of using renewable energy instead of fossil fuels.
2. Summarise the costs and benefits of using hydrogen as an alternative to fossil fuels.

Tip Look back to page 282. Use some of the key language there, such as 'stock resources' and 'flow resources', to add precision to your answer.

Did you know?

Solar power uses PV cells (photovoltaic cells), which convert light into electrical energy. The amount of electrical energy generated depends on the amount and intensity of daylight that falls on the PV material. The cells do not require direct sunlight to work.

9 Consuming Energy Resources

How are attitudes to energy and environmental issues changing?

> **Learning objectives**
> - To appreciate why different groups have contrasting views about energy futures
> - To understand how attitudes are changing towards unsustainable energy consumption and reducing carbon footprints
> - To know how to calculate carbon and ecological footprints

How do attitudes to the exploitation and consumption of energy vary?

It is estimated that from 2013 to 2035 the global demand for energy will increase by 37%, driven mainly by population growth and rising living standards in emerging and developing economies. While technological solutions to increasing energy supply are possible, if fossil fuels continue to dominate the energy mix, the consequence will be catastrophic climate change. Different stakeholders have contrasting views on what our 'energy future' holds, ranging from a 'business as usual' approach to more 'sustainable' approaches (see Figure 15).

How are attitudes changing?

In 2015, it was predicted that by 2020 the use of non-renewable energy resources could drop to 76%. This change could be linked to a number of key factors.

- **Rising affluence** – although rising incomes increase energy demand, they can also encourage alternative sources because more people support the investment needed for clean and sustainable energy.
- **Environmental concerns** – greater research and awareness of the impact fossil fuels are having on the world's environments, particularly on climate change, has led to worldwide demands for a rapid shift to sustainable energy production and use.
- **Education** – improving people's awareness of the need for more sustainable energy is an important goal for international organisations like the UN, governments and organisations like energy suppliers. Schools and young people have a key role in preparing for a more sustainable energy future.

> **Decision-making exam-style question**
> Assess the reasons why opinions about the use of renewable energy vary. **(8 marks)**

TNCs – As a global company our main aim is to maintain a profitable business that meets the challenging targets set by our shareholders. Whilst we appreciate sustainability is important we don't believe our operations alone have a direct impact on the planet.

Climate scientists – Evidence shows how the world's climate has changed in the last 50 years due to human activities. Trends show that if nothing changes there will be a considerable impact on the ability of our planet to support humanity. We must look at energy alternatives.

Governments – Whilst we see the importance of investing in renewable energy resources, our main aim is to obtain and maintain energy security as cheaply as possible. We believe reliable, affordable energy is vital for economic growth and for the improvement of living standards.

Consumers – I want to be able to use energy resources that are cheap and reliable. I am now increasingly aware of the contributions I make to carbon emissions, but will my individual changes actually make a difference on a global scale?

Environmental groups – We want world leaders to invest time and money in the use of renewable energy as there is increasing concern over the impact fossil fuels are having and will have on our planet.

Figure 15 The different views about energy futures

Individuals

Individuals can find out the impact of their personal energy use by measuring their **carbon footprints**. These show the amount of greenhouse gases produced by using fossil fuels for electricity, heating and transport in people's daily lives, expressed as kilograms of carbon dioxide. Calculating this raises people's awareness of how much energy they use and can lead them to make changes which reduce carbon emissions.

Activity

1. Calculate your carbon footprint using the World Wildlife Fund (WWF) footprint calculator.
2. List the factors that make up your footprint. Explain why they have an impact on the environment, then think about how you might reduce the impact.

Carbon footprints help identify where energy use can be made more efficient.

- Domestic heating contributes 15% to the individual carbon footprint. Heat is lost through walls, windows and roofs, so improved insulation in the loft and walls reduces energy consumption.
- Powering the home contributes 12%. Electricity for most homes comes from fossil-fuel power stations. Individuals can reduce their carbon footprints by turning off appliances not in use, or even installing solar panels on their roofs.
- Private transport contributes 10%. Individuals can reduce car use by using public transport, walking or riding a bike, or car-sharing with others.

Organisations

In recent years large organisations have applied a different approach to their business operations by adopting sustainable practices – examples are McDonald's and Google. However, because energy from fossil fuels is often cheaper than renewable energy, many other organisations are not inclined to add extra costs by using renewables.

Many environmental organisations want change to be much more significant. For example, NGOs like Greenpeace have strong views on energy futures, arguing for a more sustainable approach to our extraction and consumption of resources.

Governments

In December 2015, the UK was one of the 195 nations at the United Nations climate change summit in Paris that pledged to limit the global temperature rise to below 2°C. Each country set out its own targets towards this aim, and developed countries also agreed to put together a £100 billion fund to help developing countries transfer their economies to renewable energy. For the UK this involves:

- setting carbon budgets to limit the amount of greenhouse gases the UK is allowed to emit
- investing in low-carbon energy technologies and boosting the share of renewables in the UK's energy mix so that, by 2050, the UK produces 80% less carbon than it did in 1990
- helping to reduce the demand for energy with smart meters and other energy-efficient measures for industry, businesses and individuals
- public reporting of carbon emissions to allow people to assess their impact on climate change.

However, governments in some developing and emerging countries like India face a difficult choice. They recognise the need to tackle climate change, but need cheap energy to fuel economic growth and improve people's living standards.

An **ecological footprint** shows the impact people have on the planet in order to provide all the resources we use and dispose of our waste.

Checkpoint

Now it is time to review your understanding of energy efficiency and conservation, the costs and benefits of using alternatives to fossil fuels and the views of different groups.

Strengthen

S1 What is the difference between a carbon footprint and an ecological footprint?

S2 Give two examples each of energy efficiency and energy conservation in the home, then do the same for transport.

Challenge

C1 Discuss the advantages and disadvantages of individuals, organisations or governments taking the lead in a more sustainable energy future.

Decision-making exercise

Consuming Energy Resources

Topic 9 explores the consumption of energy resources by people, examining renewable and non-renewable energy patterns and energy security. It also considers how future energy needs can be met, and how energy consumption can be managed to achieve a sustainable energy supply in the future.

Practise making geographical decisions

Section 1: The background

1. What is a resource? **(1 mark)**
2. What is a finite resource? **(2 marks)**
3. Study Figures 2 and 7.
   a. Which areas of the world have few resources? **(2 marks)**
   b. Name **two** countries that have a lot of resources. **(2 marks)**
4. Study Figures 3 and 8.
   a. Which world regions consume the most energy? **(3 marks)**
   b. Explain why these regions consume the most energy. **(4 marks)**

> **Exam tips**
>
> Questions 1 and 2: Definitions need to be accurate and concise.
>
> Question 3: (a) Identify the information from the figures provided and add your basic understanding. Sometimes a question may not directly refer to figures and tables and you may have to search for the information yourself – it is very helpful to take time at the start of the examination to read the Resource Booklet thoroughly. (b) Use the figures provided to help.
>
> Question 4: (a) Similar to Question 3; identify places by name, making sure to use names of world regions, not just continents and countries. (b) Link the characteristics of countries to their high use of energy resources. You should explain **two** links well.

Section 2: The issues

5. Use Figures 6, 7, 9, 10 and 11 to help you.
   a. Explain why oil companies are searching for oil in remote and difficult places. **(4 marks)**
   b. Why are pipelines often used to transport oil? **(2 marks)**
6. Evaluate the range of problems that may be created by oil extraction. **(8 marks)**
7. Study Figures 1, 3 and 8. Explain why the consumption of energy has increased rapidly over the last 50 years. **(4 marks)**

> **Exam tips**
>
> Question 5: (a) Think about what is motivating more oil exploration and the influences on oil companies from wider culture and society. (b) Consider transport costs, distance and the nature of the resource.
>
> Question 6: 'Evaluate' means that you must consider the value or success of something using the evidence available, particularly identifying strengths and weaknesses, and conclude which one (or ones) is best. Justify your decision and give reasons for your choice. Identify several problems caused by extracting oil from the ground, then place these into a rank order with the worst problem first. Then make a judgement and give your reasons for how serious the problems are.
>
> Question 7: Quote some data from the figures in your answer but focus on why the energy consumption of people and businesses has increased over time. You must explain not just describe changes.

Decision-making exercise

Consuming Energy Resources

Section 3: The options and opinions

8. Explain why Japan, Russia and China are in favour of transporting large quantities of oil. **(4 marks)**

9. Explain why some homeowners are in favour of lowering their eco-footprint (including carbon footprint) while others are against. **(4 marks)**

10. Assess the following statement 'Ordinary people hold the key to solving the energy issues of the world.' **(8 marks)**

> **Exam tips**
>
> Question 8: Consider why the named countries are interested in oil. 'Transporting' suggests the import or export of oil. Remember that the marks allocated (and the allocation of space in the exam answer booklet) indicate how much to write.
>
> Question 9: Consider why different homeowners have different views and motives. Think about what influences them, such as lifestyle, costs and being eco-friendly.
>
> Question 10: Your answer needs to consider a range of organisations and groups of people so that you can assess the truth of the statement.

Section 4: The decision

11. Several options exist for managing future energy supplies in a sustainable way. Three possibilities are:

    Option 1: Develop all the renewable energy sources as quickly as possible.

    Option 2: Use technology to improve the efficiency of fossil fuel use.

    Option 3: Change consumer use patterns in homes and transport.

    Select the option that you think would be best for ensuring an adequate energy supply for the future. Justify your choice. **(12 marks + 4 SPAG)**

> **Exam tip**
>
> Question 11: Decision questions are usually worth the most marks so ensure you leave enough time to complete them properly. All the questions in Sections A, B and C (and the information in the Resource Booklet) direct your thoughts towards this decision-making question. Usually you will be directed to choose **one** best option for solving or reducing the scale of a problem, but there is no one correct answer. Choose the option that you can best justify. To justify, you must identify the strengths of your choice and state clearly how each would help reduce the problem (or meet the aim). Include facts from the Resource Booklet. You should also identify major weaknesses in the other options and acknowledge that your choice has weaknesses too. Four marks are for spelling, punctuation, grammar and use of geographical terminology (SPAG), so provide a well-structured, prose answer.

WRITING GEOGRAPHICALLY

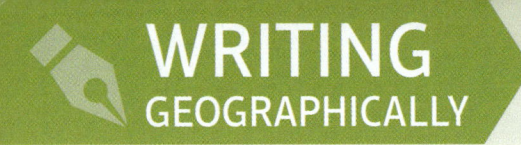

Writing geographically: selecting vocabulary

The best geographical writing uses carefully selected vocabulary to express ideas formally, clearly and precisely.

Learning objectives

- To understand how to select nouns and verbs which can help you to express your ideas clearly and precisely
- To be able to build noun phrases which can help you add more detailed information to your ideas

Definitions

Determiner: a word which precedes a noun and determine definiteness (e.g. *a*, *the*), quantity (*some*, *many*, *two*), possession (*my*, *your*), etc.

Adjective: a word giving additional information about a noun, e.g. *clear*, *precise* writing.

Prepositional phrase: a phrase which begins with a preposition, often giving information about position or time, e.g. *in* the river, *on* the bank, *after* an hour.

How can I add detail to my writing?

> Assess the reasons why some groups are against the development of oil and gas. **(8 marks)**

Look at the first sentence of one student's response to the above exam-style question. The key nouns and verbs in the sentence have been highlighted:

> People are bothered about oil and gas because of the pollution they make. For example, smoke given off from burning fossil fuel adds to global warming.

1. How could you improve this sentence? Would you add more detail? Or would you express the same information more formally and precisely? Or both?
2. Rewrite the sentence using more precise, accurate nouns and verbs. You could use the thesaurus extracts below to help you.

people	bothered	make	smoke	given off	adds to
scientists	worried	create	gases	released	contributes to
environmentalists	concerned	give off	fumes	produced	increases
ecologists	upset	cause	CO_2	generated	escalates
conservationists	perturbed	produce	vapour	emitted	builds up

3. Now look at the next two sentences from the same student's response.

> With oil and gas being used up, there is a rush to find and get oil and gas from deeper water like the Gulf of Mexico. People are worried about oil spills in these places as they will damage things.

(a) Identify any nouns or verbs which could be replaced with more formal and precise choices.
(b) For each noun and verb you have identified, note down two or three alternative choices.
(c) Rewrite the sentences above, choosing more formal, precise nouns and verbs.

WRITING GEOGRAPHICALLY

How can I add detail to my writing in different ways?

One way in which you can add more information to your answer is by expanding noun phrases, using determiners, adjectives, prepositional phrases and other nouns.

Compare these two versions of the same sentence from a student's response to the exam-style question on page 300.

> People are concerned about vehicles which create gases and toxins such as nitrogen oxide that can cause problems when inhaled.

> Many people in cities are concerned about air pollution from vehicles which create dangerous levels of harmful gases and toxins such as nitrogen oxide that can cause significant health problems when inhaled.

In the second version, the student has made his assessment more precise and detailed by modifying some of the nouns using determiners, adjectives, prepositional phrases and nouns.

This is the head noun in this noun phrase.

> Many people in cities

This determiner and this prepositional phrase give more information about the people.

This is the head noun in this noun phrase.

> dangerous levels of harmful gases and toxins

This adjective and this prepositional phrase give more information about the levels.

This is the head noun in this noun phrase.

> air pollution from vehicles

This additional noun and this prepositional phrase give more information about the pollution.

4. What **kinds** of information and detail can determiners, adjectives, prepositional phrases and nouns add to geographical writing?

Improving an answer

5. Now look at the next section of this student's response. How could you expand some of this writer's noun phrases, using determiners, adjectives, prepositional phrases or additional nouns to make the evaluation more precise and detailed? Use the examiner's notes to help you.

> What kind of pressure? On whom?

> What kinds of environments?

> With fossil fuels running out, there is pressure to extract oil and gas from environments such as the Arctic Ocean. Conservation groups are greatly concerned about spills as they will damage ecosystems. The Deep Water Horizon incident of 2010 was an example.

> What kind of example?

> What kind of spills? Where?

301

Glossary

1% flood event a 1% flood event has a 1 in 100 chance or greater of happening each year, or a probability of 0.01

abiotic the non-living parts of an ecosystem

abrasion caused by the river picking up material in the river and rubbing it against the bed and banks of the channel in the flow

absorption the process of taking something in, such as moisture in the soil by the roots of plants

acid precipitation also called acid rain. When industrial air pollution causes water vapour in the atmosphere to become acidic and fall as acid precipitation

affluence great wealth or abundance

afforestation the planting of trees where there were none before, or they had been cut down

aid assistance in the form of grants or loans at below market rates

air pollution adding harmful substances, such as carbon dioxide, into the atmosphere

alluvium fine sediments which are deposited by rivers

andesitic lava a thick and sticky lava erupted from composite volcanoes

annotate to add notes and explanations to a photograph, map or diagram

antecedent condition conditions in a drainage basin in the period before a rainfall event, such as saturated or frozen ground

arable the farming of crops like wheat and barley

arch the rock bridge formed over a passage through a headland eroded by the waves

area how much space something occupies

arid a region with little or no regular precipitation

asthenosphere the upper layer of the Earth's mantle, below the lithosphere, in which convection currents cause tectonic plate movement

attrition a type of erosion where particles carried by rivers or waves are worn down as they collide with each other, so they become smaller and rounded

backwash the movement of a wave down a beach back to the sea

bar a ridge of sand or shingle across the entrance of a bay or river mouth

basaltic lava/rock lava/rock that is low in silica, fluid and flows easily

base isolators flexible pads on which a building is built to help it withstand earthquakes by isolating it from the moving ground

bay an area of sea, curved in shape which has been eroded between two headlands

beach a sloping area of sand or pebbles between the low and high water marks

beach replenishment the process of adding sand or shingle to widen or improve a beach

bedding plane the surface between two layers (or strata) in sedimentary rock

berm a ridge of sediment found towards the back of a beach

bio-chemical weathering the process of rocks being broken down by chemicals produced by living things, such as acidic droppings

biodiversity the variety of living species in an ecosystem or area

biofuel is made from plant oils and waste materials and can be used to power diesel vehicles and generate electricity

biological weathering the process of rocks being broken down by living things

bio-physical weathering the process of rocks being physically broken up by living things such as tree roots

biomass the mass (weight) of all the living things in an ecosystem

biome a global-scale ecosystem, such as tropical rainforest or taiga forest

biotic the living parts of an ecosystem

birth rate the number of live births per 1000 population per year

bitumen a black, sticky, tarry substance

bivariate data data with two sets of variables

boreal a type of forest found in high northern latitudes, also called the taiga

bottom-up development an approach to development that involves people and communities in decision-making, often involving small-scale projects for the poorest

BRICS a group of large and influential emerging countries: Brazil, Russia, India, China and South Africa

brownfield site a term used in urban planning to describe land previously used for industrial purposes or some commercial uses

call centre office where a group of people answer telephone queries from customers; employees use a computer to give them information that helps them answer questions

canopy the continuous layer of tall trees which shades the forest floor

capitalism the social and economic system which relies on the market mechanism to distribute the factors of production (land, labour, capital) in the most efficient way

carbon footprint measurement of all the greenhouse gases an individual produces expressed as tonnes (or kilogram) of carbon dioxide equivalent

Glossary

carbon sink something that absorbs more carbon from the atmosphere than it releases, such as a forest

carboniferous limestone deposited rocks that were formed between 363 and 325 million years ago

carrying capacity the maximum population of a species an ecosystem can support

caste a traditional Indian system of segregation by birth and social class

cave a hollow at the base of a cliff which has been eroded backwards by waves

Central Business District (CBD) the central area of a city, where land use is dominated by department stores, specialist and variety goods stores, offices, cinemas, theatres and hotels

cirrus a type of cloud that appears as thin wisp-like formations at high altitude

CITES Convention on International Trade in Endangered Species of Wild Fauna and Flora

climate the average weather conditions of an area occurring over many years

climate change a long-term change in the Earth's climate, especially changes in temperature

climate graph a graph showing the average temperature and rainfall at a particular place

clint the large blocks of rock on a limestone pavement, separated by grykes

clitter slope the trail of deposited rocks from the action of freeze thaw weathering on tors

closed economy a country which does little trade beyond its borders

colonialism acquiring control over another country, occupying it with settlers and exploiting it economically

colony a country or region under the political control of another country and occupied by settlers from that country

combined heat and power (CHP) generator an efficient method of generating electricity and using the heat from the process

commercial agriculture farming in which crops are grown for sale

composite index an index, such as the HDI, which is calculated from several different measures

composite volcano a steep-sided volcano that is made up of a variety of materials, such as lava and ash

Comprehensive Development Areas (CDAs) areas, usually in the inner city, where the whole urban landscape was demolished before being rebuilt on a planned basis

concordant coast the type of coast where the rock type runs parallel to the coastline

congestion a large volume slow-moving traffic that clogs up roads

coniferous having needles instead of leaves: most coniferous trees have cones and are evergreen

conservative plate boundary where two plates are sliding alongside each other

constructive wave a gently breaking wave with a strong swash and weak backwash. It adds more material to the beach than it removes

consumerism an economy or society based on people consuming large amounts of goods or services

continental crust thick crust forming the Earth's land masses

contour a line on a map joining places of equal height above sea level

conurbation an area in which a number of existing urban areas have grown and merged into a single large urban area

convection current circular current of heat in the mantle

convergent plate boundary where two plates are moving towards each other, resulting in one plate sinking beneath the other

coppice woodland where the trees or shrubs are cut back every few years for firewood or timber

core the central part of the Earth's structure, made up of a solid inner and a liquid outer core

Coriolis effect the deflection of air movement by the Earth's rotation

correlation when two variables in the data set are linked

corrosion chemical erosion caused by the dissolving of rocks and minerals by water

Corruption Perceptions Index a ranking of countries according to perceived levels of corruption

cost-benefit analysis a way of reaching a decision by comparing the costs of a project with the benefits it will bring

counter-urbanisation the movement of people and employment from major cities to smaller settlements and rural areas located beyond the city, or to more distant towns and cities

cove a small bay with a narrow inlet

crater a depression in the ground formed by volcanic activity, often circular in shape with steep sides

Cretaceous Period a period of the Mesozoic Era, from 140 million to 65 million years ago

cross-bracing a system of supports built diagonally inside buildings to help them withstand earthquakes

cross section a diagram showing the shape of a feature or landscape as if it was cut through sideways

crust the outer layer of the Earth

cultivation the action of using the land for agricultural purposes

cumulonimbus very tall, dense clouds that often bring heavy rain, thunder and lightning

death rate the number of deaths per 1000 population per year

Glossary

debt money owed by a country to another country, to private creditors (e.g. commercial banks) or to international agencies such as the World Bank or IMF

decentralisation the movement of people, factories, offices and shops away from city centres to suburban and edge-of-city locations

deciduous having leaves that fall off in the autumn and grow again in spring

deforestation permanently removing forest so the land can be used for something else

degradation the decline of an area, especially the environment, through erosion of land or soil, or loss of soil fertility

de-industrialisation the decline of industrial activity in a region or in an economy

delta formed where layers of sediment are deposited at river mouths faster than the sea can erode them. Deltas are usually roughly triangular in shape, and the river splits into several channels.

demographic indicators measures related to the population, such as birth and death rate and rate of natural increase

demographic transition a model of how countries' population structures often change over time as they develop

density the number of people or things per unit area

dependency theory a theory which blames the relative underdevelopment of the developing world on exploitation by the developed world, first through colonialism and then by neo-colonialism

deposition a process where sediments are dropped by the river, glacier or waves that carried them

desertification where land becomes increasingly arid and less and less useful for farming

destructive wave a strong wave that removes material from the coastline

developed country a country with very high human development

developing country a country with low human development

development the economic or social progress a country or people makes

development gap the difference in income and the quality of life in general between the richest and poorest countries in the world

diaspora the dispersion of a people from their original homeland

dip slope land that follows the same gentle slope as the layers of rocks underneath

direct threat when there is a direct cause between one thing happening and damage being caused to something else

discharge the amount of water flowing in a river, made up of its volume and speed, and measured in cubic metres per second (m^3/sec, or cumecs)

discordant coast a coast where bands of hard and soft rocks lie at right angles to the coastline forming headlands and bays

distributaries a smaller river channel created where a river splits, often to form a delta

diurnal temperature range the difference between the highest day temperature and lowest night temperature

divergent plate boundary where two plates are moving apart

drainage basin the area of land drained by a river and its tributaries

earthquake a sudden and often violent shift in the rocks forming the Earth's crust, which is felt at the surface

ecological footprint a measure of the impact of human activities, expressed as the area of productive land and water required to produce the goods consumed and the wastes generated

economic core the centre of a country or region economically, where businesses thrive, people have opportunities and are relatively wealthy; a highly developed area

economic development improvements in a country's or people's employment, income and living standards

economic periphery the edge of a country or region in terms of economics; a more remote, difficult area where people tend to be poorer and have fewer opportunities; a less well developed area

ecosystem the connections between living things (plants and animals) and non-living things (water, soil) in a particular place

ecosystem stress factors, which can be natural or human-produced, which put pressure on ecosystem productivity and processes; ecosystems can tolerate some changes but if the change is too big, or goes on too long, then damage starts to occur

ecotourism tourism that minimises harmful impacts on the environment and which aims to use tourism to help local communities

effusive a type of eruption where runny lava flows steadily out of a fissure or vent

emergency response how people react during a disaster and immediately afterwards

emergent very high trees that grow another ten metres or more above the tropical rainforest canopy

emerging country a country with high or medium human development

enhanced greenhouse effect the trapping of heat radiation around the Earth by excess greenhouse gases produced through human activity

epicentre the point at the Earth's surface directly above an earthquake's focus

epidemic an outbreak of disease that spreads rapidly to many people

Glossary

equatorial climate the constantly hot and wet climate of regions near the Equator

equilibrium in balance

erosion the wearing away and removal of material by a moving force, such as a river, a breaking wave or a glacier

erratic a rock or boulder that differs from the surrounding rock, brought from a distance by glacial action

estuary the mouth of a river which broadens into the sea and is affected by tides

evacuation moving people from somewhere dangerous to a safer place

extrapolate to estimate a value outside a range of values

eye the centre of a tropical cyclone; an area of clear conditions created by air converging at the centre of the storm and then sinking

eye wall a thick bank of cloud around the eye with high wind speeds and heavy rain

fair trade farmers and producers in developing countries are given a fair deal by buyers in developed countries; prices paid are always higher than their costs of production

fault a fracture or break in rocks

fauna animals

Ferrel cell circulation cell that brings warm air north towards the UK

fertiliser chemical added to soil to increase its fertility

fetch the distance a wave has travelled towards the coastline over open water, the longer the fetch the more powerful the wave

fissure a crack in the crust which lava comes out of

flood plain the flat land in the valley floor each side of a river channel, which is sometimes flooded

flora plants

flow resource resources such as wind, HEP or tidal energy that is used as it occurs and then replaced

focus the point in the Earth's crust where the earthquake begins

fold mountains long, high mountain range formed by upfolding of sediments

food web nutrients and energy absorbed by plants are passed along a line of living things

foreign direct investment (FDI) overseas investment in physical capital by transnational corporations

foreign exchange reserves the amount of foreign money, usually US dollars, held by a government in its central bank

formal employment jobs where people work for regular pay, have employment rights and pay taxes

fossil fuel energy resource such as coal, oil or natural gas that was formed from the remains of plants and animals that lived millions of years ago

fracking a process that involves drilling down into the Earth and using a high-pressure water mixture to release gas trapped inside rock

freeze thaw weathering the process of rocks breaking up from repeated freezing and thawing

frequency the number of times an event or data value occurs

gabion a large wire basket filled with rocks used to prevent coastal erosion

geology the different types of rocks that make up an area

geopolitical influence the way in which a country's geography and economy affect its relations with other countries

Gini coefficient a way of measuring inequality in a country: the higher the value of the Gini coefficient, the more unequal a country is

glacial a period of time with lower average temperatures causing widespread glaciations

global warming a rise in average global temperatures

globalisation the increasing interconnectedness and interdependence of the world economically, culturally and politically

gorge a steep, narrow valley with rocky sides

gradient how steep a slope, river channel or valley is

granitic a rock with a similar composition to granite: high in silica, with quartz crystals.

Green Revolution a 20th century development where new varieties of crops and better technology led to dramatic increases in crop yields in some developing countries

grid reference a four or a six figure reference number used to locate features on an OS map

Gross Domestic Product (GDP) the total value of goods and services produced by a country in a year

Gross Domestic Product (GDP) per capita the total value of goods and services produced by a country in a year per head of population

Gross National Income (GNI) per capita the total income of the country, including that made outside the country by its companies and corporations, divided by the number of inhabitants, to give average income per person

groundwater water stored underground in rocks and soil

groyne a wooden barrier built at right angles to the coast, used to break waves and reduce the movement of sediment along the coast

gryke a vertical joint, enlarged by weathering, between the blocks in a limestone pavement

Glossary

guano bird droppings, sometimes used as a fertiliser

Hadley Cell a circulation cell near the Equator responsible for storms at the Equator and desert belts north and south of the Equator

hard engineering strategies using artificial structures (e.g. concrete) to prevent river or coastal flooding

hazard a short-term event that threatens lives and property

headland an area of more resistant rock jutting out into the sea from the cliff-line

high and low water marks the points reached on a coast by the highest and lowest tides

hotspot a section of the Earth's crust where plumes of magma rise, weakening the crust; these are usually away from plate boundaries

hub the centre of a network, where good communications help economic and social development

Human Development Index (HDI) a measure of people's quality of life using social measures of development, based on life expectancy, education and standard of living

humus organic material in soil, made from decayed plants or animals

hydraulic action this results from the sheer force of moving water wearing away the river bed and banks, or waves wearing away sea cliffs

hydro-electric power (HEP) the use of fast flowing water to turn turbines which produce electricity

hydrograph a graph showing changes in a river's discharge and rainfall over time

ice core a section of ice drilled from a glacier showing the layers of ice created over time

impermeable rocks that are impermeable, like clay, do not allow water to pass through them

Index of Economic Freedom how open a country is to free-market capitalism (the index is devised by The Heritage Foundation)

Index of Multiple Deprivation (IMD) measures 38 items grouped under seven main headings: income, employment, health, education, crime, access to services and living environment

indigenous communities that have rights based on their historical ties

indigenous people the original human inhabitants of an area

indirect threat when there is not a direct cause between one thing happening and another thing being damaged

industrialisation the move from an economy dominated by the primary sector to one dominated by manufacturing (the secondary sector)

infant mortality rate the number of deaths of infants under one year of age per 1000 live births per year

infiltration the process whereby water soaks into the soil and rock

informal employment unofficial work, often without regular pay and employment rights (or payment of taxes)

infrastructure the basic services such as roads and power supplies which are needed to keep a country or region running

Integrated Coastal Zone Management (ICZM) a way to manage the coast and the land behind it sustainably, by involving everyone involved in using it

Intercept/interception the process where vegetation catches rainfall on its leaves and branches

interglacial a period of time between two glaciations with higher average temperatures

interlocking spurs areas of higher land jutting out of steep valley sides in a river's upper course

intermediate technology often small-scale technology that the local community can use without too much training or high costs

international aid the giving of resources (money, food, goods, technology) by one country or organisation to another poorer country

internet a global system of interconnected computer networks

interpolate to estimate a value inside a sequence of values

inter-quartile range the difference between the upper and lower quartiles

Inter-tropical Convergence Zone a belt of low pressure around the Earth just north and south of the Equator, where warm, moist trade winds come together

irrigation addition of water to farmland by artificial means

isobars lines on a weather map that indicate areas of equal atmospheric pressure.

jet stream a fast-moving current of air in the upper atmosphere

joint a vertical crack within a layer of rock

kinetic energy energy generated as a result of movement

lag time the difference in time between the peak rainfall and the river's peak discharge on a hydrograph

lagoon a fresh water lake formed when a bay is cut off from the sea by a beach bar

lahar a mudflow resulting from ash mixing with melting ice or water – a secondary hazard of a volcano

landfall the point at which a tropical storm reaches land

landslip the movement of rocks or soil down a slope due to gravity

lateral erosion erosion where a river cuts sideways into its banks

lava molten rock that erupts from a volcano or fissure

Glossary

lava bomb fragments of molten lava blown out of a volcano during an eruption

leaching when minerals are washed downwards through the soil by rainwater

levees the naturally raised bank of sediment along a river bank, which may be artificially strengthened or heightened

ley a fresh water lake or lagoon on the coast

life expectancy average number of years that a newborn child can expect to live

limestone pavement a horizontal or gently sloping area of limestone, comprised of large blocks (clints) separated by deep eroded fissures (grykes)

line of best fit a line going through the middle of the points on a scatter graph

liquefaction the process where sediments shaken by an earthquake behave like a liquid and so lose strength

lithosphere made up of the Earth's crust and upper mantle

litter a layer on the forest floor made up of leaves and other dead organic material

long profile the shape and gradient of a river bed from source to mouth

longshore drift the movement of material along a beach transported by wave action

long-term response reaction that happens in the weeks, months and years after an event

lower quartile divides the bottom half of the data in two halves; the bottom quarter of a set of values

magma semi-molten rock found in the mantle layer of the Earth

magma chamber an underground pool of magma that feeds a volcano

magnitude the quantifiable size of an event or piece of data

major city a city with a population of at least 200,000 inhabitants

mantle the dense, mostly solid layer of the Earth between the outer core and the crust

marginal minimal or barely sufficient to support something, e.g. poor quality land that makes farming harder

mass movement the movement of material down a slope due to gravity

maternal mortality rate the annual number of deaths of women from pregnancy-related causes per 100,000 live births

mean the sum of the data values divided by their number, often called the average

meander a bend formed in a river as it winds across the landscape

median the middle value when a set of values in a data set is written in order

megacity a very large city with a population of over ten million people

metamorphic rock a rock formed from other rock changed by extreme pressure or heat. It is usually formed from layers or bands of crystals and is very hard

microcredit/microfinance tiny loans and financial services to help the poor – mostly women – start businesses and escape poverty

mid-ocean ridge an underwater mountain range formed by diverging tectonic plates

migrate the process of people changing their place of residence, either within or between countries; the process of movement of features such as meanders

migration the long-term movement of people (or animals) within or between countries

Milankovitch cycle a long-term change in the Earth's orbit that causes natural climate change

millibar a unit of measurement of atmospheric pressure - 1000 millibars is approximately 'average' pressure

modal class the most frequent class in a data set

mode the most frequent value in a data set

modernisation theory a theory based on the economic history of a number of developed countries, which go through distinct economic and social changes and move from one stage to another

moment magnitude scale (Mw) the scale usually used today to measure the strength of an earthquake

monsoon a seasonal prevailing wind in South and South East Asia; it blows from the south-west between May and September (the wet monsoon), and from the north-east between October and April (the dry monsoon)

mouth the point where a river leaves its drainage basin and reaches the sea

multiplier effect spin-offs from one growing business, allowing other businesses to grow as well

National Park a large area of natural land protected by the government because of its natural beauty, plants or animals

natural population decrease death rate higher than birth rate, declining population

natural population increase birth rate higher than death rate, growing the population

neck the narrow strip of land between the two closest banks of a meander

neo-colonialism the dominance of poor countries by rich countries, not by direct political control (as in *colonialism*), but by economic power and cultural influence

non-governmental organisation (NGO) a national or international private organisation, which is distinct from governmental or inter-governmental agencies

Glossary

non-renewable sources of energy such as coal, oil or natural gas – that cannot be 'remade', because it would take millions of years for them to form again

number used to describe how much of a measured value there is

nutrient mineral or chemical that plants and animals need to grow and thrive

nutrient cycle the transfer of nutrients around different parts of an ecosystem

oceanic crust the Earth's crust beneath the oceans, thinner but denser than continental crust

ocean trench deep section of the ocean, usually where an oceanic plate is sinking below a continental plate

open-cast mining type of mining that extracts resources from open quarries rather than digging tunnels underground to reach mineral deposits

open economy a country with few trade barriers, which encourages trade with other countries

outsourcing the concept of taking internal company functions and paying an outside firm to handle them

oxbow lake a semicircular lake on a river flood plain, which has been cut off by a meandering river

peat bog a wet, spongy area where the soil is made up of decayed plant material

percentage the proportion or ratio expressed as a fraction (the ratio or proportion expressed per hundred)

peridotite a dense, coarse grained rock found in the upper mantle

period a large section of geological time

permeable rocks that are permeable, like chalk, allow water to pass through them

pesticide a chemical used on crops to kill unwanted insects

photosynthesis the chemical process in plants where water, carbon dioxide and sunlight are used to produce glucose

photovoltaic (PV) (cell) used in solar panels to convert light energy from the Sun into electricity

plane a flat two-dimensional surface

plate boundary the margin at which two plates meet

plunge pool a hollow in the river bed caused by erosion underneath a waterfall

point bar sediment laid down on the inside of a meander bend where the river flows slowly

Polar Cell a circulation cell furthest from the Equator that brings cold air south towards the UK

political development improvements in a country's system of government, or the involvement of the people, for example through greater democracy

population pyramid a bar chart arranged vertically, which shows the distribution of a population by age and sex

population structure the make-up (age and sex) of a population, usually shown in a population pyramid

precipitation water vapour condensed in the atmosphere which falls as rain, snow, sleet or hail

prediction attempt to forecast an event (where and when it will happen) based on current knowledge

prehensile able to grip. For example, a monkey with a prehensile tail can hold on to branches with its tail

preparation organising activities and drills so that people know what to do if an earthquake happens

prestige project a project which is often costly and attention-grabbing but may not meet people's needs

prevailing wind direction in which the wind blows most frequently

primary data data that you collect first hand

primary hazard a hazard which is the direct result of an earthquake, volcano or cyclone

primary impact the immediate effects of a natural hazard, caused directly by it

primate city the largest city in a country which dominates its economy, politics and often infrastructure

privatisation the sale of state-owned assets to the private sector

productivity a measure of the biomass of an ecosystem: all its biotic components

profile a cross section of the landscape, for example a river valley or beach

projection an estimate of future numbers or situation based on the trend at the moment

proportion expresses one part as a fraction of the whole

protection constructing buildings so that they are safe to live in and will not collapse

pull factor something that attracts people to a place

purchasing power parity (PPP) a way of adjusting Gross National Income to allow for the differences in what US$1 can buy in different countries

push factor something that encourages people to leave a place

pyroclastic flow a lethal hot mixture of broken rocks and gases that races down the sides of a volcano

qualitative data without numbers based on people's opinions or ideas, for example an interview or field sketch

quality of life the degree of well-being (physical and psychological) felt by an individual or group of people in a particular area. This may relate to jobs, wages, food and access to services such as health and education

quantitative data which contains numbers and figures, for example a pedestrian count

Quaternary period the current period of geological time

Glossary

quintile a way of analysing the distribution of income in a country for each fifth (quintile) of the population

radioactive decay the process where natural radioactive materials in the Earth's rocks break down, giving out energy and heat as they do so

random sampling data that is collected so each has an equal chance of being selected, for example by using random numbers

range the difference between the smallest and biggest values

ratio shows the number of times one value occurs compared with another

recyclable energy resources, including biofuels and nuclear, that can be reused, so will last into the future

REDD Reducing Emissions from Deforestation and Forest Degradation

regeneration reviving the economy or environment of a run-down area

regulate to bring under control through rules or laws

relict a landscape that has survived from an earlier period

relief the height and shape of the land

remittance money sent back by migrants to their families in the home community or country

remote sensing using satellites or aerial photography to provide information on land use over large areas

renewable a natural resource such as timber or solar energy that will be regenerated by the environment

replacement level fertility the level at which each generation has just enough children to replace themselves

reserve the estimated amount of resources left which can be extracted

residual heat the heat in the Earth's core remaining from its formation

retrofit to fit a new device or technology to make an old system work better

re-urbanisation the movement of people back towards the city

Richter scale a numerical scale showing the magnitude of an earthquake based on readings from a seismometer

rift valley a long, narrow valley created between two parallel faults caused by divergent tectonic plates

rip rap large boulders of resistant rock placed at the bottom of cliffs that dissipate wave energy

river cliff a steep section of river bank, caused by fast-flowing water eroding the outside of a meander

river erosion the action of water wearing away the rocks and soil on the valley bottom and sides

runoff water running across the land surface *or* the proportion of rainfall that flows in rivers

rural–urban migration the movement of people from the countryside to towns and cities

saltation a process where sediment is transported by being bounced along a river bed or sea floor

saltmarsh an area of mud flats formed by deposition of sediment in the low wave energy area behind a spit

saturate soil becomes saturated when it has absorbed as much water as is possible. If any more water is added, it cannot be absorbed

savanna tropical grassland with scattered bushes and trees, one of the world's major biomes

scale the relationship between dimensions on a map or diagram to those in the real world. On OS maps this is shown as 1:25,000 or 1:50,000

scarp slope a steep slope that cuts through the layers of rock underneath

scrub encroachment the gradual invasion of bushes due to lack of management

sea walls a curved or straight wall built along the coastline to prevent waves eroding the coastline

seasonal distribution how something such as rainfall occurs at different times of the year

secondary data data that has been collected and published by someone else

secondary hazard a hazard which occurs indirectly as a result of the primary impacts of a hazard

secondary impact the knock-on, or indirect, effects of a volcanic eruption or earthquake that take place on a longer timescale

sediment material such as mud, sand and pebbles carried and deposited by rivers or waves

sediment load the sediment particles carried by a river

sedimentary rock rock formed of small particles that have been eroded, transported, and deposited in layers, such as sandstone or from the remains of plants and animals

seismometer an instrument that measures movements of the ground, especially during earthquakes

selective plant breeding developing plants with particular characteristics, such as resistance to drought or pests

shield volcano a broad volcano that is mostly made up of lava

shock wave seismic wave generated by an earthquake that passes through the Earth's crust

Shoreline Management Plan (SMP) a plan which assesses the risks to a piece of coastline and how to manage these

Silurian rock rock from the Silurian Period, from about 440 to 420 million years ago

site the actual location of a settlement on the Earth, composed of the physical characteristics of the landscape specific to the area

Glossary

situation the location of a place relative to its surroundings and other places

slip-off slope the gentle slope on the inside of a meander bend formed by deposition

slum a run-down and often overcrowded urban area with poor quality housing and services

slumping a type of mass movement where soil or rock slides down a slope, often rotating as it moves

social development improvements in people's lives in health, education, culture

socialism a means of social organisation in which the main sectors of the economy are owned and controlled by the government rather than by individual people and companies

socio-economic process change which is related to people and jobs, money or trade

soft engineering flood defences that work with natural processes to reduce the risk and impact of coastal or river flooding

soil the layer above bedrock in which plants grow

solution the process where some rock minerals slowly dissolve in water, which is slightly acid

source the starting point of a stream or river, often a spring or a lake

source area the region in which a tropical storm first forms

spatial how features, resources and activities are arranged on the Earth's surface

spit a ridge of sand or shingle deposited by the sea. It is attached to the land at one end but ends in a bay or river mouth

spring-line settlement found where there is a ridge of permeable rock lying over impermeable rock; with a line of springs along the boundary between the two layers

stack an isolated column of rock, standing just off the coast that was once attached to the land

stock resource a non-renewable resource like coal that can be used only once, so will eventually run out

storm beach a beach affected by large destructive waves often with an angle over 45 degrees

storm surge an increase in the height of the sea due to a storm

strategic realignment the planned movement of the coastline inland because it can no longer be protected, also known as managed retreat

stratified sampling data that is collected from different parts of a population, for example different age groups

stump a short piece of rock found at the end of a headland formed after a stack has collapsed

sub-aerial processes acting on the Earth's surface, including weathering and mass movement

subarctic climate a climate zone that runs around the northern hemisphere, just south of the Arctic Circle (at a latitude of around 66° north)

subduction the process of one plate sinking beneath another

subduction zone the zone where one tectonic plate sinks (subducts) under another

subsistence agriculture farming in which crops are grown for the farmer's own use, to feed their family

suburbanisation the outward spread of the built-up area, often at a lower density compared with the older parts of the town

succulent plant a plant with thick leaves that can store water

supervolcano a colossal volcano that erupts at least 1000 km^3 of material

surface runoff water running across the land surface into streams and rivers

suspension the process where small particles of sediment are held up and carried along by moving water

sustainability development which meets the needs of the present without compromising (limiting) the ability of future generations to meet their own needs

sustainable able to continue without causing damage to the environment

sustainable development development which meets the needs of the present without compromising (limiting) the ability of future generations to meet their own needs

sustainable forestry when trees are cut down for timber and they are replaced by new trees, ideally with species that are naturally part of that ecosystem rather than non-native species

sustainable management planning ahead and controlling development for a long future

sustainable rainforest management managing a rainforest so that the way it is used now does not use up its resources and will allow future generations to use it in the same way

swash the movement of a breaking wave up a beach

systematic sampling data that is collected at regular intervals, for example every 500 metres

taiga a forest ecosystem in the sub-arctic regions of Canada, Russia, Scandinavia and Alaska (USA); also known as boreal forest

tectonic plate large areas of rock that make up the Earth's crust

tectonic processes the theory related to the seismic movement of the Earth's plates

thermal expansion the increase in volume created when a fluid (e.g. seawater) is heated and expands

Glossary

three Ps the collective term for prediction, protection and preparation

tiltmeter an instrument that measures small changes in the angle of the ground or buildings

top-down development an approach to development where decisions are made by governments or large companies, sometimes with little consultation; such programmes often involve large-scale, expensive projects

tor a block of granite found at the top of a hill

total fertility rate the average number of children born per woman in a country

track the path followed by a tropical cyclone

traction the transport of sediment along a river bed or the sea floor through a rolling action

transnational corporation (TNC) a firm that owns or controls productive operations in more than one country through foreign direct investment

transpiration the release of water vapour through a plant's leaves

transportation the movement of sediment by rivers, glaciers or waves

tree rings marks on the inside of tree's trunk that show individual growing seasons. The thickness of the rings varies depending on climatic conditions during the seasons

trench a long, deep depression in the ocean floor formed in the subduction zone between two tectonic plates

trend general direction of change

trend line shows the overall change in the data

tributary a stream or small river that joins a larger one

tropical cyclone a weather system that forms over the ocean in tropical areas and can produce high winds and heavy rain

tropical rainforest forest that grows in the constantly hot and wet climate zone near the Equator

Tropics of Cancer and Capricorn 23½ degrees north and south of the Equator; they are the farthest point north and south where the Sun's rays strike the Earth's surface at 90 degrees

tsunami giant sea wave travelling at high speed

upper quartile divides the top half of the data in two halves, the top quarter of a set of values

urban economy the structure of businesses and jobs in a city

urbanisation the increase in the percentage of people living in towns and cities, causing them to grow

urban–rural fringe the area around the edge of a city where urban and rural land uses mix

V-shaped valley a valley with a V-shaped cross section formed by river erosion

variable a number or amount that can be measured and can change in value

velocity the speed at which a river flows; river velocity is often measured in metres per second

vent an opening on the Earth's surface which emits lava or gas

vertical erosion downward erosion of the river bed

viscosity the fluidity of a lava (or other substance) – how 'sticky' it is

vog volcanic smog caused by sulphur dioxide mixing with sunlight, oxygen, water and dust particles

volcano cone-shaped mountain formed by surface eruptions of magma from inside the Earth

volcanologist a geologist who studies volcanoes

wave cut notch a small overhang at the base of the cliff formed where wave action is greatest

wave cut platform a flat area of rock at the bottom of cliffs seen at low tide

weather the day-to-day conditions of the atmosphere, e.g. temperature, precipitation, cloud cover, etc.

weathering the breakdown and decay of rock by natural processes acting on rocks, on cliffs and valley sides

wildlife corridor a link of wildlife habitat, normally native vegetation, which joins two or more larger areas of similar wildlife habitat

yield the amount of crops produced by a particular area of land

Index

A

abiotic activity	264
abrasion	136, 159
acid precipitation	138, 158, 273
adaptation	265, 267
affluence	256
afforestation	167
age	83, 201
Agora Microfinance India	120
agriculture	
arable farming	132
coastal erosion	144
commercial	270
subsistence	270
aid	69, 72–3, 80
air pollution	84, 276
alluvium	161
altitude	250
andesitic lava	42
annotated sketches	160
appropriate technology	71
arable farming	132
arches	136
Arctic sea ice	21
area	236
arid areas	14
assisted areas	189
asthenosphere	38, 39
atmosphere, regulation of	255
atmospheric circulation	12–13
atmospheric pressure	14–15, 32
attrition	136, 159
axial tilt	16

B

backwash	134
bars	141
basaltic lava	38, 43
base isolators	51
bays	135
beaches	140
bedding plane	138
berm	140
bio-chemical weathering	252
biodiversity	133, 265, 266
biofuels	254–5, 270, 295
biological weathering	138, 158, 252
biomass	264, 283
biomes	246–7
biotic and abiotic components	252–3
distribution and characteristics	248–9
local factors	250–1
bio-physical weathering	252
biosphere	245–61
as life support system	254–5
biotic activity	264
Birmingham	196–213
birth rate	64
bitumen	291
bivariate data	94
boreal forests	247, 249
Boserupian theory of population growth	258–9
bottom-up strategies	71, 120–1
Bradshaw's Model	163
BRICS nations	86
brownfield sites	207

C

call centres	80–1
canopy	265
capitalism	68
carbon dioxide	21, 85
carbon footprint	297
carbon sink	85
carboniferous limestone	129
carrying capacity	258
castes	77
caves	136
Central Business District (CBD)	103, 198
chalky soil	250
chawls	114
chemical weathering	138, 158, 273
cirrus cloud	24
CITES	274
cities *see* urban environments	
Clark-Fisher model of changing employment	101
clay soil	250
cliffs	135, 137
climate	13, 248
equatorial	264–5, 268–9
international negotiations	87
subarctic	266–7, 268–9
climate change	85, 170, 171, 271
consequences	22–3
human causes	20–1
natural causes	16–19
climate graphs	14, 15, 268
climate modelling	32
clints	130
clitter slopes	130
closed economies	66
coastal defences	148–9
coastal deposition	140–1
coastal erosion	146
case study	145
human causes	144
landforms	136–7
management	146–7
rate of	137
wave action	134
coastal flooding	146
coastal landscapes	134–57
fieldwork	150–5
flood risk	146
management	146–7
OS maps	142–3
sub-aerial processes	138–9
colonialism	66
colonies	75
combined heat and power generators	292
communications	81
comparisons	165
composite index	63
composite volcanoes	40, 42–3
Comprehensive Development Areas (CDAs)	198, 204
concordant coast	134–5
congestion charge	293
coniferous trees	247
connectivity	196
conservative plate boundaries	41
construction	144
constructive waves	134
consumerism	256, 277
continental crust	38
contours	165
conurbations	108

Index

convection currents 39
convergent plate boundaries 40, 48–9
coppices 133
core 38
Coriolis effect 13, 25, 26
correlation 93
Corruption Perception Index 63
cost-benefit analysis 174
counter-urbanisation 102
coves 135
craters 42
Cretaceous Period 131
cross-bracing 51
cross section 160
crust 38
cultivation 132
cyclones, tropical 24–5
    dissipation 27
    formation 24–5
    impact 28–9
    intensity 26–7
    landfall 31
    preparation for 32–5
    response to 33–5
    seasonal distribution 25
    source areas/tracks 25
    spin 25
    vulnerability to 30–1

D

death rate 64
debt 63
debt relief 73
decentralisation 205
deciduous trees 247, 249
deforestation 85, 257, 270–1, 274–5
de-industrialisation 102, 203, 205
deltas 161
demographic change 65, 82
demographic data 54–5
demographic indicators 64
deposition 140–1, 159
deprivation 201, 202
desertification 85
destructive waves 134
developed countries 63, 96

developing countries 62, 96
development
    bottom-up 71
    case study 74–89
    contributing factors 72–3
    definition 62
    levels of 63
    measurement of 62–3
    top-down 70–1
development gap 62–3
development theories 68–9
diaspora 77
dip slope 131
discharge 159
discordant coast 134–5
distributaries 161
diurnal temperature range 247
divergent plate boundaries 40–1
Dorset coast 145
drainage 251
drainage basins 158

E

earthquakes 39
    convergent plate boundaries 48–9
    impact and response 50–1
    measurement 49
eastings 142
East Siberia–Pacific Ocean (ESPO) oil pipeline 289
eccentricity 16
eco-footprint 210, 297
eco-housing 211
economic change 98, 192–3
economic core 69
economic decline 205
economic development 62, 284
    environmental effects 84–5
economic growth 206
economic periphery 69
economic vulnerability 31
ecosystems 246
    stress on 271
ecotourism 275
education 83
emergents 265
emerging countries 63, 96

employment 115, 221
    formal 100
    informal 100
energy 281–301
    changing attitudes 296–7
    consumption 282
    demand 292
    management 292–3
    use 284–5
enhanced greenhouse effect 20
enterprise zones 189, 209
environment
    degradation 67
    and economic development 84–5
    and inequality 66
epicentre 48
epidemics 258
equatorial climate 264–5
equilibrium 252
erosion 252
    coastal *see* coastal erosion
    lateral 160
    vertical 160
erratics 131
estuary 162
ethnicity 201
exploitation 254–7
extrapolation 92
extreme weather events 23, 24–7
eye, of cyclone 24
eye wall 24

F

fair trade 72
faults 40, 128, 135
fauna 252
Federal Emergency Management Agency (FEMA) 33
Ferrel Cells 13, 14
fertilisers 259
fetch 134
fieldwork 239–41
    coastal landscapes 150–5, 240
    river landscapes 176–81, 240
    rural environments 226–31, 241
    urban environments 214–19, 241

Index

fissures 43
flood defences
    construction 174
    hard engineering 172
    reducing impact 175
    soft engineering 173
flooding
    causes 168–9
    coastal 28
    riverine 168–9
flood plains 160, 161
flood risk
    coastal landscapes 146
    management 171–2
    river landscapes 168–75
flora 252
flow resources 282
flows 194
fold mountains 40
food webs 268–9
foreign direct investment (FDI) 70, 79, 194–5
foreign exchange gap 72
foreign exchange reserves 86
foreign investment 87
forest biomes 263–79
forest fires 273
forestry 133, 277
    sustainable 277
formal employment 100
fossil fuels 20, 21, 243, 273, 282
fracking 290
Frank's dependency theory 68–9
free trade 194
freeze thaw weathering 130, 138, 158
frequency 60

G

G-20 nations 86
gabions 149
gender 83
gentrification 207
geographical decision-making 243–4
geography 74–5, 193
geology 28, 128, 129
geopolitical influence 86
geothermal energy 283
Gini coefficient 63
glacial periods 16
glaciers 128–9
global circulation cells 12, 13
global inequalities 66–7
globalisation 67, 80, 194
global players 194
global warming 147
gorges 160
gradient 159
granitic rock 38
grasslands 249
greenfield sites 212
greenhouse effect 20
greenhouse gases 85
Green Revolution 258
green spaces 211
green transport 210
grid references 142
gross domestic product (GDP) 62–3, 78, 83, 256, 257
gross national income (GNI) 62–3, 78
groundwater 291
groynes 144, 148, 149, 150
grykes 130
guano 252

H

Hadley Cells 14, 26
Haiti earthquake 52–3
Hamara Foundation 120
hard engineering 148, 172
headlands 135
health 83
high atmospheric pressure areas 14
high water mark 137
honeypot sites 225, 226, 230
hotspots 38, 39, 43
housing 109, 114–15, 201
    affordable 222
    demand for 220
human activity
    coastal erosion 144–5
    landscapes 132–3
human causes of climate change 20–1
human development index (HDI) 63
humus 255
Hurricane Katrina 34
hydraulic action 136, 159
hydro-electric power 282, 295
hydrogen energy 295
hydrographs 166–7
hydrological cycle 253

I

ice cores 18
igneous rocks 128, 129
impermeable rocks 138, 167, 250
Index of Economic Freedom 89
Index of Multiple Deprivation 201, 223
India 74–89
    economic development 78–85
    environment 76
    geography 74–5
    international role 86–7
    regional contrasts 83
    social and religious composition 76–7
    views on development 87–8
indigenous peoples 254, 277
industrialisation 256–7
    slum industries 112–13
inequality 202–3
infant mortality rate 64
infiltration 167
informal employment 100
infrastructure 113, 144, 171
interception 167
interglacial periods 16
interlocking spurs 160
international climate negotiations 87
international migration 97, 191
interpolation 92
inter-quartile range 186
Inter-tropical Convergence Zone 24, 26, 248
investment 195
irrigation 259
isobars 14

314

Index

J
jet stream	13, 147, 168
job losses	205
joints	130, 135

K
Kilauea volcano	44–5
kinetic energy	294

L
labour force	193
lagoons	141
lahars	42
landslides	28
landslip	137
lateral erosion	160
lava	42
lava bombs	42
leaching	265
leisure	221, 225
levees	161
ley	149
life expectancy	63
limestone	
carboniferous	129
pavements	130, 250
line of best fit	93
liquefaction	50
literacy	80
lithosphere	38
litter	264
Little Ice Age	16, 18, 19
logging	270, 272
long profile	162, 163
longshore drift	140
low atmospheric pressure areas	15
low water mark	137

M
magma	40, 129
magma chamber	42
magnitude	60
major cities	97
Malthusian theory of population growth	258
mantle	38
maritime air masses	15
mass movements	138, 159
maternal mortality rate	64
mean	184
meanders	160, 161
median	184, 229
Medieval Warm Period	19
megacities	97, 105
Mumbai	105–21
metamorphic rocks	128, 129
microcredit	71
microfinance	120
mid-ocean ridges	40
migration	67, 82, 96, 161, 190–1, 200–1, 276
birds	267
international	97, 191
national	97, 190–1
rural–urban	96, 98, 190
Milankovitch cycles	17
millibars	14
mining	270, 277
mode	184
moment magnitude scale	49
monorails	119
monsoons	76
mouth (of river)	162
multiplier effect	71
Mumbai	105–21

N
national migration	97, 190–1
national parks	276
natural causes of climate change	16–19
evidence for	18–19
natural gas	282, 290
natural population increase	65, 82
neck (of meanders)	161
neo-colonialism	66
networks	194
non-governmental organisations (NGOs)	71
non-renewable energy	282
North Downs	131–3
North East England	192–3
northings	142
number	236
nutrient cycle	253
taiga	266
tropical rainforests	264

O
oceanic circulation	13
oceanic crust	38
ocean trenches	40
oil	272, 286–9
new sources	290–1
1% flood event	169
open-cast mining	257
open economies	66
Ordinance Survey maps	
Birmingham	206
coastal landscapes	142–3
river landscapes	164–5
symbols	143
outsourcing	80
oxbow lakes	161

P
peat bogs	250, 251
percentage	49–50, 58
peridotite	38
periods, historical	16
permeable rocks	138, 167, 250
pesticides	259
photosynthesis	248, 253
Pinatubo volcano	46–7
planes	130
plate boundaries	38, 39–41
plate tectonics	38–41
plunge pools	160
point bar	160
Polar Cells	13–19
political development	62
pollution	
air	84, 276
water	84, 291
population	75, 201
population growth	110–11, 206–7, 220, 258–9
Boserupian theory	258–9
Malthusian theory	258
population pyramids	64, 65, 189
poverty	67, 88
Power's scale of roundness	151
precession	16–17

Index

precipitation 247
prehensile 265
prevailing winds 22, 139
primary data 151, 177, 215
primate cities 97
privatisation 194
productivity 266
profile 140
proportion 49–50, 58
pull factors 97, 111
purchasing power parity (PPP) 63
push factors 97, 111
pyroclastic flows 42

Q

qualitative studies 151, 177, 215
quality of life 116–17, 121, 223
   Index of Multiple
      Deprivation 201, 223
quantitative studies 151, 177, 215
quartiles 186
quaternary industries 101, 193, 194
Quaternary period 16
quintile 66

R

radar 32
radioactive decay 39
rainfall 14
random sampling 151, 177, 215, 227
ratio 49–50, 58
rebranding 209
recyclable energy 282
recycling 210
REDD 274
redevelopment 204, 221
refugees 259
regeneration 102, 208
regional contrasts 83, 189, 192–3
relict glacial landscape 129
remittances 72, 73
remote sensing 274
renewable energy 282
replacement level fertility 82
reservoirs 295
residual heat 39
respiration 253

retirement migration 190
retrofitting 51
Richter scale 49
rift valleys 40
rip rap 148, 149
risk assessment 152, 216
river cliffs 160
river erosion 159
river landscapes 158–83
   effects on 162–3
   fieldwork 176–81
   flood risk 168–75
   landforms 160–1
   long profile 162, 163
   OS maps 164–5
River Severn 162–3, 168–9
rock falls 138, 139
rocks 128, 131, 138, 250
   impermeable 138, 167, 250
   permeable 138, 167, 250
Rostow's modernisation theory 68
runoff 162
rural diversification 224–5
rural environments 87, 188
   fieldwork 226–31
   Worcestershire 220–5
rural–urban migration 96, 190

S

Saffir–Simpson wind scale 29, 60
saltation 140
saltmarshes 141
sandy soil 250
satellite tracking 32
savanna 247, 248
savings gap 72
scale 142, 236
scarp slope 131
scatter graphs 93
scrub encroachment 132
sea levels 21, 22–3, 147
sea walls 144, 145, 148, 149
secondary data 151, 177, 215
sediment 159
sediment load 162
sedimentary rocks 128, 129
seismometry 49
selective plant breeding 259

service sector 80, 112
settlements 133, 144
shanty towns 46
shield volcanoes 40, 43
shock waves 48
Shoreline Management
   Plan (SMP) 145, 148
Silurian rock 131
site 106, 196
situation 106, 196
sliding 138, 139
slip-off slope 160
slope stabilisation 149
slum clearance 204
slum industries 112–13
slumping 138, 139, 159
slums 108, 115
   improving quality of life 121
social development 62
social investment 66
social vulnerability 31
socialism 69
socio-economic processes 98
soft engineering 148, 173
soil 250, 264
   health of 255
soil creep 159
solar power 294
solar radiation 12
solar variation 17
solution 136, 140, 159
South Downs 131–3
South East England 193
SPARC toilet blocks 120
spits 141
spring-line settlements 133
squatter settlements 115
stacks 136
statistics
   correlation 93
   cost–benefit analysis 174
   inter-quartile range 186
   line of best fit 93
   mean 184
   median 184
   mode 184
   percentage 49–50
   quartiles 186

Index

ratio 49–50
    trend lines 92–3
storm beaches 140
storm hydrographs 166–7
storm surges 28, 147
storms 147
strategic realignment 149
stratified sampling 151, 177, 215, 227
studentification 207
stumps 136
sub-aerial processes 138–9
subarctic climate 266–7
subduction 40
subsidence 291
suburbanisation/suburbs 102, 108
succulent plants 253
supervolcanoes 43
surface impacts 17
surface runoff 253
suspension 140
sustainability 171, 211
    energy 292–3
    forestry 277
    rainforest management 275
    transport 210, 293
    urban living 211
    water 255
sustainable cities 118, 211
swash 134
systematic sampling 151, 177, 215, 227

T

taiga 258–9, 266–7
    animals 267
    plants 267
    protection 276–7
    threats to 272–3
technical gap 72
tectonic plates 38, 39
    movement of 40–1
temperature 21, 23
    diurnal variation 247
tertiary industries 71, 101, 205
thermal expansion 21
tiltmeters 47
top-down strategies 70–1, 118–19

tors 130
total infertility rate 64
tourism 144
traction 140
trade 78–9, 195
traffic congestion 114, 293
transnational corporations (TNCs) 70–1, 194, 195, 207
transpiration 253
transport 193, 205
    green 210, 293
    infrastructure 81
    rural environments 222
transportation (of material)
    coastal landscapes 140
    river landscapes 159
tree rings 18–19
trend lines 92–3
tributaries 158
tropical cyclones see cyclones, tropical
tropical rainforests 248, 266–7
    animals 265
    biodiversity 265
    deforestation 270–1, 274–5
    importance of 264–5
    plants 265
    protection 274–5
Tropic of Cancer 76
tsunamis 49
tundra 249
Typhoon Haiyan 35

U

unemployment 205
urban economy 100–1
urban environments 82, 87, 95–125, 188, 196–213
    Birmingham 196–213
    challenges 204–5
    developed countries 96
    developing/emerging countries 96
    fieldwork 214–19
    growth 206–7, 220
    inequality 202–3
    interdependence with rural areas 212–13

    megacities see megacities
    migration 200–1
    quality of life 210–11
urban land use 103–4
urbanisation 256–7
urban-rural fringe 108, 212–13
U-shaped valleys 129

V

variables 93
velocity 159
vents 42
vertical erosion 160
volcanic smog (vog) 45
volcanism 17
volcanoes 39, 40, 42–3
    composite 40, 42–3
    impact 44–7
    responses to eruption 44–7
    shield 40, 43
volcanology 45
V-shaped valleys 162

W

waterfalls 160
water management 255
water pollution 84, 291
wave action 134
wave cut notch 137
wave cut platform 137
weather 13, 139
weathering 136, 158
    bio-chemical 252
    biological 138, 158, 252
    bio-physical 252
    chemical 138, 158, 273
    freeze thaw 130, 138, 158
wildlife corridors 132
wind power 294
winds
    prevailing 22, 139
    Saffir–Simpson wind scale 29, 60
Worcestershire 220–5
world biome map 246

Y

yields 259

Acknowledgements

Picture Credits
The publisher would like to thank the following for their kind permission to reproduce their photographs:

(Key: b-bottom; c-centre; l-left; r-right; t-top)

123RF.com: 248, Bruce Robbins 297, im_kenneth 4t, Joop Hoek 252l, Sam D Cruz 132, Steven Heap 226
Alamy Images: Andrew Holt 187, Babelon Pierre-Yves 271b, christopher Pillitz 46, CNP Collection 47, Colin Underhill 199r, David Bagnall 198, David Burr 138, David Levenson 84, Dinodia Photos 109tl, 119, dmark 160t, Douglas Peebles Photography 44, Dual Aspect 148b, Flirt 188r, George S de Blonsky 272t, Greg Vaughn 11, Hira Punjabi 112r, Ian Dagnall 239, imageBROKER 265r, Images of Birmingham Premium 102, 209, Images of Birmingham Premium 102, 209, James Osmond Photography 252r, JG Photography 265l, Joerg Boethling 87, John Sylvester 277, Jon Helgason 19, LA/AeroPhotos 95, Les. Ladbury 175, Michael Hoyer 199l, Midland Aerial Pictures 4tc, 160b, Mike Hughes 188l, MPAK 51, NorthernExposure 267t, Patrick Eden 144, Paul Andrew Lawrence 294, Peter Carey 113r, RGB Ventures/SuperStock 34, Robert Holmes 107, robertharding 61, 147, RosaIreneBetancourt 6 113l, RosaIreneBetancourt 9 109br, Shaun Higson/India 109bl, Simon Rawles 72, Simon Whaley 176, Sylvain Leser/Le Pictorium 112l, The Photolibrary Wales 53, Universal Images Group North America LLC 111, Visuals Stock 109tr
Corbis: Roger Ressmeyer 45, Serguei Fomine/ZUMA Press 272b
Derek Harper: Geograph, Derek 148t
Fotolia.com: acceleratorhams 150, Ali Safarov 99, David Woolfenden 135, lenisecalleja 5b, 136, Sapsiwai 105
Getty Images: Anselmo Garrido 245, Bloomberg 29l, Chris Hepburn/robertharding 127, Daniel Berehulak 255, David Goddard 168, Larry Dale Gordon 29r, Nicolas Asfouri 30
Greenpeace UK: Jiri Rezac 295
NASA: 27, Data courtesy Marc Imhoff of NASA GSFC and Christopher Elvidge of NOAA NGDC. Image by Craig Mayhew and Robert Simmon, NASA GSFC. 6, Jesse Allan using EO-1 ALI data 285
P K Das & Associates, Planners, Architects & Designers, Mumbai : 116
Rex Shutterstock: Rebecca Vale 146
Science Photo Library Ltd: British Antarctic Survey 18, Gary Hincks 158
Shutterstock.com: Andrew Williams 249l, AustralianCamera 4b, 271t, Dmytro Pylypenko 249r, kevin wise 130t, Matt Gibson 130b, nialat 267b, ODM 263, R.M. Nunes 81
Skyscan Photolibrary: 145, Brenda Marks 141r, J Farmar 141l

Cover images: *Front:* **Corbis:** Partha Pal/2/Ocean

All other images © Pearson Education

Picture Research by: Jane Smith

We are grateful to the following for permission to reproduce copyright material:

Figures
Figure 8, p.16 adapted from 'Changes in the Earth's average temperature during the last million years', www.planetseed.com. http://www.seed.slb.com/subcontent.aspx?id=3750, copyright © 2016 Schlumberger Excellence in Educational Development, Inc. Reproduced with permission; Figure 13, p.20 adapted from 'The Greenhouse Effect' adapted from *UKCIP 09: The Climate of the UK and recent trends*, www.ukcip.org.uk, Source: Met Office; Figure 1, p.60 adapted from 'Frequency of hurricanes from 1 to 5 on the Saffir–Simpson Scale making landfall at New Orleans from 1910 to 2009', https://coast.noaa.gov/hurricanes/, Source: USA National Hurricane Centre, National Oceanic and Atmospheric Administration, NOAA; Figure 2, p.78 adapted from "The political economy of economic growth in India, 1993-2013", December 2014, published in *ESID Working Paper No 44*, Fig 7, www.effective-states. org, Source: National Accounts Statistics (NAS), CSO, CSO accessible free of charge and licensed under Creative Commons Attribution (version 4.0 cc); Figure 14, p.79 from 'What is the trade balance for India? (1995-2013)', http:// atlas.media.mit.edu/en/profile/country/ind/, Source: AJG Simoes, CA Hidalgo. The Economic Complexity Observatory: An Analytical Tool for Understanding the Dynamics of Economic Development. Licensed under a Creative Commons Attribution-ShareAlike 3.0 Unported License; Figures 16, 21, pp.82, 89 adapted from Population Reference Bureau, September 2015, *Population Bulletin 70.1*, p.7, Fig 4; p.13, Fig A, www.prb.org/pdf15/india-population-bulletin.pdf, Source: India, 2011 Census; Figure 18, p.86 adapted from 'Average annual growth rates for the BRICS and three major developed economies, 2001–11 and 2010–14', calculated from the IMF World Economic Outlook database, October 2014, https://www.imf.org/external/pubs/ft/weo/2014/02/weodata/index.aspx copyright © IMF. Reproduced with permission of the International Monetary Fund; Figure 4a,b, p.94 from data concerning water supply, life expectancy and child mortality, 2013, http://data.worldbank.org/indicator/SP.DYN.LE00.IN, http://data.worldbank.org/indicator/SH.DYN.MORT, copyright © 2016 The World Bank Group, All Rights Reserved, © 2016 The World Bank Group, All Rights Reserved; Figures 1, 2, p.96 adapted from *The urban and rural population of the world, 1950–2030* and *Average annual rate of change in major urban areas, 1950–2050*, Department of Economic and Social Affairs, World Urbanization Prospects: 2014 Revision, United Nations, p.7, Fig 2; Figure 4, p.9, http://esa.un.org/unpd/wup/highlights/wup2014-highlights.pdf, copyright © 2014 United Nations. Reprinted with the permission of the United Nations; Figure 4, p.98 adapted from 'Population of London', *Census 2001* and *2011*, Crown copyright, Office for National Statistics licensed under the Open Government Licence v.3.0; Figure 14, p.111 adapted from 'Greater Mumbai's spatial development over the past century' from *Mumbai: India's global city*, December 2014, p.11 by Greg Clark and Tim Moonen, https://www.jpmorganchase.com/corporate/Corporate-Responsibility/document/gci_mumbai_02.pdf. Reproduced with permission from JP Morgan Chase & Co; Figures 1, 2, pp.129, 135 adapted from 'Geological map of the Swanage coast' as found on *Geology of Britain Viewer* http://mapapps.bgs.ac.uk/geologyofbritain/home.html © BGS, and 'Geological map of the UK and Ireland', http://www.thegeologytrusts.org/pub/our-earth-heritage/, CP16/017, CP16/025 British Geological Survey © NERC 2015. All rights reserved. Reproduced by permission; Figure 6, p.161 adapted from "Formation of an ox-bow lake" by Rob Chambers, copyright © Rob Chambers. Reproduced with kind permission; Figure 13, p.166 from "River Severn hydrograph", Bewdley Case Study, July 2007, www.geography.org, copyright © Geographical Association; Figures 3, 4, p.189 from 'London Population' and 'Cornwall Population' from *2011 Census*, http://www.ons.gov.uk/census/2011census, ONS © Crown copyright 2014, Office for National Statistics licensed under the Open Government Licence v.3.0; Figure 6, p.190 from 'Net flows

of internal migrants by local authority, year ending June 2014, per 1,000 mid-2013 population, local authorities in England and Wales', Map 1, http://www.ons.gov.uk, Office for National Statistics licensed under the Open Government Licence v.3.0. Contains OS data @ Crown copyright and database right 2015; Figure 10, p.195 from 'UK Inward FDI Stock – Major Source Countries' from *UKTI Inward Investment Report 2014 to 2015,* https://www.gov.uk, Sources: Office for National Statistics (ONS); 2014 estimate from the OECD stats (May 2015), licensed under the Open Government Licence v.3.0; Figure 15, p.200 from "Black and minority ethnic groups by ward in Birmingham in May 2010", https://placeexplorer.wordpress.com/2011/09/18/about-birminghams-residents-and-their-social-struggles/, Birmingham City Council, copyright © 2010; Figures 16-18. pp.201, 202 from "Birmingham wards showing index of Multiple Deprivation", "Out of Work Benefit Claimants, February 2014", and "Estimated Population growth in Birmingham's Wards (2011-2031)" from *The way forward: an independent review of the governance and organisational capabilities of Birmingham City Council: Supporting Analysis,* December 2014, pp.5, 13, https://www.gov.uk, Strategic Analysis Team, DCLG and ABS Analysis Team © Crown copyright and database rights 2012, Ordnance Survey 100018986, 2013, Ordnance Survey 100024857, Source: Office for National Statistics licensed under the Open Government Licence v.3.0; Figure 19, p.204 adapted from 'Comprehensive Development Areas in Birmingham, 1975' from *The post-war redevelopment of the central area of Birmingham* by J. M. H. Parke, 1975, unpublished MA thesis, Department of Geography, University of Birmingham. Reproduced by kind permission of the author; Figure 22, p.210 adapted from *Blueprint for a Green Planet* by John Seymour and Herbert Girardet, Dorling Kindersley, 1987, copyright © John Seymour & Herbert Girardet, 1987. Reproduced by permission of Penguin Books Ltd; Figure 25, p.220 from "2014 mid-year population estimate: Birmingham and England age pyramid", ONS mid-2014 population estimates, www.birmingham.gov.uk, © Crown copyright 2015, Source: Office for National Statistics licensed under the Open Government Licence v.3.0; Figure 26, p.223 from 'Deprivation in Worcestershire by Lower Super Output Area' from *English Indices of Deprivation 2015,* source: IMD Index of Multiple Deprivation (IMD), Department for Communities & Local Government © Crown copyright, licensed under the Open Government Licence v.3.0; Figure 1, p.237 adapted from *Population Statistics, Total Population, A Vision of Britain through Time,* GB Historical GIS/University of Portsmouth, London GovOf through time, http://www.visionofbritain.org.uk/unit/10097836/cube/TOT_POP, Census data 1961 to 2001, copyright © Office for National Statistics, for England and Wales, 2011 data and Great Britain Historical GIS Project 2004-12; Figure 2, p.238 from 'Map of all 32 London boroughs and the City of London', https://en.wikipedia.org/wiki/List_of_London_boroughs, licensed under the Creative Commons Attribution-Share Alike 3.0 Unported license; Figure 1, p.246 adapted from 'World distribution of biomes' from *This dynamic earth,* http://www.usgs.gov, Source: US Geological Survey; Figure 6, p.250 adapted from 'An area close to the equator', Topic 3: Battle for the Biosphere, *Edexcel GCSE Geography B, Unit 1: Dynamic Planet, Foundation Tier, SAM, 5GB1F/01,* p.6, Fig 3, http://qualifications.pearson.com, copyright © 2010 Edexcel Limited; Figure 14, p.256 from 'World-Population-1800-2100' 2012, https://commons.wikimedia.org/wiki/File:World-Population-1800-2100.svg, licensed under the Creative Commons Attribution-Share Alike 3.0

Unported license; Figure 15, p.257 adapted from 'Projected GDP levels', pre January 2014. Source: World Bank and Goldman Sachs. Reproduced with permission; Figure 17, p.259 adapted from *Beyond the Limits* by Donella H. Meadows and Dennis L. Meadows, 1992, copyright © 1992 Donella H. Meadows, Dennis L. Medows, Jørgen Randers. Used with permission from Chelsea Green Publishing, www.chelseagreen.com; Figure 6, p.268 adapted from Climate Graph, http://en.climate-data.org/location/1882/. Reproduced by permission of AmbiWeb GmbH; Figure 13, p.275 from "Slowing Amazon deforestation through public policy and interventions in beef and soy supply chains" by Daniel Nepstad et al, *Science,* Vol. 344 (6188), pp.1188-1123, copyright © American Association for the Advancement of Science (AAAS). Figure 1, p.282 adapted from *BP Statistical Report of World Energy, 2015,* http://www.bp.com, copyright © BP, 2016; Figure 3, p.284 adapted from *Collins Student World Atlas,* Collins, *2nd Revised edition,* 2007. Reproduced by permission of HarperCollins Publishers Ltd; Figures 6-8, pp.286, 287 with data adapted from 'The world's remaining oil reserves, as of 2014', 'World's top oil producers', and 'World Petroleum consumption by Region, 1980-2010', Source: US Energy Information Administration, 2012, 2014, 2016; Figure 13, p.292 adapted from 'Oak Tree House, Woking's demonstration house', http://www.actionsurrey.org, copyright © Action Surrey. Reproduced with permission.

Maps
Figure 3, p.97 adapted from 'World's Largest Cities: Population', *World Urban Areas, 11th Annual Edition, 2015:01* www.demographia.com/db-worldua.pdf copyright © Demographia, Wendell Cox Consultancy. Reproduced with permission; Ordnance Survey Maps, pp.131, 142, 143, 164, 169, 206 © Crown copyright 2016, OS 100030901 and supplied by courtesy of Maps International; Figure 5, p.189 from 'Assisted Areas Map for the UK 2014-2020 Under Consideration by the European Commission' from 2014-2020 Assisted Areas Map', April 2014, https://www.gov.uk/government/consultations/assisted-areas-map-2014-to-2020-stage-2, Department for Business, Innovation & Skills © Crown copyright and database rights (March 2014). Ordnance Survey (100037028), licensed under the Open Government Licence v.3.0.

Tables
Figure 4, p.29 from 'The Saffir-Simpson scale' by Pamela Ho, https://grade7geography.wikispaces.com/The+Saffir-Simpson+scale © Creative Commons licence Attribution-ShareAlike 3.0 Unported; Table 2, p.59 adapted from 'Average rainfall data for Valley in Anglesey', www.metoffice.gov.uk/public/weather/climate, Source: MET Office, 2015; Table 3, p.60 adapted from 'Hurricane wind speed on the Saffir-Simpson Scale', https://coast.noaa.gov/hurricanes/. Source: USA National Hurricane Centre, National Oceanic and Atmospheric Administration, NOAA; Table 1, p.236 adapted from *Population of London 2012-2015,* https://www.ons.gov.uk/, ONS © Crown copyright 2015, Source: Office for National Statistics licensed under the Open Government Licence v.3.0; Table 2, p.237 adapted from *Population Statistics, Total Population, A Vision of Britain through Time,* GB Historical GIS/University of Portsmouth, London GovOf through time, http://www.visionofbritain.org.uk/unit/10097836/cube/TOT_POP, Census data 1961 to 2001, copyright © Office for National Statistics, for England and Wales, 2011 data and Great Britain Historical GIS Project 2004-12.

Acknowledgements

Text

Extracts on pp. 158–161, 172–173, 291 adapted from *Edexcel GCSE Geography A: Geographical Foundations*, revised edition by Andy Palmer, Michael Witherick, Phil Wood, Nigel Yates, Pearson Edexcel, 2012, pp.72–76, 82, 117, 118 copyright © Pearson Education Limited; Exam Questions on pp.56, 124, 234, 300 from *Pearson Edexcel Level 1/2 GCSE (9-1), Geography B,* Sample Assessment Materials, First Teaching 2016, Paper reference 1GB0/02, Paper 1: Global Geographical Issues, SECTION A Hazardous Earth and SECTION C Challenges of an Urbanising World, Paper 2: UK Geographical Issues, SECTION B The UK's Evolving Human Landscape and Paper 3: People and Environment Issues – Making Geographical Decisions, SECTION C Consuming energy resources, pp.10, 23, 58, 114, copyright © Pearson Education Limited 2015. Reproduced by permission of Edexcel.